CAPITAL

AND OTHER WRITINGS
OF KARL MARX

CAPITAL

THE COMMUNIST MANIFESTO

AND OTHER WRITINGS

BY KARL MARX

Edited, with an introduction, by **MAX EASTMAN**

With an essay on Marxism by **V. I. LENIN**

**THE
MODERN LIBRARY
NEW YORK**

Random House IS THE PUBLISHER OF

THE MODERN LIBRARY

BENNETT A. CERF · DONALD S. KLOPFER · ROBERT K. HAAS

Manufactured in the United States of America

By H. Wolff

CONTENTS

		PAGE
INTRODUCTION . . . . . *By Max Eastman*		vii
THE THREE SOURCES AND THREE CONSTITUENT PARTS OF MARXISM . . . *By V. I. Lenin* (1913)		xxi

PART I
OUTLINES OF A FUTURE SOCIETY

1. From "The German Ideology" (1845-6) . . . — 1
2. From "The Poverty of Philosophy" (1847) . . 2
3. From "The Criticism of the Gotha Program" (1875) 2

PART II
ANALYSIS OF THE MATERIALS

A. The Theory of History
1. From "The German Ideology" (1845-6) . . . 8
2. From the Introduction to "Critique of Political Economy" (1859) 10

B. The Existing Society
1. Capital: An Analysis of Capitalist Production (1867-1883) 11
2. The Theory of Crises 302

PART III
THE METHOD AND THE CALL TO ACTION

1. The Communist Manifesto (1848) . . . 315
2. From the "Criticism of The Gotha Program" (1875) 355
3. Address of the Central Authority to the Communist League, April (1850) 355
4. The Civil War in France (1871) 367

INTRODUCTION

IT took a revolution in Russia to wake up the English-speaking world to the importance of Karl Marx. Marx regarded England as a model of the mature workings of that capitalist system which he analyzed, and he would regard present-day America as a super-model. Nevertheless it is just in England and America that Marxism never found a home. It never took firm root among our radical minded intellectuals; it never became the official philosophy of our organizations of the working class, as it has almost everywhere else in the world. There must be some reason why in the countries most advanced economically this most advanced economic theory and program never took hold. I think the principal reason is that Marx was educated in the atmosphere of German metaphysics. He began life as a follower of Hegel, and he never recovered from that German philosophical way of going at things which is totally alien to our minds. Hegel scorned the English for speaking of Isaac Newton as a great philosopher—for regarding his discoveries, that is, as the highest kind of knowledge. We, on the other hand, regard the professorial apostle of "German thoroughness," who cannot even suggest a plan for building a dam across a creek without starting in with the creation of the world, and getting us to agree about the essential nature of being and the relations between Pure Reason and the Categories of the Understanding, as a comic type to be caricatured on the stage. In this methodological difference of opinion we are right. Our methodology, like our economic development, is the more advanced. Science in its mature forms casts loose from philosophy, just as earlier it cast loose from religion and magic. It contents itself on the theoretic side with specific solutions of specific problems, and on the practical side with methods of procedure for accomplishing specific things. If these solutions and methods *imply* some general attitude toward the universe at large, then that is conceded tentatively and with some reluctance. A quick recourse to scepticism, a readiness to say "I don't know" when large general questions come up about being and the nature of the universe—a readiness to say "I don't know" whenever as a simple matter of fact *you do not know*—is the surest mark of an advanced scientific mind, whether practical or theoretical.

Marx gave the world as important a gift of scientific knowledge as any man of the modern era; he is one of the giants of science. Nevertheless, he did not have this mental attitude. His approach to his problems was philosophical. It was German-professorial in the very sense that seems unnatural to us more sceptical and positivistic Anglo-Saxons. He wanted to revolutionize human society and make it intelligent and decent, and he studied its history and its present constitution with that end in view, and drew up a plan by which the thing might be accomplished. But instead of presenting his thoughts in this simple and clear form as a specific plan for the solution of a specific problem, he started in by deciding in general what the universe is made of and how it operates, and then gradually worked down towards a demonstration that by the very nature of its being and laws of its operation this universe is inevitably going to revolutionize itself, and it is going to revolutionize itself in just the manner outlined in his plan, and therefore as intelligent parts of a universe of such a kind it behooves us to get to work on the job. That method of approaching a job is alien to the Anglo-Saxon mind—especially to the hard-headed and radical specimens of the Anglo-Saxon mind. That is surely one reason—and I think it is the main reason—why Marxism does not take firm root in our culture where its lessons are most directly applicable.

In this I do not mean to boast of any inherent superiority of the Anglo-Saxon brain cells. The more advanced simplicity of logic with which Englishmen like John Stuart Mill approached social problems, however tame their solution of them, was doubtless closely associated with that more advanced industrial development of which Marx himself was so clearly aware. It is important, however, that those young Americans who wish to approach Marx as a teacher—and they all ought to—should not be "buffaloed" by his philosophic mode of approach. They are very likely to in these days, because those most interested in propagating the ideas of Marx, the Russian Bolsheviks, have swallowed down his Hegelian philosophy along with his science of revolutionary engineering, and they look upon us irreverent peoples who presume to meditate social and even revolutionary problems without making our obeisance to the mysteries of Dialectic Materialism, as a species of unredeemed and well-nigh unredeemable barbarians. They are right in scorning our ignorance of the scientific ideas of Karl Marx and our indifference to them. They are wrong in scorning our distaste for having practical programs presented in the form of systems of philosophy. In that we simply represent a more progressive intellectual culture than that in which Marx received his education —a culture farther emerged from the dominance of religious attitudes.

For it is the relic of a religious attitude to attribute your plan for changing the world to the world itself, and endeavor to prove that the "inner law" of this world is engaged in realizing your ideals. Marx was an implacable enemy of religion, and he was also—or thought he was—in revolt against philosophy. He liked to repeat the saying of Ludwig Feuerbach that "the metaphysician is a priest in disguise"; and he expressed many times the desire to get philosophy out of the way of his revolutionary science. It was with this motive that he so vigorously insisted that the world consists of matter and not spirit. But the essence of philosophy in its kinship with religion is not to declare that the world is spirit, but to declare that this world of spirit is sympathetic to the ideals of the philosopher. Marx banished the spirit, but retained in his material world that now still more extraordinary gift of being in sympathy with his ideals. He retained, that is, the philosophic method and habit of thought. It was not that he wanted help from the universe, but he did not know how else to formulate his colossal plan for controlling social evolution except to implant it as "historic necessity" in evolution itself. The combination of affirmative and confident action in a given field with a general attitude of scientific scepticism was unknown to him.

* * *

In order to help the American student get hold of the monumental ideas of Karl Marx, which is his duty, and yet retain that sceptical poise of the scientific thinker, which is his privilege, I have devised a non-philosophic way of presenting those ideas. I present them as a system of social and political engineering.

An engineer wishing to convert a given form of society into a more satisfactory one would begin by making a very rough outline of the kind of society he proposed to build. With that rough blue-print in mind he would examine the existing society, and he would also examine all past societies, and find out what are the forces which control them and the general laws of their change. When he had finished that investigation and acquired that knowledge, he would draw up a procedure or plan of action, a scheme for getting the thing moving (supposing that his investigations had proven it possible) in the direction of his proposal. That is an engineering approach to the problems raised by Karl Marx. It separates the choice of a goal, which is primarily an act of passion, from the definition of existing facts and the discovery of their laws of motion; and it presents its plan of action as a plan of action pure and simple. It does not undertake the task of proving that the objective world is by virtue of its own inner "dialectic" destined to carry that plan out—a task impossible of accomplishment by any mortal brain. We do not know what the world is destined to do, but we know what we can in our own era try to make it do, and try with good assurance that success is possible. That is all anybody needs to know in order to act, or does indeed ever know when he acts with a hazard sufficient to make his act interesting.

My presentation of Marxism to modern readers therefore

takes this form. I present first those scant fragments in which Marx did touch the question of the kind of society which he proposed as worthy of intelligent beings, and which he deemed it possible to approach. The reader must not be surprised to find these outlines extremely sketchy, nor to find them presented in the form of a dogmatic assertion as to what the future is destined to bring forth. That is merely the philosophic way of formulating a scientific purpose. Marx's faith in the benign drift of his material universe was so great that he was for the most part ready to dispense with any plan at all. The working classes, he said in one place, "have no ideal to realize; they have only to set free the elements of the new society...." And even in that sole fragment where Marx did enter with some detail into the future plans of the communists—the Criticism of the Gotha Program—we find him demurring against any disposition to give these plans a guiding rôle. He calls them "juridical conceptions," and says that they are a mere by-product of economic evolution. His goal, he permits us to know, is a society without classes and without government by force, and one in which wealth shall be distributed according to the formula "From each according to his abilities, to each according to his needs." But he insists upon presenting the conditions which make it reasonable to strive for such a goal, and show by what stages one might move toward it, as causes of its inevitable advent.

I have shown elsewhere [1] that this failure to distinguish *condition* from *cause* is the most general of those unconscious devices by which Marx and his followers keep up the attitude of a philosopher while presenting the thoughts of an engineer. But it will be obvious upon a moment's reflection that this must be so. An engineer is compelled to regard his own act as a cause, and to distinguish this from the conditions by which his act is limited—the qualities of his material, its resistance to stresses, strains, etc. The philosopher, wishing to show that his act is identical with what the universe as a whole is doing, is equally compelled to ignore the distinction.

[1] *Marx and Lenin, the Science of Revolution* (1926).

He has no other recourse, if he intends to act creatively, but to present the conditions which make his plan possible as causes which make it inevitable.

That is why Marx's blue-prints of the proposed society are so sketchy, and yet are laid down as though Marx had prophetic insight, and were able to write a history of the remote future of the world.

* * *

After reading these rough sketches of the goal to be striven for, we turn to Marx's examination of the past history of man and the existing society. He is seeking, remember, those aspects of society and those laws of its history which will guide him in the effort to transform it in the direction of his goal. And here the great work of his genius begins. It divides itself into two sections: first, an explanation of the dominant part played in all human culture and all its history by a gradual change and development of the technique of wealth production; and second, an analysis of our contemporary capitalist method of production. I call the first section "The Theory of History"; the second section is of course Marx's famous contribution to economics, "Capital, an Analysis of Capitalist Production."

The theory of history was summarized in this way by Friedrich Engels, the close friend and co-creator of Marx's ideas: "Marx discovered the simple fact (heretofore hidden beneath ideological overgrowths) that human beings must have food, drink, clothing and shelter first of all, before they can interest themselves in politics, science, art, religion and the like. This implies that the production of the immediately requisite material means of subsistence, and therewith the existing phase of development of a nation or an epoch, constitute the foundation upon which the state institutions, the legal outlooks, the artistic and even the religious ideas are built up. It implies that these latter must be explained out of the former, whereas the former have usually been explained as issuing from the latter."

It is impossible to exaggerate the influence of this simple

idea upon the subsequent development of historic knowledge. All thoughtful men have profited by it and they will forever. It marks a turning point in the whole art of understanding history. Here again, however, the fact that Marx conceived himself to be writing a *philosophy* of history, an explanation of the whole thing as a single process, and one which was leading up to and with necessity including his proposed plan for the future, led him to state the case in a way that is unacceptable to a modern scientific mind. The fact that men have to eat and shelter and clothe themselves before they do other things, makes the productive forces a primary factor in explaining history, a factor *conditioning* all others. That is to say that no historic phenomenon can arise and endure which *runs counter* to the prevailing mode of production. This does not mean, however, that everything which arises and endures is *explained by* the prevailing mode of production. Again the idea of effective cause is confused with that of indispensable condition. It is confused by Engels in this most simple statement of the theory, and it is confused still more explicitly by Marx in his Introduction to the *Critique of Political Economy*—the classic passage. "The mode of production," he says, "*conditions* the social, political and spiritual life process . . . ," and in the very next sentence, as though but developing the same thought: "It is not the consciousness of men which *determines* their existence, but on the contrary their social existence *determines* their consciousness." There can be no doubt here that the limiting condition and the determining cause are being interchanged without discrimination, and if the reader will take my word that this is true throughout the entire Marxian system, he will find Marx infinitely easier to read.

In *Capital*, for instance—which forms the next section of our engineering presentation—Marx turns to the investigation of our present-day method of production. He does so because this conditions and limits the success of any efforts that social reformers may make to improve our society. They may talk about liberty, equality, fraternity, and so on, but if these aims are inconsistent with the mode of production, all their noble talk will merely expand in the air. Now Marx is, as we have seen, interested in liberty, equality, fraternity —in all that is implied by these abstract slogans, and more too. He is interested in forming a society in which wealth shall be distributed according to need, work demanded according to ability. He sees at a glance that our system of production renders such a dream impossible. Capitalist production involves economic classes and the exploitation of one class by another inherently and eternally. It involves class struggle inherently and eternally. But there is nothing inherently eternal about capitalist production itself. It was a product of change; it evolved out of feudalism; it may not necessarily be the end of that evolution. One need not, therefore, simply abandon one's plan for a better society as impractical, and fall back upon the sad enterprise of doctoring up in small ways the one we have. One may by further investigation and exercise of ingenuity devise a scheme by which the mode of production can again be changed, and thus new conditions created which will not be inconsistent with the ideal of a classless society. It was this latter step that Marx took, and that made him the intellectual father of the Russian revolution and one of the greatest men in human history. He devised the scheme—or the science, rather, for that is what it has become—of engineering with class forces. He pointed out that by organizing and directing the struggle of the working class against the capitalists and their associates, and by interlinking with this struggle in certain quite possible ways the struggle of the poor peasants and tenant-farmers against the landlords, and carrying it forward to a veritable "dictatorship" of these exploited classes, it would be possible to take possession of the instruments of production and change the system. It would be possible to change it in those ways necessary in order to make reasonable the effort to create a classless society in which men will receive according to need and work according to ability.

Marx saw clearly enough that this manœuvre would be possible only in a crisis, only at a moment when the system had broken down so badly that the dominant classes were unable to rule and the exploited classes were driven by suffering to forceful and imperious action—only at a moment of actual or potential civil war. He was therefore concerned to find out whether the capitalist system of production does not inevitably produce crises, any one of which may possibly become severe enough to make such action practical. There is little doubt that he did demonstrate the inevitability under a capitalist system of the recurrent crisis of overproduction, and bound up therewith the inevitability of imperialist wars. His contribution to the understanding of business crises and the causes of war will not often be denied today even by the most "bourgeois" economists. And thus he completed the scientific task set by his apparently utopian aims—the task of finding out how the existing system of wealth production might be changed in such a way as to make these utopian aims possible of attainment, and reasonable to strive after.

It was not necessary for him as an engineer to prove that this change is inevitable. It was not even necessary to prove that social evolution is tending in that direction. He might, indeed, have believed with Spengler that it is tending in an opposite direction, towards decay and disaster, and that this deliberate and informed action—this new economic engineering science—is the only thing that can save us from the fate of the older civilizations. All he had to prove was that in spite of the *limiting conditions* his method of action is practical, and the occasions for its application will arise.

That is the sum and substance of *Das Kapital* as a part of an engineering science. Owing to his philosophical mode of approach, however, his training in the school of Hegel, Marx felt obliged to prove that his whole scheme of salvation is involved with "historic necessity" in the very laws of the capitalist system which "work with iron necessity toward inevitable results." It was with this sense of his mission that he approached his studies in economics.

"As far as I am concerned," he wrote to his friend Weydemeyer in 1852, "I cannot claim to have discovered the existence of classes in modern society or their strife against one another. Petty bourgeois historians long ago described the evolution of class struggles, and political economists showed the economic physiology of the classes. I have added as a new contribution the following propositions: 1. That the existence of classes is bound up with certain phases of material production; 2. That the class struggle leads necessarily to the dictatorship of the proletariat; 3. That this dictatorship is but the transition to the abolition of all classes and to the creation of a society of the free and equal." Or to put this mode of approach in the youthful words of his friend Engels: "With the same certainty with which from a given mathematical proposition a new one is deduced, with that same certainty can we deduce the social revolution from the existing social conditions and the principles of political economy."

Such words reveal the essence of what is unscientific and untrue in the Marxian system—the reading of the desired result into the limiting conditions, the failure to realize the central rôle played in all science by the working hypothesis. *Given* these conditions, *if* such and such action is taken, then the conceived result will follow: that is the language of science, and that is as far as the knowledge of man can reach. The attempt of Marx to know more than is possible to know, to prove more than he needed to prove, is what makes his great book, *Capital*, cumbersome and obscure and something of an affliction even upon the most willing. The abridgment so skillfully effected by Julian Borchardt will reduce these features to a minimum, and if in addition the reader will remember what is the matter while he reads, he may be able to get hold of the gigantic ideas in this book without obscuring his own clear judgment as so many have before him.

* * *

That being accomplished, he will turn with a more willing mind to the third part of Marxism as an engineering science—presentation of the scientific procedure, the mode of action by which it may be possible actually to pass from the conditioning facts toward the proposed goal. Here the famous *Communist Manifesto* comes into its true place. It contains, to be sure, a good deal of the metaphysic of history. Its very first sentence—"The history of all hitherto existing society is a history of class struggles" shows that disposition to read one's own interests into the definition of facts, which distinguishes the philosopher from the scientist. "No hitherto existing society has ever been changed fundamentally except by way of a class struggle" is all that the authors needed to say. But on the whole the *Communist Manifesto,* being the program of a conspiratorial league of revolutionists who hoped it might be possible in the approaching revolutionary disturbances in Europe to overthrow the bourgeoisie and establish a communist state, contains little of the phraseology of the dialectic philosopher. Historic necessity and the logic of evolution, are here pretty well forgotten. The universe is dropped out of the picture. The Communist League declares concretely in the language of common sense and of practical science that such and such are their "views" and such their "aims," and that these aims can be attained only by such and such methods.

In order to make more detailed the method of action which Marx believed in and initiated, and which received so high a development at the hands of Lenin and Trotsky and their followers in Russia, I have added a letter of instructions written to the Communist League by Marx from London in 1850. At that time he believed that the revolutionary crisis was still present, and he confidently expected another militant action of the proletariat led by the League. This letter has never before appeared in English, and yet it will perhaps more than anything else written by Marx convey a full sense of the degree in which he was the author and creator of all the essential outlines of what we call "Bolshevism." And finally, to give the reader a sense of Marxism as an attitude of feeling as well as of judgment, I have included another address written by Marx to his followers after the fall of the Paris Commune of 1871—the first occasion in history, and the only one in Marx's life, when an organization of the revolutionary working-class did actually seize the power. In the introduction, written by Engels, will be found again that concept of a dictatorship of the proletariat which has become the battle-cry of organized millions since the victory of the Bolshevik revolution in Russia.

It is hardly necessary to say that the man who foresaw these struggles, discovered their basis in the technique of

wealth production, and also laid down the methods of organization and action, and exemplified the emotional attitude,
which have led them to victory over one-sixth of the habitable
earth, is one of the most significant minds of our race. I hope
that this volume will do something toward making that mind
more directly accessible to intelligent Americans than it
could ever be when presented with any reverence for its
Hegelian-metaphysical inheritance and mode of dress.

MAX EASTMAN.

NEW YORK,
JUNE, 1932.

NOTE

For the purpose of a preliminary survey of the subject-matter I have translated an introduction to Marxism written by Lenin in 1913 and published in a Russian magazine called *Education*. To this very orthodox statement by Lenin it might be well—in view of my own proposals—to add another remark made by him: "In no sense do we regard the Marxist theory as something complete and unassailable. On the contrary, we are convinced that this theory is only the corner-stone of that science which socialists must advance in all directions if they do not wish to fall behind life."

The *Address To The Communist League* in Part III was translated by me, and also the quotations from the *Critique of Political Economy* in Part II and from *The German Ideology* in Parts I and II. This early work, in which Marx and Engels first formulated their views, remained unpublished until 1927, when the decaying manuscript was rescued and deciphered by the Marx-Engels Institute in Moscow. This is its first peep into the English language.

The other quotations are from standard translations of Marx's writings, except for the abridgment of *Capital*, which is Stephen L. Trask's translation of Julian Borchardt's book, *The People's Marx*. This book itself has almost become a classic, and seems to me a better way to get acquainted with Marx's economic theories than merely to read through the first volume and stop, as is usually done. It is needless to say that no one but a specialist needs to read the whole three volumes of *Das Kapital*. There are too many books in the world, too many sciences, too much to be known and thought over, for these pious acts of devotion to be indulged in by live men in our day. It may bring salvation to read the Koran from cover to cover, but *Das Kapital* does not achieve its effects in that magic way. The thing is to get hold of the ideas contained in it, and get them in Marx's own language. And that is what this admirable book makes it possible to do. I owe my thanks to Stephen L. Trask for permission to use his translation.

M. E.

THE THREE SOURCES AND THREE CON-
STITUENT PARTS OF MARXISM

THROUGHOUT the whole civilized world Marxist teachings draw upon themselves the extreme hostility and hatred of all bourgeois science (both governmental and liberal). It sees in Marxism something in the nature of a harmful "sect." No other attitude could be expected, for an impartial social science is impossible in a society founded on class struggle. In one way or another every governmental and liberal science defends wage slavery, and Marxism has declared ruthless war against this slavery. To expect impartial science in a wage-slave society is rather stupidly naïve—like expecting owners to be impartial on the question whether to raise the workers' wages at the expense of the profits of capital.

But never mind that. The history of philosophy and the history of social science offer abundantly clear proof that Marxism has nothing similar to "sectarianism" in the sense of a shut-in, ossified doctrine standing apart from the main road of development of world civilization. On the contrary, the very genius of Marx lay in the fact that he gave the answer to those questions which the most advanced thought of humanity had already raised. His teachings arose as a direct and immediate continuation of the teachings of the greatest representatives of philosophy, political economy and socialism.

The teaching of Marx is all-powerful because it is true. It is complete and symmetrical, offering an integrated view of the world, irreconcilable with any superstition, with any reactionism, or with any defense of bourgeois oppression. It is the legitimate inheritor of the best that humanity created in the 19th century in the form of German philosophy, English political economy, French socialism.

Let us dwell briefly upon these three sources and therefore constituent parts of Marxism.

The philosophy of Marxism is materialism. Throughout modern European history, and especially at the end of the 18th century in France, where a decisive battle was fought against all kinds of medieval rubbish, against serfdom in institutions and ideas, materialism proved to be the only consistent philosophy, true to all the teachings of the natural sciences, hostile to superstition, bigotry, etc. The enemies of democracy tried therefore with all their might to "refute," undermine and slander materialism, defending various forms of philosophic idealism, all of which come down one way or another to a defense or support of religion.

Marx and Engels defended philosophic materialism with the utmost determination, and many times explained the profound error of any departure from this foundation. Their views are expounded most clearly and in the greatest detail in the works of *Engels, Ludwig Feuerbach,* and *Anti-Dühring,* works which, like the *Communist Manifesto,* are everyday books on the table of the class-conscious worker.

But Marx did not rest in the materialism of the 18th century. He made an advance in philosophy. He enriched materialism with the acquisitions of the German classic philosophy, especially the system of Hegel which had led in its turn to the materialism of Feuerbach. The chief of these acquisitions is the dialectic—that is, the understanding of evolution in its fullest, deepest and most universal aspect, the understanding of the relativity of human knowledge, which gives us a reflection of eternally evolving matter. The most recent discoveries of natural science, radium, the electron, the transmutation of elements, have admirably confirmed the dialectic materialism of Marx—all the teachings of the bourgeois philosophers, with their "new" ways of returning to an old and rotten idealism, to the contrary notwithstanding.

While deepening and developing philosophic materialism, Marx carried it through to the end, extending its mode of understanding nature to the understanding of human society. The historic materialism of Marx is one of the greatest achievements of scientific thought. The caprice and chaos reigning up to that time among opinions about history and politics were here replaced by a strikingly whole and symmetrical and scientific theory, showing how out of one set-up of social life, another higher one develops in consequence of a growth of the productive forces—capitalism for example out of feudalism.

Just exactly as a man's knowledge reflects a nature existing independently of him—matter, that is, in a state of development—so also the social understanding of man (that is, his various views and teachings, philosophical, religious, political, etc.) reflects the economic structure of society. Political institutions are a superstructure resting on an economic foundation. We see, for instance, how the various political forms of the contemporary European states serve as a reinforcement of the rulership of the bourgeoisie over the proletariat.

The philosophy of Marx is that finished philosophic materialism which has given humanity in general, and the working class in particular, the greatest of all instruments of understanding.

Having seen that the economic structure is the basis upon which the political superstructure arises, Marx gave most of his attention to the study of this economic structure. His chief work *Capital* is devoted to a study of the economic structure of contemporary—that is, capitalist—society.

The classic political economy up to Marx's time had been formed in England, the most highly developed capitalist country Adam Smith and David Ricardo in their investigation of the economic structure had laid down the principle of the labor theory of value. Marx continued their work. He firmly established and consistently developed this theory. He showed that the value of any commodity is defined by the quantity of socially necessary labor time involved in its production.

Where the bourgeois economist had seen a relation between things (exchange of commodity for commodity) Marx discovered a relation between people. The exchange of goods expresses the connection formed between separate producers by means of the market. Money means that this connection is becoming closer, inseparably uniting in one unit the whole industrial life of the individual producers. Capital implies a further development of this connection. The labor power of man becomes a commodity. The wage-worker sells his labor power to the owner of land, factories and the instruments of labor. One part of the working day he spends in order to meet the cost of supporting himself and his family (wages), but another part of the day he spends working for nothing, creating for the capitalist surplus value, the source of profits, the source of the wealth of the class of capitalists.

The doctrine of surplus value is the keystone of the economic theory of Marx.

Capital, created by the labor of the worker, oppresses the worker by undermining the small proprietor and creating an army of the unemployed. In industry the victory of large-scale production is obvious at once, but in agriculture too we see the same phenomenon. The superiority of big capitalistic agriculture increases; there is a growing application of machines; the peasant economy falls into the noose of money capital, declines and collapses under the weight of a backward technique. In agriculture the decline of small-scale production takes special forms, but the decline itself is an indubitable fact.

In outstripping small-scale production, capital leads to an increase of the productivity of labor and the creation of monopolies through the union of the biggest capitalists. Production itself becomes more and more social—hundreds, thousands and millions of workers are brought together in a planned, economic, industrial organism—but the product of their general labor is appropriated by a handful of capitalists. Anarchy of production increases, crises multiply, and therewith the mad search for a market and insecurity of existence for the mass of the population.

In enlarging the dependence of the workers upon capital, the capitalist structure creates the mighty power of united labor.

From the first beginnings of commodity economy, from simple barter, Marx followed the development of capitalism to its highest forms, to large-scale production.

And the experience of all capitalist countries, both old and new, proves clearly every year to a larger and larger number of workers the truth of this doctrine of Marx.

Capitalism has conquered throughout the world, but its victory is only an earnest of the victory of labor over capital.

When serfdom was overthrown and the "free" capitalist society saw the light of day, it suddenly became clear that this freedom meant a new system of oppression and exploitation of the toilers. Various socialist doctrines began to emerge as a reflection of this oppression and a protest against it. But this original socialism was a utopian socialism. It criticized the capitalist society, condemned it, cursed it, dreamed of its destruction, drew fanciful pictures of a better structure, and tried to convince the rich of the immorality of exploitation.

But utopian socialism could not show a real way out. It was unable to explain the essence of wage labor under capitalism, to discover the laws of its development, or to find that social force capable of becoming the creator of a new society.

Meanwhile the tumultuous revolutions which accompanied the fall of feudalism, of serfdom—everywhere in Europe but especially in France—were making it more and more manifest that the foundation of the whole development and its motive force was the struggle of classes.

Not one single victory of political liberty over the feudal class was gained without overcoming a desperate resistance. Not one capitalist country has been formed on a more or less free democratic basis without a life-and-death struggle between the different classes of capitalist society.

The genius of Marx lay in the fact that he was able sooner than others to make and consistently carry out the inference to which the whole of world history leads. That inference is the doctrine of class struggle.

People always have been and they always will be the stupid victims of deceit and self-deception in politics, until they learn behind every kind of moral, religious, political, social phrase, declaration and promise to seek out the interests of this or that class or classes. The partisans of reform and betterment will always be fooled by the defenders of the old régime, until they understand that every old institution, no matter how savage and rotten it may seem, is sustained by the forces of this or that dominant class or classes. And there is only one way to break the resistance of these classes: namely, to find in the very society surrounding us, to find and educate and organize for the struggle, those forces which can—and owing to their social situation must—form a power capable of sweeping away the old and creating the new.

Only the philosophic materialism of Marx has shown the proletariat a way out of that spiritual slavery in which up to now all oppressed classes have been sleeping. Only the economic theory of Marx has explained the actual situation of the proletariat in the general structure of capitalism.

Throughout the whole world, from America to Japan and from Sweden to South Africa, independent organizations of the proletariat are multiplying. The proletariat is educating and enlightening itself by waging its class struggle. In casting loose from the prejudices of bourgeois society, uniting more and more closely, learning to take the measure of its successes, it is tempering its powers and growing irresistibly.

LENIN.

PART I

OUTLINES OF A FUTURE SOCIETY

1. *From "The German Ideology"*

THE division of labor presents just the first example of the fact that so long as men find themselves in a natural-grown society, so long therefore as the split exists between the individual and the common interest, so long as activities are not divided voluntarily but by a process of natural growth, man's own act becomes to him an alien power standing over against him, dominating him, instead of being ruled by him. That is to say that according as labor begins to be divided, everyone has a definite, circumscribed sphere of activity which is put upon him and from which he cannot escape. He is hunter, fisherman or shepherd or "critical critic," and must remain so if he does not want to lose the means of subsistence —whereas in the Communist society, where each one does not have a circumscribed sphere of activity but can train himself in any branch he chooses, society by regulating the common production makes it possible for me to do this today and that tomorrow, to hunt in the morning, to fish in the afternoon, to carry on cattle-breeding in the evening, also to criticize the food—just as I please—without becoming either hunter, fisherman, shepherd or critic. This setting-fast of social activity, this consolidation of our own product into an objective power over us, which outgrows our control, thwarts our expectations, brings our calculations to nothing, is one of the principal distinguishing points in historic evolution up to this day. . . .

In all history up to now it is certainly an empiric fact that single individuals, with the expansion of their activity to a world historic scale, have become more and more enslaved to an alien power . . . a power which has become steadily more massive, and has turned out to be, in the last analysis, the *world market*. But it is just as empirically grounded that through the overthrow of the existing social order, through the Communist revolution (about which more later) and what is the same thing, the abolition of private property, this power so mysterious to the German theoreticians will be dissolved, and then the emancipation of every single individual will be achieved to the same extent that history transforms itself completely into world history. That the genuine spiritual riches of the individual depend entirely upon the richness of the actual relations in which he stands, is clear from the above. Single individuals will in this way only be freed from the various national and local limitations, put into practical relation to the productive activity (including spiritual production) of the whole world, and placed in a position to acquire the capacity to enjoy this all-sided production of the whole earth. That *all-sided* dependence, that natural-grown form of the *world historical* coöperation of individuals, will be transformed by the Communist revolution into a control and conscious domination of those powers that are born of the mutual reactions of men, and which have heretofore imposed upon them and ruled over them as powers completely alien.

2. *From "The Poverty of Philosophy"*

THE working class will substitute, in the course of its development, for the old order of civil society, an association which will exclude classes and their antagonism, and there will no longer be political power, properly speaking, since political power is simply the official form of the antagonism in civil society.

3. *From "The Criticism of the Gotha Program"*

3. The emancipation of labor demands the elevation of the means of labor to the common property of society and the coöperative regulation of the total labor of society, together with an equitable distribution of the proceeds of labor.

—THE GOTHA PROGRAM [1]

[1] This was a proposed program for the German Social Democratic party drawn up under the influence of Ferdinand Lassalle, and Marx submitted its articles one-by-one to a vigorous criticism from his own point-of-view.

By "elevation of the means of labor to common property" is probably meant their "transformation into common property." But this only in passing.

What are "proceeds of labor"? The product of labor or its value? And in the latter case, are they the total value of the product or only that part of the value which labor has newly added to the value of the consumed means of production?

"Proceeds of labor" is a loose notion which takes the place with Lassalle of definite economic conceptions.

What is "equitable distribution"?

Does not the bourgeoisie maintain that the distribution now prevailing is "equitable"? And is it not, in fact, the only "equitable" distribution on the basis of the present mode of production? Are economic relations regulated by juridical conceptions or on the contrary do not the juridical relations arise out of the economic relations? Do not the sectarian socialists also entertain the most variegated notions of what constitutes "equitable" distribution?

In order to know what to understand in this instance by the phrase "equitable distribution," we must connect the first sentence with it. The phrase assumes a society in which the means of labor are common property and the total social labor is regulated coöperatively, whereas we learn from the first sentence that the "proceeds of labor belong to all the members of society, uncurtailed and with equal right."

"To all the members of society"? Even to those who do not work? Then what becomes of the "uncurtailed proceeds of labor"? Only to the working members of society? Then what becomes of the "equal right" of all the members of society?

Obviously, "all the members of society" and the "equal right" are only methods of expression. The essence of the matter consists in this, that in this Communistic society every worker must receive the "uncurtailed" Lassallean "proceeds of labor."

In the first place, if we take the phrase "proceeds of labor" in the sense of the product of labor, then the coöperative proceeds of labor are the "totality of the social product."

From this must be deducted:

First: what is required for the replacement of the consumed means of production.

Secondly: a supplementary portion for the extension of production.

Thirdly: a reserve or insurance fund against accidents, disturbances due to natural causes, etc.

These deductions from the "uncurtailed proceeds of labor" are an economic necessity and their magnitude will be determined according to the existing means and forces, in part by the calculation of the probabilities, but they can in no way be calculated by justice.

There remains the other portion of the total product, destined to serve as means of consumption.

Before this can be distributed among the individuals, there is still to be deducted:

First: *the general costs of administration which are not part of production.*

This portion is very considerably reduced at the very outset in comparison with present society and diminishes in the same measure as the new society develops.

Secondly: *what is destined to satisfy the needs of the community, such as schools, sanitary provisions, etc.*

This portion grows considerably from the very outset in comparison with present society and increases in the same measure as the new society develops.

Thirdly: *a fund for those incapable of working, etc., in short, for what today belongs to so-called official public charity.*

Only now do we arrive at the only "distribution" which the program, under the influence of Lassalle and in a narrow manner, has in view, namely, the portion of the means of consumption which is distributed among the individual producers of the community.

The "uncurtailed proceeds of labor" have already been transformed under our very eyes into the "curtailed"—although what is taken from the producer as an individual benefits him directly or indirectly as a member of society.

Just as the phrase "uncurtailed proceeds of labor" has

By "elevation of the means of labor to common property" is probably meant their "transformation into common property." But this only in passing.

What are "proceeds of labor"? The product of labor or its value? And in the latter case, are they the total value of the product or only that part of the value which labor has newly added to the value of the consumed means of production?

"Proceeds of labor" is a loose notion which takes the place with Lassalle of definite economic conceptions.

What is "equitable distribution"?

Does not the bourgeoisie maintain that the distribution now prevailing is "equitable"? And is it not, in fact, the only "equitable" distribution on the basis of the present mode of production? Are economic relations regulated by juridical conceptions or on the contrary do not the juridical relations arise out of the economic relations? Do not the sectarian socialists also entertain the most variegated notions of what constitutes "equitable" distribution?

In order to know what to understand in this instance by the phrase "equitable distribution," we must connect the first sentence with it. The phrase assumes a society in which the means of labor are common property and the total social labor is regulated coöperatively, whereas we learn from the first sentence that the "proceeds of labor belong to all the members of society, uncurtailed and with equal right."

"To all the members of society"? Even to those who do not work? Then what becomes of the "uncurtailed proceeds of labor"? Only to the working members of society? Then what becomes of the "equal right" of all the members of society?

Obviously, "all the members of society" and the "equal right" are only methods of expression. The essence of the matter consists in this, that in this Communistic society every worker must receive the "uncurtailed" Lassallean "proceeds of labor."

In the first place, if we take the phrase "proceeds of labor" in the sense of the product of labor, then the coöperative proceeds of labor are the "totality of the social product."

From this must be deducted:

First: what is required for the replacement of the consumed means of production.

Secondly: a supplementary portion for the extension of production.

Thirdly: a reserve or insurance fund against accidents, disturbances due to natural causes, etc.

These deductions from the "uncurtailed proceeds of labor" are an economic necessity and their magnitude will be determined according to the existing means and forces, in part by the calculation of the probabilities, but they can in no way be calculated by justice.

There remains the other portion of the total product, destined to serve as means of consumption.

Before this can be distributed among the individuals, there is still to be deducted:

First: *the general costs of administration which are not part of production.*

This portion is very considerably reduced at the very outset in comparison with present society and diminishes in the same measure as the new society develops.

Secondly: *what is destined to satisfy the needs of the community, such as schools, sanitary provisions, etc.*

This portion grows considerably from the very outset in comparison with present society and increases in the same measure as the new society develops.

Thirdly: *a fund for those incapable of working, etc., in short, for what today belongs to so-called official public charity.*

Only now do we arrive at the only "distribution" which the program, under the influence of Lassalle and in a narrow manner, has in view, namely, the portion of the means of consumption which is distributed among the individual prolucers of the community.

The "uncurtailed proceeds of labor" have already been transformed under our very eyes into the "curtailed"—although what is taken from the producer as an individual benefits him directly or indirectly as a member of society.

Just as the phrase "uncurtailed proceeds of labor" has

disappeared, the phrase "proceeds of labor" in general now also disappears.

Within the coöperative society, based upon the common ownership of the means of production, the producers do not exchange their products; just as little does the labor employed upon these products appear here *as the value* of these products, as a material quality possessed by them, since now, in contrast to capitalist society, the labor of the individual becomes, no longer in a roundabout way, but directly, a component part of the total labor. The phrase, "proceeds of labor," to be condemned even today because of its ambiguity, thus loses all meaning.

What we are dealing with here is a Communist society, not as it has *developed* upon its own foundation, but on the contrary, just as it is *emerging* out of capitalist society; consequently, a society which still bears, in every respect, economic, moral and intellectual, the birthmarks of the old society from whose womb it is issuing. Accordingly, the individual producer gets back—once the deductions are made —exactly as much as he has given it. What he has given is his individual amount of labor. For example, the social working day consists of the sum of the individual working hours; the individual working time of each producer is the portion of the social working day supplied by him, his share of it. He receives from society a check signifying that he has supplied so much labor (after deduction of his work done for the common fund), and with this check he draws from the social stores as much of the means of consumption as costs an equal amount of labor. The same quantity of labor which he has given society in one form, he receives back in another.

Evidently the same principle prevails here that today regulates the exchange of commodities in so far as it is an exchange of equal values. Substance and form are changed because under the changed conditions no one can give anything except his labor and because, on the other hand, nothing can become the property of the individual except the individual means of consumption. But so far as the distribution of the latter among the individual producers is concerned, the same principle prevails as in the exchange of equivalent commodities: an equal quantity of labor in one form is exchanged for an equal quantity of labor in another form.

Equal right, therefore, is here still according to the principle of *bourgeois right,* although principle and practice are no longer at odds, whereas today the exchange of equivalents in the exchange of commodities exists only for the average and not for individual cases.

Notwithstanding this progress, the *equal right* is still encumbered with bourgeois limitations. The right of the producers is *proportional* to the labor they supply; the equality consists in measuring this right by an *equal standard:* labor.

But one individual is physically or mentally superior to another and consequently supplies more labor in the same time or can work for a longer time; and in order to serve as a measure, labor must be determined according to its duration or its intensity, otherwise it would cease to be a standard. This *equal* right is an unequal right for unequal labor. It recognizes no class distinctions because everyone is only a worker like everybody else; but it tacitly recognizes the inequality of individual endowment and therefore productive capacity, as natural privileges. *It is therefore a right of inequality, in its substance, as is all right.* By its very nature, right can only consist in the application of an equal standard; but the unequal individuals (and they would not be different individuals if they were not unequal) can be measured by an equal standard only in so far as they are considered from the same point of view, or are regarded from a *definite* aspect, for example, in the given instance, if they are regarded *only as workers,* no more than that and regardless of anything else. Furthermore: one worker is married, the other is not; one has more children than the other, etc., etc. Hence, with an equal contribution of labor and consequently an equal share of the social consumption fund, one actually gets more than the other, one is richer than the other, etc. In order to avoid all these shortcomings, right would have to be unequal, and not equal.

But these shortcomings are unavoidable in the first phase of Communist society, as it issues forth from capitalist society after a long and painful travail. Right can never be on a higher level than the economic state of society and the stage of social civilization conditioned by it.

In a higher phase of Communist society, after the enslaving subordination of the individual to the division of labor shall have disappeared, and with it the antagonism between intellectual and manual labor, after labor has become not only a means of life but also the primary necessity of life; when, with the development of the individual in every sense, the productive forces also increase and all the springs of collective wealth flow with abundance—only then can the limited horizon of bourgeois right be left behind entirely and society inscribe upon its banner: "From each according to his abilities, to each according to his needs!"

PART II
ANALYSIS OF THE MATERIALS

A. The Theory of History

1. *From "The German Ideology"*

THE first premise of all human history is of course the existence of living human individuals. The first matter of fact to be established is therefore the bodily organization of these individuals and their relation thus given to the rest of nature. We cannot here, of course, go into the physical constitution of men themselves nor into the natural conditions found by them—the geologic, oro-hydrographic, climatic and other conditions. All historical writing must set out from these natural bases, and their modification in the course of history by the action of men.

We can distinguish men from animals by consciousness, religion, or whatever we like. They themselves begin to distinguish themselves from animals as soon as they begin to *produce* the means of life, a step which is conditioned by their bodily organization. In producing their means of life, men indirectly produce their material life itself.

The manner in which men produce their means of life depends first of all upon the nature of the means which they have found and have to reproduce.

The mode of production is not to be considered as being merely a reproduction of the physical existence of the individuals. It is much rather a definite kind of activity of these individuals, a definite way in which they express their lives, one of their definite *modes of living*. As individuals express their lives, so are they. Therefore what they are coincides with their production, both in the sense of *what* they produce and *how* they produce it. Thus what individuals are, depends upon the material conditions of their production. . . .

The fact therefore is this: definite individuals, who are productively active in a definite manner, enter into these definite social and political relations. Empiric observation must in every single case reveal the connection between the social and political organization and the mode of production—reveal it empirically and without any mystification or speculation. The social organization and the state issue perpetually from the life-process of definite individuals, but from these individuals not as they may appear in their own or another's imagination, but as they *really* are, that is, as they act, as they materially produce—thus, as they act under definite material limitations, premises and conditions independent of their will.

The production of ideas and conceptions, of consciousness, is, to begin with, directly interwoven with the material activity and the material intercourse of men, language of real life. Men's conceptions, thoughts, spiritual intercourse, here still appear as the direct emanation of their material conduct. The same holds for spiritual production, as represented in the language of the politics, laws, morality, religion, metaphysics, etc., of a people. Men are the producers of their conceptions, ideas, etc.—but this means real, functioning men, as they are determined by a definite development of their productive forces and the intercourse corresponding to the same up to its remotest formations. Consciousness can never be anything but the conscious being, and the being of men is their actual life-process. . . .

Wholly in contrast to German philosophy, which comes down from heaven to earth, we here ascend from earth to heaven. That is, we do not proceed from what men say, imagine and represent to themselves, nor from the men who are said, thought, imagined and represented, in order from out of and by them to arrive at the bodily men. We proceed from the really active men and set forward the development out of their real life-process of the ideological reflexes and echoes of this life-process. The phantasmagorias in the brains of men are necessary supplements also of their material life-process as empirically establishable and bound up with material premises. Morals, religion, metaphysics and other ideologies, and the forms of consciousness corresponding to them, here no longer retain a look of independence. They have no history, they have no development, but men in developing their material production and their material intercourse, alter along with this reality of theirs their thought and the products of their thought. It is not consciousness that determines life, but life that determines consciousness. In the first view, one proceeds from the consciousness as the living individual; in the second, which conforms to real life, one proceeds from the really living individuals themselves and regards consciousness only as *their* consciousness.

This view is not without premises. It proceeds from the real premises, not abandoning them for a second. Its premises are men, not in some fantastic seclusion and state of fixation, but in their actual empirically visible process of development under definite conditions. As soon as this active life-process is presented, history ceases to be a collection of dead facts, as it is even with the still abstract empiricists, or an imaginary activity of imaginary creatures, as with the idealists.

For where speculation ceases, at real life, there begins the real, positive science, a presentation of the practical activity, of the practical process of development of men. Phrases about consciousness cease, and real knowledge must take their place. With the presentation of the reality independent philosophy loses its medium of existence. Its place can be taken, at the most, by a summing up of the most general results to be abstracted from a consideration of the historical development of men. . . .

2. *From the Introduction to "Critique of Political Economy"*

In the social production of their subsistence men enter into determined and necessary relations with each other which are independent of their wills—production-relations which correspond to a definite stage of development of their material productive forces. The sum of these production-relations forms the economic structure of society, the real basis upon which a juridical and political superstructure arises, and to which definite social forms of consciousness correspond. The mode of production of the material subsistence, conditions the social, political and spiritual life-process in general. It is not the consciousness of men which determines their existence, but on the contrary it is their social existence which determines their consciousness. At a certain stage of their development the material productive forces of society come into contradiction with the existing production-relations, or what is merely a juridical expression for the same thing, the property relations within which they have operated before. From being forms of development of the productive forces, these relations turn into fetters upon their development. Then comes an epoch of social revolution. With the change in the economic foundation the whole immense superstructure is slowly or rapidly transformed. In studying such a transformation one must always distinguish between the material transformation in the economic conditions essential to production—which can be established with the exactitude of natural science— and the juridical, political, religious, artistic, or philosophic, in short ideological forms, in which men become conscious of this conflict and fight it out. As little as one judges what an individual is by what he thinks of himself, so little can one judge such an epoch of transformation by its consciousness; one must rather explain this consciousness by the contradictions in the material life, the conflict at hand between the social forces of production and the relations in which production is carried on. No social formation ever disappears before all the productive forces are developed for which it has room, and new higher relations of production never appear before the material conditions of their existence are matured in the womb of the old society.

B. THE EXISTING SOCIETY

1. *Capital: An Analysis of Capitalist Production.*

Abridged edition of Marx's three volumes by **Julian** Borchardt. Translated by Stephen L. Trask.

CAPITAL

CONTENTS

		PAGE
	Editor's Preface	15
CHAPTER		
I.	Commodities, Prices, Profits	20
II.	Profit and Value in Circulation	24
III.	Value in Use and Exchange Value. The Socially Necessary Labour	29
IV.	Purchase and Sale of Labour Power . . .	34
V.	How Surplus-Value Arises	39
VI.	Constant Capital and Variable Capital. Fixed Capital and Circulating Capital . . .	47
VII.	How Uniform Profit Is Obtained	54
VIII.	Methods by Which Surplus-Value Is Increased	59
IX.	How Capital Revolutionises the Mode of Production	63
X.	The Influence of Industrial Progress on the Working Classes	99
XI.	Decrease of the Rate of Profit	141
XII.	The Accumulation of Capital	146
XIII.	Influence of the Accumulation of Capital on the Working Class. The Industrial Reserve-Army. The Theory of the Growing Impoverishment of the Masses	161
XIV.	The So-called Primitive Accumulation . .	182
XV.	What Capitalist Accumulation Leads To . .	202
XVI.	Money	205

XVII. The Circular Course of Capital and the Time Requisite for Its Circulation 223

XVIII. Commercial Activity 233

XIX. Commercial Capital and the Work of the Commercial Employés 239

XX. The Influence of Commercial Capital on Prices 253

XXI. The Historical Development of Commercial Capital 257

XXII. Interest and the Profit Derived from Industrial Undertakings 268

XXIII. Credit and Banks 280

XXIV. Crises 293

Supplement. The Essence of Marx's Theory of Crises 302

EDITOR'S PREFACE

THE November revolution in Germany in 1918 marked the beginning of the era of Socialism. Socialism and Socialisation are the catchwords of the hour. But what does Socialism signify? It is urgently necessary that everyone, and not merely the intellectuals, should become familiar with the fundamental teachings of Socialism.

The founder of scientific Socialism was Karl Marx, who was born in Treves in 1818, and who died in London in 1883. The fundamental teachings of Socialism are contained in Marx's principal work: *Das Kapital*. It is therefore today the imperative duty of everyone who is anxious to understand the trend of our present social development—and *a forteriori* of everyone desirous of contributing actively to such development—to acquire a knowledge of that work.

But this duty is by no means easy to fulfil. Whoever wishes to read Marx's *Capital,* encounters a superabundance of difficulties. We may, indeed, go further, and say that it is quite incomprehensible for the layman. And the majority of mankind are composed of laymen.

In the first place there is the enormous size of the work —not less than 2200 large printed pages filling three volumes. Who can be expected to read this, if he be not a specialist in political economy, and if he have professional business to attend to? Secondly, there is Marx's manner of expressing himself, which is uncommonly difficult to grasp. Sycophants, anxious to praise everything done by a great man, have maintained that Marx's style is clear, precise, and easy of comprehension. This does not even hold good of his short essays destined for newspapers. And when such assertions are put forward in regard to his books on political economy, these assertions are absolutely false. In order to understand Marx, various conditions must be postulated:

not only is it necessary that the reader penetrate deeply into, and meditate with heart and soul on, the great thinker's work, but he must also subject himself to intense intellectual strain; and, furthermore, he must be in possession of a sound and thorough-going economic training. It is easy to understand the reasons for Marx's obscurity. Marx achieved a colossal intellectual labour. He had a thorough grasp of everything taught before him by the science of political economy, and by dint of his own research he increased immensely the material already accumulated. He studied minutely all economic problems, and discovered entirely new solutions precisely for the most important of them. His whole attention and energy was so taken up by the *content* of economic science, that he attached no importance to the *form* in which his ideas were expressed. The number of ideas continuously occupying him was so great, that he was indifferent to the manner of expressing such ideas. And he evidently did not realise the fact, that a number of things with which he was familiar and which appeared to him self-evident, must needs be extremely difficult of comprehension for persons lacking his extensive knowledge. All the more so, as he had no intention of writing for amateurs. He intended, on the contrary, composing a strictly scientific work.

However this may be, it is certain that, in order to understand Marx, a much greater amount of time and labour is necessary, than a mere layman can be expected to devote to the task.

And now we come to the third and greatest difficulty. From beginning to end, Marx's work is from one and the same mould; the various parts of his teaching are so intimately interwoven that no single part can be rightly understood without acquiring a knowledge of the others. The reader of the first chapters cannot, of course, be aware of the contents of the subsequent ones, and must therefore obtain a false impression of the master's teaching as long as he has not achieved the study of all three volumes of *Capital*.

This difficulty is increased by reason of the fact that Marx himself was unable to complete the work. Only the first volume of *Capital*, published in 1867, was completely achieved and made ready for press by him. The two other volumes were published after his death by his friend Friedrich Engels —the second volume in 1885, the third, in two parts, in 1894. But neither of these two volumes was in any way ready for press when Marx died, so that Engels had frequently to include in them the sketches in which Marx first put his ideas into writing. Countless repetitions are the result. The reader who is unaware of this—and the amateur cannot possibly be aware of it—sees to his astonishment the same idea, clothed in different words, constantly recurring, ten or fifteen times or even more; and the reason for this is not clear to him. The consequence is that even professional *savants* as a rule confine themselves to the first volume, and therefore naturally misunderstand the author. *A forteriori* is this the case with laymen, for instance with the Socialist workingman, who, even if he devote almost the whole of his leisure time to reading the first volume to the end, carefully avoids perusing the second and third volumes.

For all these reasons it has long since been clear to me that there was an urgent need for rendering Marx's *Capital* accessible to the vast number who are eager to know its contents, but who are unable to make such a study a part of their life-work. It must clearly be understood that there is no question here of "popularising" Marx's teaching in the sense that another author exposes in his own words that teaching, in such a way as to render the latter comprehensible. There are already enough expositions of the sort. (They are moreover often incomplete, seeing that the author himself was acquainted with the first volume only, and considered it superfluous to consult the others.) In my case, *Marx himself speaks;* it is his own work, in his own words, which I am laying before the reader in such a manner as to render it comprehensible to everyone willing to expend on it a little time and trouble.

This task I had assigned to myself many years ago.[1] The

[1] Consequently a quite different task to the one assigned themselves by Kautsky and Eckstein when publishing the so-called "people's editions" of Marx's *Capital*. This edition confines itself, in its German version, to "germanising" a number of words of foreign extraction and

war with the enforced leisure resulting from it for me, gave me the necessary time. I considered myself competent to undertake the work for the reason that I have been studying Marx's *Capital* most closely and carefully for some 30 years past; over twenty years ago I translated—at the request of the *Institut des Sciences Sociales* in Brussels, and in cooperation with my Belgian comrade Vanderryrlt—the second and third volumes into French.[1]

* * *

I will add a few words concerning the manner in which I have sought to fulfil my task. Necessarily I was anxious above all things, as already stated, to let Marx's own words remain as far as possible, and to confine myself to *omissions* and *transpositions*. I have remarked above that the difficulty of understanding Marx is attributable, to a large extent, to the fact that, in order to rightly understand one part of his work, all the other parts must be known. It is hardly exaggerated to say that the first sections must seem to the novice bold enough to venture to read them, as if they were written in Chinese. This is due to the fact that he can have, as yet, no notion of the spirit in which the book was conceived, of the author's method of thinking and reasoning. In order to obtain such a notion, he must be acquainted with important discussions in the third volume. For this reason it was, from the beginning, evident to me that I should have to entirely transpose the order of Marx's ideas, consequently the order of treatises containing those ideas. A considerable portion of the contents of the third volume had to be placed right at the beginning. Treatises which, in the original, are distributed over a number of chapters sometimes wide apart from each other, had often to be joined together; others, on

translating the quotations reproduced in a foreign tongue in the original. And the "people's edition" contains, in a space of 700 large pages, only the first volume. It would scarcely be possible to edit in this way the other volumes, which present much greater difficulties. But even if it were possible, the only result would be a new book of 2000 pages, which only those persons could afford to study, who had the necessary leisure and money.

[1] Paris, Giard & Brière, 1901.

the contrary, had to be taken asunder. I had, therefore, frequently to write connecting sentences. But, on the whole, the exact wording of the original has been rigidly adhered to.

Numerous advantages were already obtained thereby. Whoever gives himself the trouble to compare the present edition with the original one, will see to his surprise how many orders of ideas, otherwise extremely difficult of comprehension, have been rendered clear by merely transposing them.

The omissions will be seen to be not less valuable. It was evident that one version only of the innumerable repetitions contained in the second and third volumes had to be selected. But, over and above this, it was by no means my intention to reproduce the entire work in all its details. On the contrary, a selection had to be made in such a way, that the reader be able to study all Marx's fundamental ideas in the author's own words, without being alarmed or overtired by the excessive dimensions of the book. Anyone can, at any time, verify by comparison if anything essential has been omitted. In order to facilitate this control, I have indicated at the beginning of each chapter, and also elsewhere when needed, those parts of the original I have reproduced.[1]

True, an appreciable number of passages are to be found in this edition, the wording of which differs from the wording in the original. This was inevitable; for otherwise they would have remained incomprehensible.

In conclusion, I would venture to express the hope that this edition may not only prove useful in so far as conducive to a better understanding of Marx, but that it may develop the interest in, and increase the comprehension of, economic science generally, and thus be profitable to the cause of Socialism.

I should be particularly happy if the present abridged edition would serve as an incitement to study the original work.

Berlin-Lichterfelde, April, 1919.

JULIAN BORCHARDT.

[1] Where no edition is specified, reference is always made to the English edition (William Glaisher, 1920).

CHAPTER I

COMMODITIES, PRICES, PROFITS

(Extracted from vol. III, part. 1, sections 1 & 2; vol. III, part. 2, pp. 356—358 & 398—402. German edition.)

POLITICAL ECONOMY deals with the economic supply to mankind of the commodities needed by the latter in order to live. In modern capitalist States this process is accomplished exclusively by means of the sale and purchase of commodities, of which human beings become the proprietors by buying such commodities for the money that constitutes their income. There are various categories of income, which, however, can be divided into three main groups: every year *capital* brings in profit for the capitalist; *the soil* brings in ground rents for the landowner; and *labour power*—under normal conditions, and as long as such labour power can be utilized—earns wages for the worker. Thus capital appears to the capitalist, the soil to the landowner, and his labour power—or rather, his labour itself—to the labourer, as the three different sources of their respective incomes, *i. e.*, of profits, ground rents, and wages. All such incomes would seem to resemble the fruit of a tree that never withers, fruit which is consumed every year—or, to be precise, of three trees which furnish the annual income of three social classes: of the capitalist class, the landowning class, and the labouring class. The wealth which constitutes all categories of income appears to be derived from three distinct and independent sources: namely, capital, ground rents, and labour.

But the amount of income possessed by each class is not the only decisive factor in the supply of economic commodities. The price of such commodities is likewise a decisive element of the process; and the question as to what causes determine prices has, consequently, always formed the subject of searching inquiry on the part of economists.

At first sight this question does not appear to present any difficulty. If we take any product of industry, its price is determined by the manufacturer adding to the cost of production such profit as is customary in his particular branch. The price depends, in consequence, on the amount of the cost of production and on the amount of profit.

The manufacturer reckons as cost of production everything spent by him for the purpose of producing a given commodity. Such expenditure consists, in the first place, of the sums spent on raw materials and such auxiliary materials as are needed (*e. g.* cotton, coal, etc.); and, further, on machines, tools, and buildings. The expenditure consists, secondly, of the ground rent (*e. g.* the rent due for the premises), and, thirdly, of the wages paid for labour. We can therefore divide the manufacturer's costs of production into the three following categories:

1) the means of production (*e. g.* raw materials, auxiliary materials, machinery, tools, and buildings);
2) the ground rent (which will also be calculated in the event of the factory standing on its own ground);
3) wages.

If we analyse these three categories somewhat closer, we shall find ourselves confronted by unforeseen difficulties. Let us first of all take the wages. According as to whether the latter are high or low, the total costs of production—and, consequently, the price of the finished article—will be high or low. But what determines the rate of wages? Let us say, after labour power has been offered and demanded. The demand for labour power comes from the capitalist, who needs labourers for his undertaking. A large demand for labour power implies therefore a large increase of capital. What does capital consist of? It consists of money and commodities. Or, rather, seeing that money—as we shall point out in detail later on—is itself only a commodity, we may say that capital simply consists of commodities. The more valuable such commodities are, the larger is the capital, and the greater is the demand for labour power with its ensuing influence alike on the rate of wages and—as a further consequence—on the price of the finished article. Now let us see what determines the value (or price) of the commodities which constitute capital. That value is determined by the costs necessary for their own production. And among such costs of production we find wages! So that in the long run the rate of wages is, according to this theory, determined by— the rate of wages! And the price of commodities by—the price of commodities!

Or else it is stated that wages are determined by the price of the food needed by the labourer. But such foodstuffs are themselves commodities, and their price is in part determined by wages; and thus the error is obvious.

A second factor of the manufacturer's costs of production was seen to be the *means of production*. It is not necessary to go into details in order to understand that cotton, machinery, coal, etc., are also commodities, of which exactly the same holds good as of those commodities which constitute the food of the labourer or the capital of the employer of labour.

The attempt to explain prices by referring to the costs of production has thus proved a sorry failure. It has just simply resulted in "determining" prices by themselves!

To the cost of production the manufacturer adds the customary profit. It would seem as if, in this case, all difficulties were overcome, seeing that the percentage (or rate) of profit which he must calculate is known to the manufacturer as the amount customary in his particular branch of industry. This, of course, does not prevent an individual manufacturer, by reason of special circumstances, sometimes calculating his profit at a higher or lower rate than the customary one. But on an average the rate of profits is the same in all the undertakings in a given branch of industry. In every branch there is thus a common average rate of profit.

But not only that. Owing to competition, the rates of profit in different branches are brought into a certain harmony with each other. And it cannot be otherwise, for, as soon as extraordinary high profits are reaped in any given branch, capital emigrates from those branches which are less lucrative, and is invested in the more lucrative one. Or else new capital, which is continually being formed and which seeks profitable investment, will strongly favour such lucrative branches; production in the latter must in consequence increase considerably; and in order to sell the greatly increased number of commodities, prices—and therefore profits—must be reduced. Just the contrary will take place if in any branch extraordinarily low profits are made. Capital will emigrate from such a branch as rapidly as possible; production will thus be diminished to the extent of such emigration; and this, in turn, tends to increase prices and profits.

Competition thus tends to establish an equilibrium between the rates of profit in all branches; and we are justified in speaking of a general average rate of profit, which, if not identical, is at all events more or less similar in all branches of production. True, this phenomenon is not as obvious as is the equality of profits within one and the same branch, seeing that the general costs, the wear of the machinery, the use to which the latter is put, etc., are liable to vary very considerably from branch to branch. In order to bring about a balance between such variations it is possible that the brutto profit —*i. e.* the percentage actually calculated by the manufacturer over and above the costs of production—be appreciably higher (or lower) in one branch than in others. This phenomenon tends to obscure the real facts. But after deduction of the different costs of production there none the less remains, in the various branches of industry, a net profit rate which is approximately similar in all cases.

As a general average rate of profit thus exists, the amount of profit accruing in reality to any given undertaking depends on the amount of capital sunk in the latter. It is true that— as previously mentioned—it is not entirely indifferent whether a factory produce guns or cotton stockings, seeing that the profits vary a little according to the security of the investment, to the greater ease or difficulty with which the commodity produced is sold, etc. But such differences are unimportant. Let us suppose the general average rate of profit to be 10 per cent, and it is evident that a capital of $1,000,000— must reap a profit which will be 10 times greater than that reaped by a capital of $100,000—(We assume, of course, the existence of proper business methods, just as we make abstraction of all those particular instances of luck or ill-luck which may possibly occur in the history of any individual undertaking).

We must further bear in mind that profits are made not only by industrial undertakings, which *produce* commodities; but also by commercial undertakings, which merely act as a medium between the producer and the consumer for the sale of such commodities to the latter; and likewise by banks, carriers and forwarding agents, railways, etc. In the case of all these undertakings—always assuming efficient business management—profits are determined by the amount of capital invested. It is no wonder that those persons who are concerned in the practical conduct of such undertakings should be convinced that profits arise, so to speak, spontaneously out of capital—that capital produces them just as the tree, if properly cultivated, produces fruit. And in so far as profits are not regarded as a natural characteristic inherent to capital, they are looked upon as the result of the work accomplished by the capitalist. As a matter of fact, we have invariably had to start, in our discussion, from the presumption that the management of the business is an efficient one. Much depends on the personal efficiency of the manager. Should the latter prove inefficient, the profit of any individual undertaking can easily sink below the general average rate, whereas a capable manager may succeed in raising it above that average.

CHAPTER II

PROFIT AND VALUE IN CIRCULATION

(Extracted from vol. III, part. 1, sections 1 & 2, German ed. —Vol. I, ch. 5.)

BUT how can profit derive "spontaneously" from capital? For the production of any given commodity the capitalist needs a certain sum, say $25.00. In this sum are included all the costs of production, *i. e.* raw and auxiliary materials, wages, the wear of the machinery, tools, buildings, etc. He subsequently sells the finished commodity for $27.50. If we conclude that the finished commodity is really worth $27.50, we must necessarily conclude that this increased value, which has accrued during the process of production, has arisen out of nothing, seeing that all the values for which the capitalist has paid $25.00 existed previous to the existence of the commodity in question. The idea of something being thus created out of nothing is unacceptable to human reason. Hence economists have always held in the past, and still hold to-day, that the value of the commodity does not increase during the process of production, but that when this process is finished the capitalist has only in his possession an object of the same value as previously—that is to say, in the case assumed by us, of the value of $25.00.

But from what then do the surplus $2.50 derive, which he receives out of the sale of the commodity? The simple fact that the commodity passes out of the hands of the seller into those of the buyer, cannot enhance its value; for this would likewise be equivalent to the creation of something out of nothing.

Two courses are generally adopted in order to get out of the difficulty. Some maintain that in the hands of the purchaser the commodity is really more valuable than in those of the vendor, seeing that it satisfies a want of the purchaser which is non-existent in the case of the vendor. Others say that the commodity does not, as a matter of fact, possess the value represented by the price paid, and that the purchaser has to pay the surplus without obtaining any equivalent.

Let us analyse the two views. The French economist Condillac wrote in 1776, in an essay on Commerce and Government: "It is false that, in the exchange of commodities, equal value is given and obtained. The contrary is true. Each of the two contracting parties, invariably gives a smaller value for a greater one. . . . If, as a matter of fact, equal values were always exchanged, neither of the contracting parties would earn a profit. But both profit, or at any rate both should do so. Why? The value of things resides solely in their relation to our wants. What is more to one man, is less to the other and *vice-versa*. . . . We wish to give away a thing which is useless for us, in order to obtain something necessary; in other words, we wish to give less in order to obtain more. . . ."

Truly a singular example of arithmetical reasoning! When two persons exchange something, does each give the other more than he receives? That would imply that if I buy a coat from the tailor for $5.00, the coat in question is worth less than $5.00 as long as it remains in the hands of the tailor, but that its value rises to $5.00 when I take possession of it! Neither do we get any further with the makeshift argument that the value of commodities resides exclusively in their relation to our wants. For (apart from the confusion of *value in use* and *value in exchange,* which we shall come to later) even if the coat be more valuable than the money for the purchaser, the money is more valuable than the coat for the vendor.

If, on the other hand, we accept the hypothesis that commodities in general are sold for a higher price than they are worth, the consequences which ensue are stranger still. Let us provisionally admit that through some inexplicable privilege the vendor is able to sell the goods at a price over and above their value, for $27.50 when they are worth but $25.00, *i. e.* at a premium of 10%. The vendor thus obtains an increase of value of 10%. But after having been the vendor, he becomes purchaser. He now meets a third owner of commodities; and the latter, in his capacity as vendor, enjoys in his turn the privilege of selling the commodity 10% too dear. Our man has thus gained $2.50 as vendor, and lost $2.50 as purchaser. As a matter of fact, the whole process resolves itself into this: every owner of commodities sells every other owner his goods at the rate of 10% over and above their value; and this is exactly the same as if they had sold them at their exact value; the prices of the commodities increase, but the real relation of their values to each other remains unchanged.

Let us suppose, on the other hand, that it is the privilege of the purchaser to buy commodities below their value. In this case it is not even necessary to recall the fact that the purchaser becomes again later-on a vendor, just as he was a vendor before becoming a purchaser. He had already lost 10% as vendor, before gaining 10% as purchaser. Everything thus remains as it was.

It may be objected that such a counterbalancing of a previous loss by a subsequent profit only takes place in the case of purchasers who afterwards become vendors, and that there are persons who have nothing to sell. The consistent representatives of the illusion according to which increase of value derives from a nominal increase of prices, or from the privilege of the vendor to sell the commodity too dear— these representatives take for granted the existence of a class which only purchases and does not sell, *i. e.* which only consumes and does not produce. But the money with which such a class is able to keep on continually purchasing must be obtained from the owners of commodities themselves—without any exchange, gratuitously, on the strength of any given legal or non-legal titles. To sell such a class commodities above their value thus simply means recovering, in part and by fraudulent means, money given away gratuitously. For instance, in ancient times the towns in Asia Minor paid annually money tributes to Rome. With this money Rome purchased commodities from them and purchased them too dear. The inhabitants of Asia Minor defrauded the Romans by retaking a part of the tribute money in the course of trade. But none the less were those inhabitants swindled in the long run. Their commodities, both before and after, were paid them with their own money. This is not the way to increase one's wealth or to create surplus-value.

Of course we do not contest that the individual owner of commodities may enrich himself by selling too dear. The owner A may be smart enough to take-in his colleagues B or C, whereas the latter are unable to obtain a *revanche*, despite all their efforts. A sells wine for $10.00 to B, and obtains in exchange corn to the value of $12.50. A has transformed his $10.00 into $12.50 or in other words has made more money out of less. But let us examine the matter more closely. Previous to the exchange A possessed $10.00 worth of wine, and B $12.50 worth of corn, the total value thus amounting to $22.50. After the exchange, the same total value of $22.50 remains. The value in circulation has not been increased by a single farthing; merely the proportion in which the sum total was divided between A and B has been reversed. The same change would have taken place if A, instead of veiling the transaction by having recourse to an exchange.

had purely and simply stolen the $2.50 from B. The total value of the commodities in circulation can manifestly not be increased by changes in the proportion of their distribution; just as little as a Jew can increase the quantity of precious metals in a given country by selling a copper coin of the 18th century for a gold coin. The totality of the capitalist class in a given country cannot impose on itself.

We may thus twist and turn the matter as much as we will—the result remains the same. If commodities of equal value are exchanged, no surplus-value arises; and neither does such a surplus-value arise in the event of commodities of unequal value being exchanged. The circulation or exchange of commodities in itself creates no value.

The increase of value, which is visible after the sale of a commodity, cannot in any case be derived from the sale. It cannot be explained as the result of the discrepancy between the price of a commodity and its value. If the price really differs from the value we must reduce the former to the latter —in other words we must eliminate this phenomenon as a purely accidental one, so as not to let ourselves be confused by disturbing side-issues. Such a process of reduction is moreover not limited to the domain of science. The continual fluctuations of the market prices, their increase and decrease, neutralise each other and reduce themselves to an average price as their internal determining principle. The latter serves as guide to the merchant or the industrial undertaker in every enterprise of long duration. The merchant thus knows that, if we contemplate a long period of time in its entirety, commodities are in reality sold for their average price, and neither above nor below that price. The origin of profit, the creation of a surplus-value, must hence be explained on the presumption that commodities are sold at their real value. But in this case the surplus value must manifestly have its origin in the process of production. Already in the minute when the commodity is finished, and before it leaves the hands of its first vendor, it must be worth as much as the final purchaser, *i. e.* the consumer, pays for it at the end. In other words its value must exceed the manufacturer's costs of pro-

duction; during the process of production of the commodity
a new value must have been created.

This leads us to the question as to how the value of
commodities arises.

CHAPTER III

VALUE IN USE AND EXCHANGE VALUE
THE SOCIALLY NECESSARY LABOUR

(Extracted from vol. 1, ch. 1 & 2.)

A COMMODITY is primarily an external object, which by
reason of its qualities satisfies some sort of human want.
Every useful thing, such as iron, paper, etc., must be considered from a double point of view—according to quality,
and according to quantity. Every such thing has numerous
qualities, and can thus be useful in many ways. The usefulness of the thing implies that it is a *value in use*. But this
usefulness is not, so to speak, something hanging indefinitely
in the air. Conditioned by the physical qualities of the commodity, it cannot exist apart from the latter. The substance
itself of the commodity—such as iron, wheat, diamond, etc.—
possesses therefore a value in use.

Exchange Value appears primarily as the quantitative relation in which values in use of one kind are exchanged
against values in use of another kind. A definite quantity of
one commodity is regularly exchanged for a specific quantity of another: that constitutes its exchange value—a relation which changes constantly according to time and locality.
Thus does exchange value seem to be something accidental
and purely relative, *i. e.* (as Condillac expressed it) it seems
"to consist solely in the relation of the commodities to our
wants." A value in exchange inherent in commodities appears
thus an impossibility. Let us consider the question more
closely.

A given commodity, let us say a ton of wheat, is exchanged
for a specific amount of boot-blacking, silk, or gold, etc., in
a word, for other commodities in varying proportions. Corn

has thus a number of different exchange values. But as those specific amounts of boot-blacking, silk, gold, etc. represent the exchange value of a ton of wheat, they must themselves possess an equal exchange value. It ensues therefore, first of all, that the valid exchange values of the same commodity express something identical; and, secondly, there must be something behind the exchange value—something of which the latter is but the mode of expression.

Let us further take two commodities, e. g. wheat and iron. Whatever the proportions in which these commodities are exchangeable, it is always possible to express them by means of an equation, in which a given quantity of corn is equal to a certain quantity of iron. For instance, let us suppose a ton of wheat to be equivalent to two tons of iron. What does this equation mean? It means that a common property of the same dimension exists in two different things—in a ton of wheat and also in two tons of iron. The two things are thus equal to a third, which in itself is neither the one nor the other. So far as constituting exchange values, each of the two must therefore be reducible to the third in question.

This property possessed in common cannot be a natural quality inherent in commodities. Their natural physical qualities only come under consideration at all in so far as such qualities render these commodities useful, i. e. in so far as they confer on the latter a value in use. In the exchange of commodities, abstraction is to all intents and purposes made of the value in use of such commodities. In this case one value in use is worth just as much as any other, if only it be available in the proper proportion. Or as the old economist Barbon wrote in 1696: "The one kind of commodity is as good as the other, if the respective exchange values are equal. There is no difference, and no possibility of differentiation, between things of equal exchange value. . . . $25.00 worth of lead or iron have the same exchange value as $25.00 worth of silver and gold." Heterogeneity of quality is the main characteristic of commodities, when we regard the latter from the point of view of their value in use; when we consider their value in exchange, there can only be heterogeneity of quantity.

If we make abstraction of the value in use of commodities,

they appear henceforth under one single aspect, namely as *products of labour*. But the product of labour also undergoes a change as soon as it is finished. If we leave out of consideration its value in use, we likewise make abstraction of the material elements and shapes which confer on it a value in use. It is no longer a table or house or yarn, or, indeed, a useful object of any kind. All its concrete qualities have been put out of sight. Neither is it any longer the product of the labour of a carpenter or stonemason or spinner, or of any other definite productive worker. It is, on the contrary, henceforth merely the product of human labour *per se*, abstract human labour, *i. e.* a product of the expenditure of human labour power considered independently of the shape assumed by such expenditure. I mean that it is quite indifferent whether the labour power in question was expended by a carpenter, a stonemason, or a spinner. All products of labour —considered from this point of view—merely demonstrate that human labour power has been expended in their production and that labour is accumulated in them.

The exchange value of a commodity thus only exists because, and in so far as abstract human labour is embodied in that commodity. How are we to measure the amount of such value? According to the quantity of "value-creating substances," *i. e.* of labour, contained in it. The quantity of labour will itself be measured by its duration, and working-time is, in turn, measured according to definite time-standards, such as hours, days, etc.

If the value of a commodity be determined by the quantity of labour expended in its production, it might seem that the lazier and more unskilful a man is, the more valuable the commodity produced by him would be, seeing that more time was required for its manufacture. But the labour which constitutes the substance of the values is homogeneous human labour, expenditure of the same uniform human labour power. The total labour power of society which is embodied in the sum total of the values of all commodities existing at any given moment, is to be considered as one homogeneous mass of human labour power, although it consists in the labour power of innumerable individuals. The labour power of each of these individuals is the same, in so far as it constitutes the average labour power of society, and operates as such—. *i. e.* in so far as it needs the working-time necessary on an average, or socially necessary, for the production of a commodity. Socially necessary is only such working-time as is required for producing a value in use under existing normal conditions of production and with the average amount of skill and intensity prevalent at the time. After the introduction of steam weaving-looms in England, for instance, perhaps only half the labour needed previously was henceforth necessary in order to transform a given quantity of yarn into a textile fabric. The English hand-weaver still needed the same amount of time for effecting such a transformation; but the product of his individual hour's work represented henceforth only half an hour's social labour, and lost in consequence half its former value.

Thus it is only the quantity of labour or of working-time socially necessary for its production, which determines the exchange value of a commodity. The individual commodity is in this case merely an average sample of its kind. Therefore those commodities which represent an equal sum of labour, or which can be produced in the same amount of working-time, possess the same value. The value of a commodity is to the value of every other commodity as the working-time necessary for the production of one commodity to the working-time necessary for the production of the others. "Considered in terms of value, all commodities are but a definite quantity of congealed working-time." [1]

Thus the total value of a commodity would remain unchanged, if the working-time necessary for its production were to remain the same. But the latter changes with every variation in the productiveness of labour. The productiveness of labour is determined by various circumstances—amongst others by the average amount of skill of the labourers, by the degree in which science is developed and applicable for technical purposes, the manner in which the process of production is organized, the extent and efficiency of the means

[1] Karl Marx: Zur Kritik der politischen Oekonomie, Berlin, 1859. New edition, Stuttgart 1897, p. 5.

of production, and by natural conditions. For instance, the same quantity of labour is, in the favourable season of the year, embodied in double the quantity of wheat obtained in the unfavourable season. The same quantity of labour extracts greater quantities of metal from rich mines than from poor ones. And so forth. Diamonds are seldom to be found on the earth's surface, and their discovery requires, therefore, as a general rule, much working-time. Consequently they represent a large amount of labour in but a small compass. In the case of richer mines the same quantity of labour would be embodied in a larger quantity of diamonds, and the value of the latter would fall. If it were possible to transform carbon into diamonds with but a slight expenditure of labour, the value of such diamonds might fall below that of bricks. In general we may say that the greater the productiveness of labour, the shorter will be the working-time necessary for the production of an article, the smaller will be the mass of labour contained in it, and the smaller will be its value. Conversely, the less the productiveness of labour, the longer will be the working-time necessary for the production of an article, and the greater will be the value of that article.

A thing can possess value in use, without having value. This is the case when no labour is required in order to make it useful to mankind. Such are air, virgin soil, natural pastures, wild-growing wood, etc. A thing can be both useful and the product of human labour, without constituting a commodity. Whoever satisfies his own wants by the produce of his own labour creates, it is true, values in use, but no commodity. In order to produce commodities he must not only create values in use *per se*, but values in use for others, *i. e.* social values in use. Lastly, nothing can have value without being an object of utility. If it be useless, the labour contained in it is useless, cannot be reckoned as labour, and cannot therefore create value.

CHAPTER IV

PURCHASE AND SALE OF LABOUR POWER

(Extracted from vol. 1, ch. 6.)

Now that we have seen that the value of commodities is constituted solely by the human labour contained in them, let us return to the question as to how it is possible for the manufacturer to obtain from his commodities a greater value than that invested by him in them.

We will put the case once more before the reader: a capitalist needs a definite sum, say $25.00, for the production of a certain commodity. He subsequently sells the finished product for $27.50. As our investigation has shown that the surplus value of $2.50 cannot have arisen in the process of circulation (*i. e.* in the turnover of the commodities), it must have its origin in the process of production. It is now incumbent on us to show how this comes about.

The problem, it is true, is partly solved, once we know that value is created by socially necessary labour. In order to produce yarn with the available means of production, *e. g.* spinning-frames and cotton, labour is performed in the spinning-mill. In so far as such labour is socially necessary, it creates value It therefore adds a new value to the already existing means of production—in this case raw cotton—by transmitting at the same time the value of worn-out machinery, etc. to the yarn. But the difficulty remains, that the capitalist would also seem to have included payment for the newly performed labour in his costs of production, seeing that wages are likewise reckoned among such costs of production along with the value of the machines, buildings, raw materials, and other requisites. And these wages are paid precisely for the labour performed in spinning. It appears therefore as if all the values available after the process of production were also available previously.

But it is clear that the value which has been newly created by the work of spinning is not necessarily identical with the value paid by the capitalist in the shape of wages. It can be

larger or smaller. If it be larger, we should then have discovered the origin of the surplus-value.

Have we not, however, proceeded from the assumption
that in all purchases and sales the exact value is paid? Have
we not satisfied ourselves that price often deviates from
value, but that such deviations explain nothing? For this
reason must the case of the capitalist paying the labourer
less than the latter's value—however often such cases may
occur—be here considered only as an exception. The origin
of the surplus-value must also be explained in the normal
case of the capitalist paying the full value of what he purchases for the purpose of labour. This particular transaction
of purchase and sale, such as it takes place between capitalist
and labourer, must hence be more closely scrutinised.

That which the capitalist obtains by paying wages, consequently that which he purchases from the labourer, is the
latter's faculty, or power, of working. But in order that the
capitalist may be able to purchase labour power, various
conditions must be fulfilled. Labour power can only appear
as a commodity on the market in so far, and because, it is
offered for sale by its owner. In order to sell it as a commodity, the owner of such labour power must be able to
dispose of it, that is to say he must be a free person, the
free proprietor of his working faculty. He and the capitalist
meet on the market and come into contact with each other
as proprietors of commodities of equal rights—differing from
each other only in that the one is purchaser and the other
vendor—consequently as legally equal persons. In order to
ensure the continuity of these relations it is necessary that
the proprietor of labour power sell the latter only for a
specified length of time. For should he sell it in the bulk,
once and for all, he would be selling himself, and converting
himself from a free man into a slave; he would cease to be
a proprietor of commodities and would become a commodity
himself.

The second essential condition, if the capitalist is to find
labour power as a commodity on the market, is that its proprietor, instead of being able to sell commodities in which
his labour is incorporated. is obliged to offer his labour power

itself, which exists solely in his living body. This is the case when he owns none of the means of production, *e. g.* raw materials, tools, etc., necessary for the manufacture of commodities, and no foodstuffs to keep him alive until the process of manufacture is completed and the commodities sold.

The capitalist must therefore find a free labourer on the market, free in a double sense of the word: namely, a free man able to dispose of his labour power as his own commodity; and, on the other hand, a man having no other commodities to sell, without ties of any sort, free from everything necessary to utilise his labour power.

The question as to why this free labourer meets him on the commodities market, does not interest the capitalist. And for the present it does not interest us either. But one thing is clear: Nature does not produce on the one hand capitalists and proprietors of commodities, on the other proprietors solely of their own individual labour power. This state of things is not a natural one, nor indeed a social one in the sense of being common to all periods of history. Manifestly it is the result of an antecedent historical development, the product of numerous economic revolutions, of the disappearance of a number of older forms of social production.

This peculiar commodity, labour power, must now be considered more closely. Like every other commodity it possesses value. How is this value determined?

The value of labour power, like that of every other commodity, is determined by the working-time necessary for its production, consequently also for its reproduction. Labour power exists solely as an attribute of a live individual, and hence it presupposes the latter's existence. A live individual needs a certain amount of necessaries in order to sustain himself. The working-time necessary for the production of labour power resolves itself therefore into the working-time required for the production of such necessaries of life, in other words: *the value of labour power is the value of the necessaries required to sustain its proprietor.*

The amount of necessaries must be sufficient to maintain the working individual in his normal condition of life. The natural wants themselves. such as food, clothing, heating, lodging, etc. vary according to the natural conditions prevailing in every country. On the other hand the extent of the so-called natural wants, and the manner in which they are satisfied, depend to a large extent on the degree of civilisation attained by any given country—especially on (amongst other factors) the conditions under which the class of free labourers has been formed, consequently on the customs and pretensions concerning the standard of life of this class. In the case of labour power a historical and moral element thus enter into the determination of its value, contrary to the case of all other commodities. But for a given country at any given time, the average quantity of indispensable staple articles of food is practically known.

The proprietor of labour power is mortal. If such proprietors are to appear permanently on the market, and the unceasing demands of capital require this, then must that amount of labour power which is lost to the market in consequence of wear and tear or death be continually replaced by at least an equal amount of new power. The sum total of the necessaries required for the production of labour power thus includes those required by future (substitute) power, *i. e.* by the labourer's children. Likewise included in the sum total are the costs necessitated by learning the skill and dexterity requisite for a given branch of labour—costs which, however, are insignificant in so far as ordinary labour power is concerned.

The value of labour power consists in the value of a definite amount of necessaries of life. It varies according as to how such necessaries vary—*i. e.* according to the length of working-time needed for their production. Part of these necessaries, *e. g.* foodstuffs, fuel, etc., is consumed daily and must be replaced daily. Other necessaries, such as clothes, furniture, etc., take longer to consume and need hence to be replaced only at longer intervals. Commodities of one kind must be bought or paid for daily, others weekly, quarterly, etc. But however the sum total of these costs be distributed over the course, say, of a year, it must be covered by the average income, taking one day with another. The real daily value of labour power will thus be ascertained by reckoning the value of all the necessaries of life required by the labourer during an entire year, and then dividing this sum by 365. If we assume that in the commodities required for an average day six hours social labour is contained, then does labour power represent half a day's average social work daily—or in other words, half a working-day is required for the daily production of labour power.[1] This quantity of labour necessary for the daily production of labour power constitutes the daily value of such power—or, if one likes, the value of daily reproduced power. If half a day's average social labour be incorporated also in a quantity of gold worth 75 cents, then is this sum the price corresponding to the daily value of labour power. If the proprietor of labour power offers it for 75 cents a day, then is the selling price equal to the value of such power; and we have assumed that the capitalist pays this value.

To the peculiar nature of the commodity we call labour power is due the fact that when the contract between buyer and seller has been concluded, the value in use of the commodity in question has not really been transferred to the buyer. The value in use of labour power consists in the subsequent exercise of force. The sale of labour power and the exercise of the latter are thus separated from each other in time. But in the case of commodities, the sale of whose value in use is separated in time from their effective transfer to the buyer, payment is as a general rule made subsequently. In all countries with capitalist production the power of labour is paid only after it has exercised itself, e. g. at the end of the week. The labourer thus everywhere advances the capitalist the value in use of labour power; he lets the latter be consumed by the buyer before receiving payment of its price. Therefore does the labourer everywhere give credit to the capitalist.

---

[1] The reader is particularly requested to read this attentively. Dr. Friedrich Kleinwächter, Professor of Political Economy at the University of Czernowitz, has understood this passage as meaning that Marx maintains that a labourer produces in about six hours everything needed by him for his sustenance! (Vide Kleinwächter, Lehrbuch der National-ökonomie, p. 153). EDITOR'S NOTE.

CHAPTER V

HOW SURPLUS-VALUE ARISES

(Extracted from vol. i, ch. 7.)

LABOUR power in use is labour itself. The purchaser of labour power consumes it by letting its vendor work. With the eye of a connoisseur the capitalist has selected the means of production and the labour power best adapted to his special line of business—spinning-mill, shoe manufactory, etc.—and he now lets the labourer consume the means of production by his labour. He must begin by taking the labour power just as he finds it; consequently also with a kind of labour as would be found at a time in which capitalists did not exist. Transformations of the forms of production due to the subordination of labour to capital can take place only later, and must therefore be considered later.

The labour process, considered as the consumption of the labour power sold to the capitalist, shows us two peculiarities.

The labourer works under the control of the capitalist. The latter takes care that the work is carried-on properly, and that the means of production are put to a suitable use. In other words: the freedom and independence of the worker during the labour process do not exist.

Secondly, the product is the property of the capitalist, not of the labourer. As the capitalist—according to our hypothesis—pays the daily value of the labour power, it appertains to him to employ this power. Similarly the other elements essential for the manufacture of the product, namely the means of production, belong to him. Consequently the labour process is carried-on amongst things which have all been purchased by the capitalist; and thus the product is his property.

This product constitutes a value in use—yarn, boots, etc. But although boots, for example, are to a certain extent the basis of social progress, our capitalist, a decidedly progressive man, does not manufacture them for their own sake. Values in use are produced solely because, and in so far as, they are exchange values. Our capitalist has two purposes in view: firstly, he wishes to produce a value in use having an exchange value—an article destined for sale, a commodity; secondly, he wishes to produce a commodity having a higher value than that of the means of production and the labour power, for which he advanced his money on the market. He does not want merely to produce a value in use, but value; and not only value, but surplus-value.

We know that the value of every commodity is determined by the quantity of labour contained in it. This applies also to the product resulting for our capitalist from the process of labour. We must therefore first and foremost calculate the labour thus materialised in the work.

Let us take, for example, yarn. For the production of yarn raw materials, e. g. 10 lbs. of cotton, were first of all necessary. It is superfluous to inquire at present as to the value of the cotton, seeing that we assume the capitalist purchased the latter at its value, e. g. $2.50. In the price of the cotton, the labour required for its production is already expressed as average social labour. We will further assume that the instruments of labour used-up during the manufacture of the cotton—spindles, etc.—have a value of 50 cents. If an amount of gold equivalent to $3.00 be the product of 24 working-hours or two working-days, it ensues firstly that two working-days are incorporated in the yarn. The working-time necessary for the production of the cotton is a part of the working-time needed for the production of the yarn, the raw material of which it constitutes, and is consequently included in the yarn. The same holds good of the working-time necessary for the production of the spindles, without the wear and tear of which the cotton cannot be spun. But we start from the assumption that only such working-time is spent as is indispensable under given social conditions of production. Thus if only 1 lb. of cotton be needed for spinning 1 lb. of yarn, only 1 lb. of cotton may be used in the manufacture of 1 lb. of yarn. The same applies to the spindle. If the capitalist has the phantasy to use golden spindles instead of iron ones, nevertheless only the socially necessary labour is reckoned in the value of the yarn, i. e. the working-time necessary for the production of iron spindles.

We come next to the question of what amount of value the labour of the spinner himself adds to the cotton. We assume that the labour of spinning is simple, unskilled labour, the average labour of a given state of society. Subsequently we shall see, that, even should we assume the contrary, the question would remain unchanged.

Now it is vitally important that no more time be consumed in the work of spinning than is necessary under given social conditions. If under normal conditions of production 1⅔ lbs. of cotton be transformed during a working-hour into 1⅔ lbs. of yarn, then only that working-day counts as a 12 hours day, in which 12 × 1⅔ lbs. of cotton are converted into 12 × 1⅔ lbs. of yarn. For only the socially necessary working-time counts as creative of value.

The fact that the labour consists in spinning, that its material is cotton and its product yarn, is absolutely indifferent as regards the creation of value. If the labourer, instead of working in a spinning-mill were employed in a coal mine, the object of the labour, *i. e.* coal, would be furnished by Nature, but all the same a definite quantity of coal picked from the seam, *e. g.* 1 cwt., represents a definite quantity of absorbed labour.

When the labour power was sold, it was assumed that its daily value totals 75 cents, and that in these 75 cents, 6 working-hours are incorporated—that consequently 6 working-hours are required to produce the average amount of necessaries of life needed by the labourer every day. If now our spinner transforms during one working-hour 1⅔ lbs. of cotton into 1⅔ lbs. of yarn,[1] in 6 working-hours he transforms 10 lbs. of cotton into 10 lbs. of yarn. During the process of spinning, the cotton thus absorbs 6 working-hours. This working-time is represented by a quantity of gold worth 75 cents. Owing therefore to the spinning, the value of the cotton is enhanced to the extent of 75 cents.

Let us now turn to the total value of the product, *i. e.* of the 10 lbs. of yarn. In them are incorporated 2½ working-days, of which 2 are contained in cotton and instruments of labour, and one half is absorbed during the process of spin-

[1] The figures are here wholly arbitrary.

ning. The same working-time is represented by a quantity of gold worth $3.75. The price corresponding to the value of the 10 lbs. of yarns amounts thus to $3.75, the price of 1 lb. of yarn amounts to 37½ cents.

Our capitalist is taken aback. The value of the product is equal to the capital advanced. The value advanced has not been remunerative, has not produced a surplus-value. The price of 10 lbs. of yarn is $3.75, and $3.75 have been laid out—$2.50 for cotton, 50 cents for the consumed instruments of labour, and 75 cents for labour power.

Perhaps the capitalist will say that he advanced his money with the intention of making more money out of it. But the road to hell is paved with good intentions, and he may just as well have had the intention to make money without producing at all. He threatens. He will never be caught again. In future he will buy the finished commodity on the market instead of manufacturing it himself. But if all his fellow-capitalists were to do the same, how would he find commodities on the market? And money he cannot eat. He becomes unctuous. His sacrifice should be appreciated. He might have squandered his $3.75. Instead of which, he has laid-out the latter productively and made yarn out of them. But precisely for that reason he is in possession of good yarn instead of an evil conscience. Moreover, there where nothing is to be had, the King himself forfeits his rights. However meritorious his renunciation, there is nothing available wherewith to pay special remuneration for it, seeing that the value of the commodity resulting from the process of production is but equal to the sum total of the values invested in that process. He should therefore console himself with the reflection that virtue is its own reward. Instead of which he becomes importunate. The yarn is useless for him. He has produced it for sale. He may therefore sell it, or, still better, may in future only produce commodities for his own use. He defiantly shows his teeth. Could the labourer produce commodities from nothing, merely with his own limbs? Did the capitalist not furnish the materials with which alone the labourer could work, and in which alone his work could he incorporated? Seeing that the greater part of society is composed of persons who possess nothing, has he not rendered society, through his means of production, *i. e.* his cotton and his spindles, an invaluable service? Has he not rendered the labourer himself such a service, having furnished him with necessaries of life into the bargain? And shall he not count this service for something? But, on the other hand, has not the labourer in his turn rendered him the service of transforming cotton and spindle into yarn? Moreover there is here no question of services. A service is nothing but the useful effect produced by a value in use, be it a commodity or be it labour. But here there is only question of the exchange value. The capitalist paid the labourer the value of 75 cents. The labourer gave him back exactly the same value, in the shape of a value of 75 cents added to the cotton. Thus value is returned for value. Our friend, just now so purse-proud, suddenly assumes the modest attitude of his own labourer. Has the capitalist not worked himself? Has he not performed the work of superintending and controlling the spinners? Does not such work also produce value? His own foreman and his business manager shrug their shoulders. But meanwhile he has already resumed his former smiling face. He bamboozled us with the whole rigmarole. But he does not care a straw. He leaves these and similar hollow subterfuges and shifts to the professor of Political Economy, who is especially paid to repeat them. The capitalist himself is a practical man, who, it is true, does not always reflect on what he says outside his office, but who always knows what he does inside the latter.

Let us consider the matter more closely. The daily value of the labour power amounted to 75 cents, seeing that half a day's labour is incorporated in it—*i. e.* because the necessaries of life required daily for the production of labour power cost half a working-day. But the past labour incorporated in the labour power, on the one hand; and the living work which it can put into action, on the other: are two very different magnitudes. The fact that half a day's work is necessary to keep him alive for 24 hours by no means prevents the labourer working the entire day. The value of labour power and the utilisation of that power in the labour

process are two different things. The capitalist had this difference of value in view when buying the labour power. The
latter's useful quality, *i. e.* the capacity for producing yarn
or boots, was merely an indispensable secondary condition,
because in order to create value labour in an useful shape
must be performed. What was decisive was the peculiar value
in use of this commodity, *which is a source of value, and of
value greater than it possesses itself*. This is the service which
the capitalist expected from it. And he acted in conformity
with the eternal laws governing the exchange of commodities.
For it is a fact that the vendor of labour power, like the
vendor of every other commodity, obtains its exchange value
and sells its value in use. The value in use of his labour
power, *i. e.* the labour itself, belongs just as little to the
vendor as the value in use of oil which has been sold belongs
to the oil dealer. The capitalist has paid the daily value of
labour power; consequently its use during the day, the whole
day's labour belongs to him. The circumstance that the daily
sustenance of labour power only costs half a working-day,
although such labour power can be in action the entire day—
that consequently the value which its employment creates
in a single day is double its own daily value; this circumstance
is doubtless particularly lucky for the purchaser, but by no
means an injustice towards the vendor.

Our capitalist has foreseen this state of things, which
was the cause of his hilarity. The labourer therefore finds in
the workshop not only the means of production necessary for
working six hours, but also those necessary for working
twelve hours. If 10 lbs. of cotton absorbed 6 working hours
and be transformed into 10 lbs. of yarn, then 20 lbs. of
cotton will absorb 12 working hours and be transformed into
20 lbs. of yarn. Let us consider the product of this prolonged labour process. Five working days are now materialised
in the 20 lbs. of yarn, *i. e.* four in the cotton and the lost
steel of the spindle, and one absorbed by the cotton during
the process of spinning. Expressed in gold, the value of five
working days is $7.50. That is therefore the price of the 20
lbs. of yarn. The latter still costs $37\frac{1}{2}$ cents per lb. But the
total value of the commodities entering into the process was

$6.75, whereas the value of the yarn is $7.50. The value of the product has increased to the extent of one-ninth over and above the value advanced for its production. $6.75 have been transformed into $7.50. A surplus value of 75 cents has been obtained. The trick has succeeded at last.

All the conditions of the problem are satisfied, and the laws of the exchange of commodities have in no wise been broken. Equal value was exchanged for equal value. The capitalist paid as purchaser the value of every commodity—cotton, spindles, labour power. He did what every other purchaser of commodities does—he consumed their value in use. The consumption of labour power yielded 20 lbs. of yarn, worth $7.50. The capitalist now returns to the market and sells commodities after having bought them. He sells the yarn for 37½ cents per lb., not a farthing either above or below its value. And yet he obtains from circulation 75 cents more than he originally threw into it.

If we compare the process of creating value with that of creating surplus-value, we see the latter to be but the continuation of the former beyond a definite point. If the process be only carried as far as the point where the value paid by capital for labour power be replaced by an exact equivalent, then it is simply a process of producing value. But if the process be continued beyond that point, it becomes a process of creating surplus-value.

But labour is only creative of value in the measure in which the time needed for the production of a value in use is socially necessary. Labour power must be expended under normal conditions. If a self-acting mule be the implement in general use for spinning, the labourer must not be supplied with a distaff and spinning-wheel. He must not, instead of cotton of normal quality, be furnished with rubbish susceptible of tearing any moment. In both cases he would consume more working-time than is socially necessary for the production of 1 lb. of yarn; and this extra time would not produce value or money. Further, labour power must itself be normal. In that branch of production in which it is expended, it must possess the general average amount of skill, dexterity, and celerity. It must be expended with the general average amount of exertion and with the degree of intensity usual in society at any given moment. And the capitalist is as careful to see that this is done, as that his workmen are not idle for a single moment. He has purchased the labour power for a specific length of time and he insists on his rights. He will not let himself be robbed. Neither may the raw materials and tools be put to a wrong use, because those raw materials or tools which are wasted represent a useless expenditure of labour, and do not, consequently, count in the product nor enter into its value.

We have already observed that in the production of surplus-value it is indifferent whether the labour bought by the capitalist be simple unskilled labour of average quality or more complicated labour. The labour which is of a higher kind and more complicated is the manifestation of a labour power which has cost more to develop, whose production has cost therefore more working-time, and which has consequently a higher value than unskilled labour power. This power being of greater value, it will be expended in labour of a higher class; it will, therefore, materialise itself in an identical length of time in proportionately higher values than unskilled labour. But whatever differences in skill may exist between the labour of a spinner and that of a jeweller, the portion of his labour by which the jeweller merely replaces the value of his own labour power, does not in any way differ in quality from the additional portion by which he creates surplus-value.[1]

---

[1] The differences between skilled and unskilled labour rest in part on mere illusions, or, to say the least, on differences which have long ceased to exist in reality, and only survive by virtue of a traditional convention; in part on the helpless condition of some categories of the working class, a condition that prevents them exacting equally with their comrades the value of their labour power; accidental circumstances play here so great a part, that both forms of labour can sometimes change places. Where, for instance, the physique of the working class has deteriorated, and is relatively speaking exhausted—and this is the case in all countries characterised by highly developed capitalist production—the lower forms of labour, which demand great muscular strength, are in general considered as skilled by comparison with much more delicate forms, which sink down to the level of unskilled labour. Take the case of a stonemason in England, whose labour is on a much

CHAPTER VI

CONSTANT CAPITAL AND VARIABLE CAPITAL
FIXED CAPITAL AND CIRCULATING CAPITAL

(Extracted from vol. I, ch. 8 & 9.—Vol. III, part 1, ch. 8-10; vol. II, ch. 8, German ed.)

Now that we know that surplus-value arises during the production of commodities, and, further, how it arises, it is clear that the surplus-value obtained in every individual undertaking must differ in its amount independently of the amount of capital. For we have seen that surplus-value is exclusively derived from living, newly performed labour, and not from the pre-existing means of production. To revert to our example of the cotton spinner, the capitalist paid $6.00 for all the means of production (cotton and instruments of labour), and 75 cents wages for labour. The labour of spinning has not changed the value of the $6.00—*i. e.* of the means of production; such labour has transmitted exactly the same value to the yarn. The 75 cents paid for wages have, on the other hand, been consumed, and in their stead we find a new value of $1.50.

higher level than that of a damask-weaver. On the other hand, although the work of a fustian cutter demands great bodily exertion and is very unhealthy into the bargain, yet it counts only as unskilled labour. And we must not forget that the so-called skilled labour occupies only a small space in the total labour of a nation. Laing calculates that in England and Wales the livelihood of 11 million persons depends on unskilled labour. If from the total population of 18 million people living at the time when he wrote, we deduct 1,000,000 for the genteel population, and another 1,000,000 for paupers, vagrants, criminals, prostitutes, etc., there remain 4,000,000 who compose the middle-class, including people that live on the interest of small investments, officials, authors, artists, schoolmasters and the like. In order to obtain this last figure of 4,000,000, he includes all better paid factory operatives among the working category of the middle-class—from which, however, bankers, etc. are excluded! The stonemasons, too, figure among the skilled labourers. There remain the above mentioned 11,000,000. (S. Laing: "National Distress," &c., London, 1844). "The great class who have nothing to give for food but ordinary labour, are the great bulk of the people." (James Mill, in article: "Colony." Supplement to the Enyclop. Brit., 1831).

The value of that part of the capital expended by the capitalist for procuring means of production—*i. e.* raw and auxiliary materials, and instruments of labour—is therefore not altered in the course of process of production. We consequently call it *constant capital.*

On the other hand, the value of that part of the capital expended on buying labour power is altered during the process of production. It reproduces its own value and yields a surplus-value over and above the latter; and this surplus-value can be greater or less as the case may be. This part of the capital is being continually transformed from a constant (unchangeable) magnitude into a variable (changeable) one. We therefore call it *variable capital.*

Now it is clear that in the different branches of production the proportions in which the means of production (constant capital) stand to one and the same amount of wages (variable capital) can be different. In an engine-works the quantity of instruments of production to be utilised and transformed by labour power will be different to what it is in a cotton spinning-mill or in a coal mine, &c. The "organic composition" of capital (as we will call this relation of the constant and variable parts of capital to each other) differs therefore from branch to branch. The most varied relations are here not only conceivable, but they also really exist.

Let us assume the existence of three different capitals (in 3 different branches) having the following organic composition:

$$\text{I. } 80\,c \text{ (constant)} + 20\,v \text{ (variable)}$$
$$\text{II. } 50\,c \qquad\qquad\quad + 50\,v$$
$$\text{III. } 20\,c \qquad\qquad\quad + 80\,v$$

If we assume that the exploitation of labour power is identical in all three branches, *e. g.* that in each case labour power furnishes exactly twice the amount of value which it receives in the shape of wages, we obtain the following result:

$$
\begin{array}{lllll}
\text{capital} & \text{I gains} & 20 \text{ dollars surplus-value} \\
\text{"} & \text{II "} & 50 & \text{"} & \text{"} & \text{"} \\
\text{"} & \text{III "} & 80 & \text{"} & \text{"} & \text{"}
\end{array}
$$

This means—seeing that profits, as percentage of the surplus-balance, are calculated on the entire consumed capital —profits of 20%, 50%, and 80% respectively. We must also bear in mind that the exploitation of the labourers is not everywhere the same, but that it is greater in some undertakings and less in others. Further, there are other circumstances which enter into the determination of the amount of surplus-value in the various branches and even in individual undertakings—*e. g.* the rapidity of the turnover of the capital, of which we shall speak later. It ensues that the amount of surplus-value really produced cannot be the same in two different undertakings, much less in two different branches. How, in spite of this, is the equality of the rate of profit— which, as a matter of fact, exists—brought about?

Let us take five different branches of production, each having a different organic composition of the capitals invested therein (and on the assumption that labour power in each case supplies 100% of its own value as surplus-value):

Capital	Surplus-Value	Value of Product	Rate of Profit
I. 80 c + 20 v	20	120	20%
II. 70 c + 30 v	30	130	30%
III. 60 c + 40 v	40	140	40%
IV. 85 c + 15 v	15	115	15%
V. 95 c + 5 v	5	105	5%

We have here very different rates of profit for different branches, the exploitation of labour remaining the same in all cases.

The total capital invested in the five branches is equal to 500; the total amount of surplus-value produced by it = 110; the total value of the manufactured commodities = 610. If we assume that the figure 500 represents one single capital, merely divided into the categories I to V (*e. g.* as in a cotton manufactory, where a different proportion of variable and constant capital is to be found in the different departments such as the carding room, the roving room, the spinning and weaving rooms, where the average proportion for the entire factory must first be calculated)—if we assume this, we shall find that the average composition of the capital of 500 = 390 c + 110 v, or, calculated per hundred, 78 c + 22 v. If we regard each capital of 100 as representing only one-fifth of the total capital, its composition would be this average one of 78 c + 22 v; in the same way an average surplus-value of 22 would be obtained by every fraction of 100. The average rate of profit would consequently be equal to 22 per cent, and, finally, the price of each fifth part of the total product would equal 122. The product of each fifth part of the total capital advanced must therefore be sold for 122.

In order not to come to false conclusions, another circumstance must be taken into account. The constant capital, i. e. the means of production, is in its turn composed of two essentially different parts. The means of production, which constitute the constant capital, are of various kinds. The principal means of production consist of buildings, machinery, tools, raw and auxiliary materials—i. e. of the instruments by means of which labour is performed, and the objects to which labour is applied. It is evident, that, in the process of production, the former play an essentially different part to the latter. The coal utilised for heating the machine completely disappears; so does the oil used for greasing the axle of a wheel; and so forth. Colours and other auxiliary materials likewise disappear, but manifest themselves in the qualities of the product. The raw material constitutes the substance of the product, but changes its form. In short, the raw and the auxiliary materials are completely consumed in the course of the process of production. Nothing remains of the form they had at the beginning of this process. It is different in the case of the means of production. A tool, a machine, a factory, a receptacle etc. are only useful as long as they retain their original form, as long as they are utilisable to-morrow in the labour process under the same form as they possess to-day. And just as they retain their own original form in regard to the product during the whole labour process, they also retain it after they are worn-out. The forms of machines, tools, factories, etc. always exist independently of the products they helped to manufacture. If we consider the whole length of time during which such an instrument of labour serves, from the day of its entry into the workshop to the day when it is relegated to the lumber-room, we find that during this period its value in use has been completely consumed by labour, and that its exchange value has consequently been entirely transferred to the product. For instance, if a spinning-machine has been worn-out in ten years, its total value has, during the ten years labour process, been transferred to the products manufactured during that time. The life period of an instrument of labour thus comprises a greater or smaller number of labour processes which are being continually repeated. In this respect there is similarity between the instrument of labour and the human being. Every day that passes brings the latter 24 hours nearer death, but it is impossible to ascertain, by merely looking at a man, how much nearer that final goal he already is. This fact does not prevent life insurance companies from drawing very accurate, and moreover very profitable, conclusions from a study of the average length of human life. It is the same with instruments of labour. Experience teaches us, how long a given instrument of labour, *e. g.* a specific sort of machine, last on an average. If we assume that its use value in the labour process lasts only six days, this means that it loses on an average $\frac{1}{6}$th of its use value daily, and thus transfers $\frac{1}{6}$th of its value to the daily product. The wear and tear of every instrument of labour is calculated in this way.

It is thus evident that an instrument of production never transfers to the product a greater sum of value than it loses itself through destruction of its own value in use. If it had no value to lose, *i. e.* if it were itself not a product of human labour, it would not transfer any value to the product. It would serve as a creator of value in use, but would not create any value in exchange. This is consequently the case with all those means of production which exist independently of human labour, such as the soil, the wind, water, coal in the mine, wood in the virgin forest, etc.

The instrument of labour must always cooperate with its full corporeal power in the process of production, even if the exchange value be less. Let us assume, for instance, that a machine is worth 1000 dollars and wears itself out in 1000 days. In this case $\frac{1}{1000}$th part of the value of the machine is transferred daily from the latter to its daily product. The total machine operates nevertheless in the labour process, although with diminishing vitality.

What is peculiar about this part of the constant capital, *i. e.* the instrument of labour, is thus that simultaneously with its entering into activity and with its wear and tear, a part of its value is transferred to the product, whereas another part remains fixed in the instrument of labour, consequently in the process of production. The value thus fixed constantly diminishes, until the instrument of labour is worn out and has thus distributed its value among a quantity of products, which are the result of a number of continuously repeated labour processes. But as long as it still serves as instrument of labour, *i. e.* as long as it need not be replaced by another instrument of the same sort, constant capital remains fixed in it, whereas another part of the value originally fixed in it is transferred to the product and consequently circulates as a component part of the value of the commodity.

This part of the capital which is fixed in the instruments of labour circulates just the same as any other. The entire capital value is in continual circulation, and in this sense all capital is thus circulating capital. But the circulation of that part of the capital we have just been considering, is a peculiar one. It does not circulate in its use form, but its value alone circulates—gradually, piecemeal, in the measure in which it is transferred to the product in circulation as commodity. During the whole period of its activity, part of its value remains invariably fixed in itself, and is independent in regard to the commodities which it helps to produce. Owing to this peculiarity, this part of the constant capital assumes the form of fixed capital. All other components of the capital advanced constitute, in contradistinction herewith, circulating capital.

It is clear that the difference in the manner in which the various component parts of the capital transfer their respective value to the product must also influence the amount of surplus-value produced by each individual capital. The said peculiarity likewise tends to obscure the genesis of surplus-value.[1]

When the capitalist contemplates the finished commodity, the difference between constant capital (means of production) and variable capital (wages) does not strike him. He knows, it is true, that a part of his costs of production (of the cost price of the commodity) has been spent on instruments of production, and another part on wages; he also knows that, if the production is to be continued, he must again apply in the same way the money derived from the sale of the commodity to purchasing instruments of production and labour power. But this tells him nothing concerning the origin of value and surplus-value. On the contrary, he only sees that the value of the means of production recurs again in the cost-price of the commodity just as it was before the beginning of the process of production, and that the same holds good of wages. The characteristic difference between constant and variable capital is thus obscured by appearances; and the surplus-value available at the end of the process of production seems to derive equally from all component parts of the capital.

The difference between fixed and circulating capital is on the contrary very obvious. Let us assume that the value of instruments of labour was originally 1200 dollars, exclusive of raw materials worth 380 dollars, and of wages worth 100 dollars. Let us further assume that during the process of production 20 dollars' worth of instruments of labour are worn-out; in this case the cost-price of the product will amount to 20 dollars for wear and tear + 380 dollars for raw and auxiliary materials + 100 dollars for wages = total 500 dollars. The capitalist holds this value of 500 dollars in the shape of the finished product in his hand, independently of the surplus-value. But machines, factories etc. exist into the bargain, and their total value is 1180 dollars.[2] Their value can certainly not be neglected, and to the mind of the capitalist the matter appears consequently as follows: 20 dollars of the value of the commodity have originated through wear and tear of instruments of labour (fixed capital), 480 dollars through wear and tear of raw materials and payment of wages

[1] From here on vol. III, part. 1, ch. 1, German ed.

[2] These figures are, all of them, quite arbitrarily selected.

(circulating capital). Or in other words: everything that I (the capitalist) invest in the production in the shape of raw materials and wages returns to me again through a single process of production; the sum invested in the instruments of labour remains longer within the process and only returns little by little; it must therefore be accumulated again little by little, in order that, once the machines etc. are completely worn-out, the equivalent for replacing them be available. The difference between fixed and circulating capital is thus, so to speak, hammered into the head of the capitalist. But in this sense wages are also regarded, without further ado, as circulating capital. Just like the expenses for raw materials, must wages be recouped from out of the single process of production, and be available for the purchase of fresh labour power. In this way wages (*i. e.* variable capital) are confounded, owing to appearances, with raw materials (*i. e.* a part of the constant capital) and both are set up in common contradistinction to the instruments of labour (*i. e.* the other part of the constant capital). For the superficial observer, the buildings, machines, etc., stand on the one side as fixed capital; whereas on the other side there are the raw and auxiliary materials and the wages of circulating capital. In this way, the essential differences between wages, on the one hand, and the other parts of the circulating capital, on the other, are entirely obscured.

CHAPTER VII

HOW UNIFORM PROFIT IS OBTAINED

(Extracted from vol. III, part 1, ch. 9, German ed.)

LET us now return to the question as to the influence exerted by the difference between fixed and circulating capital on the rate of profit. In our schedule (p. 49) we assumed that the whole of the constant capital reappears immediately in the value of the product (*i. e.* that is entirely circulating capital). This may occasionally be the case, but it is not the rule. We must therefore take into consideration the fact that, in general, only a part of the constant capital is consumed, whereas the rest remains. According as to whether this remaining part is large or small, the surplus-value actually produced by several capitals of equal size will—other conditions being identical—naturally vary. Let us take the following figures—always on the assumption that the surplus-value amounts to 100%, *i. e.* that labour power, over and above its own value, produces exactly as much surplus-value:

Capital	Surplus-Value	Rate of Profit	Consumed constant Capital	Value of Commodities	Cost-price	
I. 80 c + 20 v	20	20%	50	90	70	
II. 70 c + 30 v	30	30%	51	111	81	
III. 60 c + 40 v	40	40%	51	131	91	
IV. 85 c + 15 v	15	15%	40	70	55	
V. 95 c + 5 v	5	5%	10	20	15	
390 c + 110 v	110	110%				Total
78 c + 22 v	22	22%				Average

If we regard the capitals I—V once more as a single total capital, we shall find that in this case also the composition of the five capitals is 500 = 390 c + 110 v; that the average composition 78 c + 22 v, thus remains the same; consequently that the average surplus-value 22% likewise remains unchanged. If this surplus-value were uniformly distributed among capitals I—V, the following would be the prices of the commodities:

Capital	Surplus-Value	Value of commodities	Cost-price	Price of commodities	Rate of Profit	Difference between Price & Value
I. 80 c + 20 v	20	90	70	92	22%	+ 2
II. 70 c + 30 v	30	111	81	103	22%	— 8
III. 60 c + 40 v	40	131	91	113	22%	— 18
IV. 85 c + 15 v	15	70	55	77	22%	+ 7
V. 95 c + 5 v	5	20	15	37	22%	+ 17

Taken all together the commodities will be sold:

$$+ \quad 2 \qquad \text{and} \ - \quad 8$$
$$+ \quad 7 \qquad \qquad - \quad 18$$
$$+ \ 17$$
_____
26 above   26 below their value.

Thus the differences of price are mutually compensated by means of a uniform distribution of the surplus-value, or by the addition of the average profit of 22% on the capital advanced to the various cost-prices of the commodities I—V. In the same proportion in which part of the commodities is sold above its value, another part is sold below the latter. And their sale at such prices alone renders it possible that the rate of profit for all the categories I—V is a uniform one (22%), regardless of the heterogeneous organic composition of capitals I—V. The prices which are obtained in this way are the *prices of production*.[1] Consequently the price of production of the commodity = its cost-price + the average profit.

When selling their commodities, the capitalists in the different branches thus withdraw exactly those capital values which have been consumed in the process of production. Not so in the case of the surplus-value or profit. Of this, the individual capitalist does not obtain the amount realised in the course of the production of his commodities, but as much of the total surplus-value of the entire class of capitalists as is apportioned to his own capital according to the prevailing average rate of profit. Every capital advanced, whatever be its composition, obtains *per centum* each year the profit reaped *per centum* that year by the totality of capital. The various capitalists resemble, in so far as profit is concerned, mere shareholders of a joint-stock company in which the profit-sharing is uniformly distributed *per centum;* such profit-sharing varies, in the case of the individual capitalists, merely according to the size of the capital invested by each one in the whole undertaking—*i. e.* according to the number

_____

[1] We call thus the prices obtained by the addition of the average profit to the cost price paid by the capitalist.

of his shares. In this way, if we consider all the branches of production in their totality, the total price of production of all commodities is, in Society itself, equal to their total value.

This assertion would appear to be contradicted by the fact that the commodities which serve one capitalist as means of production—*i. e.* machines, raw materials, etc.—have, as a rule, been purchased from another capitalist and include therefore the latter's profit in their price, or, in other words, that the profit of one branch of industry is included in the cost-price of another branch. But if we add, on the one side, all the cost-prices of the whole country together; and, on the other side, all the profits, we shall find the calculation to be exact. For instance, linen is required for the manufacture of linen coats, and linen, in turn, requires flax. A number of capitalists apply themselves therefore to the production of flax, and invest therein a capital of, let us say, 100 (*e. g.* $100,000). If the rate of profit be 10%, the linen manufacturers must purchase this flax for 110, and then sell it to the tailors for 121. The total capital utilised in these three branches thus amounts to the following sum:

in the production of flax . . .	100
in the production of linen . . .	110
in the production of coats . . .	121

$$331$$

This sum must yield a profit of 33.1, which is realised by selling the coats in the final instance for 133.1.[1] But of this profit the coat manufacturers obtain only the sum of 12.1. When purchasing the linen they must pay over the surplus amount of 21 to its producers; these, in their turn, retain only 11, and hand on the remaining 10 to the producers of flax. Thus each of the capitals interested receives that share of profit due to it in proportion to its size.

As soon as a general rate of profit has been established, with the result that the average profit in all branches adapts

---

[1] In reality the price of the coats must of course be much higher. We are only considering that part of the capital required for the purchase of the linen.

itself to the size of the invested capital, it is only by accident that the surplus-value really produced in any given branch corresponds to the profit contained in the selling-price of the commodity. As a general rule, profit and surplus-value are really two different magnitudes. The question as to how much surplus-value is produced in a given branch is of direct interest only in so far as the total average profit of all capitals is concerned. This question affects but indirectly individual branches of production and individual capitalists; an increased surplus-value in a particular branch causes an increase of the total available surplus-value, and, in consequence, an increased average profit. But this process goes on, so to speak, behind the back of the individual capitalist; he neither sees nor understands it, nor, indeed, does it interest him. The difference between profit and surplus-value in the various branches of production completely conceals the origin and the real nature of profit—not only from the capitalist, who has an interest in deceiving himself, but also from the labourer. The mere fact that, as far as practical experience is concerned, profit and cost-price are opposed to each other, tends to confuse the capitalist as to the real meaning of value; for he has not in view the total amount of labour necessary for the production of the commodity, but only that part of it which he has paid in the shape of dead or live means of production; and thus does profit appear to him as something distinct from the inner value of the commodity. The capitalist is confirmed and hardened in this mistaken idea, seeing that, as a matter of fact, the profit which is added to the cost-price—in the case of the individual branches of production, which the capitalist naturally enough alone has in view—is not determined by the formation of the value going on within itself, but is quite extraneously established against it. As far as practical experience is concerned, each part of the capital yields a uniform profit. Whatever may be the composition of capital—whether ¼ dead and ¾ live, or ¾ dead and ¼ live labour be set in motion by it, whether it absorbs in the one case three times as much surplus-labour and produces three times as much surplus-value as in the other—it yields in either case the same profit, equal exploitation of labour being assumed, and abstraction being made of individual differences which disappear anyhow, seeing that each time we have only the average composition of the whole branch before us. The individual capitalist, whose horizon is limited, rightly believes that his profit does not derive exclusively from the labour employed by him personally or in his branch of industry. This is quite right in so far as his average profit is concerned. But he is wholly ignorant as to how far this profit is adjusted by the total exploitation of labour by the total capital, *i. e.* by all his capitalist comrades; and he is all the more ignorant of this, seeing that the bourgeois theorists themselves, the professors of political economy, have up to now not revealed it. Economy of labour—not only of the labour necessary to produce a given commodity, but also of the number of labourers employed—and increased utilisation of dead labour (*i. e.* constant capital), appear as economically justifiable operations. How could therefore live labour be the only source of profit, seeing that the reduction of the quantity of labour necessary for production appears under certain circumstances as the primary source of the increase of profit—at any rate for the individual capitalist?

CHAPTER VIII

METHODS BY WHICH SURPLUS-VALUE IS INCREASED

(Extracted from vol. I, ch. 10, 11, 12.)

SURPLUS-VALUE is produced by the employment of labour power. Capital buys the labour power and pays the wages for it. By means of his work the labourer creates new value which does not belong to him, but to the capitalist. He must work a certain time merely in order to reproduce the equivalent value of his wages. But when this equivalent value has been returned, he does not cease work, but continues to do so for some further hours. The new value which he produces during this extra time, and which exceeds in consequence the amount of his wage, constitutes surplus-value.

Capital thus extorts surplus-value in the first place simply

by prolonging the duration of the working day beyond the
"necessary" working-time ("necessary" in so far as the reproduction of the wages paid for labour power is concerned).
Capital at first subordinates labour on the basis of those technical conditions in which it historically finds it. Consequently
it does not alter immediately the mode of production. The
creation of surplus-value by means of the simple prolongation
of the duration of the working day was not less active in an
old-fashioned bakery, than it is in a modern cotton-spinning-
mill.

But the working-day has a maximum limit. It cannot be
prolonged beyond a certain point. This maximum limit is conditioned by two things. First, by the physical bounds of labour
power. Within 24 hours a human being can only expend a definite quantity of his vital force. A horse in like manner, can
only work, on an average, 8 hours daily. During part of the
day the vital force must rest, sleep; during another part the
human being must feed, wash, clothe himself, etc. Besides
these purely physical limitations, the prolongation of the
working day encounters moral ones. The labourer needs time
for satisfying his intellectual and social wants, the extent and
number of which are conditioned by the general state of social
advancement. But both the physical and social limiting conditions are of a very elastic nature, and allow the greatest lati-
tude. So we find working days of 8, 10, 12, 14, 16, 18 hours,
i. e. of the most different lengths.

The constant efforts made by capital to prolong the working-day roused the opposition of the labouring class, and led in
England—in the country in which capitalist production was
first established—to bitter social and political struggles, which
lasted for centuries.

But there are also other methods of increasing surplus-
value—in the first place, the more intense utilisation of labour
power, in view of obtaining more from the latter within a
specified time. In the second place, by lowering the wages of
the labourer below the value of his labour power. Despite the
important part which this method plays in actual practice, we
are excluded from considering it in this place by our assump-

tion that all commodities, including labour power, are bought and sold at their full value.

There remains, finally, the increase of the so-called "relative" surplus-value. In this case, the following is the position of affairs;

If the working-day, let us say, lasts 10 hours, of which 6 are spent in replacing the value of labour power, a definite quantity of surplus-value is produced during the remaining 4 hours. If it be possible to increase the duration of the working-day to 11 hours, or to increase the output of labour during the 10 hours, or to combine both proceedings, the amount of surplus-value will be increased in proportion. An *absolute* increase of surplus-value is thereby obtained.

If, on the other hand, it be impossible to prolong the working-day beyond 10 hours, and likewise impossible to intensify the production, it may nevertheless perhaps be feasible to shorten the "necessary" working-time. We assumed the latter to last 6 hours, because this time was needed to produce those necessaries of life requisite for the upkeep of labour power. If such necessaries can be produced within a shorter time and with less expenditure of labour, 5 hours may perhaps suffice instead of 6, and in the 10 hours working-day 5 hours would then be available for the production of surplus-value instead of 4. The surplus-value would in this case have been increased "relatively" to the working-day.

In order to obtain such a "relative" increase of surplus-value, those commodities destined for the consumption of the labourers must be produced in a shorter time. In other words: the productive force of labour must be increased, so that a lesser amount of labour may produce the same quantity of commodities. For this purpose it by no means suffices for capital to take over the labour process in the form under which it has been historically handed down, and then simply to prolong the duration of that process. The technical and social conditions of the process and consequently the very mode of production, must be revolutionized, before the productiveness of labour can be increased. By that means alone the value of labour power can be made to sink, and the portion of the working-day necessary for the reproduction of that value be shortened.

In order to effect a fall in the value of labour power, the increase in the productiveness of labour must seize upon those branches of industry whose products determine the value of labour power, and consequently either belong to the class of customary means of subsistence, or are capable of supplying the place of those means. Such industries include, not only those which produce themselves the means of subsistence, but also those which supply the former with the means of production. For instance, the value of a pair of boots depends, not only on the cobbler's labour, but also on the value of the leather, wax, thread, etc. But an increase in the productiveness of labour in those branches of industry which supply neither the necessaries of life nor the means of production for such necessaries, leaves the value of labour power undisturbed.

Whenever an individual capitalist cheapens, for instance, shirts, by increasing the productiveness of labour, he by no means necessarily aims at reducing the value of labour power. But it is only in so far as he ultimately contributes to this result that he assists in raising the general rate of surplus-value. Hence there is imminent in capital an inclination and constant tendency to heighten the productiveness of labour, in order to cheapen commodities, and by such cheapening to cheapen the labourer himself.

Since one and the same process cheapens commodities and augments the surplus-value contained in them, we have here the solution of the riddle: why does the capitalist, whose sole concern is the production of exchange value, continually strive to depress the exchange value of commodities? The object of all development of the productiveness of labour, within the limits of capitalist production, is to shorten that part of the working-day during which the labourer must work for his own benefit, and by that very shortening to lengthen the other part of the day, during which he works gratis for the capitalist.

CHAPTER IX

HOW CAPITAL REVOLUTIONISES THE MODE OF PRODUCTION

(A) *Cooperation*

(Extracted from vol. I, ch. 13.)

CAPITALIST production begins when each individual capital employs simultaneously a comparatively large number of labourers. A greater number of labourers working together at the same time in one place (or, if you will, in the same field of labour), in order to produce the same sort of commodity, constitutes both historically and logically the starting point of capitalist production. With regard to the mode of production itself, manufacture (for instance) is originally hardly to be distinguished from the handicraft trades of the guilds, otherwise than by the greater number of labourers simultaneously employed by one and the same individual capital. The workshop of the master handicraftsman is simply enlarged.

At first, therefore, the difference is purely quantitative. Nevertheless, within certain limits, a material modification takes place. In every industry each individual labourer, be he Peter or Paul, differs more or less from the average labourer. These individual differences compensate one another and vanish, whenever a certain number of labourers are employed together. Edmund Burke asserted (in the 18th century) on the strength of his practical experiences as farmer, that even if only five farm labourers work together, all individual differences vanish, and that consequently any given five adult farm labourers taken together will in the same time do as much work as any other five. But however that may be, it is clear that the collective working-day of a large number of labourers simultaneously employed gives one day of average social labour. If, for instance, the capitalist employs 12 labourers during 12 hours each, this means for the capitalist a working-day of 144 hours. And although the labour of each of the dozen men may deviate more or less from average social labour, and each of them require a different time for the same operation—the capitalist reckons the working-day of each individual as $\frac{1}{12}$th of the total working-day of 144 hours. But if the 12 men are employed in six pairs by as many different small masters, it will be a matter of chance whether each of these masters produces the same value, and consequently realises the general rate of surplus-value. Deviations would occur in individual cases. If one labourer required considerably more time for the production of a commodity than is socially necessary, his labour would not count as average labour. Of the six small masters, one would therefore squeeze out more than the average rate of surplus-value, another less. The inequalities would be compensated for society at large, but not for the individual masters.

Even if the system of working remains the same, the simultaneous employment of a large number of labourers brings about a total change in the material conditions of the labour process. Buildings in which many are at work, storehouses for raw materials, receptacles, implements, utensils, etc., which serve, simultaneously or otherwise, the purpose of many labourers, are now consumed in common. The increased utilisation of the value in use of these means of production does not raise their exchange-value; they do not cost more. And this advantage increases in proportion to the amount of the capital. A room where 20 weavers work at 20 looms must be larger than the room of a single independent weaver with two apprentices. But it costs less to construct a single workshop for 20 persons than to build 10 to accommodate two persons each; thus the value of the means of production which are concentrated for use in common on a large scale does not increase in direct proportion to the expansion and the increased useful effects of those means. When consumed in common, they give up a smaller part of their value to each product. In this way, the total value of the commodity decreases. The economy in the application of the means of production is entirely owing to their being consumed in common by a large number of labourers—even if the latter merely work side by side, and do not assist one another.

When numerous labourers work systematically together or

side by side in one and the same process of production, or in different but connected processes, they are said to work in *cooperation*.

Just as the offensive power of a squadron of cavalry, or the defensive power of an infantry regiment, is essentially different from the sum of the offensive or defensive powers of each individual cavalry or infantry soldier, so the sum total of the mechanical forces exerted by isolated workmen differs from the social force that is developed when many hands take part simultaneously in the same operation, such as raising a heavy weight, turning a winch or removing an obstacle. In such cases the effect of the combined labour could either not be produced at all by isolated individual labour, or it could only be produced with a great expenditure of time, or on a very dwarfed scale. Not only have we here an increase in the productive power of the individual by means of cooperation, but the creation of a new power—namely the collective power of masses. ("As one man cannot, and ten men must strain to lift a ton of weight, yet one hundred men can do it only by the strength of a finger of each of them."—John Bellers, London, 1696.)

Apart from the new power that arises from the fusion of many forces into one collective force, the mere social contact begets, in the case of most productive labourers, an emulation and a stimulation of the animal spirits that heighten the efficiency of each individual labourer. Hence a dozen persons working together will, in their collective working day of 144 hours, produce far more than 12 isolated men working 12 hours each, or than one man who works twelve days in succession. The reason is that man, if not, as Aristotle contends, a political animal, is at all events a social one.

Although a number of men may be occupied together at the same time on the same, or the same kind of, labour—yet the labour of each, as a part of the collective labour, may correspond to a distant phase of the labour process, through all whose phases the object of their labour passes, in consequence of cooperation, with greater speed. For instance, if 12 masons line up so as to pass stones from the foot of a ladder to its summit, each of them does the same thing; nevertheless, their separate acts form connected parts of one total operation whereby the stones are carried up quicker by the 24 hands of the line of labourers than they could be if each man went separately up and down the ladder with his burden. The object is carried over the same distance in a shorter time. Again, a combination of labour occurs whenever a building, for instance, is taken in hand on different sides simultaneously; although here also the cooperating masons are doing the same, or the same kind of, work. The 12 masons in their collective working-day of 144 hours make much more progress than one mason could make working for 12 days or 144 hours. The reason is, that a body of men working in concert has hands and eyes both before and behind, and is, to a certain degree, omnipresent. The various parts of the work progress simultaneously.

If the work be complicated, then the mere number of the men who cooperate allows of the various operations being apportioned to different hands, and consequently of being carried on simultaneously. The time necessary for the completion of the whole work is thereby shortened. ("All together obtain a result which could not be obtained by a single individual. The one rows, while the other steers and a third casts the net or harpoons the fish; in this way the fishermen obtain a success which would have been impossible without cooperation."—Destutt de Tracy, Traité de la Volonté et de ses Effets. Paris, 1826. p. 78.)

In many branches of production there are critical periods, determined by the nature of the labour process, during which certain definite results must be obtained. For instance if a flock of sheep has to be shorn, or a field of wheat to be mown and harvested, the quantity and quality of the product are dependent on the labour being begun and ended within a certain time. In these cases, the time that ought to be taken by the labour process is prescribed, just as it is in herring fishing. The completion of the task within the proper time depends on the simultaneous application of numerous combined working-days; the amount of useful effect depends on the number of labourers; this number, however, is invariably smaller than the number of isolated labourers required to do the same amount of work in the same period. It is owing to the absence of such cooperation that in the western part of the United States, quantities of corn, and in those parts of East India, where English rule has destroyed the ancient communities, quantities of cotton, are yearly wasted.

On the one hand, cooperation admits of the work being carried on over an extended space; it is consequently imperatively called for in certain undertakings, such as draining, constructing dykes, irrigation works, and the construction of canals, roads, railways, etc. On the other hand, while extending the scale of production, it renders possible a relative contraction of the arena. This contraction of the arena of labour, simultaneous with extension of scale, whereby a number of expenses are saved, is owing to the conglomeration of the labourers, and to the concentration of the means of production.

The combined working-day, compared with an equal sum of isolated working-days, produces a greater quantity of values in use, and thereby diminishes the working-time necessary for the production of a given useful effect. As our analysis has shown, this increase of productive power is in all cases due to cooperation itself. But wage labourers cannot cooperate unless they are employed simultaneously by the same capital, the same capitalist, and unless therefore their labour powers are simultaneously bought by him. The total values of these labour powers, or the sum of the wages of these labourers for a day, or a week, as the case may be, must be available in the pocket of the capitalist, before the various labour powers are themselves assembled for the process of production. The payment of 300 labourers at once, though only for one day, requires a greater outlay of capital than does the payment of a smaller number week by week, during the whole year. Hence the number of the labourers who cooperate (or the so-called "scale" of cooperation) depends in the first place on the amount of capital that the individual capitalist can advance for the purchase of labour power.

As with the variable, so it is with the constant capital. For instance, the outlay for raw materials is 30 times larger for the capitalist who employs 300 labourers, than it is for each of the 30 capitalists who employ respectively 10 men. The value and quantity of the instruments of labour used in common do not, it is true, increase at the same rate as the number of labourers employed, but they do increase considerably. The concentration of large quantities of the means of production in the hands of individual capitalists is thus a material condition for the cooperation of wage-labourers; and the extent of the cooperation (or the "scale" of production) depends on the extent of this concentration.

We saw that, at first, the subjection of labour to capital was only a formal consequence of the fact that the labourer, instead of working for himself, works for, and therefore under, the capitalist. By the cooperation of numerous wage-labourers the sway of capital develops into a requisite for carrying on the labour process itself, into a real requisite of production. That a capitalist should command on the field of production, is now as indispensable as that a general should command on the field of battle.

All combined labour on a large scale requires, more or less, a directing authority, which secures the harmonious working of the individual activities, and performs the general functions that have their origin in the action of the combined organism, as distinguished from the action of its separate organs. A single violinist is his own conductor, whereas an orchestra requires a separate one. This work of directing, superintending and adjusting, becomes a function of capital, from the moment that the labour under the latter's control becomes cooperative. Once a function of capital, it acquires special characteristics.

The directing motive, the end and aim of capitalist production is, in the first place, to extract the greatest possible amount of surplus-value; and consequently, to exploit labour power to the greatest possible extent, in the interest of the capitalist. As the number of simultaneously employed (cooperating) labourers increases, so does also their resistance, and with it, the necessity for capital to overcome this resistance by counter-pressure. Again, in proportion to the increasing mass of the means of production, now no longer the property of the wage-labourer, the necessity increases for control over the proper application of those means. The co-operation of the wage-labourers is, further, entirely brought about by the capital that simultaneously employs them. The connexion between their individual functions and their union into one single productive body are matters external to them, and are but the act of the capital that brings and keeps them together. Hence the connexion existing between their various labours appears to them, ideally, in the shape of a plan of the capitalist, and, practically, in the shape of the authority of the same capitalist, in the shape of the will of another, who subjects their activities to his aims. Hence the authority of the capitalist is despotic. As cooperation extends its scale, this despotism assumes forms peculiar to itself. The capitalist hands over the work of direct and constant supervision of the individual worker and groups of workers, to a special kind of wage labourer. An industrial army of workers, under the command of a single capitalist, requires, like a military organisation, officers (directors, managers), and non-commissioned officers (foremen, overlookers), who command in the name of the capitalist while the work is being done.

We see therefore that the subjection and supervision of labour by capital have two distinct origins; in the first place, they derive from the fact that all labour performed in common requires a directing authority; in the second place, that such labour in the capitalist period is destined to produce surplus-value for capital. It is necessary to differentiate clearly between these two origins, which must on no account be confounded with each other if we wish to rightly understand the nature of the process.

We have seen that new productive forces develop from the mere fact that many labourers work in common, and that this cooperation further increases the already existing forces. These advantages have their origin in cooperation. This cooperation begins only with the labour process, and as soon as the labourers have begun to cooperate they have ceased to belong to themselves and become incorporated with capital.

The productive power developed by the labourer when working in cooperation, is therefore the productive power of capital. This power is developed gratuitously, whenever the labourers are placed under such given conditions, and it is capital that places them under such conditions. Because the social productive power of labour (*i. e.* the productive power developed by cooperation with other labourers) costs capital nothing, and because that productive power is not developed by the labourer before his labour belongs to capital, it appears as a power with which capital is endowed by nature—a productive power that is immanent in capital.

The colossal effects of simple cooperation are to be seen in the gigantic constructions of the ancient Asiatics, Egyptians, Etruscans, etc. "It has happened in times past that these Oriental States, after supplying the expenses of their civil and military establishments, have found themselves in possession of a surplus which they could apply to works of magnificence or utility. In the construction of these, their command over the hands and arms of almost the entire non-agricultural population, and the exclusive sway of the monarch and the priesthood over the aforementioned surplus, afforded the means of erecting the mighty monuments which filled the land. . . . In moving the colossal statues and vast masses, of which the transport creates wonder, human labour, almost alone, was prodigally used. . . . The number of the labourers and the concentration of their efforts sufficed. . . . The non-agricultural labourers of an Asiatic monarchy have little but their individual bodily exertions to bring to the task, but their number is their strength, and the power of directing these masses gave rise to those gigantic structures. It is that confinement of the revenues which feed them, to one or a few hands, which makes such undertakings possible." (R. Jones, *Textbook of Lectures*, 1852, p. 77.) This power of Asiatic and Egyptian kings, Etruscan theocrats, etc., has in modern society been transferred to the capitalists.

Cooperation, such as we find it at the dawn of human development, among tribes who live by the chase, or, say, in the agriculture of Indian communities, is based, on the one hand, on ownership in common of the means of production, and, on the other hand, on the fact that in those cases each individual has no more torn himself off from the navel-string of his tribe or community, than each bee has freed itself from connexion with the hive. Such cooperation is distinguished from capitalist cooperation by both the above characteristics. The sporadic application of cooperation on a large scale in ancient times, in the middle ages, and in modern colonies reposes on relations of dominion and servitude, principally on slavery. The capitalistic form, on the contrary, presupposes from first to last the free wage-labourer, who sells his labour power to capital. Historically, however, this form is developed in opposition to peasant agriculture and to the carrying on of independent handicrafts. From the standpoint of these, capitalistic cooperation does not manifest itself as a particular historical form of cooperation; but cooperation itself appears to be a historical form peculiar to, and specifically distinguishing, the capitalist process of production.

The simultaneous employment of a large number of wage-labourers in one and the same process, forms the starting point of capitalist production. It is the first change effected in the real process of labour by its subjection to capital.

(B) *Division of Labour and Manufacture*

(Extracted from vol. I, ch. 14.)

That cooperation which is based on division of labour, assumes its typical form in manufacture, and is the prevalent characteristic form of the capitalist process of production from about the middle of the 16th to the last third of the 18th century. Manufacture takes its rise in two ways:

(1) By the assemblage in one workshop, under the control of a single capitalist, of labourers belonging to various independent handicrafts, and through whose hands a given article must pass before completion. For instance, a coach was formerly the product of the labour of a great number of independent artificers, such as wheelwrights, harness-makers, tailors, locksmiths, upholsterers, turners, fringe-makers, glaziers, painters, polishers, gilders, etc. In the manufacture of coaches all these different artificers are assembled in one

building, where they simultaneously work into one another's hands. True, a coach cannot be gilt before being made. But if a number of coaches are being made simultaneously, some may be in the hands of the gilders while others are going through an earlier process. So far, we are still in the domain of simple cooperation, which finds its materials ready to hand in the shape of men and things. But very soon an important change occurs. The tailor, the locksmith, the upholsterer, etc., being now exclusively occupied in making coaches, each gradually loses through want of practice the capacity to carry-on his old handicraft to its full extent. On the other hand, his activity, now confined to one groove, assumes the form best adapted to the narrowed sphere of action. Originally, coach manufacture appeared as a combination of independent handicrafts. It becomes gradually the splitting-up of coach making into its various detail processes, each of which crystallises into the exclusive function of a particular labourer— the manufacture, as a whole, being carried-on by the men in conjunction. In the same way, cloth manufacture and a whole series of other manufactures arose by the combination of different handicrafts under the control of one and the same capitalist.

(2) Manufacture also arises in a way exactly the reverse of this—namely, by one capitalist employing simultaneously in one workshop a number of artificers, who all do the same or the same kind of work, *e. g.* making paper, types, or needles. This is cooperation in its most elementary form. Each of these artificers (with the help, perhaps, of one or two apprentices) makes the entire commodity, and he consequently performs successively all the operations necessary for its production. He still works in his old handicraft-like way. But very soon external circumstances cause a different use to be made of the concentration of the labourers on one spot, and of the simultaneousness of their work. For instance, an increased quantity of the finished article has to be supplied within a given time. The work is therefore redistributed. Instead of each man performing successively all the different operations, each of these operations is henceforth assigned to a different artificer, and thus all of them together are carried out simultaneously. This

accidental repartition is repeated, develops advantages of its own, and gradually ossifies into a permanent systematic division of labour. The commodity, from being the individual product of an independent artificer, who does many different things, is transformed into the social product of a union of artificers, each of whom performs continuously but a single one of the constituent partial operations.

If we now go into more detail, it is, in the first place, clear that a labourer who all his life performs one and the same simple operation, converts his whole body into the automatic specialised implement of that operation, consequently, he takes less time in doing it than the artificer who performs successively a whole series of operations. But the collective labourer, who constitutes the living mechanism of manufacture, is made up solely of such specialised detail labourers. Hence, in comparison with the independent handicraft, more is produced in less time—in other words, the productive power of labour is increased. Moreover, when once this fractional work is established as the exclusive function of one person, the methods it employs become perfected. The continued repetition of the same simple act, and the concentration of his attention on it, teach the labourer by experience how to attain the desired effect with the minimum of effort. But since there are always several generations of labourers living at one and the same time, working together at the manufacture of a given article, the technical skill thus acquired becomes established, is accumulated, and is handed down. Manufacture, in fact, develops the skill of the detail labourer, by reproducing and systematically driving to an extreme within the workshop the naturally developed differentiation of trades, which it found ready to hand in society at large. "The muslins of Dakka in fineness, the calicoes and other piece goods of Coromandel in brilliant and durable colours, have never been surpassed. Yet they are produced without capital, machinery, division of labour, or any of those means which give such facilities to the manufacturing interest of Europe. The weaver is a detached individual, working a web when ordered of a customer, and with a loom of the rudest construction, consisting sometimes of a few branches or bars of wood, put roughly together.

There is even no expedient for rolling up the warp; the loom must therefore be kept stretched to its full length and becomes so inconveniently large, that it cannot be contained within the hut of the manufacturer, who is therefore compelled to ply his trade in the open air, where it is interrupted by every vicissitude of the weather." [1] It is only the special skill accumulated from generation to generation, and transmitted from father to son, that gives to the Hindu, as it does to the spider, this proficiency. And yet the work of such a Hindu weaver is very complicated, compared with that of a manufacturing labourer.

An artificer, who performs one after another the various fractional operations in the production of a finished article, must at one time change his place, at another his tools. The transition from one operation to another interrupts the flow of his labour, and creates, so to say, gaps in his working-days. These gaps close up as soon as he is tied to one and the same operation all day long; they vanish in proportion as the changes in his work diminish. The resulting increased productive power is owing either to increased intensity of labour, because more labour power is expended in a given time; or to a decrease in the amount of labour power unproductively consumed. Every transition from rest to motion requires a certain expenditure of power, and this expenditure ceases once the acquired normal velocity has lasted a certain time. On the other hand, constant labour of one uniform kind destroys the intensity and flow of a man's animal spirits, which find recreation and delight in mere change of activity.

The productiveness of labour depends not only on the proficiency of the labourer, but on the perfection of his tools. Tools of the same kind, e. g. knives, drills, gimlets, hammers, etc., may be employed in different processes; and the same instrument may serve various purposes in a single process. But as soon as the different operations of a labour process are disconnected the one from the other and each fractional operation acquires in the hands of the detail labourer a suitable and consequently peculiar form, alterations become necessary in

[1] *Historical and descriptive account of British India,* by Hugh Murray and James Wilson, etc., v. II, p. 449. Edinburgh 1832.—The Indian loom is upright, *i. e.* the warp is stretched vertically.

the implements that previously served more than one purpose. The direction taken by this change is determined by the difficulties experienced in consequence of the unchanged form of the implement. Manufacture is characterised by the differentiation of the instruments of labour. In Birmingham alone 500 varieties of hammers are produced, and not only is each adapted to one particular process, but several varieties often serve exclusively for the different operations in one and the same process. Manufacture simplifies, improves, and multiplies the implements of labour, by adapting them to the exclusively special functions of each detail labourer.[1] It thus creates at the same time one of the material conditions for the existence of machinery, which consists of a combination of simple instruments.

The detail labourer and his implements are the simplest elements of manufacture. Let us now turn to its aspect as a whole.

The organisation of manufacture has two essentially different fundamental forms, which, especially in the subsequent transformation of manufacture into modern industry carried on by machinery, play very distinct parts. This double character arises from the nature of the article produced. Such an article either results from the mere mechanical fitting together of partial products made independently, or owes its completed shape to a series of connected processes and manipulations.

A locomotive, for instance, consists of more than 5000 independent parts. It cannot, however, serve as an example of the first kind of genuine manufacture, because it is a product of modern industry. But a watch can. Formerly the individual work of a Nuremberg artificer, the watch has been

---

[1] Darwin in his epoch-making work on *The Origin of Species*, remarks, with reference to the natural organs of plants and animals: "So long as one and the same organ has different kinds of work to perform, a ground for its changeability may possibly be found in this, that natural selection preserves or suppresses each small variation of form less carefully than if that organ were destined for one special purpose alone. Thus, knives that are adapted to cut all sorts of things may, on the whole, be of one shape; but an implement destined to be used exclusively in one way must have a different shape for every different use."

transformed into the social product of an immense number of detail labourers, such as mainspring makers, dial makers, spiral spring makers, jewelled hole makers, ruby lever makers, hand makers, case makers, screw makers, gilders with numerous subdivisions, such as wheel makers (brass and steel separate), pin makers, movement makers, acheveur de pignon (fixes the wheels on the axles, polishes the facets, etc.), pivot makers, planteur de finissage (puts the wheels and springs in the works), finisseur de barillet (cuts teeth in the wheels, makes the holes of the right size, etc.), escapement makers, cylinder makers for cylinder escapements, escapement wheel makers, balance wheel makers, raquette makers (apparatus for regulating the watch), planteur d'echappement (escapement maker proper); then the repasseur de barillet (finishes the box for the spring), steel polishers, wheel polishers, screw polishers, figure painters, dial enamellers (melts the enamel on the copper), fabricant de pendants (makes the ring by which the case is hung), finisseur de charnière (puts the brass hinge in the cover, etc.), faiseur de secret (puts in the springs that open the case), graveur, ciseleur, polisseur de boite, etc., etc., and last of all the repasseur, who fits together the whole watch and hands it over in a going state. Only a few parts of the watch pass through several hands; and all these scattered parts come finally together in the hand that binds them into one mechanical whole. The external relation between the finished product and its various and diverse elements makes it, in this case as in the case of all similar finished articles, a matter of chance whether the detail labourers are brought together in one workshop or not. The detail operations may further be carried on like so many independent handicrafts, as they are in the cantons of Vaud and Neufchatel; while in Geneva there exist large watch manufactories where the detail labourers work together under the control of a single capitalist. And even in the latter case the dial, the springs, and the case are seldom made in the factory itself. To carry on the trade as a manufacture with concentration of workmen is in the watch trade profitable only under exceptional conditions, because competition is greater between the labourers who desire to work at home, and because the splitting-up of the work into a number of heterogeneous processes permits but little use of the instruments of labour in common, and the capitalist, by scattering the work, saves the outlay on workshops, etc.[1] Nevertheless the position of this detail labourer, who, though he works at home, does so for a capitalist, is very different from that of the independent artificer who works for his own customers.[2]

The second kind of manufacture, its perfected form, produces articles that go through connected phases of development, through a series of processes, step by step, like the wire in the manufacture of needles, which passes through the hands of 72, sometimes even 92 detail workmen.

If we confine our attention to some particular lot of raw materials, of rags, for instance, in paper manufacture, or of wire in needle manufacture, we perceive that it passes in succession through a series of stages in the hands of the various detail workmen until completion. On the other hand, if we look at the workshop as a whole, we see the raw material in all the stages of its production at the same time. The collective labourer, with one set of his many hands armed with one kind of tools, draws the wire, with another set, armed with different tools, he, at the same time, straightens it, with another, he cuts it, with another, points it, and so on. Hence, produc-

---

[1] In 1854 Geneva produced 80,000 watches, which is not one-fifth of the production in the canton of Neufchatel. La Chaux-de-Fonds alone, which we may look upon as a huge watch manufactory, produces yearly twice as many as Geneva. From 1850 to 1861 Geneva produced 750,000 watches. The want of connexion alone, between the processes into which the production of articles that merely consist of parts fitted together is split up, makes it very difficult to convert such a manufacture into a branch of modern industry carried-on by machinery; but in the case of a watch there are two other impediments in addition, the minuteness and delicacy of its parts, and its character as an article of luxury. Hence their variety, which is such that in the best London houses scarcely a dozen watches are made alike in the course of a year. The watch manufactory of Messrs. Vacheron & Constantin, in which machinery has been employed with success, produces at the most 3 or 4 different watches of size and form.

[2] In watch-making, that classical example of heterogeneous manufacture, we may study with great accuracy the above-mentioned differentiation and specialisation of the instruments of labour caused by the subdivision of handicrafts.

tion of a greater quantity of finished commodities in a given time. Manufacture accomplishes this social organisation of the labour process only by riveting each labourer to a single fractional detail.

Since the fractional product of each detail labourer is, at the same time, only a particular stage in the development of one and the same finished article, each labourer, or each group of labourers, prepares the raw material for another labourer or group. The result of the labour of the one is the starting point for the labour of the other. The labour-time necessary in each partial process, for attaining the desired effect, is learned by experience; and the mechanism of manufacture, as a whole, is based on the assumption that a given result will be obtained in a given time. It is only on this assumption that the various supplementary labour-processes can proceed uninterruptedly, simultaneously, and side by side. It is clear that this direct dependence of the operations, and therefore of the labourers, on each other, compels each one of them to spend on his work no more than the necessary time, and thus a continuity, uniformity, regularity, order, and especially intensity of labour, of quite a different kind, is begotten than is to be found in an independent handicraft or even in simple cooperation.

Different operations take, however, unequal periods, and yield therefore, in equal times unequal quantities of fractional products. If, therefore, the same labourer has, day after day, to perform the same operation, there must be a different number of labourers—a number exactly adapted to their mutual relations—for each operation; for instance, in type manufacture, there are four founders and two breakers to one rubber: the founder casts 2000 types an hour, the breaker breaks up 4000, and the rubber polishes 8000.

When once the most fitting proportion has been experimentally established for the numbers of the detail labourers in the various groups when producing on a given scale, that scale can be extended only by employing a multiple of each particular group. For instance, in type manufacture it is impossible to employ a single extra rubber without employing simultaneously two extra breakers and four extra founders.

There is this to boot, that the same individual can do certain kinds of work just as well on a large as on a small scale; for instance, the labour of superintendence, the carriage of the fractional product from one stage to the next, &c. The isolation of such functions, their allotment to a particular labourer, does not become advantageous till after an increase in the number of labourers employed; but this increase must at once affect every group proportionally.

In many manufactures, however, the group itself is an organised body of labour. Take, for instance, the manufacture of glass bottles. It may be resolved into three essentially different stages. First, the preliminary stage, consisting of the preparation of the components of the glass, mixing the sand and lime, &c., and melting them into a fluid mass of glass. Various detail labourers are employed in this first stage, as also in the final one of removing the bottles from the drying furnace, sorting and packing them, &c. In the middle, between these two stages, comes the glass melting proper, the manipulation of the fluid mass. At each mouth of the furnace, there works a group, called "the hole", consisting of one bottlemaker or finisher, one blower, one gatherer, one putter-up or whetter-off, and one taker-in. These five detail workers are so many special organs of a single working organism that acts only as a whole, and therefore can operate only by the direct cooperation of the whole five. The whole body is paralysed if but one of its members be wanting. But a glass furnace has several openings (in England from 4 to 6), each of which contains an earthenware melting-pot full of molten glass, and employs a similar five-membered group of workers. The organisation of each group is based directly on division of labour, but the bond between the different groups is simple cooperation, which, by using in common one of the means of production, the furnace, causes it to be more economically consumed. Such a furnace, with its 4—6 groups, constitutes a glass house; and a glass manufactory comprises a number of such glass houses, together with the apparatus and workmen requisite for the preparatory and final stages.

Finally, manufacture can develop into a combination of various manufactures. The larger English glass manufacturers, for instance, make their own earthenware meltingpots, because on the quality of these depends, to a great extent, the success or failure of the process. Thus, we find the manufacture of flint glass combined with that of glass cutting and brass founding; the latter for the metal settings of various articles of glass. The various manufactures so combined form more or less separate departments of a larger manufacture, but are at the same time independent processes, each with its own division of labour. In spite of the many advantages offered by this combination of manufactures, it never grows into a complete technical system on its own foundation. That happens only on its transformation into an industry carried on by machinery.

Early in the manufacturing period, the principle of lessening the necessary labour-time in the production of commodities, was accepted and formulated: and the use of machines, especially for certain simple first processes that have to be conducted on a very large scale, and with the application of great force, sprang up here and there. Thus at an early period in paper manufacture, the tearing up of the rags was done by paper mills; and in metal works, the pounding of the ores was effected by stamping mills. The Roman Empire had handed down the elementary form of all machinery in the waterwheel.[1] The handicraft period bequeathed to us the great inventions of the compass, of gunpowder, of typeprinting, and of the automatic clock. But, on the whole, machinery played a subordinate part in comparison with division of labour. The sporadic use of machinery supplied the great mathematicians of that time with a practical basis and stimulant to the creation of the science of mechanics.

The collective labourer, formed by the combination of a number of detail labourers, is the machinery specially characteristic of the manufacturing period. The various operations that are performed in turns by the producer of a commodity,

[1] The whole history of the development of machinery can be traced in the history of the corn mill. The factory in England is still a "mill." In German technological works of the first decade of the 19th century, the term "Mühle" is still found in use, not only for all machinery driven by the forces of Nature, but also for all manufactures where apparatus in the nature of machinery is applied.

lay claim to him in various ways. In one operation he must exert more strength, in another more skill, in another more attention &c; and the same individual does not possess all these qualities in an equal degree. After manufacture has once separated, made independent, and isolated the various oper-ations the labourers are divided, classified, and grouped according to their predominating qualities. If their natural endowments are, on the one hand, the foundation on which the division of labour is built up, on the other hand, manu-facture, once introduced, develops in them new powers that are by nature fitted only for limited and special functions. The collective labourer now possesses, in an equal degree of excellence, all the qualities requisite for production, and ex-pends them in the most suitable manner, by exclusively em-ploying all his organs, consisting of particular labourers, or groups of labourers, in performing their special functions. The one-sidedness and the deficiencies of the detail labourer become perfections when he is a part of the collective la-bourer.[1] The habit of doing only one thing, converts him into a never failing instrument, while his connexion with the whole mechanism compels him to work with the regularity of the parts of a machine.

Since the collective labourer has functions, both simple and complex, both high and low, his members, the individual labour powers, require different degrees of training, and must therefore have different values. Manufacture, therefore, de-velops a hierarchy of labour powers, to which there corre-sponds a scale of wages. Every process of production, how-ever, requires certain simple manipulations, which every man is capable of doing. They too are now severed from their con-nexion with the more pregnant moments of activity, and ossi-fied into exclusive functions of specially appointed labourers. Hence, manufacture begets, in every handicraft that it seizes upon, a class of so-called unskilled labourers, a class which handicraft industry strictly excluded. Alongside of the hier-archic gradation there steps the simple separation of the labourers into skilled and unskilled. For the latter, the cost

[1] For instance, abnormal development of some muscles, curvature of bones, &c.

of apprenticeship vanishes; for the former, it diminishes, compared with that of artificers, in consequence of the functions being simplified. In both cases the value of labour power falls. An exception to this law holds good whenever the decomposition of the labour process begets new and comprehensive functions, that either had no place at all, or only a very modest one, in handicrafts.

The division of labour in manufacture, which we have just described, was the continuation of the division of labour which has gone on ever since the earliest records of history, and which, in the pre-manufacturing period, found its most complete expression in handicraft. It is evident that the new process of division due to capital, manifested numerous analogies with the former process, and that the two processes reacted on each other mutually. None the less are the two processes—i. e. the division of labour known for many centuries past, and which organised the labourers in the various handicrafts, on the one hand, and the division within one and the same workshop caused by capital, on the other— essentially different from each other. The analogy appears most indisputable where there is an invisible bond uniting the various branches of trade. For instance, the cattle-breeder produces hides, the tanner makes the hides into leather, and the shoemaker the leather into boots. Here the thing produced by each of them is but a step towards the final form, which is the product of all their labours combined. There are, besi les, all the various industries that supply the cattle-breeder, the tanner, and the shoemaker with the means of production. But what is it that forms the bond between the independent labours of the cattle-breeder, the tanner, and the shoemaker? It is the fact that their respective products are commodities. What, on the other hand, characterises division of labour in manufactures? The fact that the detail labourer produces no commodities. It is only the common product of all the detail labourers that becomes a commodity. Division of labour in a society is brought about by the purchase and sale of the products of different branches of industry, while the connexion between the detail operations in a workshop is due to the sale of the labour power of several workmen to one capitalist, who applies it as combined labour power. The division of labour in the workshop implies concentration of the means of production in the hands of one capitalist; the division of labour in society implies their dispersion among many independent producers of commodities. While within the workshop, the iron law of proportionality subjects definite numbers of workmen to definite functions, in the society outside the workshop chance and caprice have full play in distributing the producers and their means of production among the various branches of industry. Division of labour within the workshop implies the undisputed authority of the capitalist over men, that are but parts of a mechanism that belongs to him. The division of labour within the society brings into contact independent commodity-producers, who acknowledge no other authority but that of competition, of the coercion exerted by the pressure of their mutual interests. The same bourgeois mind which praises division of labour in the workshop, life-long annexation of the labourer to a partial operation, and his complete subjection to capital, as being an organisation of labour that increases its productiveness—that same bourgeois mind denounces with equal vigour every conscious attempt to socially control and regulate the process of production, as an inroad upon such sacred things as the rights of property, freedom and unrestricted play for the bent of the individual capitalist. It is very characteristic that the enthusiastic apologists of the factory system have nothing more damning to urge against a general organisation of the labour of society, than that it would turn all society into one immense factory.

The rules of the guilds, by limiting most strictly the number of apprentices and journeymen that a single master could employ, prevented him from becoming a capitalist. Moreover, he could not employ his journeymen in any other handicraft than the one in which he was a master. The guilds jealously repelled every encroachment by the capital of merchants, the only form of free capital with which they came in contact. A merchant could buy every kind of commodity, but labour as a commodity he could not buy. He existed only on sufferance, as a dealer in the products of the handicrafts. If circumstances called for a further division of labour, the existing guilds split themselves up into varieties, or founded new guilds by the side of the old ones; all this, however, without concentrating various handicrafts in a single workshop. Hence, the guild organisation, however much it may have contributed, by separating, isolating, and perfecting the handicrafts, to create the material conditions for the existence of manufacture, excluded division of labour in the workshop. On the whole, the labourer and his means of production remained closely united, like the snail with its shell, and thus there was wanting the principal basis of manufacture, the separation of the labourer from his means of production, and the conversion of these means into capital.

While division of labour in society at large, whether such division be brought about or not by exchange of commodities, is common to the most diverse economical formations of society, division of labour in the workshop, as practised by manufacture, is a special creation of the capitalist mode of production alone.

Once manufacture has been introduced, every further progress of the division of labour requires an increase of the capital available in the hand of the individual capitalist. As we have seen, the minimum number of labourers that any given capitalist is bound to employ is here prescribed by the previously established division of labour. (We need only recall the example of type manufacture. For one rubber employed, there must be two breakers and four founders; the capitalist must employ at least these seven workmen if he wishes to keep his foundry going. Any extension of business requires the employment of at least seven new workmen.) This renders necessary a corresponding increase of the implements and materials of labour, and also an increase in the workshops, furnaces, &c., and especially in the raw materials, the call for which grows quicker than the number of workmen. For the extension of business increases the productive power of labour; a larger quantity of raw material is worked-up in the same length of time by the same number of labourers. This raw material must be available in the hand of the capitalist. In the same proportion, therefore, in which manufacture extends, the necessaries of life and the means of production existing in society must be converted into capital in the hands of the capitalist.

"It is not sufficient that capital" (the writer should have said the necessary means of subsistence and of production) "required for the sub-division of handicrafts should be in readiness in the society: it must also be accumulated in the hands of the employers in sufficiently large quantities to enable them to conduct their operations on a large scale . . . The more the division increases, the more does the constant employment of a given number of labourers require a greater outlay of capital in tools, raw material, &c." (Storch: Cours d'Econ. Polit. Paris Ed., t. I., pp. 250, 251.)

Manufacture, like simple cooperation, is due to capital. The productive power derived from the combination of labour thus appears to be the productive power of capital. But there is an essential difference between simple cooperation and manufacture. While simple cooperation leaves the mode of working by the individual for the most part unchanged, manufacture thoroughly revolutionises it, and seizes labour power by its very roots. It converts the labourer into a crippled monstrosity, by forcing his detail dexterity at the expense of a world of productive capabilities and instincts; just as in the states of La Plata they butcher a whole beast for the sake of his hide or his tallow. Not only is the detail work distributed to the different individuals, but the individual himself is made the automatic motor of a fractional operation, and the absurd fable of Menenius Agrippa, which makes man a mere fragment of his own body, becomes realised. If, at first, the workman sells his labour power to capital, because the material means of producing a commodity fail him, now his very labour power refuses its services unless it has been sold to capital. Its functions can be exercised only in an environment that exists in the workshop of the capitalist after the sale. By nature unfitted to make anything independently, the manufacturing labourer develops productive activity as a mere appendage of the capitalist's workshop. "The workman who is capable of performing an entire handicraft can everywhere exercise his industry and find the means of subsistence; the other (the manufacturing labourer) is but an accessory, who, separated from his comrades, is no longer either capable or independent, and is compelled to accept any law which the employer may find it convenient to impose on him." [1]

The knowledge, the judgment, and the will, which, though in ever so small a degree, are practised by the independent peasant or handicraftsman, are now required only for the workshop as a whole. The detail labourers lose the intellectual potencies of production, which concentrate themselves in the capital that employs them. It is a result of the division of labour in manufacture that the individual labourer is deprived of the intellectual potencies of production, which are brought face to face with him as the property of another and as a ruling power. This separation begins in simple cooperation, where the capitalist represents to the single workman, the oneness and the will of the associated labour. It is developed in manufacture which cuts down the labourer into a detail labourer. It is completed in modern industry, which makes science a productive force distinct from labour and presses it into the service of capital.

In manufacture, in order to make the collective labourer, and through him capital, rich in social productive power, each labourer must be made poor in individual productive powers. "Ignorance is the mother of industry as well as of superstition. Reflection and fancy are subject to err; but a habit of moving the hand or the foot is independent of either. Manufactures, accordingly, prosper most where the mind is least consulted, and where the workshop may . . . be considered as an engine, the parts of which are men." (J. D. Tuckett: *A History of the Past and Present State of the Labouring Population*. Lond., 1846, vol. I, p. 149.) As a matter of fact, some few manufacturers in the middle of the 18th century preferred, for certain operations that were trade secrets, to employ half idiotic persons.

Adam Smith has described graphically (in *Wealth of*

[1] Storch, 1, c. Petersb. edit. 1815, t. 1, p. 204.

Nations, 1776, vol. V, ch. 1, section 2) the intellectual crippling resulting from manufactures:

"The understandings of the greater part of men", says Adam Smith, "are necessarily formed by their ordinary employments. The man whose whole life is spent in performing a few simple operations . . . has no occasion to exert his understanding. . . . He generally becomes as stupid and ignorant as it is possible for a human creature to become."

But also the body of the detail labourer is crippled, and thus manufacture is the first to afford the materials for, and to give a start to, industrial pathology.

"To subdivide a man is to execute him, if he deserves the sentence, to assassinate him if he does not . . . The subdivision of labour is the assassination of a people." (D. Urquhart: *Familiar Words*, Lond., 1855, p. 119.)

Cooperation based on division of labour, in other words, manufacture, commences as a spontaneous formation. So soon as it attains some consistence and extension, it becomes the recognised methodical and systematic form of capitalist production. History shows how the division of labour peculiar to manufacture, strictly so called, acquires the best adapted form at first by experience, as it were behind the backs of the actors, and then, like the guild handicrafts, strives to hold fast that form when once found, and here and there succeeds in keeping it for centuries. Any alteration in this form, except in trivial matters, is solely owing to a revolution in the instruments of labour. Modern manufacture, in the large towns where it arises—I do not here allude to modern industry based on machinery—either finds the disjecta membra poetae ready to hand, and only waiting to be collected together, as is the case in the manufacture of clothes, or it can easily apply the principle of division, simply by exclusively assigning the various operations of a handicraft (such as bookbinding) to particular men. In such cases, a week's experience is enough to determine the proportion between the numbers of the hands necessary for the various functions.[1]

[1] The simple belief in the inventive genius exercised a priori by the individual capitalist in the various manipulations of the division of labour, exists now-a-days only among German professors, of the

Division of labour in manufacture consequently creates a definite organisation of the labour of society, and thereby develops at the same time new productive forces in the society. In its specific capitalist form—and under the given conditions it could take no other form than a capitalistic one —manufacture is but a particular method of begetting relative surplus-value, or of augmenting at the expense of the labourer the self-expansion of capital. It increases the social productive power of labour, not only for the benefit of the capitalist instead of that of the labourer, but it does this by crippling the individual labourers. It creates new conditions for the lordship of capital over labour. If, therefore, on the one hand, it presents itself historically as a progress, on the other hand it is a refined and civilised method of exploitation.

Political economy, which as an independent science, first sprang into being during the period of manufacture, sees in the social division of labour only the means of producing more commodities with a given quantity of labour, and, consequently, of cheapening commodities and hurrying on the accumulation of capital. In most striking contrast with this accentuation of quantity and exchange-value, is the attitude of the writers of classical antiquity, who hold exclusively by quality and use-value. In consequence of the separation of the social branches of production, commodities are better made, the various bents and talents of men select a suitable field, and without some restraint no important results can be obtained anywhere.

During the manufacturing period proper, *i. e.*, the period during which manufacture is the predominant form taken by capitalist production, many obstacles are opposed to the full development of the peculiar tendencies of manufacture. Although manufacture creates, as we have already seen, a simple separation of the labourers into skilled and unskilled, simultaneously with their hierarchic arrangement in classes, yet the number of the unskilled labourers remains very lim-

stamp of Herr Roscher, who, to recompense the capitalist from whose Jovian head division of labour sprang ready formed, dedicates to him "various wages". The more or less extensive application of division of labour depends on length of purse, not on greatness of genius.

ited. Although it adapts the detail operations to the various degrees of maturity, strength, and development of the living instruments of labour, thus conducing to exploitation of women and children, yet this tendency as a whole is wrecked by the habits and the resistance of male labourers. Although the splitting up of handicrafts lowers the cost of forming the workman, and thereby lowers his value, yet for the more difficult detail work a longer apprenticeship is necessary, and, even where it would be superfluous, is jealously insisted upon by the workmen. In England, for instance, we find the laws of apprenticeship, with their seven years' probation, in full force down to the end of the manufacturing period; and they are not thrown on one side till the advent of modern industry. Since handicraft skill is the foundation of manufacture, capital is constantly compelled to wrestle with the insubordination of the workmen. Hence throughout the whole manufacturing period there runs the complaint of want of discipline among the workmen. During the period between the 16th century and the epoch of modern industry capital failed to become the master of the whole disposable working-time of the manufacturing labourers, and manufactures had to change their locality from one country to another with the emigrating or immigrating workmen.

At the same time manufacture was unable, either to seize upon the production of society to its full extent, or to revolutionise that production to its very core. One of its most finished creations was the workshop for the production of the instruments of labour themselves, including especially the complicated mechanical apparatus then already employed. This workshop, the product of the division of labour in manufacture, produced in its turn—machines. Thus the fetters fall away, which the dependence of the work on the personal capacity of the workmen still laid on the dominion of capital.

(C) *Machinery and Modern Industry*

(Extracted from vol. II, ch. 15, sections 1 & 2.)

Applied by capital, machinery is intended to cheapen commodities, and, by shortening that portion of the working-day, in which the labourer works for himself, to lengthen the other portion that he gives without an equivalent to the capitalist. In short, it is a means for producing surplus-value.

In manufacture, the revolution in the mode of production begins with the labour power, in modern industry it begins with the instruments of labour. Our first inquiry then is, how the instruments of labour are converted from tools into machines.

Mathematicians and mechanicians call a tool a simple machine, and a machine a complex tool. They see no essential difference between them. As a matter of fact, every machine is a combination of those simple tools, no matter how they may be disguised. From the economical standpoint this explanation is worth nothing. Another explanation of the difference between tool and machine is that in the case of a tool, man is the motive power, while the motive power of a machine is something different from man, is, for instance, an animal, water, wind, and so on. According to this, a plough drawn by oxen, which is a contrivance common to the most different epochs, would be a machine, while Claussen's circular loom, which, worked by a single labourer, weaves 96,000 picks per minute, would be a mere tool. Nay, this very loom, though a tool when worked by hand, would, if worked by steam, be a machine. And since the application of animal power is one of man's earliest inventions, production by machinery would have preceded production by handicrafts.

All fully developed machinery consists of three essentially different parts, the motor mechanism, the transmitting mechanism, and finally the tool or working machine. The motor mechanism is that which puts the whole in motion. It either generates its own motive power, like the steam engine, the caloric engine, the electro-magnetic machine, &c., or it receives its impulse from some already existing natural force, like the water-wheel from a head of water, the wind-mill from wind. The transmitting mechanism, composed of fly-wheels, shafting, toothed wheels, pullies, straps, ropes, bands, pinions, and gearing of the most varied kinds, regulates the motion, changes its form where necessary, as for instance, from linear to circular, and divides and distributes it among the working machines. These two first parts of the whole mechanism are there solely for putting the working machines in motion, by means of which motion the subject of labour is seized upon and modified as desired. The tool or working-machine is that part of the machinery with which the industrial revolution of the 18th century started. And to this day it constantly serves as such a starting point, whenever a handicraft, or a manufacture, is turned into an industry carried on by machinery.

On a closer examination of the working-machine proper, we find in it, as a general rule, though often, no doubt, under very altered form, the apparatus and tools used by the handicraftsman or manufacturing workman. Either the entire machine is only a more or less altered mechanical edition of the old handicraft tool, as, for instance, the power-loom; or the working parts fitted in the frame of the machine are old acquaintances, as spindles, needles, saws and knives. The machine proper is therefore a mechanism that, after being set in motion, performs with its tools the same operations that were formerly done by the workman with similar tools. Whether the motive power is derived from man, or from some other machine, makes no difference in this respect. From the moment that the tool proper is taken from man, and fitted into a mechanism, a machine takes the place of a mere implement.

The difference strikes one at once, even in those cases where man himself continues to be the prime mover. The number of implements that he himself can use simultaneously, is limited by the number of his own natural instruments of production, by the number of his bodily organs. In Germany, they tried at first to make one spinner work two spinning wheels, that is, to work simultaneously with both hands and both feet. This was too difficult. Later, a treddle spinning wheel with two spindles was invented, but adepts in spinning who could spin two threads at once, were almost as scarce as two-headed men. The Jenny, on the other hand, even at its very birth, spun with 12-18 spindles, and the stocking-loom knits with many thousand needles at once. The number of tools that a machine can bring into play simultaneously, is from the very first emanci-

pated from the limits that hedge in the tools of a handicraftsman.

The steam-engine itself, such as it was at its invention, during the manufacturing period at the close of the 17th century,
and such as it continued to be down to 1780, did not give rise
to any industrial revolution. It was, on the contrary, the invention of machines that made a revolution in the form of
steam-engines necessary.

The machine, which is the starting point of the industrial
revolution, supersedes the workman, who handles a single tool,
by a mechanism operating with a number of similar tools, and
set in motion by a single motive power, whatever the form of
that power may be. ("The union of all these simple instruments, set in motion by a single motor, constitutes a machine."
Babbage, London, 1832.)

Increase in the size of the machine, and in the number of
the working tools, calls for a more massive mechanism to drive
it; and this mechanism requires, in order to overcome its
resistance, a mightier moving power than that of man, apart
from the fact that man is a very important instrument for
producing uniform continued motion. Natural forces can now
replace him as moving power, and thus a single mover can
simultaneously drive many machines.

There were mules and steam-engines before there were any
labourers, whose exclusive occupation it was to make mules
and steam-engines; just as men wore clothes before there were
such people as tailors. The inventions of Vaucanson, Ark-
wright, Watt, and others, were, however, practicable only because those inventors found, ready to hand, a considerable
number of skilled mechanical workmen, placed at their disposal by the manufacturing period. As inventions increased in
number, and the demand for the newly discovered machines
grew larger, the machine-making industry split up, more and
more, into numerous independent branches and division of
labour in these manufactures was more and more developed.
Here, then, we see in manufacture the immediate technical
foundation of modern industry. Manufacture produced the
machinery, by means of which modern industry abolished
the handicraft and manufacturing systems in those spheres of

production that it first seized upon. The factory system was therefore raised, in the natural course of things, on an inadequate foundation. Modern industry was crippled in its complete development, so long as its characteristic instrument of production, the machine, owed its existence to personal strength and personal skill, and depended on the muscular development, the keenness of sight, and the cunning of hand, with which the detail workmen in manufactures, and the manual labourers in handicrafts, wielded their dwarfish implements. Thus, apart from the dearness of the machines made in this way, the expansion of industries carried on by means of machinery, and the invasion by machinery of fresh branches of production, were dependent on the growth of a class of workmen, who, owing to the almost artistic nature of their employment, could increase their numbers only gradually, and not by leaps and bounds. But besides this, at a certain stage of its development, modern industry became technologically incompatible with the basis furnished for it by handicraft and manufacture. The construction of machines was confronted by tasks which manufacture was unable to fulfil. Such machines as the modern hydraulic press, the modern power loom, and the modern carding engine, could never have been furnished by manufacture.

A radical change of the mode of production in one sphere of industry involves a similar change in other spheres. Thus spinning by machinery made weaving by machinery a necessity, and both together made the mechanical and chemical revolution that took place in bleaching, printing, and dyeing, imperative. So too, on the other hand, the revolution in cotton-spinning called forth the invention of the gin, for separating the seeds from the cotton fibre; it was only by means of this invention, that the production of cotton became possible on the enormous scale at present required. But more especially, the revolution in the modes of production of industry and agriculture made necessary a revolution in the means of communication and of transport. The means of communication and transport handed down from the manufacturing period soon became unbearable trammels on modern industry, with its feverish haste of production, its enormous extent, its con-

stant flinging of capital and labour from one sphere of production into another, and its newly-created connexions with
the markets of the whole world. Hence, apart from the radical
changes introduced in the construction of sailing vessels, the
means of communication and transport became gradually
adapted to the modes of production of mechanical industry,
by the creation of a system of river steamers, railways, ocean
steamers, and telegraphs. But the huge masses of iron that had
now to be forged, to be welded, to be cut, to be bored and to
be shaped, demanded, on their part, cyclopean machines, for
the construction of which the methods of the manufacturing
period were utterly inadequate. Modern industry had therefore itself to take in hand the machine, its characteristic instrument of production, and to construct machines by
machines.

If we now fix our attention on that portion of the machinery employed in the construction of machines, which constitutes the operating tool, we find the manual implements
reappearing, but on a cyclopean scale. The boring machine
operates with the help of an immense borer which is propelled
by a steam-engine and without which, on the other hand, the
cylinders of large steam-engines and of hydraulic presses
could not be made. The mechanical lathe is only a cyclopean
reproduction of the ordinary foot-lathe; the planing machine,
an iron carpenter, that works on iron with the same tools that
the human carpenter employs on wood; the instrument that,
on the London wharves, cuts the veneers, is a gigantic razor;
the tool of the shearing machine, which shears iron as easily
as a tailor's scissors cut cloth, is a monster pair of scissors;
and the steam hammer works with an ordinary hammer head,
but of such a weight that not Thor himself could wield it.
There is one that weighs over 6 tons and strikes with a vertical
fall of 7 feet, on an anvil weighing 36 tons. It is mere child's-
play for it to crush a block of granite into power, yet it is no
less capable of driving, with a succession of light taps, a nail
into a piece of soft wood.

In simple cooperation, and even in that founded on division of labour, the suppression of the isolated, by the collective workman still appears to be more or less accidental.

Machinery, with a few exceptions to be mentioned later, operates only by means of associated labour, or labour in common. Hence the cooperative character of the labour power is, in the latter case, a technical necessity dictated by the instrument of labour itself.

We saw that the productive forces resulting from cooperation and division of labour cost capital nothing. They are natural forces of social labour. So also physical forces, like steam, water, &c., when appropriated to productive processes, cost nothing. But just as a man requires lungs to breathe with, so he requires something that is work of man's hand in order to consume physical forces productively. A water-wheel is necessary to exploit the force of water, and a steam-engine to exploit the elasticity of steam. The case of science is similar to that of natural powers. Once discovered, the law of deviation of the magnetic needle in the field of an electric current, or the law of the magnetisation of iron, around which an electric current circulates, costs never a penny. But the exploitation of these laws for the purposes of telegraphy, &c., necessitates a costly and extensive apparatus. Although, therefore, it is clear at the first glance that, by incorporating both stupendous physical forces and the natural sciences with the process of production, modern industry raises the productiveness of labour to an extraordinary degree, it is by no means equally clear that this increased productive force is not, on the other hand, purchased by an increased expenditure of labour. Machinery, like every other component of constant capital, creates no new value, but yields up its own value to the product that it serves to beget. And it is clear as noon-day, that machines and systems of machinery, the characteristic instruments of labour of modern industry, are incomparably more loaded with value than the implements used in handicrafts and manufactures. Instead of cheapening the product they render the latter dearer in proportion to their own value.

It must be observed that the machine never adds more value to the individual product than it loses on an average through wear and tear. There is thus a great difference between the value of a machine and the fraction of value transferred each time by it to the product. This fraction is smaller.

the longer the machine lasts. This holds good for every imple-ment of labour and every instrument of production. But the difference between utilisation, on the one hand, and wear and tear, on the other, is greater in the case of the machine than in that of the tool. For the former, being made of more last-ing material, is more durable; its application, governed by strictly scientific laws, permits of greater economy being real-ized; and, finally, its sphere of production is much greater than that of the tool.

Mr. Baynes, of Blackburn, in a lecture published in 1858, estimates that "each real mechanical horse-power will drive 450 self-acting mule spindles, with preparation, or 200 throstle spindles, or 15 looms for 40 inch cloth with the appliances for warping, sizing, &c." In the first case, it is the day's produce of 450 mule spindles, in the second, of 200 throstle spindles, in the third, of 15 power-looms, over which the daily cost of one horse-power, and the wear and tear of the machinery set in motion by that power, are spread; so that only a very minute value is transferred by such wear and tear to a pound of yarn or a yard of cloth. The same is the case with the steam-hammer mentioned above. Since its daily wear and tear, its coal consumption, &c., are spread over the stupendous masses of iron hammered by it in a day, only a small value is added to a hundredweight of iron, but the value would be very great if the cyclopean instrument were employed in driving in nails.

Already when considering cooperation and manufacture, we saw that certain necessities of production, such as build-ings &c. undergo less wear and tear in consequence of their use in common, and thus increase but inconsiderably the dear-ness of the product. But this reduction of dearness augments in the case of machinery; for not only is a working-machine consumed in common by its several operating tools, but the same motor-machine, together with a part of the transmitting apparatus, is consumed in common by numerous working-machines.

Given the rate at which machinery transfers its values to the product, the amount of value so transferred depends on the total value of the machinery. The less labour it contains, the less value it imparts to the product. The less value it gives up, so much the more productive it is, and so much the more its services approximate to those of natural forces.

It is evident that whenever it costs as much labour to produce a machine as is saved by the employment of that machine, there is nothing but a transposition of labour; consequently the total labour required to produce a commodity is not lessened, or the productiveness of labour is not increased. It is clear, however, that the difference between the labour a machine costs, and the labour it saves does not depend on the difference between its own value and the value of the implement it replaces. This difference lasts as long as the labour spent on a machine, and consequently the portion of its value added to the product, remains smaller than the value added by the workman to the product with his tool The productiveness of a machine is therefore measured by the human labour power it replaces. The labour saved by a machine must not, however, be confounded with wages. Suppose, then, a machine cost as much as the wages for a year of the 150 men it displaces, say $15,000; this $15,000 is by no means the expression in money of the labour added to the object produced by these 150 men before the introduction of the machine, but only of that portion of their year's labour which was expended for themselves and represented by their wages. They received $15,000 wages for the year, but they furnished in return for that sum a greater value. If now, the machine costs $15,000, in which all the labour applied during its production is included—no matter in what proportion such labour is divided into wages for the workmen and surplus-value for the capitalist—the value of the machine is less than the value formerly produced by the 150 labourers. Therefore, though a machine cost as much as the labour power displaced by it costs, yet the labour materialised in it is even then much less than the living labour it replaces.

If it were only a question of cheapening the products, the employment of the machine would be profitable as long as its production costs less labour than its employment renders superfluous. Let us illustrate this by means of figures. In the above cited case, 150 labourers received $15,000 wages per annum, and furnished in return, let us say, $30,000 of labour, the surplus-value thus amounting to 100 per cent of their wages. As long as the production of the machine, which the labour of the 150 men undertakes, costs less than $30,000, the employment of the machine would be profitable for society, seeing that it saves labour. But the capitalist cannot calculate in this way. He pays only $15,000 for the labour performed by 150 men, and the machine can therefore not be utilised by him as soon as it costs more than $15,000. (In a communist society, machinery would hence be employed on a quite different scale than in a bourgeois society.) The wages effectively paid alone play a part for the capitalist in his costs of production. These wages vary for the same amount of labour, in the different countries. They also vary by sinking below the value of labour power, or rising above it. Hence the invention nowadays of machines in England that are employed only in North-America; just as in the sixteenth and seventeenth centuries, machines were invented in Germany to be used only in Holland, and just as many a French invention of the eighteenth century was exploited in England alone. In the older countries, machinery, when employed in some branches of industry, creates such a redundancy of labour in other branches that in these latter the fall of wages below the value of labour power impedes the use of machinery. In some branches of the woollen manufacture in England the employment of children has during recent years been considerably diminished, and in some cases has been entirely abolished. Why? Because the factory Acts made two sets of children necessary, one working six hours, the other four, or each working five hours. But the parents refused to sell the "half-timers" cheaper than the "full-timers". Hence the substitution of machinery for the "half-timers". Before the labour of women and of children under 10 years of age was forbidden in mines, capitalists considered the employment of naked women and girls, often in company with men, so far sanctioned by their moral code, and especially by their ledgers, that it was only after the passing of the Act that they had recourse to machinery. The Yankees have invented a stonebreaking-machine. The English do not make use of it, because the "wretch" who does this work gets paid for such a small portion of his labour, that machinery would increase the cost of production to the capitalist. ("Wretch" is the recognised term in English political economy for the agricultural labourers.) In England women are still occasionally used instead of horses for hauling canal boats (1860), because the labour required to produce horses and machines is an accurately known quantity, while that required to maintain the women of the surplus population is below all calculation. Hence nowhere do we find a more shameful squandering of human labour power for the most despicable purposes than in England, the land of machinery.

CHAPTER X

THE INFLUENCE OF INDUSTRIAL PROGRESS ON THE WORKING CLASSES

(Extracted from vol. II, ch. 15, sections 3—7.)

(A) *Labour of Women and Children*

IN so far as machinery dispenses with muscular power, it becomes a means of employing labourers of slight muscular strength and those whose bodily development is incomplete, but whose limbs are all the more supple. The labour of women and children was, therefore, the first thing sought for by capitalists who used machinery. That mighty substitute for labour and labourers was forthwith changed into a means for increasing the number of wage-labourers, by enrolling under the direct sway of capital every member of the workman's family, without distinction of age or sex. Compulsory work for the capitalist usurped the place, not only of the children's play, but also of free labour at home within moderate limits for the support of the family.[1]

[1] Dr. Edward Smith, during the cotton crisis caused by the American Civil War, was sent by the English Government to Lancashire, Cheshire, and other places, to report on the sanitary condition of the cotton operatives. He reported, that from a hygienic point of view, and apart

The value of labour power was determined, not only by the labour time necessary to maintain the individual adult labourer, but also by that necessary to maintain his family. Machinery, by throwing every member of that family on to the labour market, depreciates the labour power of the man. To purchase the labour power of a family of four workers may, perhaps, cost more than it formerly did to purchase the labour power of the head of the family, but, in return, four days' labour takes the place of one. In order that the family may live, four people must now, not only labour, but expend surplus labour for the capitalist.

"The numerical increase of labourers has been great, through the growing substitution of female for male, and above all, of child for adult labour. Three girls of 13, at wages of from 6 shillings to 8 shillings a week, have replaced the one man of mature age, of wages varying from 18 shillings to 45 shillings." (Th. de Quincey: "The Logic of Political Econ., London, 1845.") Since certain family functions, such as nursing and suckling children, cannot be entirely suppressed, the mothers confiscated by capital must hire substitutes of some sort. Domestic work, such as sewing and mending, must be replaced by the purchase of ready-made articles. Hence, the diminished expenditure of labour in the house is accompanied by an increased expenditure of money. The cost of keeping the family increases and balances the greater income. In addition to this, economy and judgment in the consumption and preparation of the means of subsistence becomes impossible.[1]

from the banishment of the operatives from the factory atmosphere, the crisis had several advantages. The women now had sufficient leisure to give their infants the breast, instead of poisoning them with "Godfrey's cordial." They had time to learn to cook. Unfortunately the acquisition of this art occurred at a time when they had nothing to cook. But from this we see how capital, for the purposes of its self-expansion, has usurped the labour necessary in the home of the family. This crisis was also utilised to teach sewing to the daughters of the workmen in sewing schools. An American revolution and a universal crisis, in order that the working girls who spin for the whole world might learn to sew!

[1] Abundant material relating to these facts, which are concealed by official political economy, is to be found in the Reports of the Inspectors of Factories, of the Children's Employment Commission, and more especially in the Reports on Public Health.

Machinery also revolutionises the contract between labourer and capitalist, since capital buys children and young persons under age. Previously, the workman sold his own labour power, which he disposed of nominally as a free agent. Now he sells wife and child. He has become a slave dealer. The demand for children's labour often resembles in form the inquiries for negro slaves, such as were formerly to be read among the advertisements in American journals. In the reports of the Children's Employment Commission (1864-66) we find truly revolting details regarding the conduct of the operative parents in relation to the traffic in children—conduct which entirely resembles slave-dealing.

One consequence of the ensuing dissolution of family life is the enormous mortality, during the first few years of their life, of the children of the operatives. In sixteen of the registration districts into which England is divided, there are, for every 100,000 children alive under the age of one year, only 9000 deaths in a year on an average (in one district only 7000); in 24 districts the deaths are over 10,000, but under 11,000; in 39 districts, over 11,000, but under 12,000; in 48 districts over 12,000, but under 13,000; in 22 districts over 20,000; in 25 districts over 21,000; in 17 over 22,000; in 11 over 23,000; in Hoo, Wolverhampton, Ashton-under-Lyne, and Preston, over 24,000; in Nottingham, Stockport and Bradford, over 25,000; in Wisbeach 26,000; and in Manchester 26,125.[1]

As was shown by an official medical inquiry in the year 1861, the high death-rates are, apart from local causes, principally due to the employment of the mothers away from their homes, and the neglect and maltreatment consequent on her absence, such as, amongst others, insufficient nourishment, unsuitable food, and dosing with opiates; besides this, there arises an unnatural estrangement between mother and child, and as a consequence intentional starving and poisoning of the children. In those agricultural districts, "where a minimum in the employment of women exists, the death-rate is on the other hand very low."[2]

[1] Sixth Report on Public Health. Lond., 1864, p. 34.
[2] l. c. p. 454.

The moral degradation caused by the capitalistic exploitation of women and children has been so exhaustively depicted by F. Engels in his "Lage der arbeitenden Klassen Englands", and other writers, that I need only mention the subject in this place. But the intellectual desolation, artificially produced by converting immature human beings into mere machines for the fabrication of surplus-value, a state of mind clearly distinguishable from that natural ignorance which keeps the mind fallow without destroying its capacity for development, its natural fertility, this desolation finally compelled even the English Parliament to make elementary education a compulsory condition to the "productive" employment of children under 14 years, in every industry subject to the Factory Acts. The spirit of capitalist production stands out clearly in the ludicrous wording of the so-called education clauses in the Factory Acts, in the absence of an administrative machinery, in the opposition of the manufacturers even to these education clauses, and in the tricks and dodges they put in practice for evading them. The legislature "provides nothing more than that the children shall on certain days of the week, and for a certain number of hours (three) in each day, be inclosed within the four walls of a place called a school, and that the employer of the child shall receive weekly a certificate to that effect signed by a person designated by the subscriber as a schoolmaster or schoolmistress." [1] Previous to the passing of the amended Factory Act, 1844, it happened, not unfrequently, that the certificates of attendance at school were signed by the schoolmaster or schoolmistress with a cross, as they themselves were unable to write. "But it is not only in the miserable places above referred to that the children obtain certificates of school attendance without having received instruction of any value, for in many schools where there is a competent teacher, his efforts are of little avail from the distracting crowd of children of all ages, from infants of 3 years old and upwards; his livelihood, miserable at the best, depending on the pence received from the greatest number of

[1] Leonard Horner in "Reports of Insp. of Fact, for 30th June, 1857", p. 17.

children whom it is possible to cram into the space. To this is to be added scanty school furniture, deficiency of books and other materials for teaching, and the depressing effect upon the poor children themselves of a close, noisome atmosphere. I have been in many such schools, where I have seen rows of children doing absolutely nothing; and this is certified as school attendance, and, in statistical returns, such children are set down as being educated." [1] As an example of the perfidious manner in which the capitalists seek to thwart the law, we may quote the following: By the Act relating to print works and similar industries, "every child, before being employed in a print work, must have attended school for at least 30 days, and not less than 150 hours, during the six months immediately preceding such first day of employment, and during the continuance of its employment in the print works, it must attend for a like period of 30 days, and 150 hours, during every successive period of six months. . . . The attendance at school must be between 8 a. m. and 6 p. m. No attendance of less than 2½ hours, nor more than 5 hours on any one day, shall be reckoned as part of the 150 hours." How did capital carry out these legal obligations? "Under ordinary circumstances the children attend school morning and afternoon for 30 days, for at least 5 hours each day, and upon the expiration of the 30 days, the statutory total of 150 hours having been attained, having, in their language, made up their book, they return to the print work, where they continue until the six months have expired, when another instalment of school attendance becomes due, and they again seek the school until the book is again made up. . . . Many boys having attended school for the required number of hours, when they return to school after the expiration of their six months' work in the print work, are in the same condition as when they first attended school as print-work boys. They have lost all they gained by their previous school attendance. . . . In other print works the children's attendance at school is made to depend altogether upon the exigencies of the work

[1] L. Horner in "Reports &c., for 31st Oct., 1856", pp. 17, 18. Sir J. Kincaid in "Reports, &c., 31st Oct. 1856", pp. 66.

in the establishment. The requisite number of hours is made up each six months, by instalment consisting of from 3 to 5 hours at a time, spreading over, perhaps, the whole six months. . . . For instance, the attendance on one day might be from 8 to 11 a. m., on another day from 1 p. m. to 6 p. m., and the child might not appear at school again for several days, when it would attend from 3 p. m. to 6 p. m.; then it might attend for 3 or 4 days consecutively, or for a week, then it would not appear in school for 3 weeks or a month, after that upon some odd days at some odd hours when the operative who employed it chose to spare it; and thus the child was, as it were, buffeted from school to work, from work to school, until the tale of 150 hours was told." [1]

By the excessive addition of women and children to the ranks of the workers, machinery at last breaks down the resistance which the male operatives in the manufacturing period continued to oppose to the despotism of capital.

(B) *Prolongation of the Working-day*

If machinery be the most powerful means for increasing the productiveness of labour—*i. e.*, for shortening the working time required in the production of a commodity, it becomes in the hands of capital the most powerful means for lengthening the working-day beyond all bounds set by human nature. It creates, on the one hand, new conditions by which capital is enabled to give free scope to this its constant tendency, and on the other hand, new motives with which to whet capital's appetite for the labour of others.

In the form of machinery, the implements of labour become automatic, things moving and working independently of the workmen. They are henceforth an industrial perpetuum mobile, that would go on producing for ever, did it not meet with certain natural obstructions in the weak bodies and the strong wills of its human attendants. Capital is therefore animated by the longing to reduce to a minimum the resistance offered. This resistance is moreover lessened by the apparent lightness of machine work, and by the more pliant and

[1] A. Redgrave in "Rep. of Insp. of Fact., 31st Oct., 1857", pp. 41-42

docile character of the women and children employed on it.

The longer the machine works, the greater is the mass of the products over which the value transmitted by the machine is spread, and the less is the portion of that value added to each single commodity. This is a sufficient reason for the capitalist to prolong the daily activity of the machine as much as possible.

The wear and tear of a machine is not exactly proportional to its working time. And even if it were so, a machine working 16 hours daily for $7\frac{1}{2}$ years, covers as long a working period as, and transmits to the total product no more value than, the same machine would if it worked only 8 hours daily for 15 years. But in the first case the value of the machine would be reproduced twice as quickly as in the latter, and the capitalist would, by this use of the machine, absorb in $7\frac{1}{2}$ years as much surplus-value as in the second case he would in 15.

The material wear and tear of a machine is of two kinds. The one arises from use, the other from non-use, as a sword rusts when left in its scabbard. The latter kind is due to the elements, and this wear and tear is, to a certain extent, inversely proportional to the use of the machine. The longer it stands still, the more it is used-up by the elements.

But in addition to the material wear and tear, a machine also undergoes what we may call a moral depreciation. It loses exchange-value, either by machines of the same sort being produced cheaper than it, or by better machines entering into competition with it. In both cases, be the machine ever so young and full of life, its value is no longer determined by the labour actually materialised in it, but by the labour-time requisite to reproduce either it or the better machine. It has, therefore, lost value more or less. The shorter the period taken to reproduce its total value, the less is the danger of moral depreciation; and the longer the working day, the shorter is that period. When machinery is first introduced into an industry, new methods of reproducing it more cheaply follow blow upon blow, and so do improvements, that not only affect individual parts and details of the machine, but its entire build. It is, therefore, in the early days of the life of machinery that this special incentive to the prolongation of the working day makes itself felt most acutely.[1]

Given the length of the working day, all other circumstances remaining the same, the exploitation of double the number of workmen demands, not only a doubling of that part of constant capital which is invested in machinery and buildings, but also of that part which is laid out in raw material and auxiliary substances. The lengthening of the working day, on the other hand, allows of production on an extended scale without any alteration in the amount of capital laid out on machinery and buildings. It is true that this takes place, more or less, with every lengthening of the working day; but in the case under consideration, the change is more marked, because the capital converted into the instruments of labour preponderates to a greater degree. "When a labourer," said Mr. Ashworth, a cotton magnate, to Professor Nassau W. Senior, in 1837, "lays down his spade, he renders useless, for that period, a capital worth eighteenpence. When one of our people (i. e. the factory workman) leaves the mill, he renders useless a capital that has cost £100,000." [2] Only fancy! making "useless" for a single moment, a capital that has cost £100,000! It is, in truth, monstrous, that a single one of our people should ever leave the factory! The increased use of machinery, as Senior after the instruction he received from Ashworth clearly perceives, makes a constantly increasing lengthening of the working day "desirable."

When machines are first introduced in an isolated fashion in a given branch of industry, the social value of the product of the machine is superior to its individual value, i. e. the product of the machine requires less labour than the product

---

[1] The improvements which took place not long ago in frames for making patent net was so great that a machine in good repair which had cost £1200, sold a few years after for £60.... Improvements succeeded each other so rapidly, that machines which had never been finished were abandoned in the hands of their makers, because new improvements had superseded their utility. (Babbage, London 1832.) In these stormy, go-ahead times, therefore, the tulle manufacturers soon extended the working day, by means of double sets of hands, from the original 8 hours to 24.

[2] Senior, "Letters on the Factory Act. London, 1837", pp. 13, 14.

of competitors working without machinery. The value, however, is determined by the "socially necessary" labour, in this
case the greater amount of labour requisite when no machine
is available. The machine-made product can consequently
be sold at a much higher price than its own value represents.
During this transition period, when the use of machinery is
a sort of monopoly, the profits are therefore exceptional, and
the capitalist endeavors to exploit thoroughly "the sunny time
of this his first love," by prolonging the working day as much
as possible. The magnitude of the profit whets his appetite for
more profit.

As the use of machinery becomes more general in a particular industry, the social value of the product sinks down to its
individual value, and the law that surplus-value does not arise
from the labour power that has been replaced by the machinery, but from the labour power actually employed in
working with the machinery, asserts itself. Surplus-value
arises from variable capital alone, *i. e.* from living labour;
it must therefore be greater in the measure in which living
labour is employed by capital, and less in the measure in which
the amount of such labour is reduced. But the object of the
machine is to eliminate living labour and to act as a substitute
for the latter. Machinery increases the power of production,
and cheapens the product, seeing that it manufactures this
product with less expenditure of labour. It thereby reduces
the cost of living, and consequently the value of labour power.
It obtains all these results, however, only by reducing the number of labourers employed by a given capitalist, or in other
words by transferring a part of the formerly variable capital
employed in paying wages to the purchase and upkeep of
machines, *i. e.* by transforming variable capital into constant
capital which produces no surplus-value. Let us illustrate this
by a concrete example. Before the introduction of machinery
a capital of $25,000 had to be applied to the extent of 40 per
cent to the purchase of labour implements and raw material,
the other 60 per cent serving for the remuneration of human
labour. When machinery is introduced, the productiveness of
the undertaking is tripled. Henceforth only 20 per cent of the
capital is applied for the remuneration of labour, and two-

thirds of the labourers hitherto employed are discharged. That share of the capital which formerly served to remunerate them serves in future for the purchase of machines and of the raw material to be worked-up by the latter.

It is impossible, however, to squeeze as much surplus-value out of 2 as out of 24 labourers. If each of these 24 men gives only one hour of surplus-labour in 12, the 24 men give together 24 hours of surplus-labour, while 24 hours is the total labour of the two men. Hence, the application of machinery to the production of surplus-value implies a contradiction which is immanent in it, since the rate of surplus-value cannot be increased, except by diminishing the number of workmen. It is this contradiction, that in its turn drives the capitalist, without his being conscious of the fact, to excessive lengthening of the working day, in order that he may compensate the decrease in the number of labourers exploited, by an increase of the absolute surplus-value of each individual labourer.

If, then, the capitalistic employment of machinery, on the one hand, supplies new and powerful motives to an excessive lengthening of the working day, and radically changes methods of labour, in such a manner as to break down all opposition to this tendency, on the other hand it produces, partly by employing women and children, partly by setting free the labourers it supplants, a surplus working population, which is compelled to submit to the dictation of capital. Hence that remarkable phenomenon in the history of modern industry, that machinery sweeps away every moral and natural restriction on the length of the working day. Hence, too, the economical paradox, that the most powerful instrument for shortening labour-time becomes the most unfailing means for placing every moment of the labourer's time and that of his family, at the disposal of the capitalist for the purpose of expanding the value of his capital.[1]

There followed on the birth of machinism and modern industry in the last third of the 18th century, an immense extension of the working-day like an avalanche in its intensity and extent. All bounds of morals and nature, age and sex, day and

[1] From here on vol. I, ch. 10, section 6.

night, became so confused that an English judge, as late as 1860, needed a quite Talmudic sagacity to explain "judicially" what was day and what was night. Capital celebrated its orgies. "The fact is, that prior to the Act of 1833, young persons and children were worked all night, all day, or both ad libitum." [1]

Now let us cast a glance at certain branches of production in which the exploitation of labour is either free from fetters to this day (1863-1865) or was so yesterday.[2]

Mr. Broughton Charlton, county magistrate, declared, as chairman of a meeting held at the Assembly Rooms, Notting ham, on the 14th January, 1860, "that there was an amount of privation and suffering among that portion of the population connected with the lace trade, unknown in other parts of the civilised world. . . . Children of nine or ten years are dragged from their squalid beds at two, three, or four o'clock in the morning and compelled to work for a bare subsistence until ten, eleven, or twelve at night, their limbs wearing away, their frames dwindling, their faces whitening, and their humanity absolutely sinking into a stonelike torpor, utterly horrible to contemplate. . . . What can be thought of a town which holds a public meeting to petition that the period of labor for men shall be diminished to eighteeen hours a day?" [3] . . .

The potteries of Staffordshire have, during the last 22 years, (before 1860), been the subject of three parliamentary inquiries. For my purpose it is enough to take, from the reports of 1860 and 1863, some depositions of the exploited children themselves. From the children we may form an opinion as to the adults, especially the girls and women, and that in a branch of industry by the side of which cotton-spinning appears an agreeable and healthy occupation.

William Wood, 9 years old, was 7 years and 10 months when he began to work. He "ran moulds" (carried readymoulded articles into the drying room, afterwards bringing back the empty mould). He came to work every day in the

---

1 "Report of Insp. of Fact.", 30th April, 1860, p. 50.
2 Form here on vol. I, ch. 10, section 3.
3 "Daily Telegraph", 15. 1. 1860.

week at 6 a. m. and left off about 9 p. m. "I work till 9 o'clock at night six days in the week. I have done so seven or eight weeks." Fifteen hours of labour for a child 9 years old! J. Murray, 12 years of age, says: "I turn jigger, and run moulds. I come at 6. Sometimes I come at 4. I worked all night last night, till 6 o'clock this morning. I have not been in bed since the night before last. There were eight or nine other boys working last night. All but one have come this morning. I get 3 shillings and sixpence [88 cents]. I do not get any more for working at night. I worked two nights last week."

Dr. Greenhow states that the average duration of life in the pottery districts of Stoke-on-Trent and Wolstanton is extraordinarily short. Although in the district of Stoke only 36.6% and in Wolstanton only 30.4% of the adult male population above 20 are employed in the potteries, among the men of that age in the first district more than half, in the second nearly two-fifths of all the deaths are the result of pulmonary diseases among the potters. Dr. Boothroyd, a medical practitioner at Hanley, says: "Each successive generation of potters is more dwarfed and less robust than the preceding one." In like manner another doctor, Mr. McBean: "Since he began to practise among the potters 25 years ago, he had observed a marked degeneration, especially shown in diminution of stature and breadth." These statements are taken from the report of Dr. Greenhow in 1860.[1]

From the report of the Commissioners in 1863, the following: Dr. J. T. Arledge, senior physician of the North Staffordshire Infirmary, says: "The potters as a class, both men and women, represent a degenerated population, both physically and morally. They are, as a rule, stunted in growth, ill-shaped, and frequently ill-formed in the chest; they become prematurely old, and are certainly short-lived; they are phlegmatic and bloodless, and exhibit their debility of constitution by obstinate attacks of dyspepsia, and disorders of the liver and kidneys, and by chest disease, pneumonia, phthisis, bronchitis, and asthma. One form would appear peculiar to them and is known as potter's asthma, or potter's consumption. Scrofula attacking the glands, or bones, or other parts of

[1] Public Health, 3rd report, etc., p. 102, 104, 105.

the body, is a disease of two-thirds or more of the potters.
... That the 'degenerescence' of the population of this district is not even greater than it is, is due to the constant recruiting from the adjacent country, and intermarriages with
more healthy races.'

Mr. Charles Pearson, late house surgeon of the same institution, writes in a letter to Commissioner Longe, amongst
other things: "I can only speak from personal observation and
not from statistical data, but I do not hesitate to assert that
my indignation has been aroused again and again at the sight
of poor children whose health has been sacrificed to gratify
the avarice of either parents or employers." He enumerates
the causes of the diseases of the potters, and sums them up
in the phrase, "long hours." And all that holds of the potteries
in England is true of those in Scotland.

The manufacture of lucifer matches dates from 1833, from
the discovery of the method of applying phosphorus to the
match itself. Since 1845 this manufacture has rapidly developed in England, and has extended especially amongst the
thickly populated parts of London as well as in Manchester,
Birmingham, Liverpool, Bristol, Norwich, Newcastle and
Glasgow. With it has spread the form of lockjaw, which a
Vienna physician in 1845 discovered to be a disease peculiar
to lucifer-matchmakers. Half the workers are children under
thirteen, and young persons under eighteen. The manufacture is on account of its unhealthiness and unpleasantness
in such bad odour that only the most miserable part of the
labouring class, half-starved widows and so forth, deliver up
their children to it, "the ragged, half-starved, untaught children". Of the witnesses that Commissioner White examined
(1863), 270 were under 18, 50 under 10, 10 only 8, and 5
only 6 years old. A range of the working day from 12 to 14
or 15 hours, night labour, irregular meal times, meals for the
most part taken in the very workrooms that are pestilent with
phosphorus. Dante would have found the worst horrors of his
Inferno surpassed in this manufacture.

In the manufacture of paper-hangings the coarser sorts
are printed by machine; the finer by hand (block-printing).
The most active business months are from the beginning of

October to the end of April. During this time the work goes on fast and furious without intermission from 6 a. m. to 10 p. m. or further into the night.

G. Apsden deposes (1862): "That boy of mine ... when he was 7 years old I used to carry him on my back to and fro through the snow, and he used to have 16 hours a day. . . . I have often knelt down to feed him as he stood by the machine. for he could not leave it or stop." Smith, the managing partner of a Manchester factory: "We (he means his 'hands' who work for 'us') work on, with no stoppage for meals, so that the day's work of 10½ hours is finished by 4:30 p. m., and all after that is overtime." (Does this Mr. Smith take no meals himself during 10½ hours?) "We (this same Smith) seldom leave off working before 6 p. m. . . . For all these, children and adults alike (152 children and young persons and 140 adults), the average work for the last 18 months has been at the very least 7 days, 5 hours, or 78½ hours a week. For the six weeks ending May 2nd this year (1863), the average was higher—8 days or 84 hours a week." Still this same Mr. Smith adds with a smile, "Machine work is not great." So the employers in the block-printing say: "Hand labour is more healthy than machine-work." On the whole, manufacturers declare with indignation against the proposal "to stop the machine at least during meal times".

In January 1866, three railway men are standing before a London coroner's jury—a guard, an engine-driver, a signal-man. A tremendous railway accident has hurried hundreds of passengers into another world. The negligence of the employés is the cause of the misfortune. They declare with one voice before the jury that ten or twelve years before, their labour only lasted eight hours a day. During the last five or six years it had been screwed up to 14, 18, and 20 hours, and under a specially severe pressure of holiday-makers, at times of excursion trains, it often lasted for 40 or 50 hours without a break. They were ordinary men, not Cyclops. At a certain point their labour power failed. Torpor seized them. Their brain ceased to think, their eyes to see. The thoroughly "respectable" British jurymen answered by a verdict that sent them to the next assizes on a charge of manslaughter, and.

in a gentle "rider" to their verdict, expressed the pious hope that the capitalistic magnates of the railways would, in future, be more extravagant in the purchase of a sufficient quantity of labour power, and more "abstemious", more "self-deny-ing", more "thrifty", in the draining of paid labour power.[1]

From the motley crowd of labourers of all callings let us take two more figures whose striking contrast proves that before capital all men are alike—a milliner and a blacksmith.

In the last week of June, 1863, all the London daily papers published a paragraph with the "sensational" heading, "Death from simple over-work." It dealt with the death of the milli-ner, Mary Anne Walkley, 20 years of age, employed in a highly-respected dressmaking establishment, exploited by a lady with the pleasant name of Elise. The old, often-told story, was once more recounted.[2] This girl worked, on an average, 10½ hours, during the season often 30 hours, with-out a break, whilst her failing labour power was revived by occasional supplies of sherry, port, or coffee. It was just now the height of the season. It was necessary to conjure up in the twinkling of an eye the gorgeous dresses for the

---

[1] "Reynolds Newspaper," January 20th, 1866.—Every week this same paper has, under sensational headings, a whole list of fresh rail-way catastrophes. On these an employé on the North Staffordshire line comments (4. 2. 1866): "Everyone knows the consequences that may occur if the driver and fireman of a locomotive engine are not con-tinually on the lookout. How can that be expected from a man who has been at such work for 29 or 30 hours, exposed to the weather, and without rest. The following is an example which is of very frequent occurrence:—One fireman commenced work on the Monday morning at a very early hour. When he had finished what is called a day's work, he had been on duty 14 hours 50 minutes. Before he had time to get his tea, he was again called on for duty.... He worked a total of 29 hours 15 minutes without intermission. The rest of the week's work was made up as follows:—Wednesday, 15 hours; Thursday, 15 hours 35 minutes; Friday, 14½ hours; Saturday, 14 hours 10 minutes, mak-ing a total for the week of 88 hours 40 minutes. Now, sir, fancy his astonishment on being paid 6 days for the whole. Thinking it was a mistake, he inquired what they considered a day's work, and was told 13 hours (or 78 hours per week). But what about the payment for the extra 10 hours and 40 minutes? After long bargaining he re-ceived 10 d.—"

[2] Cf F. Engels. Lage der arbeitenden Klassen in England pp. 253, 254.

noble ladies bidden to the ball in honour of the newly imported Princess of Wales. Mary Anne Walkley had worked
without intermission for 26½ hours, with 60 other girls, 30
in one room, that only afforded one-third of the cubic feet of
air required for them. At night, they slept in pairs in one
of the stifling holes into which the bedroom was divided by
partitions of board. And this was one of the best millinery
establishments in London. Mary Anne Walkley fell ill on the
Friday, died on Sunday, without, to the astonishment of
Madame Elise, having previously completed the work in hand.
The doctor, Mr. Keyes, called too late to the death bed, duly
bore witness before the coroner's jury that "Mary Anne
Walkley had died from long hours of work in an overcrowded
workroom, and a too small and badly ventilated bedroom."
In order to give the doctor a lesson in good manners, the
coroner's jury thereupon brought in a verdict that "the de-
ceased had died of apoplexy, but there was reason to fear that
her death had been accelerated by overwork in an overcrowded workroom, &c."

Dr. Richardson, Senior Physician to one of the London
Hospitals: "With needlewomen of all kinds, including milli-
ners, dressmakers, and ordinary sempstresses, there are three
miseries—over-work, deficient air, and either deficient food
or deficient digestion. . . . But the mischiefs of the trade, in
the metropolis especially, are that it is monopolised by some
twenty-six capitalists. . . . This power tells throughout the
whole class of female workers. If a dressmaker can get a little
circle of customers, such is the competition that, in her home,
she must work to the death to hold together, and this same
over-work she must of necessity inflict on any who may assist
her. If she fail, or do not try independently, she must join an
establishment, where her labour is not less, but where her
money is safe. Placed thus, she becomes a mere slave, tossed
about with the variations of society. Now at home, in one
room, starving, or near to it, then engaged 15, 16, aye, even 18
hours out of the 24, in an air that is scarcely tolerable, and on
food which, even if it be good, cannot be digested in the absence of pure air. On these victims, consumption, which is
purely a disease of bad air, feeds." (Dr. Richardson: "Work

and Overwork" in "Social Science Review," 18th July, 1863).

The same Dr. Richardson continues: "It is not only in dressmakers' rooms that working to death is the order of the day, but in a thousand other places; in every place I had almost said, where a 'thriving business' has to be done. . . . We will take the blacksmith as a type. If the poets were true, there is no man so hearty, so merry, as the blacksmith; he rises early and strikes his sparks before the sun; he eats and drinks and sleeps as no other man. Working in moderation, he is, in fact, in one of the best of human positions, physically speaking. But we follow him into the city or town, and we see the stress of work on that strong man, and what then is his position in the death-rate of his country? In Marylebone, blacksmiths die at the rate of 31 per thousand per annum, or 11 above the mean of the male adults of the country in its entirety. The occupation, instinctive almost as a portion of human art, unobjectionable as a branch of human industry, is made by mere excess of work the destroyer of the man. He can strike so many blows per day, walk so many steps, breathe so many breaths, produce so much work, and live an average, say of fifty years; he is made to strike so many more blows, to walk so many more steps, to breathe so many more breaths per day, and to increase altogether a fourth of his life. He meets the effort; the result is, that producing for a limited time a fourth more work, he dies at 37 for 50."

(C) *Intensification of Labour* [1]

The immoderate lengthening of the working day, produced by machinery in the hands of capital, leads to a reaction on the part of society, the very sources of whose life are menaced; and, thence, to a normal working day whose length is fixed by law. On the basis of such a normal day, the intensity of labour was greatly increased.

It is self-evident, that in proportion as the use of machinery spreads, and the experience of a special class of workmen habituated to machinery accumulates, the rapidity and intensity of labour increase as a natural consequence. Thus in

[1] From here on once more vol. II, ch. 15, section 3 sq.

England, during half a century, lengthening of the working day went hand in hand with increasing intensity of factory labour. Nevertheless the reader will clearly see, that where we have labour, not carried on by fits and starts, but repeated day after day with unvarying uniformity, a point must inevitably be reached, where extension of the working day and intensity of the labour mutually exclude one another, in such a way that lengthening of the working day becomes compatible only with a lower degree of intensity, and a higher degree of intensity only with a shortening of the working day. So soon as the gradually surging revolt of the working class compelled Parliament to shorten compulsorily the hours of labour, and to begin by imposing a normal working day on factories proper, so soon consequently as an increased production of surplus-value by the prolongation of the working day was once for all put a stop to, from that moment capital threw itself with all its might into the production of such surplus-value, by hastening on the further improvement of machinery.

Henceforth surplus-value is increased not only by cheapening the product and thereby reducing the value of labour power, but at the same time by intensifying the labour, *i. e.* by increasing the tension of labour power, so that in a shorter time it must perform as much or even more labour than formerly in a longer time. The more intensive 10 hours day contains henceforth as much labour (or expended labour power) as the porous working-day of 12 hours. The product therefore of one of the former hours has as much or more value than has the product of $1\frac{1}{5}$ of the latter hours. Apart from the increased yield of relative surplus-value through the heightened productiveness of labour, the same mass of value is now produced for the capitalist say by $3\frac{1}{3}$ hours of surplus labour, and $6\frac{2}{3}$ hours of necessary labour, as was previously produced by four hours of surplus labour and eight hours of necessary labour.

We now come to the question: How is the labour intensified?

The first effect of shortening the working-day results from the self-evident law, that the efficiency of labour power is in an inverse ratio to the duration of its expenditure. The shorter a labourer works, the more intensively can he work. Hence, within certain limits, what is lost by shortening the duration is gained by the increasing tension of labour power. That the workman moreover really does expend more labour power, is ensured by the mode in which the capitalist pays him.[1] In those industries, such as potteries, where machinery plays little or no part, the introduction of the Factory Acts has strikingly shown that the mere shortening of the working-day increases to a wonderful degree the regularity, uniformity, order, continuity, and energy of the labour.[2] It seemed, however, doubtful whether this effect was produced in the factory proper, where the dependence of the workman on the continuous and uniform motion of the machinery had already created the strictest discipline. Hence, when in 1844 the reduction of the working-day to less than twelve hours was being debated, the masters almost unanimously declared "that their over-lookers in the different rooms took good care that the hands lost no time," that "the extent of vigilance and attention on the part of the workmen was hardly capable of being increased", and therefore, that the speed of the machinery and other conditions remaining unaltered, "to expect in a well managed factory any important result from increased attention of the workmen was an absurdity." [3] This assertion was contradicted by experiments. Mr. Robert Gardner reduced the hours of labour in his two large factories at Preston, on and after the 20th April, 1844, from twelve to eleven hours a day. The result of about a year's working was that "the same amount of product for the same cost was received, and the workpeople as a whole earned in eleven hours as much wages as they did before in twelve." [4] In the weaving department where, moreover, many sorts of figured fancy articles were woven, there was not the slightest alteration in the conditions of the work. The result was: "From 6th January to 20th April, 1844, with a twelve hours day, average weekly wages

[1] Especially by piece-work.

[2] See Rep. of Insp. of Fact. for 31st October, 1865.

[3] Rep. of Insp. of Fact. for 1844 and the quarter ending 30th April 1845. pp. 20-21.

[4] l. c., p. 19. Since the wages for piece-work were unaltered, the weekly wages depended on the quantity produced.

of each hand 10s. 1½d. [$2.53]; from 20th April to 29th June, 1844, with a day of eleven hours, average weekly wages 10s. 3½d.[$2.57]." Here we have more produced in eleven hours than previously in twelve, and entirely in consequence of more steady application and economy of time by the work-people. While they got the same wages and gained one hour of spare time, the capitalist got the same amount produced and saved the cost of coal, gas, and other such items, for one hour. Similar experiments, and with the like success, were carried out in the mills of Messrs. Horrocks and Jackson. (Report for 1844, p. 21.)

The moral element played an important part in the above experiments. The workpeople told the factory inspector: "We work with more spirit, we have the reward ever before us of getting away sooner at night, and one active and cheerful spirit pervades the whole mill, from the youngest piecer to the oldest hand, and we can greatly help each other."

So soon as that shortening becomes compulsory, machinery becomes in the hands of capital the objective means, sytematically employed, for squeezing out more labour in a given time. This is effected in two ways: by increasing the speed of the machinery, and by giving the workman more machinery to tend.

The improvements in the steam-engine have increased the piston speed, and at the same time have made it possible, by means of a greater economy of power, to drive with the same or even a smaller consumption of coal more machinery with the same engine. The improvements in the transmitting mechanism have lessened friction and, what so strikingly distinguishes modern from the older machinery, have reduced the diameter and weight of the shafting to a constantly decreasing minimum. Finally, the improvements in the operative machines have, while reducing their size, increased their speed and efficiency, as in the modern powerloom; or, while increasing the size of their frame-work, have also increased the extent and number of their working parts, as in spinning mules, or have added to the speed of these working parts by imperceptible alterations of detail, such as those which ten years ago increased the speed of the spindles in self-acting mules by one-fifth (*i. e.* about 1855).

The reduction of the working day to 12 hours dates in England from 1832. In 1836 a manufacturer stated: "The labour now undergone in the factories is much greater than it used to be ...—compared with thirty or forty years ago ...owing to the greater attention and activity required by the greatly increased speed which is given to the machinery." In 1844 Lord Ashley made in the House of Commons the following statements, supported by documentary evidence:

"The labour performed by those engaged in the processes of manufacture, is three times as great as in the beginning of such operations. Machinery has executed, no doubt, the work that would demand the sinews of millions of men; but it has also prodigiously multiplied the labour of those who are governed by its fearful movements. ... In 1825, the labour of following a pair of mules spinning cotton yarn of No. 40—reckoning 12 hours to the working-day—involved a necessity of walking 8 miles. In 1832, the distance travelled in following a pair of mules, spinning cotton yarn of the same number, was 20 miles, and frequently more. In 1825, the spinner put up daily, on each of these mules, 820 stretches, making a total of 1640 stretches in the course of the day. In 1832, the spinner put upon each mule 2200 stretches, making a total of 4400. In 1844, 2400 stretches, making a total of 4800; and in some cases the amount of labour required is even still greater. ... I have another document sent to me in 1842, stating that the labour is progressively increasing—increasing not only because the distance to be travelled is greater, but because the quantity of goods produced is multiplied, while the hands are fewer in proportion than before; and, moreover, because an inferior species of cotton is now often spun, which it is more difficult to work ... In the carding-room there has also been a great increase of labour. One person there does the work formerly divided between two. ... In the weaving-room, where a vast number of persons are employed, and principally females .. the labour has increased within the last ten years fully 10 per cent, owing to the increased speed of the machinery. In 1838, the number of hanks spun per week was 18,000, in 1843 it amounted to 21,000. In 1819 the number of picks in power-loom-weaving per minute was 60—in 1842 it was 140, showing a vast increase of labour."

In the face of this remarkable intensity of labour which had already been reached in 1844 under the Twelve Hours' Act, there appeared to be a justification for the assertion made at that time by the English manufacturers, that any further progress in that direction was impossible, and therefore that every further reduction of the hours meant a lessened production. But let us come to the period that follows the introduction of the Ten Hours' Act in 1847 into the English cotton, woollen, silk, and flax mills.

"The speed of the spindles has increased upon throstles 500, and upon mules 1000 revolutions a minute, *i. e.*, the speed of the throstle spindle, which in 1839 was 4500 times a minute, is now (1862) 5000; and of the mule spindle, that was 5000, is now 6000 times a minute.[1] James Nasmyth, the eminent civil engineer of Patricroft, near Manchester, explained in a letter to Leonard Horner, written in 1852, the nature of the improvements in the steam-engine that had been made between the years 1848 and 1852. He goes on to say: "I am confident that from the same weight of steam-engine machinery, we are now obtaining at least 50 per cent. more duty or work performed on the average, and that in many cases the identical steam-engines which in the days of the restricted speed of 220 feet per minute, yielded 50 horse-power, are now yielding upwards of 100." . . . "The modern steam-engine of 100 horse-power is capable of being driven at a much greater force than formerly, arising from improvements in its construction, the capacity and construction of the boilers, &c." . . . "Although the same number of hands are employed in proportion to the horse-power as at former periods, there are fewer hands employed in proportion to the machinery." [2] "The facts brought out by the return (of 1856)

---

[1] "Rep. of Fact. for 31st October, 1862", p. 62.

[2] "Rep. of Insp. of Fact. for 31st October, 1856", pp. 13-14, 20, and 1852, p. 23.

appear to be that the factory system is increasing rapidly; that although the same number of hands are employed in proportion to the horse-power as at former periods, there are fewer hands employed in proportion to the machinery; that the steam-engine is enabled to drive an increased weight of machinery by economy of force and other methods, and that an increased quantity of work can be turned off by improvements in machinery, and in methods of manufacture, by increase of speed of the machinery, and by a variety of other causes." [1]

"The great improvements made in machines of every kind have raised their productive power very much. Without any doubt, the shortening of the hours of labour ... gave the impulse to these improvements. The latter, combined with the more intense strain on the workman, have had the effect, that at least as much is produced in the shortened (by two hours or one-sixth) working-day as was previously produced during the longer one." [2]

But however great the progress of English industry had been during the 8 years from 1848 to 1856 under the influence of a working-day of 10 hours, it was far surpassed during the next period of 6 years from 1856 to 1862.

In silk factories there were, for instance

	Spindles	Looms	Operatives
1856	1,093,799	9,260	56,131
1862	1,388,544	10,709	52,428

These figures show

an increase in the spindles of 26.9%
an increase in the looms of 15.6%
a decrease in the operatives of 7%.

In worsted mills were employed
1850 ..... 875,830 spindles
1856 ..... 1,324,549 spindles (increase 51.2%)
1862 ..... 1,289,172 spindles (decrease 2.7%)

[1] l. c., pp. 14-15.
[2] Reports, &c., for 31st October, 1858, pp. 9-10.

But if we deduct the doubling spindles that figure in the numbers for 1856, but not in those for 1862, it will be found that after 1856 the number of spindles remained nearly stationary. On the other hand, after 1850, the speed of the spindles and looms was in many cases doubled.

In worsted mills were employed:

	Power-looms	Operatives	Including Children under 14
1850	32,617	79,737	9,956
1856	38,956	87,794	11,228
1862	43,048	86,063	13,178

In spite, therefore, of the greatly increased number of looms in 1862, compared with 1856, the total number of the workpeople employed decreased, and that of the children exploited increased.[1]

On the 27th April, 1863, Mr. Ferrand said in the House of Commons: "I have been informed by delegates from 16 districts of Lancashire and Cheshire, in whose behalf I speak, that the work in the factories is, in consequence of the improvements in machinery, constantly on the increase. Instead of as formerly one person with two helps tending two looms, one person now tends three looms without helps, and it is no uncommon thing for one person to tend four. Twelve hours' work, as is evident from the facts adduced, is now compressed into less than 10 hours. It is therefore self-evident, to what an enormous extent the toil of the factory operative has increased during the last 10 years."

On 2 modern power-looms a weaver now (1867), makes in a week of 60 hours 26 pieces of certain quality, length, and breadth; while on the old power-looms he could make no more than 4 such pieces. The cost of weaving a piece of such cloth had already soon after 1850 fallen from 68 cents to 11 cents.

"Thirty years ago (1841) one spinner with three piecers

[1] "Report of Insp. of Fact. for 31st Oct., 1862", pp. 100 and 130.

was not required to attend to more than one pair of mules with 300-324 spindles. At the present time (1871) he has to mind with the help of 5 piecers 2200 spindles, and produces not less than seven times as much yarn as in 1841." (Alex. Redgrave, Factory Inspector, in the Journal of Arts, 5th January, 1872.)

Although, therefore, the Factory Inspectors unceasingly and with justice commend the results of the Acts of 1844 and 1850, yet they admit that the shortening of the hours of labour has already called forth such an intensification of the labour as is injurious to the health of the workman and to his capacity for work. "In most of the cotton, worsted, and silk mills, an exhausting state of excitement necessary to enable the workers satisfactorily to mind the machinery, the motion of which has been greatly accelerated within the last few years, seems to me not unlikely to be one of the causes of that excess of mortality from lung disease, which Dr. Green-how has pointed out in his recent report on this subject."[1] There cannot be the slightest doubt that the tendency that urges capital so soon as a prolongation of the hours of labour is once for all forbidden, to compensate itself by a systematic heightening of the intensity of labour, and to convert every improvement in machinery into a more perfect means of exhausting the workman, must soon lead to a state of things in which a reduction of the hours of labour will again be inevitable.

(D) Blunting of the Labourer's Intelligence. Increase of Accidents

When considering manufacture carried-on without machinery, we saw that it is entirely based on the personal capacity of the labourer, on the skill with which he manipulates his tool, and that consequently a hierarchy arises—the result of the inequalities prevailing among the labourers. We further saw that the difference between such primitive manufacture and modern industry, lies precisely in the fact that the

[1] Rep. of Insp. of Fact. for 31st Oct., 1861. pp. 25, 26.

tool which shapes the raw material is withdrawn from the workman and passes over to the machine; so that the latter, and not the workman, henceforth shapes the raw material, whereas the workman has only to superintend the activity of the machine. The capabilities of the tool are emancipated from the restraints that are inseparable from human labour power. In manufacture, the tool can only operate as long as the workman who manipulates it, and with intensity, skill, and strength corresponding to those displayed in his labour. In modern industry, one workman can easily replace another in the task of superintending the machine; and the latter can continue to operate even when the workman is sleeping or eating. Thereby the technical foundation on which is based the division of labour in manufacture, is swept away. Hence, in the place of the hierarchy of specialised workmen that characterises manufacture, there steps, in the automatic factory, a tendency to equalise and reduce to one and the same level every kind of work that has to be done by the minders of the machines; in the place of the artificially produced differentiations of the detail workmen, step the natural differences of age and sex.

Although then, technically speaking, the old system of division of labour is thrown overboard by machinery, it hangs on in the factory, as a traditional habit handed down from manufacture, and is afterwards systematically re-moulded and established in a more hideous form by capital, as a means of exploiting labour power. The life-long speciality of handling one and the same tool, now becomes the life-long speciality of serving one and the same machine. Machinery is put to a wrong use, with the object of transforming the workman, from his very childhood, into a part of a detail-machine. In this way, not only are the expenses of his reproduction considerably lessened, but at the same time his helpless dependence upon the factory as a whole, and therefore upon the capitalist, is rendered complete. Here as everywhere else, we must distinguish between the increased productivness due to the development of the social process of production, and that due to the capitalist exploitation of that process.

In handicrafts and manufacture, the workman makes use of a tool, in the factory, the machine makes use of him. There the movements of the instrument of labour proceed from him, here it is the movement of the machine that he must follow. In manufacture the workmen are parts of a living mechanism. In the factory we have a lifeless mechanism independent of the workman, who becomes its mere living appendage. "The miserable routine of endless drudgery and toil in which the same mechanical process is gone through over and over again, is like the labour of Sisyphus. The burden of labour, like the rock, keeps ever falling back on the worn-out labourer."[1] At the same time that factory work exhausts the nervous system to the uttermost, it does away with the many-sided play of the muscles, and confiscates every atom of freedom, both in bodily and intellectual activity. The lightening of the labour, even, becomes a sort of torture, since the machine does not free the labourer from work, but deprives the work of all interest. The separation of the intellectual powers of production from the manual labour, and the conversion of those powers into the might of capital over labour, is finally completed by modern industry erected on the foundation of machinery. The special skill of each individual insignificant factory operative vanishes as an infinitesimal quantity before the science, the gigantic physical forces, and the mass of labour that are embodied in the factory mechanism and, together with that mechanism, constitute the power of the "master". This "master", therefore, in whose brain the machinery and his monopoly of it are inseparably united, whenever he falls out with his "hands", contemptuously tells them: "The factory operatives should keep in wholesome remembrance the fact that theirs is really a low species of skilled labour; and that there is none which is more easily acquired, or of its quality more amply remunerated, or which by a short training of the least expert can be more quickly, as well as abundantly, acquired. . . . The master's machinery really plays a far more important part in the business of production than the labour

[1] F. Engels, *Lage der arbeitenden Klassen in England,* 2nd ed., p. 180

and the skill of the operative, which six months' education can teach, and a common labourer can learn."[1]

The technical subordination of the workman to the uniform motion of the instruments of labour, and the peculiar composition of the body of workpeople, consisting as it does of individuals of both sexes and of all ages, give rise to a barrack discipline, which is elaborated into a complete system in the factory, and which fully develops the before-mentioned labour of overlooking, thereby dividing the workpeople into operatives and overlookers, into private soldiers and sergeants of an industrial army. "The main difficulty (in the automatic factory) ... lay ... above all in training human beings to renounce their desultory habits of work, and to identify themselves with the unvarying regularity of the complex automaton." But the difficulty was overcome, and discipline was established. The place of the slave driver's lash is taken by the overlooker's book penalties. All punishments naturally resolve themselves into fines and deductions from wages, and the law-giving talent of the factory Lycurgus so arranges matters, that a violation of his laws is, if possible, more profitable to him than the keeping of them. "The slavery in which the bourgeoisie has bound the proletariat, comes nowhere more plainly into daylight than in the factory system. In it all freedom comes to an end both at law and in fact. The workman must be in the factory at half past five. If he come a few minutes late, he is punished; if he come 10 minutes late, he is not allowed to enter until after breakfast, and thus loses a quarter of a day's wage. He must eat, drink and sleep at the word of command.... The despotic bell calls him from his bed, calls him from breakfast and dinner. And how does he fare in the mill? There the master is the absolute law-giver. He makes what regulations he pleases; he alters and makes additions to his code at pleasure; and if he insert the veriest nonsense, the courts say to the workman: Since you have entered into this contract voluntarily, you must now carry it

[1] "The Master Spinners' and Manufacturers' Defence Fund. Report of the Committee." Manchester, 1854, p. 17. We shall see hereafter, that the "master" can sing quite another song, when he is threatened with the loss of his "living" automaton.

out. . . . These workmen are condemned to live, from their ninth year till their death, under this mental and bodily tor-ture." (F. Engels, l. c. p. 217, sq.)

We shall here merely allude to the material conditions under which factory labour is carried on. Every organ of sense is injured in an equal degree by artificial elevation of the temperature, by the dust-laden atmosphere, by the deafening noise, not to mention danger to life and limb among the thickly crowded machinery, which, with the regularity of the seasons, issues its list of the killed and wounded in the industrial battle. Economy of the social means of production, matured and forced as in a hothouse by the factory system, is turned, in the hands of capital, into systematic robbery of what is necessary for the life of the workman while he is at work, robbery of space, light, air, and of protection to his person against the dangerous and unwholesome accompaniments of the productive process, not to mention the robbery of appliances for the comfort of the workman.

The protection afforded by the Factory Acts against dangerous machinery has had a beneficial effect. "But . . . there are other sources of accident which did not exist twenty years since; one especially, viz., the increased speed of the machinery. Wheels, rollers, spindles and shuttles are now propelled at increased and increasing rates; fingers must be quicker and defter in their movements to take up the broken thread, for, if placed with hesitation or carelessness, they are sacrificed. . . . A large number of accidents are caused by the eagerness of the workpeople to get through their work expeditiously. It must be remembered that it is of the highest importance to manufacturers that their machinery should be in motion uninterruptedly, i. e., producing yarns and goods. Every minute's stoppage is not only a loss of power, but of production, and the workpeople are urged by the overlookers, who are interested in the quantity of work turned off, to keep the machinery in motion; and it is not less important to those of the operatives who are paid by the weight or piece, that the machines should be kept in motion. Consequently, although it is strictly forbidden in many, nay in most factories, that machinery should be cleaned while in motion, it is nevertheless the constant practice in most if not in all. . . . Thus from this cause only, 906 accidents have occurred during the last six months. . . . Although a great deal of cleaning is constantly going on day by day, yet Saturday is generally the day set apart for the thorough cleaning of the machinery, and a great deal of this is done while the machinery is in motion. . . . Since cleaning is not paid for, the workpeople seek to get done with it as speedily as possible. Hence the number of accidents which occur on Fridays, and especially on Saturdays, is much larger than on any other day. On the former day the excess is nearly 12 per cent. over the average number of the four first days of the week, and on the latter day the excess is 25 per cent. over the average of the preceding five days; or, the number of working-hours on Saturday being taken into account—7½ hours on Saturday as compared with 10½ on other days—there is an excess of 65 per cent. on Saturdays over the average of the other five days." (Rep. of Insp. of Fact., 31st. Oct., 1866, pp. 9, 15, 16, 17.)

I will further quote the following from the official report of Leonard Horner of October 31st, 1855: "I have heard some millowners speak with inexcusable levity of some of the accidents; such, for instance, as the loss of a finger being a trifling matter. A working-man's living and prospects depend so much upon his fingers, that any loss of them is a very serious matter to him. When I have heard such inconsiderate remarks made, I have usually put this question: suppose you were in want of an additional workman, and two were to apply, both equally well qualified in other respects, but one had lost a thumb or a forefinger, which would you engage? There never was a hesitation as to the answer." . . .

It must nevertheless be observed that in those factories that have been longest subject to the Factory Acts, with their compulsory limitation of the hours of labour, and other regulations, many of the older abuses have vanished. The very improvement of the machinery demands to a certain extent improved construction of the buildings and this is an advantage to the workpeople (See "Rep. of Insp. of Fact. for 31st. Oct., 1863," p. 109).

(E) *Starvation of the Wage-Earners*

The contest between the capitalist and the wage-labourer dates back to the very origin of capital. It raged on throughout the whole manufacturing period. But the writers of the manufacturing period treat the division of labour chiefly as a means of virtually supplying a deficiency of labourers, and not as a means of actually displacing those in work. If it be said that 100 millions of people would be required in England to spin with the old spinning-wheel the cotton that is now spun with mules by 500,000 people, this does not mean that the mules took the place of those millions who never existed. If, on the other hand, we say that in England the power-loom threw 800,000 weavers in the streets, we refer to a number of weavers in existence who were actually replaced or displaced by the looms. During the manufacturing period, handicraft labour, altered though it was by division of labour, was yet the basis. The demands of the new colonial markets could not be satisfied owing to the relatively small number of town operatives handed down from the middle ages, and the manufactures proper opened out new fields of production to the rural population, driven from the land by the dissolution of the feudal system. At that time, therefore, division of labour and co-operation in the workshops were viewed from the positive aspect, that they made the workpeople more productive. The instrument of labour, when it takes the form of a machine, immediately becomes a competitor of the workman himself. The self-expansion of capital by means of machinery is thenceforward directly proportional to the number of the workpeople, whose means of livelihood have been destroyed by that machinery. So soon as the handling of the tool becomes the work of a machine, then, with the use-value, the exchange-value too, of labour power vanishes; the workman becomes unsaleable, like paper-money thrown out of currency. That portion of the working class, thus by machinery rendered superfluous, *i. e.*, no longer immediately necessary for the self-expansion of capital, either goes to the wall in the unequal contest of the old handicrafts and manufactures with machinery, or else floods all the more easily accessible branches of industry, swamps the labour market, and sinks the price of labour power below its value. It is impressed upon the work-people, as a great consolation, first, that their sufferings are only temporary, secondly, that machinery acquires the mastery over the whole of a given field of production only by degrees, so that the extent and intensity of its destructive effect is diminished. The first consolation neutralises the second. When machinery seizes on an industry by degrees, it produces chronic misery among the operatives who compete with it. When the transition is rapid, the effect is acute and felt by great masses. History discloses no tragedy more horrible than the gradual extinction of the English handloom weavers, an extinction that was spread over several decades, and finally sealed in 1838. Many of them died of starvation, many with families vegetated for a long time on 5 cents a day. On the other hand, the English cotton machinery produced an acute effect in India. The Governor General reported 1834-35: "The misery hardly finds a parallel in the history of commerce. The bones of the cotton-weavers are bleaching the plains of India."

But even in modern industry the continual improvement of machinery has an analogous effect. "The object of improved machinery is to diminish manual labour." [1] "The adaptation of power to machinery heretofore moved by hand, is almost of daily occurrence . . . the minor improvements in machinery having for their object economy of power, the production of better work, the turning off of more work in the same time, or in supplying the place of a child, a female, or a man, are constant, and although sometimes apparently of no great moment, have somewhat important results." [2] "Whenever a process requires peculiar dexterity and steadiness of hand, it is withdrawn, as soon as possible, from the cunning workman, who is prone to irregularities of many kinds, and it is placed in charge of a peculiar mechanism, so self-regulating that a child can superintend it." Who, in 1860, the Zenith year of the English cotton-industry, would have dreamt of the galloping improvements in machinery, and the

[1] "Rep. Insp. Fact. for 31st October, 1858", p. 43.
[2] "Rep. Insp. Fact. for 31st October, 1856", p. 15.

corresponding displacement of working people, called into being during the following 3 years, under the stimulus of the American Civil War? A couple of examples from the Reports of the Inspectors of Factories will suffice on this point. A Manchester manufacturer states: "We formerly had 75 carding engines, now we have 12, doing the same quantity of work of equal if not better quality. . . . We are saving in wages £10 [$50.00] a week. Our estimated saving in waste is about 10% in the quantity of cotton consumed." "In another fine spinning mill in Manchester, I was informed that through increased speed and the adoption of some self-acting processes, a reduction had been made, in the number of workmen, of a fourth in one department, and of above half in another, and that the introduction of the combing machine in place of the second carding, had considerably reduced the number of hands formerly employed in the carding-room." Another spinning mill is estimated to effect a saving of labour of 10%. The Messrs. Gilmore, spinners at Manchester, state: "In our blowing-room department we consider our expense with new machinery is fully one-third less in wages and hands . . . in two other departments about one-third less in expense, and likewise one-third less in hands; in the spinning-room about one-third less in expense. But this is not all; when our yarn goes to the manufacturers, it is so much better by the application of our new machinery, that they will produce a greater quantity of cloth, and cheaper than from the yarn produced by old machinery." [1]

The following table shows the total result of the mechanical improvements in the English cotton industry due to the American civil war.

Number of

	Factories	Power-Looms	Spindles	Persons Employed
1858	2,210	298,847	28,010,217	379,213
1861	2,887	399,992	30,387,494	451,569
1868	2,549	379,329	32,000,014	301,064

[1] "Rep. Insp. Fact., 31st Oct., 1863", pp. 108, 109.

Hence, between 1861 and 1868, 338 cotton factories disappeared, in other words more productive machinery on a larger scale was concentrated in the hands of a smaller number of capitalists. The number of power-looms decreased by 20,663; but since their product increased in the same period, an improved loom must have yielded more than an old one. Lastly the number of spindles increased by 1,612,541, while the number of operatives decreased by 50,505. The "temporary" misery, inflicted on the work-people by the cotton-crisis, was heightened and from being temporary made permanent, by the rapid and persistent progress of machinery.

But machinery not only acts as a competitor who gets the better of the workman, and is constantly on the point of making him superfluous. It is the most powerful weapon for repressing strikes, those periodical revolts of the working class against the autocracy of capital. According to Gaskell, the steam engine was from the very first an antagonist of human power, an antagonist that enabled the capitalist to tread under foot the growing claims of the workmen, who threatened the newly-born factory system with a crisis.[1] It would be possible to write quite a history of the inventions, made since 1830, for the sole purpose of supplying capital with weapons against the revolts of the working class.

Nasmyth, the inventor of the steam hammer, gives the following evidence before the Trades Union Commission, with regard to the improvements made by him in machinery and introduced in consequence of the wide-spread and long strike of the engineers in 1851: "The characteristic feature of our modern mechanical improvements is the introduction of self-acting tool machinery. What every mechanical workman has now to do, and what every boy can do, is not to work himself but to superintend the beautiful labour of the machine. The whole class of workmen that depend exclusively on their skill, is now done away with. Formerly, I employed four boys to every mechanic. Thanks to these new mechanical combinations, I have reduced the number of grown-up men from 1500 to 750. The result was a considerable increase in my profits."

[1] Gaskell, *The Manufacturing Population of England*. London, 1833, pp. 3, 4.

A whole series of bourgeois political economists insist that all machinery that displaces workmen, simultaneously and necessarily sets free an amount of capital adequate to employ the same identical workmen.

Suppose a capitalist to employ 100 workmen, at $150 a year each, in a carpet factory. The variable capital annually laid out (in wages) amounts, therefore, to $15,000. Suppose, also, that he discharges 50 of his workmen, and employs the remaining 50 with machinery that costs him $7,500. To simplify matters, we take no account of buildings, coal, &c. Further suppose that the raw material annually consumed costs $15,000, both before and after the change. Is any capital set free by this metamorphosis? Before the change, the total sum of $30,000 consisted half of constant, and half of variable capital. After the change it consists of $22,500 constant ($15,000 raw material and $6,500 machinery), and $7,500 variable capital. The variable capital (converted into living labour power) instead of being one half, is only one quarter of the total capital. Instead of being set free, a part of the capital is here locked up in such a way as to cease to be exchanged against labour power: variable has been changed into constant capital. Other things remaining unchanged, the capital of $30,000 can, in future, employ no more than 50 men. With each improvement in the machinery, it will employ fewer.

But suppose the newly introduced machinery had cost less than did the labour power and implements displaced by it. What happens then? Let us assume that, instead of costing $7,500, it had cost only $5,000. Of the $15,000, which were paid originally as wages, $7,500 serve this purpose further, $5,000 are employed in purchasing machinery, and $2,500 are effectively set free. At the best, the latter sum (supposing wages unchanged) would only suffice to employ 16 men instead of 50. In reality, even less than 16, for a part of the $2,500, if this sum is to be applied to employing labour, must be laid-out in implements and raw material.

But suppose, besides, that the making of the new machinery affords employment to a greater number of mechanics, can that be called compensation to the carpet makers, thrown on the streets? At the best, its construction employs fewer men than its employment displaces. The sum of $7,500 that formerly represented the wages of the discharged carpet-makers, now represents in the shape of machinery: (1) the value of the means of production used in the construction of that machinery, (2) the wages of the mechanics employed in its construction, and (3) the surplus-value falling to the share of their "masters". Thus only a part of the $7,500 is henceforth laid-out in wages. Further, the machinery need not be renewed till it is worn out. Hence, in order to keep the increased number of mechanics in constant employment, one carpet manufacturer after another must displace workmen by machines.

As a matter of fact, the apologists do not mean this sort of setting free of capital. They have in their minds the means of subsistence of the liberated workpeople. It cannot be denied, in the above instance, that the machinery not only liberates 50 men, thus placing them at others' disposal, but, at the same time, it withdraws from their consumption and sets free means of subsistence to the value of $7,500. The simple fact, by no means a new one, that machinery cuts off the workmen from heir means of subsistence is, therefore, in economical parlance tantamount to this, that machinery liberates means of subsistence for the workman, or converts those means into capital for his employment. The mode of expression, you see, is everything.

This theory implies that the $7,500 worth of means of subsistence was capital that was being expended by the labour of the 50 men discharged. That, consequently, this capital falls out of employment so soon as they commence their forced holidays, and never rests till it has found a fresh investment, where it can again be productively consumed by these same 50 men. That sooner or later therefore, the capital and the workmen must come together again, and that, then, the compensation is complete. That the sufferings of the workmen displaced by machinery are therefore as transient as are the riches of this world.

In relation to the discharged workmen, the $7,500 worth of means of subsistence never was capital. What really confronted them as capital, was the sum of $7,500, afterwards laid out in machinery. On looking closer it will be seen that this sum represented part of the carpets produced in a year by the 50 discharged men, which part they received as wages from their employer in money instead of in kind. With the carpets in the form of money, they bought means of subsistence to the value of $7,500. These means, therefore, were to them not capital, but commodities, and they, as regards these commodities, were not wage-labourers, but buyers. The circumstance that they were "freed", by the machinery, from the means of purchase, changed them from buyers into non-buyers. Hence a lessened demand for those commodities. If this diminution be not compensated by an increase from some other quarter, the market price of the commodities falls. If this state of things lasts for some time, and extends, there follows a restriction in the production of these commodities. Some of the capital that was previously devoted to production of necessary means of subsistence, has to become reproduced in another form, and thus the labourers employed in the production of necessary means of subsistence are in their turn "freed" from a part of their wages. The result is that machinery throws workmen on the streets, not only in that branch of production in which it is introduced, but also in those branches in which it is not introduced.

The real facts are as follows: The labourers, when driven out of the workshop by the machinery, are thrown upon the labour market, and there add to the number of workmen at the disposal of the capitalists. In another chapter of this book it will be seen that this effect of machinery, which, as we have seen, is represented to be a compensation to the working class, is on the contrary a most frightful scourge. For the present I will only say this: The labourers that are thrown out of work in any branch of industry, can no doubt seek for employment in some other branch. If they find it, and thus renew the bond between them and the means of subsistence, this takes place only by the intermediary of a new and additional capital that is seeking investment; not at all by the intermediary of the capital that formerly employed them and was afterwards converted into machinery. And even should they find employment, what a poor look-out is theirs! Crippled as they are by division of labour, these poor devils are worth so little outside their old trade, that they cannot find admission into any industries, except a few of inferior kind, that are over-supplied with underpaid workmen. Further, every branch of industry attracts each year a new stream of men, who furnish a contingent from which to fill up vacancies, and to draw a supply for expansion. So soon as machinery sets free a part of the workmen employed in a given branch of industry, the reserve men are also diverted into new channels of employment, and become absorbed in other branches; meanwhile the original victims, during the period of transition, for the most part starve and perish.

It is an undoubted fact that machinery, as such, is not responsible for "setting free" the workman from the means of subsistence. It cheapens and increases production in that branch which it seizes on, and at first makes no change in the mass of the means of subsistence produced in other branches. Hence, after its introduction, the society possesses as much, if not more, of the necessaries of life than before, for the labourers thrown out of work; and that quite apart from the enormous share of the annual produce wasted by the non-workers. And this is the point relied on by our apologists! The contradictions and antagonisms inseparable from the capitalist employment of machinery, do not exist, they say, since they do not arise out of machinery, as such, but out of its capitalist employment! Since therefore machinery, considered alone, shortens the hours of labour, but, when in the service of capital, lengthens them; since in itself it lightens labour, but when employed by capital, heightens the intensity of labour; since in itself it is a victory of man over the forces of nature, but in the hands of capital, makes man the slave of those forces; since in itself it increases the wealth of the producers, but in the hands of capital, makes them paupers—for all these reasons and others besides, says the bourgeois economist without more ado, when we regard machinery itself, it is as clear as noonday that all these contradictions are a mere semblance of the reality, and that, as a matter of fact, they have neither an actual nor a theoretical existence. Thus he saves himself from all further puzzling of

the brain, and what is more, implicitly declares his opponent
to be stupid enough to contend against, not the capitalistic
employment of machinery, but machinery itself.

No doubt he is far from denying that temporary inconvenience may result from the capitalist use of machinery.
But where is the medal without its reverse! Any employment
of machinery, except by capital, is to him an impossibility.
Exploitation of the workman by the machine is therefore, with
him, identical with exploitation of the machine by the workman. Whoever, therefore, exposes the real state of things in
the capitalistic employment of machinery, is against its employment in any way, and is an enemy of social progress.
Exactly the reasoning of the celebrated Bill Sykes: "Gentlemen of the jury, no doubt the throat of this commercial
traveller has been cut. But that is not my fault, it is the
fault of the knife. Must we, for such a temporary inconvenience, abolish the use of the knife? Only consider! Where
would agriculture and trade be without the knife? Is it not
salutary in surgery, as it is knowing in anatomy? And in
addition a willing help at the festive board? If you abolish
the knife—you hurl us back into the depths of barbarism."

Although machinery necessarily throws men out of work
in those industries into which it is introduced, yet it may,
notwithstanding this, bring about an increase of employment
in other industries. True, if the total quantity of the article
produced by machinery be equal to the total quantity of the
article previously produced by a handicraft or by manufacture, and now made by machinery, then the total labour
expended is diminished. The new labour spent on the instruments of labour, on the machinery, on the coal, and so on,
must necessarily be less than the labour displaced by the
use of the machinery; otherwise the product of the machine
would be as dear, or dearer, than the product of the manual
labour. But, as a matter of fact, the total quantity of the
article produced by machinery by far exceeds the total quantity of the hand-made article that has been displaced. The
result must be that, at first, an increase of employment takes
place in other branches of labour. Let us suppose that a given
number of workmen has produced by handicraft 100,000

yards of cloth. Now the machine appears on the scene, throws a number of workmen out of employment, but enables the remainder to produce 400,000 yards. In the quadrupled product there lies four times as much raw material. Hence the production of raw material must be quadrupled. And also the production of buildings, coal, machinery, &c., may demand, when 400,000 yards are produced, more labour than is saved in the case of 100,000.

Hence, as the use of machinery extends in a given industry, the immediate effect is to increase production in the other industries that furnish the first with means of production. How far employment is thereby found for an increased number of men, depends on the extent to which machinery has already seized on, or is then seizing on, those trades. The number of the men condemned to work in coal and metal mines increased enormously owing to the progress of the English factory system; but during the last few decades this increase of number has been less rapid, owing to the use of new machinery in mining. A new type of workman springs into life along with machine, namely its maker. As to raw material, there is not the least doubt that the rapid strides of cotton spinning not only pushed on with tropical luxuriance the growth of cotton in the United States, and with it the African slave trade, but also made the breeding of slaves the chief business of the border slave-states. When, in 1790, the first census of slaves was taken in the United States, their number was 697,000; in 1861 it had nearly reached four millions. On the other hand, it is no less certain that the rise of the English woollen factories, together with the gradual conversion of arable land into sheep pasture, brought about the superfluity of agricultural labourers that led to their being driven in masses into the towns. Ireland, having during the last twenty years reduced its population by nearly one half, is at this moment (1867) undergoing the process of still further reducing the number of its inhabitants, so as exactly to suit the requirements of its landlords and of the English woollen manufacturers.

When machinery is applied to any of the preliminary or intermediate stages through which the subject of labour has to pass on its way to completion, and when the half-finished or intermediary product is produced in great quantities, whereas the finished product (of which the former is the preparatory stage) is still supplied by handicraft, an increased demand for labour arises in consequence of the greater quantity of material available. Spinning by machinery, for example, supplied yarn so cheaply and so abundantly that the hand-loom weavers were, at first, able to work full time without increased outlay. Their earnings accordingly rose. Hence a flow of people into the cotton-weaving trade, till at length the 800,000 weavers, called into existence by the Jenny, the throstle and the mule, were overwhelmed by the power-loom. So also, owing to the abundance of clothing materials produced by machinery, the number of tailors, seamstresses and needle-women went on increasing until the appearance of the sewing machine.

Machinery causes, at first, a further increase of employment in the industries that produce luxuries. For it augments surplus-value and the mass of products in which surplus-value is embodied. Thus the wealth of the capitalist class increases. And as the number of workmen necessary for the production of the necessaries of life diminishes relatively, with the rise of new and luxurious wants arise the means of satisfying those wants. In other words, the production of luxuries increases. The refined and varied forms of the products are also due to new relations with the markets of the world, relations that are created by modern industry. Not only are greater quantities of foreign articles of luxury exchanged for home products, but a greater mass of foreign raw materials, ingredients, and intermediate products, are used as means of production in the home industries. Owing to these relations with the markets of the world, the demand for labour increases in the carrying trades, which split up into numerous varieties.[1]

The increase of the means of production and subsistence, accompanied by a relative diminution in the number of labourers, causes an increased demand for labour in making

[1] In 1861, in England and Wales, there were 94,665 sailors in the merchant service.

canals, docks, tunnels, bridges, and so on, works that can
only bear fruit in the far future.

Lastly, the extraordinary productiveness of modern industry, accompanied as it is by both a more extensive and a
more intense exploitation of labour power in all other spheres
of production, allows of the unproductive employment of a
larger and larger part of the working class, and the consequent reproduction, on a constantly extending scale, of the
ancient domestic slaves under the name of a servant class,
including men-servants, women-servants, lackeys, &c. According to the census of 1861, the population of England and
Wales included:

	Persons:
Agricultural labourers	1,100,000
All who are employed in textile factories . . .	643,000
All who are employed in coal mines and metal mines	565,000
All who are employed in metal works (blast-furnaces, rolling mills, &c.), and metal manufactures of every kind	400,000
The servant class	1,210,000

None are included in the 1,210,000 who do not serve in
private houses.

Nevertheless, in spite of the mass of hands actually displaced and virtually replaced by machinery, we can understand how the factory operatives, through the building of
more mills and the extension of old ones in a given industry,
may become more numerous than the manufacturing workmen and handicraftsmen that have been displaced. Suppose,
for example, that in the old mode of production a capital of
$2,500 is employed weekly, $1,000 being laid out in means
of production, and $1,500, say $5 per man, in labour-power.
On the introduction of machinery only $500 is now laid out
in labour power. Consequently, two-thirds of the workmen
are discharged. If now the business extends, and the total
capital employed grows to $7,500 under unchanged condi-
tions, the number of operatives employed will increase to
300, just as many as before the introduction of the machinery.

If the capital further grows to $10,000, 400 men will be employed, or one-third more than under the old system. Their numbers have, in point of fact, increased by 100, but relatively, *i. e.*, in proportion to the total capital advanced, they have diminished by 800, for the $10,000 capital would, in the old state of things, have employed 1,200 instead of 400 men. Hence, a relative decrease in the number of hands is consist*ent with an actual increase.

CHAPTER XI

DECREASE OF THE RATE OF PROFIT

(Extracted from vol. III, part 1, ch. 13-15. German ed.)

THE continuous relative decrease of the number of labourers employed, must have a peculiar effect on the rate (or percentage) of profit.

The aim of machinery (as also of the technical discoveries of former times) is to save labour. The same quantity of commodities—or a larger one—is produced by less labourers. Living labour becomes more productive and more fertile. The Alpha and Omega of economic progress is the increase of productiveness.

But this means that the same number of workmen work-up an ever increasing mass of raw materials and utilise an ever increasing number of implements of labour. For instance, when the workman, with the help of the machine, is able to produce 10 times as much cotton yarn in the same time as he formerly did, he consumes also 10 times as much cotton, to say nothing of the immense and costly machine, which is far more valuable than the simple tool formerly in use. In other words, every economic progress—but in by far the largest measure the progress due to machinery—increases the quantity of constant capital consumed by a given number of labourers. But at the same time such progress diminishes, as a necessary consequence, the percentage of profit, as is clearly illustrated by the following table.

In order to simplify the calculation, we have everywhere

assumed the rate of surplus-value to amount to 100%. In other words, we assume that labour, over and above the restitution of wages, yields a surplus-value for capital which is exactly as large as the wages paid. For instance, if the variable capital, *i. e.* wages (represented by *v*) equals 100, and consequently the surplus-value (represented by *s*) likewise equals 100, the percentage of this surplus of 100 *s* will be quite different, according as to whether *c* (the constant capital constituted by raw material, implements of labour, etc.) be large or small.

If for 100 *v* we take

50c,	the total capital will be	150,	of which the	100s	=	66⅔%
100c	" "	" " "	200,	" " "	100s	=	50 %
200c	" "	" " "	300,	" ; "	100s	=	33⅓%
300c	" "	" " "	400,	" " "	100s	=	25 %
400c	" "	" " "	500,	" " "	100s	=	20 %

Consequently it is always the same quantity of surplus-value, which, with every increase of the total capital, yields a smaller rate of profit. The result of technical progress—a result which manifests itself most clearly with the introduction, and with every subsequent improvement of, machinery—is thus to gradually augment the constant capital in proportion to the variable capital, and therefore to reduce gradually the rate of profit. The same number of workmen and the same amount of labour power consume a constantly increasing quantity of implements of labour, of machines, of raw and auxiliary materials, *i. e.* a constant capital of continuously increasing value.

A progressive cheapening of the product corresponds to this increasing value of the constant capital. Every single fraction of the product, regarded by itself, contains a smaller amount of labour than is the case in more primitive stages of production. The constant tendency of the general rate of profit to decrease is thus only a manifestation, peculiar to the capitalist mode of production, of the constant development of the productive power of labour. This does not mean that the rate of profit cannot temporarily decrease also for other reasons; but it may be regarded as a self-evident necessity, appertaining to the essence of capitalist production, that as the latter progresses, the general average rate of surplus value must find expression in a general decrease of the rate of profit. As the quantity of applied living labour constantly decreases in proportion to the quantity of the means of production set in motion by it, that part of living labour which is unpaid and incorporated in surplus-value, must likewise decrease in proportion to the value of the applied total capital.

This law of the progressive decrease of the rate of profit in no wise excludes the fact that the *absolute* quantity of labour set in motion and exploited by capital—and consequently also the absolute quantity of surplus-labour appropriated by capital—increases. For instance, if in any given country the number of labourers employed—and consequently the amount of wages paid for such labour—should increase from 2 to 3 millions, the quantity of surplus-labour and surplus-value likewise increases by one half. But if the productive power of labour simultaneously increases in such a manner that the means of production (*i. e.* the constant capital) consumed by it increase from 4 to 15 millions, the increased quantity of surplus value would none the less be smaller than before in proportion to the total capital.

We would have

in the first case: $4\ c + 2\ v = 6$; $2\ s = 33\frac{1}{3}\%$ profit
in the second case: $15\ c + 3\ v = 18$; $3\ s = 16\frac{2}{3}\%$ profit.

Whereas the quantity of surplus value has increased by one half, the rate of profit has fallen by one half. Thus the absolute amount of profit, its totality, has increased to the extent of 50% in spite of an enormous decrease in the proportion of this amount of profit to the total capital advanced—or in spite of the enormous decrease in the general rate of profit. The number of labourers employed by capital, hence the amount of labour and surplus-labour performed by them, and consequently the amount of surplus-value, can thus increase progressively, in spite of the progressive decrease of the rate of profit. But not only is this phenomenon possible, it is inevitable, on the basis of capitalist production (if we except temporary fluctuations).

As we shall show in the next chapter, capitalist production requires—precisely on account of the decrease of the rate of profit—constant expansion; the labour process must take place on constantly increasing scale, and consequently the capital advanced must constantly increase, in every individual factory or workshop. We can thus understand, as far as the individual capitalist is concerned, that his sway extends over an ever increasing number of workmen, and that the quantity of surplus-value appropriated by him increases simultaneously with, and in spite of, the decrease in the rate of profit. The same reasons which lead to the concentration of vast masses of workmen under the command of a single capitalist, lead also to the increase of the quantity of applied fixed capital and raw and auxiliary materials, in ever greater proportion to the amount of living labour employed.

The law according to which the fall in the rate of profit due to the development of productive labour is accompanied by an increase in the total quantity of profit, finds likewise its expression in the fact that the fall in the price of commodities is accompanied by a relative increase of the amount of profit contained in such commodities, and realised by their sale.

As the development of productive power results in setting in motion a constantly increasing quantity of means of production by a constantly decreasing quantity of labour, each fraction of the total product, i. e. each individual commodity contains less labour and its price decreases. But the total number of commodities produced augments accordingly. Viewed superficially, we thus witness a decrease of the amount of profit realised on the individual commodity, a decrease of its price, and an increase of the amount of profit realised on the increased total amount of commodities produced by the total capital, either of society or of the individual capitalist. This phenomenon is then taken to signify that the capitalist of his own free will realises less profit on the individual commodity, but indemnifies himself by means of the larger total quantity of commodities produced by him.

When we contemplate the immense development of productive power, even during the last 30 years (previous to 1867); and especially when we contemplate the immense amount of fixed capital applied over and above the machinery proper, it appears astonishing that the rate of profit has not decreased more and with greater rapidity than is, as a matter of fact, the case. Opposing forces must be at work, of which the following are the most important.

The capitalist naturally seeks to counterbalance the decrease of the rate of profit by an increased exploitation o labour power. More must be extracted from the individual workman, consequently more value must be yielded by him, by means of a prolongation of the working-day and an increased strain upon his working-power. In the previous chapter we saw how this is effected by means of machinery. But it is evident that limits, and not very wide ones, are set to this process. Two workmen, working daily 12 hours, cannot supply the same amount of surplus-value as 24 workmen working two hours each, even if they could live on fresh air and received no wages. By such means, the decrease of the rate of profit can be checked, but not suppressed.

Another means of intensifying the exploitation of labour, and thereby of increasing the amount of surplus-value extracted from each individual workman, the total number of workmen being reduced, is to force down wages to a point below the value of labour power. As a matter of fact, this is one of the chief causes which tend to check the decrease of the rate of profit.

There comes further the circumstance that the value of the constant capital does not increase as rapidly as its quantity. For instance, the quantity of cotton which a single European spinner works-up in a modern factory, has immensely increased in proportion to the amount formerly worked-up by a European spinner by means of the spinning-wheel. But the value of the cotton thus worked-up has not increased in the same proportion. The same holds of machines and other fixed capital.

But the most important means of checking the decrease of the rate of profit, and of thus escaping ruin, consists in the unceasing increase of capital. If economic progress causes the rate of profit to decrease from 20 to 10%, it is, it is true, impossible to prevent 100 capital from yielding henceforth but 10 surplus-value. But the individual capitalist can make good his loss by doubling the amount of his capital. As he now applies everywhere 200 instead of 100, the amount of his profit remains the same. He can even increase his profit, should he still further augment his capital.

The constant increase and accumulation of capital plays, therefore, an important part. We will now turn our attention to this phenomenon.

CHAPTER XII

THE ACCUMULATION OF CAPITAL

(A) *The Uninterrupted Continuation of Production (Reproduction)*

(Extracted from vol. II, ch. 23.)

A SOCIETY can no more cease to produce than it can cease to consume. No society can continually produce, unless it constantly reconverts a part of its products into means of production. All other circumstances remaining the same, the only mode by which it can reproduce its wealth, and maintain it at one level, is by replacing the means of production—*i. e.* the instruments of labour, the raw material, and the auxiliary substances—consumed in the course of the year by an equal quantity of the same kind of articles; these must be separated from the mass of the yearly products, and thrown afresh into the process of production, and must be applicable for this purpose.

In a capitalist society all means of production serve as capital, for they all enable their proprietor to reap surplus-value by employing wage-labour. As a matter of fact the capitalist

does not intend reaping surplus-value only once, but continually, from the capital advanced by him.

If such surplus-value were to be completely consumed every
year by the capitalist, there would be a simple repetition of
production, *i. e.* simple reproduction. But even this simple
continued repetition gives a new character to the process.

The purchase of labour power for a fixed period is the
prelude to the process of production. But the labourer is not
paid until after he has expended his labour power, and realised in commodities not only its value, but surplus-value. He
has, therefore, produced not only surplus-value, but he has
also produced, before it flows back to him in the shape of
wages, the fund out of which he himself is paid; and his employment lasts only so long as he continues to reproduce this
fund. Hence, wages are but a portion of the product that is
continuously reproduced by the labourer himself. The capitalist, it is true, pays him in money, but this money is merely
the transmuted form of the product of his labour. It is his
labour of last week, or of last year, that pays for his labour
power this week or this year. The illusion begotten by the
intervention of money vanishes immediately, if, instead of
taking a single capitalist and a single labourer, we take the
class of capitalists and the class of labourers as a whole. The
capitalist class is constantly giving to the labouring class
order-notes, in the form of money, on a portion of the commodities produced by the latter and appropriated by the
former. The labourers give these order-notes back just as constantly to the capitalist class, and in this way get their share
of their own product. The transaction is veiled by the commodity form of the product and the money form of the
commodity.

True, the illusion that wages are advanced out of the capitalist's funds only disappears when we view the process of
capitalist production in the flow of its constant renewal. But
that process must have had a beginning of some kind. We assume, therefore, for the present, that the capitalist, once upon
a time, became possessed of money, independently of the unpaid labour of others, and that this was how he was enabled
to buy labour power. However this may be, the mere con-

tinuity of the process, the simple reproduction, brings about some other wonderful changes, which affect not only the variable, but the total capital.

If a capital of $5,000 beget yearly a surplus-value of $1,000, and if this surplus-value be consumed every year, it is clear that at the end of 5 years the surplus-value consumed will amount to $5 \times \$1,000$ or the $5,000 originally advanced. If only a part, say one half, were consumed, the same result would follow at the end of 10 years, since $10 \times \$500 = \$5,000$. General rule: at the end of a certain number of years, according to the amount of the capital advanced and of the surplus-value consumed, the capital originally advanced has been consumed by the capitalist and has disappeared. The capitalist thinks that he is consuming the produce of the unpaid labour of others, *i. e.* the surplus-value, and is keeping intact his original capital; but what he thinks cannot alter facts. After the lapse of a certain number of years, the capital value he then possesses is equal to the sum total of the surplus-value appropriated by him during those years, and the total value he has consumed equal to that of his original capital. It is true, he has in hand a capital whose amount has not changed, and of which a part, *viz.*, the buildings, machinery, &c., were already there when the work of his business began. But what we have to do with here, is not the material elements, but the value, of that capital. When a person gets through all his property, by taking upon himself debts equal to the value of that property, it is clear that his property represents nothing but the sum total of his debts. And so it is with the capitalist; when he has consumed the equivalent of his original capital, the value of his present capital represents nothing but the total amount of the surplus-value appropriated by him without payment. Not a single atom of the value of his old capital continues to exist.

The mere continuity of the process of production, in other words simple reproduction, thus sooner or later, and of necessity, converts every capital into capitalised surplus-value. Even if that capital was originally acquired by the personal labour of its employer, it sooner or later becomes value appropriated without an equivalent—the unpaid labour of others materialised either in money or in some other object.

In order to convert his money into capital, for the purpose of exploiting the labour of others, the capitalist had originally to confront, on the labour market, the labourer lacking all means of production and subsistence. This was the real foundation in fact, and the starting point, of capitalist production. But, by the mere continuity of the process, by simple reproduction, these conditions are perpetually reproduced. On the one hand, the process of production incessantly converts material wealth into capital, into means of creating more wealth and means of enjoyment for the capitalist. On the other hand the labourer, on quitting the process, is what he was on entering it, a source of wealth, but devoid of all means of making that wealth his own. Since, before entering on the process, his own labour has already been alienated from himself by the sale of his labour-power, has been appropriated by the capitalist and incorporated with capital, the product also belongs to the capitalist. This incessant reproduction, this perpetuation of the proletarian labourer, is an indispensable condition of capitalist production.

The labourer consumes in a twofold way. While producing he consumes by his labour the means of production, and converts them into products with a higher value than that of the capital advanced. This is his productive consumption. It is at the same time consumption of his labour power by the capitalist who bought it. On the other hand, the labourer turns the money paid to him for his labour-power, into means of subsistence: this is his individual consumption. The labourer's productive consumption, and his individual consumption, are therefore totally distinct. In the former, he acts as the motive power of capital, and belongs to the capitalist. In the latter, he belongs to himself, and performs his necessary vital functions outside the process of production. The result of the one is, that the capitalist lives; of the other, that the labourer lives.

True, the labourer is often compelled to make his individual consumption a mere incident of production. In such a case, he supplies himself with necessaries in order to maintain his labour power, just as coal and water are supplied to the steam engine and oil to the wheel. This, however, appears to be an abuse not essentially appertaining to capitalist production.

The matter takes quite another aspect, when we contemplate, not the single capitalist, and the single labourer, but the capitalist class and the labouring class, not an isolated process of production, but capitalist production in its totality, and on its actual social scale. By converting part of his capital into labour power, the capitalist augments the value of his entire capital. He kills two birds with one stone. He profits, not only by what he receives from, but by what he gives to, the labourer. The capital given in exchange for labour power is converted into necessaries, by the consumption of which the muscles, nerves, bones, and brains of existing labourers are reproduced, and new labourers are begotten. Within the limits of what is strictly necessary, the individual consumption of the working class is, therefore, the reconversion of the means of subsistence given by capital in exchange for labour power, into fresh labour power at the disposal of capital for exploitation. It is the production and reproduction of that means of production so indispensable to the capitalist: the labourer himself. The individual consumption of the labourer, whether it proceed within the workshop or outside it, whether it be part of the process of production or not, forms therefore a factor of the production and reproduction of capital; just as cleaning machinery does, whether it be done while the machinery is working or while it is standing. The fact that the labourer consumes his means of subsistence for his own purposes, and not to please the capitalist, has no bearing on the matter. The consumption of food by a beast of burden is none the less a necessary factor in the process of production, because the beast enjoys what it eats. The maintenance and reproduction of the working-class is, and must ever be, a necessary condition to the reproduction of capital. But the capitalist may safely leave its fulfilment to the labourer's instincts of self-preservation and of propagation. All the capitalist cares for, is to reduce the labourer's individual consumption as far as possible to what is strictly necessary, and he is far away from imitating those brutal South-Americans, who force their labourers to take more substantial food.[1]

Hence both the capitalist and his ideological representative, the political economist, consider that part alone of the labourer's individual consumption to be productive, which is requisite for the perpetuation of the class, and which therefore must take place in order that the capitalist may have labour-power to consume; what the labourer consumes for his own pleasure beyond that part, is unproductive consumption.[2]

From a social point of view, therefore, the working-class, even when not directly engaged in the labour-process, is just as much an appendage of capital as the ordinary instruments of labour. Even its individual consumption is, within certain limits, a mere factor in the process of the reproduction of capital. That process, however, takes good care to prevent these self-conscious instruments from leaving it in the lurch, for it constantly transforms their product, as fast as it is made, into the property of capital. Individual consumption provides, on the one hand, the means for their maintenance and reproduction: on the other hand, it secures by the annihilation of the necessaries of life the continued reappearance of the workman in the labour-market. The Roman slave was held by fetters: the wage-labourer is bound to his owner by invisible threads. The appearance of independence is kept up by means of a constant change of employers, and by the fictio juris of a contract.

In former times, capital resorted to legislation, whenever necessary, to enforce its proprietary rights over the free labourer. For instance, down to 1815, the emigration of

[1] "The labourers in the mines of S. America, whose daily task (the heaviest perhaps in the world) consists in bringing to the surface on their shoulders a load of metal weighing from 180 to 200 pounds, from a depth of 450 feet, live on bread and beans only; they themselves would prefer the bread alone for food, but their masters, who have found out that the men cannot work so hard on bread, treat them like horses, and compel them to eat beans; beans, however, are relatively much richer in bone-earth (phosphate of lime) than is bread" (Liebig, *Chemistry in its application to Agriculture and Physiology,* 7th German ed., 1862, vol. I, p. 194, note).

[2] James Mill, *Elements of Political Economy,* French translation by Parissot. Paris, 1823, p. 238, sqq.

mechanics employed in machine making was, in England, forbidden, under heavy pains and penalties.

The reproduction of the working class carries with it the transmission and accumulation of skill, that is handed down from one generation to another. To what extent the capitalist reckons the existence of such a skilled class among the factors of production that belong to him by right, is seen so soon as a crisis threatens him with its loss. In consequence of the civil war in the United States and of the accompanying cotton famine, the majority of the cotton operatives in Lancashire were, as is well known, thrown out of work. Both from the working-class itself, and from other ranks of society, there arose a cry for State aid, or for voluntary subscriptions, in order to enable the "superfluous" hands to emigrate to the colonies or to the United States. Thereupon, the *Times* published on the 24th March, 1863, a letter from Edmund Potter, a former president of the Manchester Chamber of Commerce. This letter was rightly called, in the House of Commons, the manufacturers' manifesto. We cull here a few characteristic passages, in which the proprietary rights of capital over labour-power are unblushingly asserted.

"He" (the man out of work) "may be told the supply of cotton-workers is too large ... and ... must ... in fact be reduced by a third, perhaps, and that then there will be a healthy demand for the remaining two-thirds. . . . Public opinion ... urges emigration. . . . The master (*i. e.* the cotton manufacturer) cannot willingly see his labour supply being removed; he may think, and perhaps justly, that it is both wrong and unsound. . . . But if the public funds are to be devoted to assist emigration, he has a right to be heard, and perhaps to protest." Mr. Potter then shows how useful the cotton trade is, how the "trade has undoubtedly drawn the surplus-population from Ireland and from the agricultural districts," how immense is its extent, how in the year 1860 it yielded $5/13$ths of the total English exports, how, after a few years, it will again expand by the extension of the market, particularly of the Indian market, and by calling forth a plentiful supply of cotton at 6 d. per lb. He then continues: "Time . . , one, two, or three years, it may be, will produce the quantity.... The question I would put then is this: Is the trade worth retaining? Is it worth while to keep the machinery (he means the living labour machines) in order, and is it not the greatest folly to think of parting with that? I think it is. I allow that the workers are not a property, not the property of Lancashire and the masters; but they are the strength of both; they are the mental and trained power which cannot be replaced for a generation; the mere machinery which they work might much of it be beneficially replaced, nay improved, in a twelvemonth.[1] Encourage or allow (!) the working-power to emigrate, and what of the capitalist? ... Take away the cream of the workers, and fixed capital will depreciate in a great degree, and the floating will not subject itself to a struggle with the short supply of inferior labour.... We are told the workers wish it (emigration). Very natural it is that they should do so.... Reduce, compress the cotton trade by taking away its working power and reducing their wages expenditure, say one-fifth, or five millions, and what then would happen to the class above, the small shopkeepers; and what of the rents, the cottage rents.... Trace out the effects upward to the small farmer, the better householder, and ... the landowner, and say if there could be any suggestion more suicidal to all classes of the country than by enfeebling a nation by exporting the best of its manufacturing population, and destroying the value of some of its most productive capital and enrichment.... Can anything be worse for landowners or masters than parting with the best of the workers, and demoralising and disappointing the rest by an extended de-

[1] It will not be forgotten that this same capital sings quite another song, under ordinary circumstances, when there is a question of reducing wages. Then the masters exclaim with one voice: "The factory operative should keep in wholesome remembrance the fact that theirs is really a low species of skilled labour; and that there is none which is more easily acquired, or of its quality more amply remunerated, or which, by a short training of the least expert, can be more quickly, as well as abundantly, acquired.... The master's machinery" (which we now learn can be replaced with advantage in 12 months) "really plays a far more important part in the business of production than the labour and skill of the operative" (who cannot now be replaced under 30 years), "which six months' education can teach, and a common labourer can learn." (See ante, p. 126.)

pletive emigration, a depletion of capital and value in an entire province?"

Potter, the chosen mouthpiece of the manufacturers, distinguishes two sort of "machinery," each of which belongs to the capitalist, and of which one stands in his factory, the other at night-time and on Sundays is housed outside the factory, in cottages. The one is inanimate, the other living. The inanimate machinery not only wears out and depreciates from day to day, but a great part of it becomes so quickly superannuated, by constant technical progress, that it can be replaced with advantage by new machinery after a few months. The living machinery, on the contrary, gets better the longer it lasts, and in proportion as the skill, handed from one generation to another, accumulates. The *Times* answered the cotton lord as follows:

"Mr. Edmund Potter is so impressed with the exceptional and supreme importance of the cotton masters that, in order to preserve this class and perpetuate their profession, he would keep half a million of the labouring class confined in a great moral workhouse against their will. 'Is the trade worth retaining?' asks Mr. Potter. Certainly by all honest means it is, we answer. 'Is it worth while keeping the machinery in order?' again asks Mr. Potter. Here we hesitate. By the 'machinery' Mr. Potter means the human machinery, for he goes on to protest that he does not mean to use them as an absolute property. We must confess that we do not think it 'worth while,' or even possible, to keep the human machinery in order—that is to shut it up and keep it oiled till it is wanted. Human machinery will rust under inaction, oil and rub it as you may. Moreover, the human machinery will, as we have just seen, get the steam up of its own accord, and burst or run amuck in our great towns. It might, as Mr. Potter says, require some time to reproduce the workers, but, having machinists and capitalists at hand, we could always find thrifty, hard, industrious men wherewith to improvise more master manufacturers than we can ever want. Mr. Potter talks of the trade reviving 'in one, two, or three years,' and he asks us not 'to encourage or allow (!) the working power to emigrate.' He says that it is very natural the workers should wish to emigrate; but he thinks that in spite of their desire, the nation ought to keep this half million of workers, with their 700,000 dependents, shut up in the cotton districts; and as a necessary consequence, he must of course think that the nation ought to keep down their discontent by force, and sustain them by alms and upon the chance that the cotton masters may some day want them. . . . The time is come when the great public opinion of these islands must operate to save this 'working power' from those who would deal with it as they would deal with iron, and coal, and cotton."

The *Times* article was only a *jeu d'esprit*. The "great public opinion," was in fact of Mr. Potter's opinion, that the factory operatives are part of the movable fittings of a factory. Their emigration was prevented.[1] They were locked up in that "moral workhouse", the cotton districts, and they form, as before, the "strength" of the cotton manufacturers of Lancashire.

Capitalist production, therefore, of itself reproduces the separation between labour power and the means of labour. It thereby reproduces and perpetuates the condition for exploiting the labourer. It incessantly forces him to sell his labour power in order to live, and enables the capitalist to purchase labour power in order that he may enrich himself. It is no longer a mere accident, that capitalist and labourer confront each other in the market as buyer and seller. It is the process itself that incessantly hurls back the labourer on to the market as a vendor of his labour power, and that incessantly converts his own product into a means by which another man can purchase him.

Capitalist production, therefore, under its aspect of a continuous connected process, of a process of reproduction, produces not only commodities, not only surplus-value, but it also

---

[1] Parliament did not vote a single farthing in aid of emigration, but simply passed some Acts empowering the municipal corporations to keep the operatives in a half-starved state, *i. e.*, to exploit them at less than the normal wages. On the other hand, when 3 years later, the cattle disease broke out, Parliament broke wildly through its usages and voted, straight off, millions for indemnifying the millionaire landlords, whose farmers in any event came off without loss, owing to the rise in the price of meat.

produces and reproduces the capitalist relation: on the one side the capitalist, on the other the wage-labourer.

(B) *Increase of Capital by Means of Surplus-Value. Capitalist Property*

(Extracted from vol. II, ch. 24, section 1.)

Hitherto we have investigated how surplus-value emanates from capital; we have now to see how capital arises from surplus-value. Employing surplus-value as capital, reconverting it into capital, is called accumulation of capital.

First let us consider this transaction from the standpoint of the individual capitalist. Suppose a spinner to have advanced a capital of $50,000, of which four-fifths ($40,000) are laid out in cotton, machinery, &c., and one-fifth ($10,000) in wages. Let him produce 240,000 lbs. of yarn annually, having a value of $60,000. The rate of surplus-value being 100%, the surplus-value lies in the surplus or net product of 40,000 lbs. of yarn, one-sixth of the gross product, with a value of $10,000 which will be realised by a sale. $10,000 is $10,000. We can neither see nor smell in this sum of money a trace of surplus-value. When we know that a given value is surplus-value, we know how its owner came by it; but that does not alter the nature either of value or of money.

In order to convert this additional sum of $10,000 into capital, the master spinner will, all circumstances remaining as before, advance four-fifths of it ($8,000) in the purchase of cotton, &c. and one-fifth ($2,000) in the purchase of additional spinners, who will find in the market the necessaries of life whose value the master has advanced to them. Then the new capital of $10,000 functions in the spinning mill, and brings in, in its turn, a surplus-value of $2,000.

The capital-value was originally advanced in money form. If the 200,000 lbs. of yarn, in which it is invested, be sold, the capital-value regains its original form. The surplus-value, on the contrary, is from the beginning the value of a definite portion of the gross product. Through the sale, therefore, the original form of the surplus-value is altered. From this moment the capital-value and the surplus-value are both of them sums of money, and their reconversion into capital takes place in precisely the same way. The one, as well as the other, is laid out by the capitalist in the purchase of commodities that place him in a position to begin afresh the fabrication of his goods, and this time, on an extended scale. But in order to be able to buy those commodities, he must find them ready in the market.

Commodities, which are to be bought on the market, must be produced beforehand. The transactions in the market effectuate only the interchange of the individual components of the annual product, transfer them from one hand to another, but can neither augment the total annual production, nor alter the nature of the objects produced.

The annual production must in the first place furnish all those objects (use-values) from which the material components of capital, used up in the course of the year, have to be replaced. Deducting these there remains the net or surplus-product, in which the surplus-value lies. And of what does this surplus-product consist? Perhaps of things destined to satisfy the wants and desires of the capitalist class? Were that the case, the cup of surplus-value would be drained to the very dregs.

We cannot, except by a miracle, convert into capital any-thing but such articles as can be employed in the labour-process (*i. e.*, means of production), and such further articles as are suitable for the sustenance of the labourer (*i. e.*, means of subsistence). Consequently, a part of the annual surplus-labour must have been applied to the production of additional means of production and subsistence, over and above the quantity of these things required to replace the capital advanced. In other words, surplus-value is convertible into capital solely because the surplus-product, whose value it is, already comprises the material elements of new capital.

Now in order to allow of these elements actually functioning as capital, the capitalist class requires additional labour. If the exploitation of the labourers already employed do not increase, either extensively or intensively, then additional labour-power must be found. For this the mechanism of capitalist production provides beforehand, since the wages suffice.

not only for the maintenance, but for the increase of the working class. It is only necessary for capital to incorporate this additional labour-power, annually supplied by the working class in the shape of labourers of all ages, with the surplus means of production comprised in the annual produce, and the conversion of surplus-value into capital is complete.

Let us now return to our illustration. It is the old story: Abraham begat Isaac, Isaac begat Jacob, and so on. The original capital of $50,000 brings in a surplus-value of $10,000, which is capitalised. The new capital of $10,000 brings in a surplus-value of $2,000, and this, too, is capitalised, converted into a second additional capital, which, in its turn, produces a further surplus-value of $400. And so the ball rolls on.

We here leave out of consideration the portion of the surplus-value consumed by the capitalist. Just as little does it concern us, for the moment, whether the additional capital is joined on to the original capital, or is separated from it to function independently; whether the same capitalist, who accumulated it, employs it, or whether he hands it over to another. This only we must not forget, that by the side of the newly formed capital, the original capital continues to reproduce itself, and to produce surplus-value, and that this is also true of all accumulated capital.

The original capital was formed by the advance of $50,000. How did the owner become possessed of it? "By his own labour and that of his forefathers," answer unanimously the spokesmen of political economy.

But it is quite otherwise with regard to the additional capital of $10,000. How that originated we know perfectly well. It is capitalised surplus-value. There is not one single atom of its value that does not owe its existence to unpaid labour. The means of production, with which the additional labour-power is incorporated, as well as the necessaries with which the labourers are sustained, are nothing but component parts of the surplus product, of the tribute annually exacted from the working class by the capitalist class. Though the latter with a portion of that tribute purchases the additional labour power even at its full price, so that equivalent is exchanged for equivalent, yet the transaction is for all that only the old dodge of every conqueror who buys commodities from the conquered with the money he has robbed them of.

If the additional capital employs the person who produced it, this producer must not only continue to augment the value of the original capital, but must buy back the fruits of his previous labour with more labour than they cost. When viewed as a transaction between the capitalist class and the working class, it makes no difference that additional labourers are employed by means of the unpaid labour of the previously employed labourers. The capitalist may even convert the additional capital into a machine which throws the workmen who made it out of work, and which replaces them by a few children. In every case the working class creates by the surplus-labour of one year the capital destined to employ additional labour in the following year.

The accumulation of the first additional capital of $10,000 presupposes a value of $50,000 belonging to the capitalist by virtue of his "primitive labour," and advanced by him. The second additional capital of $2,000 presupposes, on the contrary, only the previous accumulation of the $10,000, of which the $2,000 is the surplus-value capitalised. The ownership of past unpaid labour is henceforth the sole condition for the appropriation of living unpaid labor on a constantly increasing scale. The more the capitalist has accumulated, the more is he able to accumulate.

Owing to the process just described, i. e. the constant increase of capital by means of the surplus-value previously made, of which a part is invariably applied to the purchase of new labour power (and we will even assume that the latter is bought at its real value) it is evident that private property, based on the production and circulation of commodities, becomes changed into its very opposite. The exchange of equivalents has now become turned round in such a way that there is only an apparent exchange. This is owing to the fact, first, that the capital which is exchanged for labour power is itself but a portion of the product of others' labour appropriated without an equivalent; and, secondly, that this capital must not only be replaced by its producer, but replaced together with a

surplus. The exchange between capitalist and labourer becomes a mere form, foreign to the real nature of the transaction, and only mystifying it. The ever repeated purchase
and sale of labour power is now the mere form; what really
takes place is this: the capitalist again and again appropriates,
without equivalent, a portion of the labour of others, (already
existing in the commodities), and exchanges it for a greater
quantity of living labour. At first the rights of property seemed
to us to be based on a man's own labour. At least, some such
assumption was necessary, since only commodity owners with
equal rights confronted each other, and the sole means by
which a man could become possessed of the commodities of
others, was by alienating his own commodities; and these
could be replaced by labour alone. Now, however, property
turns out to be the right, on the part of the capitalist, to
appropriate the unpaid labour of others or its product, and
to be the impossibility, on the part of the labourer, of appropriating his own product.

We have seen that even in the case of simple reproduction,
all capital, whatever its original source, becomes converted
into capitalised surplus-value. But in the flood of production
all the capital originally advanced becomes a vanishing quantity, compared with the directly accumulated capital, *i. e.*,
with the surplus-product that is reconverted into capital,
whether it function in the hands of its accumulator, or in
those of others.

It is evident [1] that only a portion of the surplus-value can
be converted into capital, and that another portion must serve
for the sustenance of the capitalist. The larger the one of
these parts, the smaller is the other. The less the capitalist
consumes, the greater will be the accumulation.

The historical value and justification of the capitalist are
to be found in the fact that he ruthlessly forces the human
race to produce for production's sake; he thus forces the development of the productive powers of society, and creates
those material conditions, which alone can form the real basis
of a higher form of society, a society in which the full and
free development of every individual forms the ruling prin-

[1] From here on vol. II, ch. 24, section 3.

ciple. Moreover, the development of capitalist production makes it constantly necessary to keep increasing the amount of the capital laid out in a given industrial undertaking; and competition compels each individual capitalist to keep constantly extending his capital, in order to preserve it, but extend it he cannot, except by means of progressive accumulation.

CHAPTER XIII

INFLUENCE OF THE ACCUMULATION OF CAPITAL ON THE WORKING CLASS.—THE INDUSTRIAL RESERVE-ARMY.— THE THEORY OF THE GROWING IMPOVERISH- MENT OF THE MASSES

(Extracted from vol. II, ch. 25.)

WHEN a part of the surplus-value is turned into capital and employed as additional capital, it is evident that such additional capital requires, in its turn, labour. All other circumstances remaining the same, and a definite mass of means of production (constant capital) constantly needing the same mass of labour power (variable capital) to set it in motion, then the demand for labour will increase, and this the quicker the more rapidly the capital increases. Capital produces yearly a surplus-value, of which one part is yearly added to the original value; this surplus-value increases every year, because the capital (as a consequence of accumulation) increases; lastly, when a special stimulus to enrichment arises, such as the opening of new markets, or of new spheres for the outlay of capital in consequence of newly developed social wants, &c., a reduction of the private consumption of the capitalists suffices in order to accumulate a great deal more surplus-value. For all these reasons, the requirements of accumulating capital may exceed the increase of the number of labourers, and, therefore, wages may rise. This must, indeed, ultimately be the case if the conditions supposed above continue. For since in each year more labourers are employed than in its predecessor, sooner or later a point must be reached, at which the requirements of accumulation begin to surpass the customary supply of labour, and, therefore, a rise of wages takes place. A lamentation on this score was heard in England during the whole of the fifteenth, and the first half of the eighteenth centuries. The more or less favourable circumstances in which the wage-working class supports and multiplies itself, in no way alter the fundamental character of capitalist production. As simple reproduction constantly reproduces the capital-relation itself, *i. e.*, the relation of capitalists on the one hand, and wage-workers on the other, so reproduction on a progressive scale, *i. e.* accumulation, reproduces the capital-relation on a progressive scale, more capitalists or larger capitalists at this pole, more wage-workers at that. Accumulation of capital is, therefore, increase of the proletariat.[1]

As early as 1696 John Bellers says: "For if one had a hundred thousand acres of land and as many pounds in money, and as many cattle, without a labourer, what would the rich man be, but a labourer? And as the labourers make men rich, so the more labourers, there will be the more rich men ... the labour of the poor being the mines of the rich." So also Bertrand de Mandeville at the beginning of the eighteenth century (1728): "It would be easier, where property is well secured, to live without money than without poor; for who would do the work? ... As they (the poor) ought to be kept from starving, so they should receive nothing worth saving. If here and there one of the lowest class by uncommon industry, and pinching his belly, lifts himself above the condition he was brought up in, nobody ought to hinder him; nay, it is undeniably the wisest course for every person in the society, and for every private family to be frugal; but it is the interest of all rich nations, that the greatest part of the poor should almost never be idle, and yet continually spend what they get. ... Those that get their living by their daily labour ... have nothing to stir them up to be serviceable but their wants, which it is prudence to relieve, but folly to cure. The only thing then that can render the labouring man in-

---

[1] Economically speaking, the "proletarian" is none other than the wage-worker, whose labour produces and augments capital, and who is thrown out on the street as soon as capital no longer needs his services.

dustrious, is a moderate quantity of money, for as too little will, according as his temper is, either dispirit or make him desperate, so too much will make him insolent and lazy.... From what has been said, it is manifest, that, in a free nation, where slaves are not allowed of, the surest wealth consists in a multitude of laborious poor; for besides that they are the never-failing nursery of fleets and armies, without them there could be no enjoyment, and no product of any country could be valuable. To make the society ('which of course consists of non-workers') happy and people easier under the meanest circumstances, it is requisite that great numbers of them should be ignorant as well as poor; knowledge both enlarges and multiplies our desires, and the fewer things a man wishes for, the more easily his necessities may be supplied."

What Mandeville, an honest, clear-headed man, had not yet seen, is that the mechanism of the process of accumulation itself increases, along with capital, the mass of "labouring poor," *i. e.*, the wage-labourers.

Under the conditions of accumulation supposed thus far, which conditions are those most favourable to the labourers, their relation of dependence upon capital takes on an endurable form. A larger part of their own surplus-product, always increasing and continually transformed into additional capital, comes back to them in the shape of means of payment, so that they can extend the circle of their enjoyments; can make some additions to their consumption-fund of clothes, furniture, &c., and can lay by small reserve-funds of money. But just as little as better clothing, food, and treatment, and a larger peculium, do away with the exploitation of the slave, so little do they set aside that of the wage-worker. A rise in the price of labour, as a consequence of accumulation of capital, only means, in fact, that the length and weight of the golden chain the wage-worker has already forged for himself allow of a relaxation of the tension of it. An increase of wages only means at best a quantitative diminution of the unpaid labour that the worker has to supply. This diminution can never reach the point at which it would threaten the system itself. Either the price of labour keeps on rising, because its rise does not interfere with the progress of accumulation. In this there is nothing wonderful, for, says Adam Smith, (1774), "after these (profits) are diminished, stock may not only continue to increase, but to increase much faster than before. . . . A great stock, though with small profits, generally increases faster than a small stock with great profits." In this case it is evident that a diminution in the unpaid labour in no way interferes with the extension of the domain of capital.—Or, on the other hand, accumulation slackens in consequence of the rise in the price of labour, because the stimulus of gain is blunted. The rate of accumulation lessens: but, simultaneously, the extensive demand for labour power, due precisely to the large accumulation, ceases; and wages fall again. The mechanism of the process of capitalist production removes the very obstacles that it temporarily creates.

We see, thus: in the first case, it is not the diminished rate either of the absolute or of the proportional increase in labouring population, which causes capital to be in excess, but conversely the excess of capital that makes exploitable labour power insufficient. In the second case, it is not the increase in labour power or labouring population, that makes capital insufficient; but conversely, the relative diminution of capital that causes the exploitable labour power, or rather its price, to be in excess. It is these absolute movements of the accumulation of capital which are reflected as relative movements of the mass of exploitable labour power, and therefore seem produced by the latter's own independent movement. It is a grave error, to interpret the above phenomena of accumulation by saying that there are now too few, now too many wage-labourers.

It is, therefore, neither the actual extent of social wealth, nor the magnitude of the capital already functioning, that lead to a rise of wages, but only the constant growth of accumulation and the degree of rapidity of that growth. So far we have, in our study of this process, proceeded from the assumption that the productive power of labour remains the same, *i.e.* that the same amount of means of production requires the same amount of labour power to apply it; and that the division of capital into constant and variable portions, *i. e.*, the relation of c to v, remains unchanged. But this assumption is shown by a closer analysis of the process, to be erroneous.

The productive power of labour is increased by accumulation. "The same cause," says Adam Smith, "which raises the wages of labour, the increase of stock, tends to increase its productive powers, and to make a smaller quantity of labour produce a greater quantity of work." Increasing productiveness of labour implies, however, that the same quantity of labour (v) consumes a larger quantity of means of production (c). The inner, technical composition of the capital must change, in the course of the process of accumulation, in such a manner that a relatively larger portion of the capital is laid-out in means of production (c), and a relatively smaller portion in labour power (v).

There may be, *e. g.*, originally 50 per cent. of a capital laid out in means of production, and 50 per cent. in labour power; later on, with the development of the productivity of labour, 80 per cent. in means of production, 20 per cent. in labour power, and so on. This law of the progressive increase in constant capital, in proportion to the variable, is confirmed at every step (as already shown) by the comparative analysis of the prices of commodities, whether we compare different economic epochs or different nations in the same epoch.

This diminution in the variable part of capital as compared with the constant, or the altered value composition of the capital, however, only shows approximately the change in the composition of its material constituents. If, *e. g.*, the capital-value employed to-day in spinning is $7/8$ constant and $1/8$ variable, whilst at the beginning of the 18th century it was $1/2$ constant and $1/2$ variable, on the other hand the mass of raw material, instruments of labour, &c., that a certain quantity of spinning labour consumes productively to-day, is many hundred times greater than at the beginning of the 18th century. The reason is simply that, with the increasing productivity of labour, not only does the mass of the means of production consumed by it increase, but their value compared with their mass diminishes. Thus although the dif ference between constant and variable capital increases, the difference between the mass of the means of production into which the constant capital is turned, and the mass of the labour power into which the variable capital is turned, increases much more rapidly.

But, if the progress of accumulation lessens the relative magnitude of the variable part of capital, it by no means, in doing this, excludes the possibility of a rise in its absolute magnitude. Suppose that a capital-value at first is divided into 50 per cent. of constant and 50 per cent. of variable capital; later into 80 per cent. of constant and 20 per cent. of variable. If in the meantime the original capital, say $30,000, has increased to $90,000, its variable constituent has also increased. It was $15,000, it is now $18,000. But whereas formerly an increase of capital by 20 per cent. would have sufficed to raise the demand for labour 20 per cent., now this latter rise requires a tripling of the original capital.

In another chapter it was shown how the development of the productiveness of social labour presupposes co-operation on a large scale; how it is only upon this supposition that division and combination of labour can be organised, and the means of production economised by concentration on a vast scale; how instruments of labour which, from their very nature, are only fit for use in common, such as a system of machinery, can be called into being; how colossal natural forces can be placed at the service of production. On the basis of the production of commodities, where the means of production are the property of private persons, and where the artisan therefore either produces commodities, isolated from and independent of others, or sells his labour power as a commodity, because he lacks the means for independent industry, co-operation can realise itself only in the increase of individual capitals, only in proportion as the means of social production and the means of subsistence are transformed into the private property of capitalists. The basis of the production of commodities can admit of production on a large scale in the capitalistic form alone. A certain accumulation of capital, in the hands of individual producers of commodities, forms therefore the necessary preliminary of the specifically capitalistic mode of production. But all methods for raising the social productive power of labour that are developed on this basis, are at the same time methods for the increased production of surplus-value or surplus-product, which in its turn is the formative element of accumulation. They are, therefore, at the same time methods of the accelerated accumulation of capital. The continual retransformation of surplus-value into capital now appears in the shape of the increasing magnitude of the capital that enters into the process of production. This in turn is the basis of an extended scale of production, of the methods for raising the productive power of labour that accompany it, and of accelerated production of surplus-value. If, therefore, a certain degree of accumulation of capital appears as a condition of the specifically capitalist mode of production, the latter causes conversely an accelerated accumulation of capital. With accumulation of capital, therefore, the specifically capitalistic mode of production develops, and with the capitalistic mode of production the accumulation of capital. Both these economic factors bring about, in the compound ratio of the impulses they reciprocally give one another, that change in the technical composition of capital by which the variable constituent becomes always smaller and smaller as compared with the constant.

Every individual capital is a larger or smaller concentration of means of production, with a corresponding command over a larger or smaller labour army. Every accumulation becomes the means of new accumulation. With the increasing mass of wealth which functions as capital, accumulation increases the concentration of that wealth in the hands of individual capitalists, and thereby widens the basis of production on a large scale and of the specific methods of capitalist production. The growth of social capital is effected by the growth of many individual capitals. At the same time portions of the original capitals disengage themselves and function as new independent capitals. Besides other causes the division of property, within capitalist families, plays a great part in this. With the accumulation of capital, therefore, the number of capitalists grows to a greater or less extent. Accumulation and the concentration accompanying it are, therefore, not only scattered over many points, but the increase of each functioning capital is thwarted by the formation of new and the sub-division of old capitals. Accumulation, therefore, presents itself on the one hand as increasing concentration of the means of production, and of the command over labour; on the other, as repulsion of many individual capitals one from another.

This splitting-up of the total social capital into many individual capitals or the repulsion of its fractions one from another, is counteracted by their attraction. This means concentration of capitals already formed, destruction of their individual independence, expropriation of capitalist by capitalist, transformation of many small into few large capitals. This process differs from the process of accumulation in this, that it only presupposes a change in the distribution of capital already to hand, and functioning; its field of action is therefore not limited by the growth of social wealth. Capital grows in one place to a huge mass in a single hand, because it has in another place been lost by many. This is centralisation proper, as distinct from accumulation and concentration.

The battle of competition is fought by cheapening of commodities. The cheapness of commodities depends, other conditions remaining the same, on the productiveness of labour, and this again, on the scale of production. Therefore, the larger capitals beat the smaller. It will further be remembered that, with the development of the capitalist mode of production, there is an increase in the minimum amount of individual capital necessary to carry on a business under its normal conditions. The smaller capitals, therefore, crowd into spheres of production which modern industry has only sporadically or incompletely got hold of. Here competition always ends in the ruin of many small capitalists, whose capitals partly pass into the hands of their conquerors, partly vanish. Apart from this, with capitalist production an altogether new force comes into play—the credit system. Not only is this itself a new and mighty weapon in the battle of competition. By unseen threads it, moreover, draws the disposable money, scattered in larger or smaller masses over the surface of society, into the hands of individual or associated capitalists. It is the specific machine for the centralisation of capitals.

The centralisation of capital becomes more intense, in proportion as the specifically capitalist mode of production develops along with accumulation. In its turn, centralisation becomes one of the greatest levers of this development. It completes the process of accumulation by enabling the capitalists to extend their business. And the extension of industrial undertakings forms the starting-point for a comprehensive organisation of the co-operation of large numbers, for a broader development of their material impulses.

But it is clear that the accumulation of capital, its gradual growth by the means of capitalised surplus-value, is a slow process in comparison with the process of centralisation, which only draws already existing capitals together and alters their grouping. The world would still to-day (1874) be without railways if it had had to wait till the accumulation of some individual capitals reached a point permitting the latter to undertake the construction of a railway line. Centralisation, through the medium of joint-stock companies, made that construction possible without delay. And, whereas centralisation thus accentuates and accelerates the effects of accumulation, it also extends the scope of, and hastens, the revolutions brought about in the technical composition of capital, which increase the latter's constant part at the expense of its variable one, thus reducing proportionately the demand for labour.

The masses of capital joined together overnight by the process of centralisation reproduce themselves and increase in the same way as other capitals, but more rapidly; and thus they become new and powerful levers of accumulation.

The increasing bulk of individual masses of capital becomes the material basis of an uninterrupted revolution in the mode of production itself. Continually the capitalist mode of production conquers branches of industry not yet wholly, or only sporadically, or only formally, subjugated by it. At the same time there grow up on its soil new branches of industry, such as could not exist without it. Finally, in the branches of industry already carried on upon the capitalist basis, the productiveness of labour is made to ripen, as if in a hothouse. In all these cases, the number of labourers falls in proportion to the mass of the means of production worked up by them. An ever increasing part of the capital is turned into means of production, an ever decreasing one into labour power. With the extent, the concentration and the technical efficiency of the means of production, the degree lessens progressively in which the latter are means of employment for labourers. A steam plough is an incomparably more efficient means of production than the ordinary plough, but the capital expended on it is an incomparably smaller means for employing men than if it were laid out in ordinary ploughs.

At first, it is the mere adding of new capital to old, which allows of the expansion and technical revolution of the material conditions of the process of production. But soon the change of composition and the technical transformation get more or less completely hold of all old capital that has reached the term of its reproduction, and therefore has to be replaced.

On the one hand, therefore, the additional capital formed in the course of accumulation attracts fewer and fewer labourers in proportion to its magnitude. On the other hand, the old capital periodically reproduced with change of composition, repels more and more of the labourers formerly employed by it.

The development of the productive power of labour, and the change thence resulting in the organic composition of capital, do not merely keep pace with the advance of accumulation, or with the growth of social wealth. They develop at a much quicker rate, because mere accumulation, the absolute increase of the total social capital, is accompanied by the centralisation of the individual capitals of which that total is made up; and because the change in the technological composition of the additional capital causes a similar change in the technological composition of the original capital. With the advance of accumulation, therefore, the proportion of constant to variable capital changes. If it was originally say

1 : 1, it now becomes successively 2 : 1, 3 : 1, 4 : 1, 5 : 1, 7 : 1, &c., so that, as the capital increases, instead of $\frac{1}{2}$ of its total value, only $\frac{1}{3}$, $\frac{1}{4}$, $\frac{1}{5}$, $\frac{1}{6}$, $\frac{1}{8}$, &c., is transformed into labour power, and, on the other hand, $\frac{2}{3}$, $\frac{3}{4}$, $\frac{4}{5}$, $\frac{5}{6}$, $\frac{7}{8}$, into means of production. Since the demand for labour is determined not by the amount of capital as a whole, but by its variable constituent alone, that demand falls progressively with the increase of the total capital, instead of, as previously assumed, rising in proportion to it. It falls relatively to the magnitude of the total capital, and at an accelerated rate, as this magnitude increases. With the growth of the total capital, its variable constituent or the labour power incorporated in it, also increases, but in a constantly diminishing proportion. The intermediate pauses are shortened, in which accumulation works as simple extension of production, on a given technical basis. It is not merely that an accelerated accumulation of total capital, accelerated in a constantly growing progression, is needed to absorb an additional number of labourers, or even, on account of the constant metamorphosis of old capital, to keep employed those already functioning. In its turn, this increasing accumulation and centralisation becomes a source of new changes in the composition of capital, of a more accelerated diminu tion of its variable, as compared with its constant constituent. This accelerated relative diminution of the variable constituent, that goes along with the accelerated increase of the total capital, and moves more rapidly than this increase makes it appear, on the other hand, as if the labouring popu lation were increasing faster than the variable capital or the means of employment. But in fact, it is capitalistic accumulation itself that constantly produces a population of greater extent than suffices for the needs of the self-expansion of capital. The labouring population therefore produces, along with the accumulation of capital produced by it, in an ever increasing degree the means by which itself is made relatively superfluous. This is a law of population peculiar to the capitalist mode of production; and in fact every special historic mode of production has its own special laws of population, historically valid within its limits alone. An abstract law of

population exists for plants and animals only, and only in so far as man has not interfered with them.

But if a surplus labouring population is a necessary product of accumulation or of the development of wealth on a capitalist basis, this surplus population becomes, conversely, the lever of capitalistic accumulation, nay, a condition of existence of the capitalist mode of production. It forms a disposable industrial reserve army, that belongs to capital quite as absolutely as if the latter had bred it at its own cost. Independently of the limits of the actual increase of population, it creates, for the changing need of the self-expansion of capital, a mass of human material always ready for exploitation. With accumulation, and the development of the productiveness of labour that accompanies it, the power of sudden expansion of capital grows also. The mass of social wealth, overflowing with the advance of accumulation, and transformable into additional capital, thrusts itself frantically into old branches of production, whose market suddenly expands, or into newly formed branches, such as railways, &c., the need for which grows out of the development of the old ones. In all such cases, there must be the possibility of throwing great masses of men suddenly on the decisive points without withdrawing them from the other branches of production. Over-population supplies these masses. The course characteristic of modern industry, viz., a decennial cycle (interrupted by smaller oscillations) of periods of average activity, production at high pressure, crisis and stagnation, depends on the constant formation, the greater or lesser absorption, and the re-formation of the industrial reserve army or surplus population.

This peculiar course of modern industry, which occurs in no earlier period of human history, was also impossible in the childhood of capitalist production. The composition of capital (c and v) changed but very slowly. With its accumulation, therefore, there kept pace, on the whole, a corresponding growth in the demand for labour. Slow as was the advance of accumulation compared with that of more modern times, it found a check in the natural limits of the exploitable labouring population, limits, which could only be got rid of by forcible means to be mentioned later. The expansion by fits and starts of the scale of production is the preliminary to its equally sudden contraction; the latter again evokes the former, but the former is impossible without disposable human material, without an increase in the number of labourers independently of the absolute growth of the population. This increase is effected by the simple process that constantly "sets free" a part of the labourers; by methods which lessen the number of labourers employed in proportion to the increased production. The whole form of the movement of modern industry depends, therefore, upon the constant transformation of a part of the labouring population into unemployed or half-employed hands. Capitalist production can by no means content itself with the quantity of disposable labour power which the natural increase of population yields. It requires for its free play an industrial reserve army independent of these natural limits.

Up to this point it has been assumed that the increase or diminution of the variable capital corresponds rigidly with the increase or diminution of the number of labourers employed. The number of labourers commanded by capital may remain the same, or even fall, while the variable capital increases. This is the case if the individual labourer yields more labour, and therefore his wages increase, and this although the price of labour remains the same or even falls, only more slowly than the mass of labour rises. It is the absolute interest of every capitalist to press a given quantity of labour out of a smaller, rather than a greater number of labourers, if the cost is about the same. In the latter case, the outlay of constant capital increases in proportion to the mass of labour set in action; in the former that increase is much slower. The more extended the scale of production, the stronger this motive. Its force increases with the accumulation of capital.

We have seen that the development of the capitalist mode of production and of the productive power of labour—at once the cause and effect of accumulation—enables the capitalist, with the same outlay of variable capital, to set in action more labour by greater exploitation of each individual labour power. We have further seen that the capitalist buys with the same capital a greater mass of labour power, as he progressively replaces skilled labourers by less skilled, mature labour power by immature, male by female, that of adults by that of young persons or children. On the one hand, therefore, with the progress of accumulation, a larger variable capital sets more labour in action without enlisting more labourers; on the other, a variable capital of the same magnitude sets in action more labour with the same mass of labour power; and, finally, a greater number of inferior labour powers by displacement of higher.

The production of a relative surplus population, or the setting free of labourers, goes on therefore yet more rapidly than the technical revolution of the process of production that is accelerated by the advance of accumulation; and more rapidly than the corresponding diminution of the variable part of capital as compared with the constant. In proportion as the productiveness of labour increases, capital increases its supply of labour more quickly than its demand for labourers. The over-work of the employed part of the working class swells the ranks of the reserve, whilst conversely the greater pressure that the latter by its competition exerts on the former, forces these to submit to over-work and to subjugation under the dictates of capital. The condemnation of one part of the working-class to enforced idleness by the over-work of the other part, and the converse, becomes a means of enriching the individual capitalists, and accelerates at the same time the production of the industrial reserve army on a scale corresponding with the advance of social accumulation. How important is this element in the formation of the relative surplus population is shown by the example of England. Her technical means for "saving" labour are colossal. Nevertheless, if to-morrow (1867) labour generally were reduced to a rational amount, and proportioned to the different sections of the working-class according to age and sex, the working population to hand would be absolutely insufficient for the carrying on of national production on its present scale. The great majority of the labourers now "unproductive" would have to be turned into "productive" ones.

Taking them as a whole, the general movements of wages

are exclusively regulated by the expansion and contraction of the industrial reserve army, and these again correspond to the periodic changes of the industrial cycle. They are, therefore, not determined by the variations of the absolute number of the working population, but by the varying proportions in which the working class is divided into active and reserve army, by the increase or diminution in the relative amount of the surplus-population, by the extent to which it is now absorbed, now set free. For modern industry with its decennial cycles and periodic phases (average activity, high pressure, crisis, and stagnation) which moreover, as accumulation advances, are complicated by irregular oscillations following each other more and more quickly, that would indeed be a beautiful law, which pretends to make the action of capital dependent on the absolute variation of the population, instead of regulating the demand and supply of labour by the alternate expansion and contraction of capital, the labour-market now appearing relatively under-full, because capital is expanding, now again over-full, because it is contracting. Yet this is the dogma of the economists. According to them, wages rise in consequence of accumulation of capital. The higher wages stimulate the working population to more rapid multiplication, and this goes on until the labour-market becomes too full. Wages fall, and now we have the reverse of the medal. The working population is little by little decimated as the result of the fall in wages, so that capital is again in excess relatively to them, or, as others explain it, falling wages which allow of an increase of profit again accelerate accumulation, whilst, at the same time, the lower wages hold the increase of the working-class in check. Then comes again the time, when the supply of labour is less than the demand, wages rise, and so on. A beautiful mode of motion this for developed capitalist production! Before, in consequence of the rise of wages, any positive increase of the population really fit for work could occur, the time would have been passed again and again, during which the industrial campaign must have been carried through, the battle fought and won.

Between 1849 and 1859, a rise of wages practically only

nominal, though accompanied by falling prices of corn, took place in the English agricultural districts. In Wiltshire, e. g., the weekly wages rose from 7s.[1] to 8s.; in Dorsetshire from 7s. or 8s. to 9s., &c. This was the result of an unusual exodus of the agricultural population caused by the demands of war, the vast extension of railroads, factories, mines, &c. The lower the wages, the higher is the proportion in which ever so insignificant a rise of them expresses itself. If the weekly wage, e. g., is 20s. and it rises to 22s., that is a rise of 10 per cent.; but if it is only 7s. and it rises to 9s., that is a rise of 28$\frac{4}{7}$ per cent., which sounds very fine. Everywhere the farmers were howling, and the "London Economist," with reference to these starvation-wages, prattled quite seriously of "a general and substantial advance." What did the farmers do now? Did they wait until, in consequence of this brilliant remuneration, the agricultural labourers had so increased and multiplied that their wages must fall again? They introduced more machinery, and in a moment the labourers were redundant again in a proportion satisfactory even to the farmers. There was now "more capital" laid out in agriculture than before, and in a more productive form. With this the demand for labour fell, not only relatively, but absolutely.

The above economic dogma confuses the laws that regulate the general movement of wages with the laws that distribute the working population over the different spheres of production. If, e. g., in consequence of favourable circumstances, accumulation in a particular sphere of production becomes especially active, and profits in it, being greater than the average profits, attract additional capital, of course the demand for labour rises and wages also rise. The higher wages draw a larger part of the working population into the more favoured sphere, until it is glutted with labour power, and wages at length fall again to their average level or below it, if the pressure is too great. Then, not only does the immigration of labourers into the branch of industry in question cease; it gives place to their emigration. Here the political

[1] s = shilling = ap. 25 cents in U. S. coin. [M. E.]

economist thinks he sees the why and wherefore of an absolute increase of workers accompanying an increase of wages, and of a diminution of wages accompanying an absolute increase of labourers. But he sees really only the local oscillation of the labour market in a particular sphere of production—he sees only the phenomena accompanying the distribution of the working population into the different spheres of outlay of capital, according to its varying needs.

The industrial reserve army, during the periods of stagna. tion and average prosperity, weighs down the active labour-army; during the periods of over-production and paroxysm, it holds its claims in check. Relative surplus-population is therefore the pivot upon which the law of demand and supply of labour works. It confines the field of action of this law within the limits absolutely convenient to the activity of exploitation and to the domination of capital. The mechanism of capitalistic production so manages matters that the in-crease of capital is accompanied by no corresponding rise in the general demand for labour.

As soon, therefore, as the labourers learn the secret, how it comes to pass that in the same measure as they work more, as they produce more wealth for others, and as the productive power of their labour increases, so in the same measure even their function as a means of self-expansion of capital becomes more and more precarious for them; as soon as they discover that the degree of intensity of the com-petition among themselves depends wholly on the pressure of the relative surplus-population; as soon as, by Trades' Unions, &c., they try to organise a regular co-operation be-tween employed and unemployed in order to destroy or to weaken the ruinous effects of this natural law of capitalistic production on their class: so soon capital and its sycophant, political economy, cry out at the infringement of the "eternal" and so to say "sacred" law of supply and demand. Every combination of employed and unemployed disturbs the "harmonious" action of this law. But, on the other hand, as soon as, e. g., in the colonies adverse circumstances pre-vent the creation of an industrial reserve army and, with it, the absolute dependence of the working class upon the capitalist class, capital, along with its scientific apologist, rebels against the "sacred" law of supply and demand, and tries to check its inconvenient action by forcible means and State interference.

The relative surplus population exists in every possible form. Every labourer belongs to it during the time when he is only partially employed or wholly unemployed. In the factories properly so-called, as in all the great workshops, where machinery enters as a factor, or where only the modern division of labour is carried out, large numbers of boys are employed up to the age of maturity. When this term is once reached, only a small number continue to find employment in the same branches of industry, whilst the majority are regularly discharged. Part of them emigrates, following in fact capital that has emigrated. One consequence is that female population grows more rapidly than the male, *teste* England. That the natural increase of the number of labourers does not satisfy the requirements of the accumulation of capital, and yet all the time is in excess of them, is a contradiction inherent to the movement of capital itself. It wants larger numbers of youthful labourers, a smaller number of adults. The contradiction is not more glaring than that other one that there is a complaint of the want of hands, while at the same time many thousands are out of work, because the division of labour chains them to a particular branch of industry. The consumption of labour power by capital is, besides, so rapid that the labourer, half-way through his life, has already more or less completely lived himself out. He falls into the ranks of the supernumeraries, or is thrust down from a higher to a lower step in the scale. It is precisely among the work-people of modern industry, that we meet with the shortest duration of life. Dr. Lee, Medical Officer of Health for Manchester, stated "that the average age at death of the Manchester . . . upper middle class was 38 years, while the average age at death of the labouring class was 17; while at Liverpool those figures were represented as 35 against 15. It thus appeared that the well-to-do classes had a lease of life which was more than double the value of that which fell to the lot of the less favoured citizens." [1]

As soon as capitalist production takes possession of agriculture and in proportion to the extent to which it does so, the demand for an agricultural labouring population falls absolutely, while the accumulation of the capital employed in agriculture advances. Part of the agricultural population is therefore constantly on the point of passing over into an urban or manufacturing proletariat, and on the look-out for circumstances favourable to this transformation. This source of relative surplus-population is thus constantly flowing. But the constant flow towards the towns presupposes, in the country itself, a constant latent surplus-population, the extent of which becomes evident only when its channels of outlet open to exceptional width. The agricultural labourer is therefore reduced to the minimum of wages, and always stands with one foot already in the swamp of pauperism.

Another category of the relative surplus-population forms a part of the active labour army, but with extremely irregular employment. Hence it furnishes to capital an inexhaustible reservoir of disposable labour power. Its conditions of life sink below the average normal level of the working class; this makes it at once the broad basis of special branches of capitalist exploitation. It is characterised by maximum of working time, and minimum of wages. Its chief form is "domestic industry." It recruits itself constantly from the supernumerary forces of modern industry and agriculture, and specially from those decaying branches of industry where handicraft is yielding to manufacture, manufacture to machinery. But it forms at the same time a self-reproducing element of the working class, taking a proportionately greater part in the general increase of that class than the other elements. In fact, not only the number of births and deaths, but the absolute size of the families stand in inverse proportion to the height of wages, and therefore to the amount of means of subsistence of which the different categories of labourers dispose. This law

[1] Opening address to the Sanitary Conference, Birmingham, January 15th, 1875, by J. Chamberlain, Mayor of the town, now (1883) President of the Board of Trade.

of capitalistic society would sound absurd to savages, or even civilised capitalists. It calls to mind the boundless reproduction of animals individually weak and constantly hunted down.

The lowest sediment of the relative surplus-population finally dwells in the sphere of pauperism. Exclusive of vagabonds, criminals, prostitutes, in a word, the "dangerous" classes, this layer of society consists of three categories. First, those able to work. One need only glance superficially at the statistics of English pauperism to find that the quantity of paupers increases with every crisis, and diminishes with every revival of trade. Second, orphans and pauper children. These are candidates for the industrial reserve-army, and are, in times of great prosperity, as 1860, *e. g.*, speedily and in large numbers enrolled in the active army of labourers. Third, the demoralised and ragged, and those unable to work, chiefly people who succumb to their incapacity for adaptation, due to the division of labour, and whose life is longer than the normal life of working-men; finally, the victims of industry, whose number increases with the increase of dangerous machinery, of mines, chemical works, &c., the mutilated, the sickly, the widows, &c. Pauperism is the hospital of the active labour-army and the dead weight of the industrial reserve-army. Its production is included in that of the relative surplus-population, its necessity in theirs; along with the surplus-population, pauperism forms a condition of capitalist production, and of the capitalist development of wealth. It enters into the *faux frais* of capitalist production; but capital knows how to throw these, for the most part, from its own shoulders on to those of the working-class and the lower middle class.

The greater the social wealth, the functioning capital, the extent and energy of its growth, and, therefore, also the absolute mass of the proletariat and the productiveness of its labour, the greater is the industrial reserve army. The same causes which develop the expansive power of capital, develop also the labour power at its disposal. The relative mass of the industrial reserve army increases therefore with the sources of wealth. But the greater this reserve army in proportion to the active labour army, the greater is the mass of a consolidated surplus-population, whose misery is in inverse ratio to its torment of labour. The more extensive, finally, the lazarus-layers of the working-class, and the industrial reserve army, the greater is pauperism. *This is the absolute general law of capitalist accumulation.* Like all other laws it is modified in its working by many circumstances, the analysis of which does not concern us here.

The folly is now patent of the economic wisdom, that preaches to the labourers the accommodation of their number to the requirements of capital. The mechanism of capitalist production and accumulation constantly effects this adjustment. The first word of this adaptation is the creation of a relative surplus-population, or industrial reserve army. Its last word is the misery of constantly extending strata of the active army of labour, and the dead weight of pauperism.

The law by which a constantly increasing quantity of means of production, thanks to the advance in the productiveness of social labour, may be set in movement by a progressively diminishing expenditure of human power, this law, in a capitalist society, is expressed thus: the higher the productiveness of labour, the greater is the pressure of the labourers on the means of employment, the more precarious, therefore, becomes their condition of existence, viz., the sale of their own labour power for the increasing of another's wealth, or for the self-expansion of capital. The fact that the means of production, and the productiveness of labour, increase more rapidly than the productive population, expresses itself, therefore, capitalistically in the inverse form that the labouring population always increases more rapidly than the conditions under which capital can employ this increase for its own self-expansion.

We saw in the 8th and 9th chapters, within the capitalist system all methods for raising the social productiveness of labour are brought about at the cost of the individual labourer; all means for the development of production transform themselves into means of domination over, and exploitation of, the producers; they mutilate the labourer into a fragment of a man, degrade him to the level of an appendage of a machine, destroy every remnant of charm in his work and turn it into a hated toil; they estrange from him the intellectual potentialities of the labour process in the same proportion as science is incorporated in it as an independent power; they distort the conditions under which he works, subject him during the labour process to a despotism the more hateful for its meanness; they transform his lifetime into working-time, and drag his wife and child beneath the wheels of the Juggernaut of capital. But all methods for the production of surplus-value are at the same time methods of accumulation; and every extension of accumulation becomes again a means for the development of those methods. It follows, therefore, that in proportion as capital accumulates, the lot of the labourer, be his payment high or low, must grow worse. The law, finally, that always equilibrates the relative surplus-population, or industrial reserve army, to the extent and energy of accumulation, this law rivets the labourer to capital more firmly than the wedges of Hephaistos did Prometheus to the rock. It establishes an accumulation of misery, corresponding with accumulation of capital. Accumulation of wealth at one pole is, therefore, at the same time accumulation of misery, agony of toil, slavery, ignorance, brutality, moral degradation, at the opposite pole.

CHAPTER XIV

THE SO-CALLED PRIMITIVE ACCUMULATION

(Extracted from vol. II, ch. 26, 27, 28, 29, 30, 31.)

WE have seen how through capital surplus-value is made, and from surplus-value more capital. But the accumulation of capital presupposes surplus-value; surplus-value presupposes capitalistic production; capitalistic production presupposes the pre-existence of considerable masses of capital and of labour power in the hands of producers of commodities. The whole movement, therefore, seems to turn in a vicious circle, out of which we can only get by supposing a primitive accumulation preceding capitalistic accumulation; an ac-

cumulation not the result of the capitalist mode of production, but its starting point.

Political Economy explains the origin of this primitive
accumulation as an anecdote of the past. In times long gone
by there were two sorts of people; one, the diligent, intelligent,
and, above all, frugal élite; the other, lazy rascals, spending
their substance, and more, in riotous living. Thus it came to
pass that the former sort accumulated wealth, and the latter
sort had at last nothing to sell except their own skins. And
from this original sin dates the poverty of the great majority
that, despite all its labour, has up to now nothing to sell but
itself, and the wealth of the few that increases constantly
although they have long ceased to work. In actual history it is
notorious that conquest, enslavement, robbery, murder,
briefly force, play the great part. In the tender annals of
Political Economy, the idyllic reigns from time immemorial.
Right and "labour" were from all time the sole means of
enrichment, the present year of course always excepted. As
a matter of fact, the methods of primitive accumulation are
anything but idyllic.

The capitalist system presupposes the complete separation
of the labourers from all property in the means by which they
can realise their labour. As soon as capitalist production is
once on its own legs, it not only maintains this separation, but
reproduces it on a continually extending scale. The process,
therefore, that clears the way for the capitalist system, can be
none other than the process which takes away from the
labourer the possession of his means of production. The so-
called primitive accumulation, therefore, is nothing else than
the historical process of divorcing the producer from the
means of production.

The economic structure of capitalistic society has grown
out of the economic structure of feudal society. The dissolution of the latter set free the elements of the former.

The labourer could only dispose of his own person after
he had ceased to be attached to the soil and ceased to be the
slave, serf, or bondman of another. To become a free seller
of labour power, who carries his commodity wherever he finds
a market, he must further have escaped from the regime of

the guilds, their rules for apprentices and journeymen, and the impediments of their labour regulations. Hence, the historical movement which changes the producers into wage-workers, appears, on the one hand, as their emancipation from serfdom and from the fetters of the guilds, and this side alone exists for our bourgeois historians. But, on the other hand, these new freemen became sellers of themselves only after they had been robbed of all their own means of production, and of all the guarantees of existence afforded by the old feudal arrangements. And the history of this, their expropriation, is written in the annals of mankind in letters of blood and fire.

The industrial capitalists, these new potentates, had on their part not only to displace the guild masters of handicrafts, but also the feudal lords, the possessors of the sources of wealth. In this respect their conquest of social power appears as the fruit of a victorious struggle both against feudal lordship and its revolting prerogatives, and against the guilds and the fetters they laid on the free development of production and the free exploitation of man by man. The *chevaliers d'industrie*, however, only succeeded in supplanting the knights of the sword by making use of events of which they themselves were wholly innocent. They have risen by means as vile as those by which the Roman freed-man once on a time made himself the master of his *patronus*.

The starting-point of the development that gave rise to the wage-labourer as well as to the capitalist, was the servitude of the labourer. The advance consisted in a change of form of this servitude, in the transformation of feudal exploitation into capitalist exploitation. To understand its march, we need not go back very far. Although we come across the first beginnings of capitalist production as early as the 14th or 15th century, sporadically, in certain towns of the Mediterranean, the capitalist era dates from the 16th century. Wherever it appears, the abolition of serfdom has been long effected, and the highest development of the middle ages, the existence of sovereign towns, has been long on the wane.

In the history of primitive accumulation, those moments are particularly important, when great masses of men are suddenly and forcibly torn from their means of subsistence, and hurled as free and "unattached" proletarians on the labour market. The expropriation of the peasant from the soil, is the basis of the whole process. We will study the latter's history in England.

In England, serfdom had practically disappeared in the last part of the 14th century. The immense majority of the population consisted then, and to a still larger extent, in the 15th century,[1] of free peasant proprietors. In the larger seignorial domains, the old bailiff, himself a serf, was displaced by the free farmer. The wage-labourers of agriculture consisted partly of peasants, who utilised their leisure time by working on the large estates, partly of an independent special class of wage-labourers few in numbers. The latter also were practically at the same time peasant farmers, since, besides their wages, they had allotted to them arable land to the extent of 4 or more acres together with their cottages. Besides they, with the rest of the peasants, enjoyed the usufruct of the common land, which gave pasture to their cattle, furnished them with timber, fire-wood, turf, &c. In all countries of Europe, feudal production is characterised by division of the soil among the greatest possible number of sub-feudatories. The might of the feudal lord, like that of the sovereign, depended not on the length of his rent roll, but on the number of his subjects, and the latter depended on the number of peasant proprietors. Although, therefore, the English land, after the Norman conquest (1066), was distributed in gigantic baronies, one of which often included some 900 of the old Anglo-Saxon lordships, it was bestrewn with small peasant properties, only here and there interspersed with great seignorial domains. Such conditions, together with the prosperity of the towns so characteristic of the 15th century, allowed of much wealth of the people; but it excluded the possibility of capitalistic wealth.

The prelude of the revolution that laid the foundation of

---

[1] Macaulay: History of England, 10th ed., London, 1854, I, pp. 333, 334. Even in the last third of the 17th century, ⅘ of the English people were agricultural (l. c., p. 413).

the capitalist mode of production, was played in the last third of the 15th, and the first third of the 16th century. A mass of free proletarians was hurled on the labour-market, by the breaking-up of the bands of feudal retainers, who everywhere uselessly filled house and castle. Although the royal power, itself a product of bourgeois development, in its striving after absolute sovereignty, forcibly hastened on the dissolution of these bands of retainers, it was by no means the sole cause of it. In insolent conflict with king and parliament, the great feudal lords created an incomparably larger proletariat by the forcible driving of the peasantry from the land, to which the latter had the same feudal right as the lord himself, and by the usurpation of the common lands. The rapid rise of the Flemish wool manufactures, and the corresponding rise in the price of wool in England, gave the direct impulse to these evictions. The old nobility had been devoured by the great feudal wars. The new nobility was the child of its time, for which money was the power of all powers. Transformation of arable land into sheep-walks was, therefore, its cry. Harrison, in his "Description of England, prefixed to Holinshed's Chronicle," describes how the expropriation of small peasants is ruining the country. The dwellings of the peasant and the cottages of the labourers were razed to the ground or doomed to decay. "If," says Harrison, "the old records of every manour be sought ... it will soon appear that innumerable houses and small farms have disappeared, that the soil feeds far less people, that many towns are decayed, though a few new ones have arisen; ... Of towns and villages pulled down for sheep-walks, and no more but the lordships now standing in them ... I could say somewhat." The complaints of these old chroniclers are always exaggerated, but they reflect faithfully the impression made on contemporaries by the revolution in the conditions of production.

Legislation was terrified at this revolution. In his history of Henry VII, Bacon says: "Inclosures at that time (1489) began to be more frequent, whereby arable land was turned into pasture, which was easily rid by a few herdsmen; and tenancies for years, lives, and at will (whereupon much of the yeomanry lived) were turned into demesnes. This bred a decay of people, and (by consequence) a decay of towns, churches, tithes, and the like. . . . In remedying of this inconvenience the king's wisdom was admirable, and the parliament's at that time. . . . They took a course to take away depopulating inclosures, and depopulating pasturage." An Act of Henry VII, 1489, cap. 19, forbade the destruction of all "houses of husbandry" to which at least 20 acres of land belonged. By an Act, 25 Henry VIII, the same law was renewed. It recites, among other things, "that many farms and large flocks of cattle, especially of sheep, are concentrated in the hands of a few men, whereby the rent of land has much risen and tillage has fallen off, churches and houses have been pulled down, and marvellous numbers of people have been deprived of the means wherewith to maintain themselves and their families." The Act, therefore, ordains the rebuilding of the decayed farm-steads, and fixes a proportion between corn land and pasture land, &c. An Act of 1533 recites that some owners possess 24,000 sheep, and limits the number to be owned to 2000. (In his *Utopia*—1516—Thomas More speaks of the remarkable country in which the sheep devour the men.)

The cry of the people and the legislation directed, for 150 years after Henry VII, against the expropriation of the small farmers and peasants, were alike fruitless.

The process of forcible expropriation of the people received in the 16th century a new and frightful impulse from the Reformation, and from the consequent colossal spoliation of the church property. The Catholic church was, at the time of the Reformation, feudal proprietor of a great part of the English land. The suppression of the monasteries, &c., hurled their inmates into the proletariat. The estates of the church were to a large extent given away to rapacious royal favourites, or sold at a nominal price to speculating farmers and citizens, who drove out, en masse, the hereditary sub-tenants and threw their holdings into one. The legally guaranteed property of the poorer folk in a part of the church's tithes was tacitly confiscated.

Even in the last decades of the 17th century, the yeomanry, the class of independent peasants, were more numerous than the class of farmers. They had formed the backbone of Cromwell's strength, and, even according to the confession of Macaulay, stood in favourable contrast to the drunken squires and to their servants, the country clergy, who had to marry their master's cast-off mistresses. Even the agricultural wage-labourers were still co-proprietors of the common land. About 1750, the yeomanry had disappeared, and so had, in the last decades of the 18th century, the last trace of the common land of the agricultural labourer.

After the restoration of the Stuarts, the landed proprietors carried, by legal means, an act of usurpation, effected everywhere on the Continent without any legal formality. They abolished the feudal tenure of land, *i. e.,* they got rid of all its obligations of the State, "indemnified" the State by taxes on the peasantry and the rest of the mass of the people, vindicated for themselves the rights of modern private property in estates to which they had only a feudal title, and, finally, passed those laws of settlement, which had the same effect on the English agricultural labourer, as the edict of the Tartar Boris Godunof on the Russian peasantry.

The "glorious Revolution" brought into power, along with William of Orange, the landlord and capitalist appropriators of surplus-value. They inaugurated the new era by practising on a colossal scale thefts of state lands, thefts that had been hitherto managed more modestly. These estates were given away, sold at a ridiculous figure, or even annexed to private estates by direct seizure. All this happened without the slightest observation of legal etiquette. The crown lands thus fraudulently appropriated, together with the robbery of the Church estates, as far as these had not been lost again during the republican revolution, form the basis of the to-day princely domains of the English oligarchy. The bourgeois capitalists favoured the operation with the view, among others, to transforming land into a commercial article, to extending the domain of modern agriculture on the large farm-system, and to increasing their supply of the free agricultural proletarians ready to hand. Besides, the new landed aristocracy was the natural ally of the new bankocracy, of the newly-hatched *haute finance,* and of the large manufacturers, then depending on protective duties.

Whilst the place of the independent yeoman was taken by small farmers on yearly leases, a servile rabble dependent on the pleasure of the landlords, the systematic robbery of the Communal lands helped especially, next to the theft of the State domains, to swell those large farms, that were called in the 18th century capital farms or merchant farms and to "set free" the agricultural population as proletarians for manu-facturing industry.

In the 19th century, the very memory of the connexion between the agricultural labourer and the communal prop-erty had, of course, vanished. To say nothing of more recent times, have the agricultural population received a farthing of compensation for the 3,511,770 acres of common land which between 1801 and 1831 were stolen from them, and by parliamentary devices presented to the landlords by the landlords?

The last process of wholesale expropriation of the agricul-tural population from the soil is, finally, the so-called clear-ing of estates, *i. e.,* the sweeping men off them. All the Eng-lish methods hitherto considered culminated in "clearing." But what "clearing of estates" really and properly signifies, we learn only in the promised land of modern romance, the Highlands of Scotland.

The Highland Celts were organised in clans, each of which was the owner of the land on which it was settled. The repre-sentative of the clan, its chief or "great man," was only the titular owner of this property, just as the Queen of England is the titular owner of all the national soil. When the English government succeeded in suppressing the intestine wars of these "great men," and their constant incursions into the Lowland plains, the chiefs of the clans by no means gave up their time-honoured trade as robbers; they only changed its form. On their own authority they transformed their nomi-nal right into a right of private property, and as this brought them into collision with their clansmen, resolved to drive them out by open force. In the 18th century the hunted-out Gaels were forbidden to emigrate from the country, with a view to driving them by force to Glasgow and other manufacturing towns. As an example of the method obtaining in the 19th century, the "clearing" made by the Duchess of Sutherland will suffice here. This person resolved on entering upon her government, to effect a radical economical cure, and to turn the whole country, whose population had already been, by earlier processes of the like kind, reduced to 15,000, into a sheepwalk. From 1814 to 1820 these 15,000 inhabitants, about 3,000 families, were systematically hunted and rooted out. All their villages were destroyed and burnt, all their fields turned into pasturage. British soldiers enforced this eviction, and came to blows with the inhabitants. One old woman was burnt to death in the flames of the hut, which she refused to leave. Thus this fine lady appropriated 794,000 acres of land that had from time immemorial belonged to the clan. She assigned to the expelled inhabitants about 6,000 acres on the sea-shore—2 acres per family. The 6,000 acres had until this time lain waste, and brought in no income to their owners. The Duchess, in the nobility of her heart, actually went so far as to let these at an average rent of 2 s. 6 d. per acre to the clansmen, who for centuries had shed their blood for her family. The whole of the stolen clan-land she divided into 29 great sheep farms, each inhabited by a single family, for the most part imported English farm-servants. In the year 1825 the 15,000 Gaels were already replaced by 131,000 sheep. The remnant of the aborigines flung on the sea-shore, tried to live by catching fish. But they had to expiate yet more bitterly their idolatry, romantic and of the mountains, for the "great men" of the clan. The smell of their fish rose to the noses of the great men. They scented some profit in it, and let the sea-shore to the great fishmongers of London. For the second time the Gaels were hunted out.

But, finally, part of the sheep-walks are turned into deer preserves. Every one knows that there are no real forests in England. The deer in the parks of the great are demurely domestic cattle, fat as London aldermen. Scotland is therefore the last refuge of the "noble passion." "In the Highlands," says Somers in 1848, "new forests are springing up like mushrooms. . . . The transformation of their land into sheep-walks

drove the Gaels on the sterile tracks of soil. Now deer are supplanting sheep; and these are once more reducing the small
remnants to more grinding penury. Deer-forests [1] and the
people cannot co-exist. One or other of the two must yield.
Let the forests be increased in number and extent during the
next quarter of a century, as they have been in the last, and
the Gaels will perish from their native soil.... This movement among the Highland proprietors is with some a matter
of ambition ... with some love of sport ... while others, of
a more practical cast, follow the trade in 'deer with an eye
solely to profit. For it is a fact, that a mountain range laid
out in forest is, in many cases, more profitable to the proprietor than when let as a sheep-walk.... The huntsman who
wants a deer-forest limits his offers by no other calculation
than the extent of his purse.... Sufferings have been inflicted
in the Highlands scarcely less severe than those occasioned
by the policy of the Norman kings.... Deer have received extended ranges, while men have been hunted within a narrower
and still narrower circle.... One after one the liberties of the
people have been cloven down.... And the oppressions are
daily on the increase.... The clearance and dispersion of the
people is pursued by the proprietors as a settled principle, as
an agricultural necessity, just as trees and brushwood are
cleared from the wastes of America or Australia; and the
operation goes on in a quiet, business-like way."

The spoliation of the Church's property, the fraudulent
alienation of the State domains, the robbery of the common
lands, the usurpation of feudal and clan property, and its
transformation into modern private property under circumstances of reckless terrorism, were just so many idyllic methods of primitive accumulation. They conquered the field for
capitalistic agriculture, made the soil part and parcel of capital, and created for the town industries the necessary supply
of an outlawed proletariat.

The proletariat thus deprived of its means of existence

---

[1] The deer-forests of Scotland contain not a single tree. The sheep
are driven from, and then the deer driven to the naked hills, and then
this is called a deer-forest. Not even timber-planting and real forest-
culture.

could not possibly be absorbed by the nascent manufactures as fast as it was thrown upon the world. On the other hand, these men, suddenly dragged from their wonted mode of life, could not as suddenly adapt themselves to the discipline of their new condition. They were turned *en masse* into beggars, robbers, vagabonds. Hence at the end of the 15th and during the whole of the 16th century, throughout Western Europe a bloody legislation against vagabondage. The fathers of the present working-class were chastised for their enforced transformation into vagabonds and paupers. Legislation treated them as "voluntary" criminals, and assumed that it depended on their own good will to go on working under the old conditions that no longer existed.

At the time when the capitalist system of production originated, the bourgeoisie, at its rise, used the power of the State to "regulate" wages, to lengthen the working-day, and to keep the labourer himself in dependence. This is an essential element of the so-called primitive accumulation.

The class of wage-labourers, which arose in the latter half of the 14th century, formed then and in the following century only a very small part of the population, well protected in its position by the independent peasant proprietary in the country and the guild-organisation in the town. In country and town master and workmen stood close together socially. Variable capital preponderated greatly over constant. The demand for wage-labour grew, therefore, rapidly with every accumulation of capital, whilst the supply of wage-labour followed but slowly.

Now that we have considered the forcible creation of a class of outlawed proletarians, the question remains: whence came the capitalists originally? For the expropriation of the agricultural population creates, directly, none but great landed proprietors. As far, however, as concerns the genesis of the farmer, we can, so to say, put our hand on it, because it is a slow process evolving through many centuries. In England the first form of the farmer is the bailiff, himself a serf. During the second half of the 14th century he is replaced by a farmer, whom the landlord provides with seed, cattle and implements. His condition is not very different from that of the peasant. Only he exploits more wage-labour. Soon he becomes a half-farmer. He advances one part of the agricultural stock, the landlord the other. The two divide the total product in proportions determined by contract. This form quickly disappears in England, to give place to the farmer proper, who makes his own capital breed by employing wage-labourers, and pays a part of the surplus product, in money or in kind, to the landlord as rent. So long, during the 15th century, as the independent peasant and the farm-labourer working for himself as well as for wages, enriched themselves by their own labour, the circumstances of the farmer, and his field of production, were equally mediocre. The agricultural revolution which commenced in the last third of the 15th century, and continued during almost the whole of the 16th (excepting, however, its last decades), enriched him just as speedily as it impoverished the mass of the agricultural people. The usurpation of the common lands allowed him to augment greatly his stock of cattle, almost without cost, whilst the cattle yielded him a richer supply of manure for the tillage of the soil. To this, was added in the 16th century, a very important element. At that time the contracts for farms ran for a long time, often for 99 years. The progressive fall in the value of the precious metals, and therefore of money, brought the farmers golden fruit. Apart from all the other circumstances discussed above, it lowered wages. A portion of the latter was now added to the profits of the farm. The continuous rise in the corn, wool, meat, in a word of all agricultural produce, swelled the money capital of the farmer without any action on his part, whilst the rent he paid, was calculated on the old value of money. Thus they grew rich at the expense both of their labourers and their landlords. No wonder therefore, that England, at the end of the 16th century, had a class of capitalist farmers, rich, considering the circumstances of the time.

The expropriation and expulsion of the agricultural population, intermittent but renewed again and again, supplied, as we saw, the town industries with a mass of proletarians entirely unconnected with the corporate guilds. The thinning-out of the independent, self-supporting peasants not only corresponded to the increasing density of the industrial proletariat. In spite of the smaller number of its cultivators, the soil brought forth as much or more produce, after as before, because the revolution in the conditions of landed property was accompanied by improved methods of culture, greater cooperation, concentration of the means of production, &c., and because not only were the agricultural wage-labourers put on the strain more intensely, but the field of production on which they worked for themselves became more and more contracted. With the setting free of a part of the agricultural population, therefore, their former means of nourishment were also set free. The peasant expropriated must buy their value in the form of wages, from his new master, the industrial capitalist. That which holds good of the means of subsistence holds with the raw materials of industry created by home agriculture. Suppose, *e. g.*, a part of the Westphalian peasants, who, at the time of Frederic II, all span flax, forcibly expropriated and hunted from the soil; and the other part that remained, turned into day-labourers of large farmers. At the same time arise large establishments for flax-spinning and weaving, in which the men "set free" now work for wages. The flax looks exactly as before. Not a fibre of it is changed, but a new social soul has popped into its body. It forms now a part of the constant capital of the master manufacturer. Formerly divided among a number of small producers, who cultivated it themselves and with their families spun it in retail fashion, it is now concentrated in the hand of one capitalist, who sets others to spin and weave it for him. The extra labour expended in flax-spinning realised itself formerly in extra income to numerous peasant families, or may be, in Frederic II's time, in taxes. It realises itself now in profit for a few capitalists. The spindles and looms, formerly scattered over the face of the country, are now crowded together in a few great labour-barracks, together with the labourers and the raw material. And spindles, looms, raw material, are now transformed, from means of independent existence for the spinners and weavers, into means for commanding them and sucking out of them unpaid labour. One does not perceive, when looking at the large manufactories and the large farms, that they have originated from the throwing into one of many small centres of production, and have been built up by the expropriation of many small independent prœ ducers.

The expropriation and eviction of a part of the agricultural population not only set free for industrial capital the labourers, their means of subsistence, and material for labour; it also created the home market.

Formerly, the peasant family produced the means of subsistence and the raw materials, which they themselves, for the most part, consumed. These raw materials and means of subsistence have now become commodities; the large farmer sells them, he finds his market in manufactures. Yarn, linen, coarse woollen stuffs—things whose raw materials had been within the reach of every peasant family, had been spun and woven by it for its own use—were now transformed into articles of manufacture, to which the country districts at once served for markets. Thus, hand in hand with the expropriation of the self-supporting peasants, with their separation from their means of production, goes the destruction of rural domestic industry. And only the destruction of rural domestic industry can give the internal market of a country that extension and consistence which the capitalist mode of production requires. Still the manufacturing period, properly so-called, does not succeed in carrying out this transformation radically and completely. Modern industry alone supplies, in machinery, the lasting basis of capitalistic agriculture, expropriates radically the enormous majority of the agricultural population, and completes the separation between agriculture and rural domestic industry, whose roots—spinning and weaving—it tears up. It therefore also, for the first time, conquers for industrial capital the entire home market.

The genesis of the industrial capitalist did not proceed in such a gradual way as that of the farmer. Doubtless many small guild-masters, and even wage-labourers, transformed themselves into small capitalists, and (by gradually extending exploitation of wage-labour and corresponding accumulation) into full-blown capitalists. The snail's pace of this method corresponded in no wise with the commercial requirements of the new world market that the great discoveries of the end of the 15th century created. But the middle ages had handed down two distinct forms of capital, usurer's capital and merchant's capital.

The money capital formed by means of usury and commerce was prevented from turning into industrial capital, in the country by the feudal constitution, in the towns by the guild organisation. Even as late as 1794, the small clothmakers of Leeds sent a deputation to Parliament, with a petition for a law to forbid any merchant from becoming a manufacturer. These fetters vanished with the dissolution of feudal society, with the expropriation and partial eviction of the country population. The new manufactures were established at sea-ports, or at inland points beyond the control of the old municipalities and their guilds. Hence in England an embittered struggle of the corporate towns against these new industrial nurseries.

The discovery of gold and silver in America, the extirpation, enslavement and entombment in mines of the aboriginal population, the beginning of the conquest and looting of the East Indies, the turning of Africa into a warren for the commercial hunting of black-skins, signalised the dawn of the era of capitalist production. These idyllic proceedings are the chief momenta of primitive accumulation. On their heels treads the commercial war of the European nations, with the globe for a theatre. It begins with the revolt of the Netherlands from Spain, assumes giant dimensions in England's anti-jacobin war, and is still going on in the opium wars against China, &c.

The different momenta of primitive accumulation distribute themselves now, more or less in chronological order, particularly over Spain, Portugal, Holland, France, and England. In England at the end of the 17th century, they arrive at a systematical combination in the colonies, the national debt, the modern mode of taxation, and the protectionist regime. These methods depend in part on brute force, *e. g.*, the colonial system. But they all employ the power of the State to hasten in hothouse fashion the process of transformation of the feudal mode of production into the capitalist mode, and to shorten the transition. Force is the midwife of every old society pregnant with a new one. It is itself an economic power.

Of the Christian colonial system, W. Howitt, a man who makes a speciality of Christianity, says: "The barbarities and desperate outrages of the so-called Christian race, throughout every region of the world, and upon every people they have been able to subdue, are not to be paralleled by those of any other race, however fierce, however untaught, and however reckless of mercy and of shame, in any age of the earth." [1] The history of the colonial administration of Holland—and Holland was the head capitalistic nation of the 17th century—"is one of the most extraordinary relations of treachery, bribery, massacre, and meanness." [2] To secure Malacca, the Dutch corrupted the Portuguese governor. He let them into the town in 1641. They hurried at once to his house and assassinated him, to "abstain" from the payment of £21,875, [3] the price of his treason. Wherever they set foot, devastation and depopulation followed. Banjuwangi, a province of Java, in 1750 numbered over 80,000 inhabitants, in 1811 only 8,000.

The English East India Company, as is well known, obtained, besides the political rule in India, the exclusive monopoly of the tea-trade, as well as of the Chinese trade in general, and of the transport of goods to and from Europe. But the coasting trade of India and between the islands, as well as the internal trade of India were the monopoly of the higher officials of the company. The monopolies of salt, opium, betel and other commodities, were inexhaustible mines of wealth. The officials themselves fixed the price and plundered at will the unhappy Hindus. The Governor General took part in this private traffic. His favourites received contracts under conditions whereby they, cleverer than the alchemists, made gold out of nothing. Great fortunes sprang up like

[1] William Howitt: "Colonisation and Christianity: A Popular History of the Treatment of the Natives by the Europeans in all their Colonies." London, 1838, p. 9.
[2] Thomas Stamford Raffles, late Lieut.-Gov. of that island. "History of Java and its dependencies." London, 1817.
[3] £ = pound = ap. $4.86 in U. S. coin. [M. E.]

mushrooms in a day; primitive accumulation went on without the advance of a shilling. The trial of Warren Hastings swarms with such cases. Here is an instance. A contract for opium was given to a certain Sullivan at the moment of his departure on an official mission to a part of India far removed from the opium district. Sullivan sold his contract to one Binn for £40,000; Binn sold it the same day for £60,000, and the ultimate purchaser who carried out the contract declared that after all he realised an enormous gain. According to one of the lists laid before Parliament, the Company and its officials between 1757-1766 got £6,000,000 from the Indians as gifts. Between 1769 and 1770, the English manufactured a famine by buying up all the rice and refusing to sell it again, except at fabulous prices.

The colonial system ripened, like a hot-house, trade and navigation. The "societies Monopolia" of Luther were powerful levers for concentration of capital. The colonies furnished a market for the budding manufactures, and, through the monopoly of the market, an increased accumulation. The treasures captured outside Europe by undisguised looting, enslavement, and murder, floated back to the mother-country and were there turned into capital. Holland, which first fully developed the colonial system, in 1648 stood already in the acme of its commercial greatness. It was "in almost exclusive possession of the East Indian trade and the commerce between the south-west and north-east of Europe. Its fisheries, marine, manufactures, surpassed those of any other country. The total capital of the Republic was probably more important than that of all the rest of Europe put together." Gülich forgets to add that by 1648 the people of Holland were more overworked, poorer and more brutally oppressed than those of all the rest of Europe put together.

To-day industrial supremacy implies commercial supremacy. In the period of manufacture properly so-called, it is, on the contrary, the commercial supremacy that gives industrial predominance. Hence the preponderant role that the colonial system played at that time. It was "the strange God" who perched himself on the altar cheek by jowl with the old Gods of Europe, and one fine day with a shove and a kick overthrew them all. It proclaimed surplus-value making as the sole end and aim of humanity.

The system of public credit, *i. e.* of national debts, whose origin we discover in Genoa and Venice as early as the middle ages, took possession of Europe generally during the manufacturing period. The colonial system with its maritime trade and commercial wars served as a forcing-house for it. Thus it first took root in Holland. National debts, *i. e.*, the alienation of the State—whether despotic, constitutional or republican—marked with its stamp the capitalistic era. The only part of the so-called national wealth that actually enters into the collective possessions of modern peoples is their national debt.

The public debt becomes one of the powerful levers of primitive accumulation. As with the stroke of an enchanter's wand it endows barren money with the power of breeding and thus turns it into capital, without the necessity of its exposing itself to the troubles and risks inseparable from its employment in industry or even in usury. The State-creditors actually give nothing away, for the sum lent is transformed into public bonds, easily negotiable, which go on functioning in their hands just as so much hard cash would. But further, apart from the class of lazy annuitants thus created, and from the improvised wealth of the financiers, middlemen between the government and the nation—as also apart from the tax-farmers, merchants, private manufacturers, to whom a good part of every State loan renders the service of a capital fallen from heaven—the national debt has given rise to joint-stock companies, to dealings in negotiable effects of all kinds, and to agiotage, in a word to stock-exchange gambling and the modern bankocracy.

From their birth on the great banks, decorated with national titles, were only associations of private speculators, who placed themselves by the side of governments, and, thanks to the privileges they received, were in a position to advance money of the State. Hence the accumulation of the national debt has no more infallible measure than the successive rise in the stock of these banks, whose full development dates from the founding of the Bank of England in 1694. The Bank of England began with lending its money to the Government at 8%; at the same time it was empowered by Parliament to coin money out of the same capital, by lending it again to the public in the form of bank-notes. It was allowed to use these notes for discounting bills, making advances on commodities, and for buying the precious metals. It was not long before this credit-money, made by the bank itself, became the coin in which the Bank of England made its loans to the State, and paid on account of the State the interest on the public debt. I was not enough that the bank gave with one hand and took back more with the other; it remained, even whilst receiving, the eternal creditor of the nation down to the last shilling advanced. Gradually it became the inevitable receptacle of the metallic hoard of the country, and the centre of gravity of all commercial credit. At the same time as England ceased burning witches, she began to hang the forgers of banknotes. What effect was produced on their contemporaries by the sudden uprising of this brood of bankocrats, financiers, rentiers, brokers, stock-jobbers, &c., is proved by the writings of that time.

With the national debt arose an international credit system, which often conceals one of the sources of primitive accumulation in this or that people. Thus the villainies of the Venetian thieving system formed one of the secret bases of the capital-wealth of Holland, to whom Venice in her decadence lent large sums of money. So also was it with Holland and England. Already at the beginning of the 18th century the Dutch manufactures were far outstripped. Holland had ceased to be the nation preponderant in commerce and industry. One of its main lines of business, therefore from 1701-1776, is the lending out of enormous amounts of capital, especially to its great rival England. The same thing is going on to-day (1867) between England and the United States.

As the national debt finds its support in the public revenue which must cover the yearly payments for interest, &c., the modern system of taxation was the necessary complement of the system of national loans. The loans enable the government to meet extraordinary expenses, without the taxpayers feeling it immediately, but they necessitate, as a consequence, increased taxes. On the other hand, the raising of taxation caused by the accumulation of debts contracted one after another compels the government always to have recourse to new loans for new extraordinary expenses. Modern fiscality, whose pivot is formed by taxes on the most necessary means of subsistence (thereby increasing their price), thus contains within itself the germ of automatic progression. Over-taxation is not an incident, but rather a principle. In Holland, therefore, where this system was first inaugurated, the great patriot, De Witt, has extolled it as the best system for making the wage-labourer submissive, frugal, industrious, and over-burdened with labour. The destructive influence that it exercises on the condition of the wage-labourer concerns us less, however, here, than the forcible expropriation resulting from it, of peasants, artisans, and in a word, all elements of the lower middle-class. On this there are not two opinions, even among the bourgeois economists. Its expropriating efficacy is still further heightened by the system of protection, which forms one of its integral parts.

The system of protection was an artificial means of manufacturing manufactures, of expropriating independent labourers, of capitalising the national means of production and subsistence, of forcibly abbreviating the transition from the mediaeval to the modern mode of production. The European states tore one another to pieces about the patent of this invention, and, once entered into the service of the surplus-value makers, did not merely lay under contribution in the pursuit of this purpose their own people, indirectly through protective duties, directly through export premiums, &c. They also forcibly rooted out, in their dependent countries, all industry, as, *e. g.*, England did with the Irish woollen manufacture. On the continent of Europe, after Colbert's example, the process was much simplified. The primitive industrial capital, here, came in part directly out of the State treasury.

Colonial system, public debts, heavy taxes, protection, commercial wars, &c., these children of the true manufacturing period increase gigantically during the infancy of modern industry.

So much trouble was thus required to complete the process of separation between labourers and conditions of labour, to transform at one pole, the social means of production and subsistence into capital, at the opposite pole, the mass of the population into wage-labourers. If money, according to Augier, "comes into the world with a congenital blood-stain on one cheek," capital comes dripping from head to foot, from every pore, with blood and dirt.[1]

CHAPTER XV

WHAT CAPITALIST ACCUMULATION LEADS TO

(Extracted from vol. II, ch. 32.)

WHAT does the primitive accumulation of capital, *i. e.*, its historical genesis, resolve itself into? In so far as it is not immediate transformation of slaves and serfs into wage-labourers, and therefore a mere change of form, it only means the expropriation of the immediate producers, *i. e.*, the dissolution of private property based on the labour of its owner.

The private property of the labourer in his means of production is the foundation of petty industry; petty industry, again, is an essential condition for the development of social production and of the free individuality of the labourer himself. Of course, this petty mode of production exists also under slavery, serfdom, and other states of dependence. But it flourishes, it lets loose its whole energy, only where the labourer is the private owner of his own means of labour set in action by himself: the peasant of the land which he cultivates, the artisan of the tool which he handles as a virtuoso.

---

[1] "Capital is said to fly turbulence and strife, and to be timid, which is very true; but this is very incompletely stating the question. Capital eschews no profit, or very small profit, just as Nature was formerly said to abhor a vacuum. With adequate profit, capital is very bold. A certain 10 per cent. will ensure its employment anywhere; 20 per cent. certain will produce eagerness; 50 per cent., positive audacity; 100 per cent. will make it ready to trample on all human laws; 300 per cent., and there is not a crime at which it will scruple, even to the chance of its owner being hanged. If turbulence and strife will bring a profit, it will freely encourage both. Smuggling and the slave-trade have amply proved all that is here stated." (T. J. Dunning, Trade-Unions and Strikes, London, 1860, p. 36.)

This mode of production presupposes parcelling of the soil, and scattering of the other means of production. As it excludes the concentration of these means of production, so also it excludes cooperation, division of labour within each separate process of production, the control over and the productive application of the forces of nature by society, and the free development of the social productive powers. It is compatible only with a system of production, and a society, moving within narrow and more or less primitive bounds. To perpetuate it, would be to decree universal mediocrity. At a certain stage of development it brings forth the material agencies for its own dissolution. From that moment new forces and new passions spring up in the bosom of society; but the old social organisation fetters them and keeps them down. It must be annihilated; it is annihilated.

Its annihilation, the transformation of the individualised and scattered means of production into socially concentrated ones, of the pigmy property of the many into the huge property of the few, the expropriation of the great mass of the people from the soil, from the means of subsistence and from the means of labour, this fearful and painful expropriation of the mass of people forms the prelude to the history of capital. Self-earned private property, that is based, so to say, on the fusing together of the isolated, independent labourer with the conditions of his labour, is supplanted by capitalistic private property, which rests on exploitation of the nominally free labour of others, *i. e.*, on wages-labour.

As soon as this process of transformation has sufficiently decomposed the old society from top to bottom, as soon as the labourers are turned into proletarians, their means of labour into capital, as soon as the capitalist mode of production stands on its own feet, then the further socialisation of labour and the further transformation of the land and other means of production, as well as the further expropriation of private proprietors, takes a new form. That which is now to be expropriated is no longer the labourer working for himself, but the capitalist exploiting many labourers. This expropriation is accomplished by the action of the immanent laws of capitalistic production itself, by the centralisation of capital. One capitalist always kill many.

Hand in hand with this centralisation, or this expropriation of many capitalists by few, develops, on an ever extending scale, the cooperative form of the labour-process, the conscious technical application of science, the economising of all means of production by combined, socialised labour, the entanglement of all peoples in the net of the world-market, and with this, the international character of the capitalistic regime.

Along with the constantly diminishing number of the magnates of capital, who usurp and monopolise all advantages of this process of transformation, grows the mass of misery, oppressions, slavery, degradation, exploitation; but with this too grows the revolt of the working-class, always increasing in numbers, and disciplined, united, organised by the very mechanism of the process of capitalist production itself. The monopoly of capital becomes a fetter upon the mode of production, which has sprung up and flourished along with, and under it. Centralisations of the means of production and socialisation of labour at last reach a point where they become incompatible with their capitalist integument. This integument is burst asunder. The knell of capitalist private property sounds. The expropriators are expropriated.

The capitalist mode of appropriation, the result of the capitalist mode of production, capitalist private property, is the first negation of individual private property, as founded on the labour of the proprietor. But capitalist production begets, with the inexorability of a law of nature, its own negation. This does not re-establish private property, but individual property based on the acquisitions of the capitalist era: *i. e.*, on cooperation and the possession in common of the land and of the means of production produced by labour itself.

The transformation of scattered private property, arising from individual labour, into capitalist private property was, naturally, a process incomparably more protracted, violent, and difficult, than the transformation of capitalistic private property, already practically resting on socialised production, into socialised property. In the former case, we had the expropriation of the mass of the people by a few usurpers; in the latter, we have the expropriation of a few usurpers by the mass of the people.

CHAPTER XVI

MONEY

(Extracted from vol. I, ch. 2 and 3.)

COMMODITIES cannot go to market and make exchanges of their own account. We must, therefore, have recourse to their guardians, the owners of commodities. The commodity possesses for the owner no immediate use-value. Otherwise, he would not bring it to the market. It has use-value for others; but for himself its only direct use-value is that of being a depository of exchange value, and, consequently, a means of exchange.[1] Therefore, he will part with it for commodities whose value in use is of service to him. All commodities are non-use-values for their owners, and use-values for their non-owners. Consequently, they must all change hands. This change of hands is what constitutes their exchange.

The sale of an object of utility first becomes possible when a greater quantity of it is available, than its proprietor needs. When this happens, the interested parties need only regard one another implicitly as the private owners of such objects. But such a state of reciprocal independence has no existence in a primitive society based on property in common, whether such a society takes the form of a patriarchal family, an ancient Indian community, or a Peruvian Inca State. The individual members of such a community, therefore, could not exchange their commodities. The exchange of commodities first begins on the boundaries of such communities, at

---

[1] "For two-fold is the use of every object.... The one is peculiar to the object as such, the other is not, as a sandal which may be worn, and is also exchangeable. Both are uses of the sandal, for even he who exchanges the sandal for the food he is in want of, makes use of the sandal as a sandal. But not in its natural way. For it has not been made for the sake of being exchanged." (Aristotle, *De Republica*, liber I, ch. 9.)

their points of contact with other similar communities, or with members of the latter. As soon as the custom of exchanging things has been established, it is extended to the internal intercourse of the community. The proportions in which they are exchangeable are at first quite a matter of chance. Meantime the need for foreign objects of utility gradually establishes itself. The constant repetition of exchange makes it a normal social act. In the course of time, therefore, some portion at least of the products of labour must be produced with a special view to exchange. From that moment the distinction becomes firmly established between the utility of an object for the purposes of consumption, and its utility for the purposes of exchange. Its use-value becomes distinguished from its exchange-value. On the other hand, the quantitative proportion in which the articles are exchangeable, becomes dependent on their production itself. Custom stamps them as values with definite magnitudes.

Every proprietor of commodities is desirous of parting with the latter only in exchange for such other commodities, the use-value of which is capable of satisfying his wants. But he would nevertheless be willing to part with them in exchange for any other sort of commodity having the same value, whether his own commodity has any use-value for the proprietor of the other commodity or not. This would be impossible, seeing that the other proprietors cannot afford to acquire commodities, the use-value of which is of no service to them. If, then, the exchange of commodities becomes customary a commodity is needed, which possesses use-value, not merely for the one or the other, but for all proprietors of commodities without exception—a commodity offering the possibility of exchanging it for every other sort of commodity. In other words, a general medium of exchange is required.

The problem arises simultaneously with the means of solving it. As soon as traffic has been developed in the course of which commodity-owners equate their goods to various others, it has already become customary for various commodities to be exchanged by their various proprietors, in the course of business, for a third, homogeneous type of commodity of equivalent value. Such last-mentioned commodity, being an exchange medium for *various* other commodities, assumes at once—although within narrow limits—the character of a general, or social, exchange medium. This character comes and goes with the momentary social contact that called it into life. Alternately and transiently it attaches itself first to this, and then to that commodity. But with the development of exchange it fixes itself firmly and exclusively to particular sorts of commodities, and becomes crystallised by assuming the money-form. Money is a commodity generally recognised by all commodity-owners as a medium of exchange for all their various commodities, and employed by them as such. The particular kind of commodity to which it sticks is at first a matter of accident. Nevertheless there are two circumstances whose influence is decisive. The money-form attaches itself either to the most important articles of exchange from outside; or else it attaches itself to the object of utility that forms, like cattle, the chief portion of indigenous alienable wealth. Nomad races are the first to develop the money-form, because all their worldly goods consist of moveable objects and are therefore directly alienable; and because their mode of life, by continually bringing them into contact with foreign communities, solicits the exchange of products. Man has often made man himself, under the form of slaves, serve as the primitive material of money, but has never used land for that purpose. Such an idea could only spring up in a bourgeois society already well developed. It dates from the last third of the 17th century, and the first attempt to put it in practice on a national scale was made a century afterwards, during the French bourgeois revolution.

In proportion as exchange bursts its local bonds, the character of money attaches itself to commodities that are by nature fitted to perform the social function of a universal equivalent. Those commodities are the precious metals. If money is to equate every other commodity to any amount, and thus to represent any exchange-value that may be wished for, a material is needed, whose every sample exhibits the same uniform qualities. On the other hand, since the difference between the magnitudes of value is purely quantitative, the money commodity must be divisible at will, and equally capable of being re-united. Gold and silver possess these properties by nature.

Although we may be aware that gold is money, and consequently directly exchangeable for all other commodities, yet that fact by no means tells how much 10 lbs., for instance, of gold is worth. Money, like every other commodity, cannot express the magnitude of its value except relatively in other commodities. This value is determined by the labour-time required for its production, and is expressed by the quantity of any other commodity that costs the same amount of labour-time. Such quantitative determination of its relative value takes place at the source of its production by means of barter. When it steps into circulation as money, its value is already given.

Throughout this work, I assume, for the sake of simplicity, gold as the money-commodity.

The first chief function of gold is to supply commodities with the material for the expression of their values, or to represent their values as magnitudes of the same denomination, qualitatively equal, and quantitatively comparable. It thus serves as a universal measure of value. And only by virtue of this function does gold become money.

It is not money that renders commodities commensurable. Just the contrary. It is because all commodities, as values, are realised human labour, and therefore commensurable, that their values can be measured by one and the same special commodity, and the latter be converted into the common measure of their values, *i. e.*, into money. Money as a measure of value is the phenomenal form that must of necessity be assumed by that measure of value which is immanent in commodities, labour-time.

The expression of the value of a commodity in gold is its money-form or price. A single equation, such as 1 ton of iron = 2 ounces of gold, now suffices to express the value of the iron in a socially valid manner, *i. e.* to indicate the value of the iron relatively to all other commodities, seeing that all other commodities likewise indicate their value in gold. But money itself has no price. Otherwise, we should be obliged to equate it to itself as its own equivalent.

The price or money-form of commodities is, like their form of value generally, a form quite distinct from their palpable bodily form; it is, therefore, a purely ideal or mental form. Although invisible, the value of iron, linen and corn has actual existence in these very articles: it is ideally made perceptible by their equality with gold. The value, or in other words, the quantity of human labour contained in a ton of iron, is expressed in imagination by such a quantity of the money-commodity as contains the same amount of labour as the iron.

Let us now accompany the owner of some commodity—say, the weaver of linen—to the scene of action, where the process of exchange takes place, the market. His 20 yards of linen has a definite price, $10. He exchanges it for the $10, and then, like a man of the good old stamp that he is, he parts with the $10 for a family Bible of the same price. The linen, which in his eyes is a mere commodity, a depository of value, he alienates in exchange for gold, which is the linen's value-form, and this form he again parts with for another commodity, the Bible, which is destined to enter his house as an object of utility and of edification to its inmates. The exchange becomes an accomplished fact by two metamorphoses of opposite yet supplementary character—the conversion of the commodity into money, and the re-conversion of the money into a commodity. For the weaver, these constitute two acts: selling and buying; and, the unity of the two acts, selling in order to buy.

The result of the whole transaction, as regards the weaver, is this, that instead of being in possession of the linen, he now has the Bible; instead of his original commodity, he now possesses another of the same value but of different utility. In like manner he procures his other means of subsistence and production. From his point of view, the whole process effectuates nothing more than the exchange of the product of his labour for the product of some one else's.

The exchange of commodities is therefore accompanied by the following changes in their form.

Commodity—Money—Commodity.
C—M—C.

The result of the whole process is, so far as concerns the objects themselves, C—C, the exchange of one commodity for another, the circulation of materialised social labour. When this result is attained, the process is at an end.

The money which serves to buy a commodity has previously been obtained by selling another one.

We will assume that the two gold pieces, in consideration of which our weaver has parted with his linen, are the metamorphosed shape of a quarter of wheat. The sale of the linen, C—M, is at the same time its purchase, M—C. But the sale is the first act of a process that ends with a transaction of an opposite nature, namely, the purchase of a Bible; the purchase of the linen, on the other hand, ends a movement that began with a transaction of an opposite nature, namely, with the sale of the wheat. C—M (linen—money), which is the first phase of C—M—C (linen—money—Bible), is also M—C (money—linen), the last phase of another movement C—M—C (wheat—money—linen). The metamorphosis of one commodity into money is therefore also invariably the retransformation of a second from money into a commodity.[1]

The same is the case in another direction. With regard to our weaver, the life of his commodity ends with the Bible, into which he has reconverted his $10. But suppose the seller of the Bible turns the $10 set free by the weaver into brandy. M—C, the concluding phase of C—M—C (linen—money—Bible), is also C—M, the first phase of C—M—C (Bible—money—brandy). The producer of a particular commodity has that one article alone to offer; this he sells very often in large quantities, but his many and various wants compel him to split up the price realised, the sum of money set free, into numerous purchases. Hence one sale leads to many purchases of various articles. The concluding metamorphosis of a commodity thus constitutes an aggregation of first metamorphoses of various other commodities.

The circuit made by every commodity with its sale and ensuing purchase of another commodity, is inextricably mixed

---

[1] The actual producer of gold or silver forms an exception. He exchanges his product directly for another commodity, without having first sold it.

up with the circuits of other commodities. The total of all the different circuits constitutes the circulation of commodities.

The circulation of commodities differs from the direct exchange of products, not only in form, but in substance. Only consider the course of events. The weaver has, as a matter of fact, exchanged his linen for a Bible, his own commodity for that of some one else. But this is true only so far as he himself is concerned. The seller of the Bible, who prefers something to warm his inside, no more thought of exchanging his Bible for linen than our weaver knew that wheat had been exchanged for his linen. B's commodity replaces that of A, but A and B do not mutually exchange those commodities. We see here, on the one hand, how the exchange of commodities breaks through all local and personal bounds inseparable from direct barter, and develops the circulation of the products of social labour; and on the other hand, how it develops a whole network of social relations entirely beyond the control of the actors. It is only because the farmer has sold his wheat that the weaver is enabled to sell his linen, only because the weaver has sold his linen that our hotspur is enabled to sell his Bible, and only because the latter has sold the water of everlasting life that the distiller is enabled to sell his *eau-de-vie*, and so on.

The process of circulation, therefore, does not, like direct barter of products, become extinguished upon the use-values changing places and hands. The money does not vanish on dropping out of the circuit of the metamorphosis of a given commodity. It is constantly being precipitated into new places in the arena of circulation vacated by other commodities. In the complete metamorphosis of the linen, for example, linen-money-Bible, the linen first falls out of circulation, and money steps into its place. Then the Bible falls out of circulation, and money again takes its place. When one commodity replaces another, the money commodity always sticks to the hands of some third person. Circulation sweats money from every pore.

As agent of the process of circulation of commodities, money acquires the function of a medium of circulation.

The movement of the labour-product C—M—C is a circuit. For its result is that a given value in the shape of a com modity shall begin the process, and shall also, in the shape of a commodity, end it. On the other hand, the movement of money is not, and cannot be, a circuit. The result is not the return of the money, but its continued removal further and further away from its starting-point. So long as the seller sticks fast to his money, which is the transformed type of his commodity, that commodity has completed only half its course. But so soon as he completes the process, so soon as he supplements his sale by a purchase, the money again leaves the hands of its possessor. It is true that if the weaver, after buying the Bible, sell more linen, money comes back into his hands. But this return is not owing to the circulation of the first 20 yards of linen; that circulation resulted in the money getting into the hands of the seller of the Bible. The return of money into the hands of the weaver is brought about only by the circulation of a fresh commodity, which new process ends with the same result as its predecessor did. Hence the movement directly imparted to money by the circulation of commodities takes the form of a constant motion away from its starting-point, of a course from the hands of one commodity owner into those of another. This course constitutes its currency (cours de la monnaie).

That this one-sided character of the money's motion arises out of the two-sided character of the commodity's motion, is a circumstance that is veiled over. The very nature of the circulation of commodities begets the opposite appearance. The first metamorphosis of a commodity (C-M) is, visibly, not only the money's movement, but also that of the commodity itself; in the second metamorphosis (M-C), on the contrary, the movement appears to us as the movement of the money alone. In the first phase of its circulation the commodity changes place with the money. Thereupon the commodity, under its aspect of a useful object, falls out of circulation into consumption. (Even when the commodity is sold over and over again, it falls, when definitely sold for the last time, out of the sphere of circulation into that of consumption.) In its stead we have its value-shape—the money. It then goes through the second phase of its circulation, not under its own natural shape, but under the shape of gold. The continuity of the movement is therefore kept up by the money alone, and the same movement that as regards the commodity consists of two processes of an antithetical character, is, when considered as the movement of the money, always one and the same process, a continued change of places with ever fresh commodities. Hence the result brought about by the circulation of commodities, namely, the replacing of one commodity by another, takes the appearance of having been effected not by means of the change of form of the commodities, but rather by the action of the money, an action, that circulates commodities, to all appearance motionless in themselves, and appears to set them in motion; and that in a direction constantly opposed to the direction of the money. Hence, although the movement of the money is merely the expression of the circulation of commodities, yet the circulation of commodities seems to be the result of the movement of the money.

Every commodity, when it first steps into circulation, and undergoes its first change of form, does so only to fall out of circulation again and to be replaced by other commodities. Money, on the contrary, as the medium of circulation, keeps continually within the sphere of circulation and moves about in it. The question therefore arises, how much money this sphere constantly absorbs?

In a given country there take place every day at the same time numerous sales and numerous purchases of commodities. And since, in the form of circulation now under consideration, money and commodities always come bodily face to face, it is clear that the amount of the means of circulation required is determined beforehand by the sum of the prices of all these commodities. If, in consequence of a rise or fall in the value of gold, the sum of the prices of commodities fall or rise, the quantity of money in currency must fall or rise to the same extent. A one-sided observation of the results that followed upon the discovery of fresh supplies of gold and silver, led some economists in the 17th, and particularly in the 18th century, to the false conclusion, that the prices of commodities had gone up in consequence of the increased quantity of gold and silver serving as means of circulation. As a matter of fact the value of the gold and silver had diminished in consequence of the increased facility of exploitation, the prices of commodities had concurrently increased, and the more expensive commodities required naturally greater quantities of money for their circulation. Henceforth we shall consider the value of gold to be given.

If now we further suppose the price of each commodity to be given, the sum of the prices clearly depends on the mass of commodities in circulation. It requires but little racking of brains to comprehend that if one quarter of wheat costs $10, 100 quarters will cost $1,000, 200 quarters $2,000, and so on, that consequently the quantity of money that changes place with the wheat, when sold, must increase with the quantity of that wheat.

If the mass of commodities remain constant, the quantity of circulating money varies with the fluctuations in the prices of those commodities. It increases and diminishes because the sum of the prices increases or diminishes in consequence of the change of price. Whether the change in the price correspond to an actual change of value in the commodities, or whether it be the result of mere fluctuations in market prices, the effect on the quantity of the medium of circulation remains the same.

This holds good for simultaneous sales and purchases, but not for successive ones.

Suppose the following articles to be sold simultaneously: say, one quarter of wheat, 20 yards of linen, one Bible and 4 gallons of brandy. If the price of each article be $10, it follows that $40 in money must go into circulation. If, on the other hand, these same articles are links in the following chain of metamorphoses: 1 quarter of wheat—$10—20 yards of Linen—$10—1 Bible—$10—4 gallons of brandy—$10, a chain that is already well known to us, in that case the $10 thus make four moves. Only ¼ of the quantity of money is required, which would have been needed in the case of a simultaneous turnover of the four commodities. The more moves the same sum of money makes in a given time, *i. e.* the greater the velocity of its currency, and the less money does the process of circulation require. Hence the quantity of money functioning as the circulating medium is equal to the sum of the prices of the commodities divided by the number of moves made by coins of the same denomination.

$$\frac{\text{Sum of prices of commodities}}{\text{Number of moves by coins of same denomination}} = \begin{array}{c}\text{Quantity of money} \\ \text{serving as circu-} \\ \text{lating medium.}\end{array}$$

This law holds generally. Hence if the number of moves made by the separate pieces increase, the total number of those pieces in circulation diminishes. If the number of the moves diminish, the total number of pieces increases. Since the quantity of money capable of being absorbed by the circulation is given for a given mean velocity of currency, all that is necessary in order to abstract a given number of five-dollar coins from the circulation is to throw the same number of five-dollar bills into it, a trick well known to all bankers.

Just as the currency of money, generally considered, is but a result and a reflex of the circulation of commodities, so, too, the velocity of that currency reflects the rapidity with which commodities circulate—not inversely. Thus the retardation of the currency reflects the stagnation in the circulation of commodities. The circulation itself, of course, gives no clue to the origin of this stagnation. The general public, who, simultaneously with the retardation of the currency, see money appear and disappear less frequently at the periphery of circulation, naturally attribute this retardation to a quantitative deficiency in the circulating medium.[1]

The total quantity of money functioning during a given period as the circulating medium, is determined, on the one hand, by the sum of the prices of the circulating commodities, and on the other hand, by the rapidity of their circulation. But the sum of the prices of the circulating commodities depends on the quantity, as well as on the prices, of the

---

[1] But if, on the one hand, it is a popular delusion to ascribe stagnation in production and circulation to insufficiency of the circulating medium, it by no means follows, on the other hand, that an actual paucity of the medium in consequence, *e. g.*, of bungling legislative interference with the regulation of currency, may not give rise to such stagnation.

commodities. These three factors, however, state of prices, quantity of circulating commodities, and velocity of money-currency, are all variable in different proportions, and can therefore compensate each other. Consequently we find, especially if we take long periods into consideration, that the deviations from the average level of the quantity of money current in any country, are much smaller than we should at first sight expect, apart of course from excessive perturbations mostly arising from industrial and commercial crises.

The erroneous opinion that it is prices that are determined by the quantity of the circulating medium, and that the latter depends on the quantity of the precious metals in a country; this opinion was based by those who first held it, on the absurd hypothesis that commodities are without a price, and money without a value, when they first enter into circulation, and that, once in the circulation, an aliquot part of the medley of commodities is exchanged for an aliquot part of the heap of precious metals.

That money takes the shape of coin, springs from its function as the circulating medium. The weight of gold represented in imagination by the prices of commodities, must confront those commodities, within the circulation, in the shape of coins or pieces of gold of a given denomination. The only difference, therefore, between coin and bullion, is one of shape, and gold can at any time pass from one form to the other. But no sooner does coin leave the mint, than it immediately finds itself on the high-road to the melting pot. During their currency, coins wear away, some more, others less. Name and substance begin their process of separation. Coins of the same denomination become different in value, because they are different in weight. Gold thereby ceases any longer to be a real equivalent of the commodities whose prices it realises. The natural tendency of circulation is thus to convert coins into a mere semblance of what they profess to be, into a symbol of the weight of metal they are officially supposed to contain. This fact implies the possibility of replacing metallic coins by tokens of some other material, by symbols serving the same purposes as coins. The practical difficulties in the way of coining extremely minute quantities of gold or silver, and the circumstance that at first the less precious metal is used as a measure of value instead of the more precious, copper instead of silver, silver instead of gold, and that the less precious circulates as money until dethroned by the more precious—all these facts explain the parts historically played by silver and copper tokens as substitutes for gold coins. Silver and copper tokens take the place of gold in those regions of the circulation where coins pass from hand to hand most rapidly, and are subject to the maximum amount of wear and tear. This occurs where sales and purchases on a very small scale are continually happening. In order to prevent these satellites from establishing themselves permanently in the place of gold, positive enactments determine the extent to which they must be compulsorily received as payment instead of gold.

The weight of metal in the silver and copper tokens is arbitrarily fixed by law. When in currency, they wear away even more rapidly than gold coins. Hence their functions are totally independent of their weight, and consequently of all value. The function of gold as coin becomes completely independent of the metallic value of that gold. Therefore things that are relatively without value, such as paper notes, can serve as coins in its place. This purely symbolic character is to a certain extent masked in metal tokens. In paper money it stands out plainly.

We allude here only to paper money issued by the State and having compulsory circulation. It has its immediate origin in the metallic currency. Money based upon credit implies on the other hand conditions, of which we have here entirely abstained from treating.

The State puts in circulation bits of paper on which their various denominations, say $5, $20, &c., are printed. In so far as they actually take the place of gold to the same amount, their movement is subject to the laws that regulate the currency of money itself. A law peculiar to the circulation of paper money can spring up only from the proportion in which that paper money represents gold. Such a law exists; stated simply, it is as follows: the issue of paper money must not exceed in amount the gold which would actually circulate if not replaced by symbols. Now the quantity of gold which the circulation can absorb constantly fluctuates about a given level. Still in a given country it never sinks below a certain minimum easily ascertained by experience. The fact that this minimum mass continually undergoes changes in its constituent parts, *i. e.* that the pieces of gold of which it consists are being constantly replaced by fresh ones, causes of course no change either in its amount or in the continuity of its circulation. It can therefore be replaced by paper symbols. If, on the other hand, all the conduits of circulation were to-day filled with paper money to the full extent of their capacity for absorbing money, they might to-morrow be overflowing in consequence of a fluctuation in the circulation of commodities. There would no longer be any standard. If the paper money exceed its proper limit, which is the amount in gold coins of the like denomination that can actually be current, it would, apart from the danger of falling into general disrepute, represent only that quantity of gold, which, in accordance with the laws of the circulation of commodities, is required, and is alone capable of being represented by paper. If the quantity of paper money issued be double what it ought to be, then, as a matter of fact, $5 would be the money-name not of $\frac{1}{4}$ of an ounce, but of $\frac{1}{8}$ of an ounce of gold. Those values that were previously expressed by the price of $5 would now be expressed by the price of $10.

With the very earliest development of the circulation of commodities, there is also developed the necessity, and the passionate desire, to hold fast the product of the first metamorphosis. Commodities are thus sold not for the purpose of buying others, but in order to replace their commodity-form by their money-form. From being the mere means of effecting the circulation of commodities, this change of form becomes the end and aim. The money becomes petrified into a hoard, and the seller becomes a hoarder of money.

Precisely in the early stages of the circulation of commodities, the surplus use-values alone are converted into money. Gold and silver thus become of themselves social expressions for superfluity or wealth.

As the production of commodities further develops, every

producer of commodities is compelled to make sure of the nervus rerum or the social pledge. His wants are constantly making themselves felt, and necessitate the continual purchase of other people's commodities, while the production and sale of his own goods require time, and depend upon circumstances. In order then to be able to buy without selling, he must have sold previously without buying. In this way, all along the line of exchange, hoards of gold and silver of varied extent are accumulated. With the possibility of holding and storing up exchange value in the shape of a particular commodity, arises also the greed for gold. Along with the extension of circulation, increases the power of money. To a barbarian owner of commodities, and even to a West-European peasant, value is the same as value-form, and, therefore, to him the increase in his hoard of gold and silver is an increase in value.

In order that gold may be held as money, it must be prevented from circulating, or from transforming itself into a means of enjoyment. The hoarder, therefore, makes a sacrifice of the lusts of the flesh to his gold fetish. He acts in earnest up to the Gospel of abstention. On the other hand, he can withdraw from circulation no more than what he has thrown into it in the shape of commodities. The more he produces, the more he is able to sell. Hard work, saving, and avarice are therefore his three cardinal virtues, and to sell much and buy little the sum of his political economy.

By the side of the gross form of a hoard, we find also its aesthetic form in the possession of gold and silver articles. This grows with the wealth of civil society. In this way there is created, on the one hand, a constantly extending market for gold and silver, unconnected with their functions as money, and, on the other hand, a latent source of supply, to which recourse is had principally in times of crisis and social disturbance.

Hoarding serves various purposes. Its first function is the following: we have seen how, along with the continual fluctuations in the extent and rapidity of the circulation of commodities and in their prices, the quantity of money current unceasingly ebbs and flows. This mass must, therefore, be capable of expansion and contraction. At one time money must be attracted in order to act as circulating coin, at another, circulating coin must be repelled. In order that the mass of money, actually current, may constantly saturate the absorbing power of the circulation, it is necessary that the quantity of gold and silver in a country be greater than the quantity required to function as coin. This condition is fulfilled by money taking the form of hoards. These reserves serve as conduits for the supply or withdrawal of money to or from the circulation, which in this way never overflows its banks.

With the development of the circulation of commodities, conditions arise under which the alienation of commodities becomes separated, by an interval of time, from the realisation of their prices. It will be sufficient to indicate the most simple of these conditions. One sort of article requires a longer, another a shorter time for its production. Again, the production of different commodities depends on different seasons of the year. One sort of commodity may be born on its own market place, another has to make a long journey to market. Commodity-owner No. 1 may therefore be ready to sell, before No. 2 is ready to buy. When the same transactions are continually repeated between the same persons, the conditions of sale are regulated in accordance with the conditions of production. On the other hand, the use of a given commodity, of a house, for instance, is sold for a definite period. Here, it is only at the end of the term that the buyer has actually received the use-value of the commodity. He therefore buys it before he pays for it. The vendor becomes a creditor, the purchaser becomes a debtor. Thus money also acquires a fresh function; it becomes the means of payment.

The character of creditor, or of debtor, results here from the simple circulation. The change in the form of that circulation stamps buyer and seller with this new die. At first, therefore, these new parts are just as transient and alternating as those of seller and buyer, and are in turns played by the same actors. But the opposition is not nearly so pleasant. The same characters can, however, be assumed independently of the circulation of commodities. The class-struggles of the ancient world, for instance, took the form chiefly of a contest between debtors and creditors, which in Rome ended in the ruin of the plebeian debtors, who were displaced by slaves. In the Middle Ages the contest ended with the ruin of the feudal debtors, who lost their political power together with the economical basis on which it was established. Nevertheless, the money relation of debtor and creditor that existed at these two periods reflected only the deeper-lying antagonism between the general economical conditions of existence of the classes in question.

Let us return to the circulation of commodities. The appearance of commodities and money has ceased to be simultaneous. The money functions now, first as a measure of value in the determination of the price of the commodity sold; the price fixed by the contract measures the obligation of the debtor, of the sum of money that he has to pay at a fixed date. Secondly, it serves as an ideal means of purchase. Although existing only in the promise of the buyer to pay, it causes the commodity to change hands. It is not before the day fixed for payment that the means of payment actually steps into circulation, leaves the hand of the buyer for that of the seller. The means of payment enters the circulation, but only after the commodity has left it. The money is no longer the means that brings about the process. It only brings it to a close.

The seller turned his commodity into money, in order thereby to satisfy some want; the hoarder did the same in order to keep his commodity in its money-shape, and the debtor in order to be able to pay; if he do not pay, his goods will be sold by auction. Money is therefore now the end and aim of a sale, and that owing to a social necessity springing out of the process of circulation itself.

The buyer converts money back into commodities before he has turned commodities into money: in other words, he achieves the second metamorphosis of commodities before the first. The seller's commodity circulates, and realises its price, but only in the shape of a legal claim upon money. It is converted into a use-value before it has been converted into money. The completion of its first metamorphosis follows only at a later period.

The obligations falling due within a given period of circulation represent the sum of the prices of the commodities, the sale of which gave rise to those obligations. The quantity of money necessary to realise this sum, depends, in the first instance, on the rapidity of currency of the means of payment. This rapidity is conditioned by two circumstances: first the relations between debtors and creditors form a sort of chain, in such a way that A, when he receives money from his debtor B, straightway hands it over to C, his creditor, and so on; the second circumstance is the length of the intervals between the different due-days of the obligations. The continuous chain of payments is essentially different from that interlacing of the series of purchases and sales which we considered on a former page. By the currency of the circulating medium, the connexion between buyers and sellers, is not merely expressed. This connexion is originated by, and exists in, the circulation alone. Contrariwise, the movement of the means of payment expresses a social relation that was already in existence before.

In proportion as payments are concentrated at one spot, special institutions and methods are developed for their liquidation. Such in the Middle Ages were the virements in Lyons. The debts due to A from B, to B from C, to C from A, and so on, have only to be confronted with each other, in order to annul each other to a certain extent. There thus remains only a single balance to pay. The greater the amount of the payments concentrated, the less is this balance relatively to that amount, and the less is the mass of the means of payment in circulation.

If we now consider the sum total of the money current during a given period, we shall find that, given the rapidity of currency of the circulating medium and of the means of payment, it is equal to

the sum of the prices to be realised
plus the sum of the payments falling due
minus the payments that balance each other
minus the number of circuits in which the same piece of coin serves in turn as means of circulation and of payment.

The peasant, for instance, sells his wheat for $10, which thus serve as circulating medium. When due, he pays his debt to the weaver, who supplied him with linen, with that sum. The same $10 now function as means of payment. The weaver, in turn, buys a Bible for cash; the sum functions once more as circulating medium, etc. Hence, the quantity of money current and the mass of commodities circulating during a given period, such as a day, no longer correspond. Money that represents commodities long withdrawn from circulation, continues to be current. Commodities circulate, whose equivalent in money will not appear on the scene till some future day. Moreover, the debts contracted each day, and the payments falling due on the same day, are quite different quantities.

Credit-money springs directly out of the function of money as a means of payment. Certificates of the debts owing for the purchased commodities circulate for the purpose of transferring those debts to others. On the other hand, to the same extent as the system of credit is extended, so is the function of money as a means of payment.

The development of money into a medium of payment makes it necessary to accumulate money against the dates fixed for the payment of the sums owing. While hoarding, as a distinct mode of acquiring riches, vanishes with the progress of civil society, the formation of reserves of the means of payment grows with that progress.

CHAPTER XVII

THE CIRCULAR COURSE OF CAPITAL AND THE TIME REQUISITE FOR ITS CIRCULATION

(Extracted from vol. II, ch. 1, 2, 3, 4, German edition.)

WE have learnt to know what constitutes the essence of money—that it represents in a material and concrete shape the exchange-value of all other commodities, *i. e.* of all the human labour incorporated in such commodities; and we have further seen the functions of money in the simple circulation of commodities. It now remains for us to investigate the nature of money in so far as the latter constitutes capital.

In doing so we must bear in mind that by "capital" we understand a sum of values, which yield, or ought to yield, surplus-value. Money capital is thus a capital which exists in the form of money, or in other words, a sum of money applied for the purpose of obtaining surplus-value. We have seen how surplus-value is obtained: in the production of commodities. Money capital must therefore be applied for the production of commodities; and, for this purpose, it is above all things necessary to purchase the objects required for the production of commodities, *i. e.* means of production and labour power. The process of production can then commence. When it is completed, its results must be sold, in order to bring back the money capital—and also the surplus-value obtained—to its previous money form.

The circular course of money capital passes therefore through the three following phases:

First Phase: The capitalist appears on the market for commodities and the labour market as purchaser. His money it turned into commodities, and thus completes the first phase of the process of circulation: Money—Commodities (M—C).

Second Phase: The commodities thus bought are applied for the purpose of production, and consumed in the process. Commodities of increased value are the result.

Third Phase: The capitalist returns to the market as seller. His commodities are turned into money, and the second phase of the process of circulation Commodities—Money (C—M) is completed.

The circular round achieved by money capital can thus be represented by the following formula:

$$M—C \dots P \dots C'—M'$$

in which the dots (....) indicate that the circulation is interrupted, whereas C' and M' indicate C and M increased to the extent of the surplus-value.

The second phase, *i. e.* that of production, has already been analysed in detail. There remain the first and third phases. We must, of course, in the first place make abstraction of all accidental non-essential circumstances. Consequently we shall here take for granted, not only that the commodities are sold for their value, but also that this takes place under circumstances which remain the same. We will therefore make abstraction of the changes of value, which may occur during the process of circulation.

The first phase of that process (M—C) is constituted by the purchase of commodities by means of the money available as capital. But the nature of the commodities is not an optional one. Such commodities must have certain definite qualities, i. e. they must be means of production and labour power. And they must, further, be adapted to each other. The means of production must be such as can be worked-up precisely by that labour power which is purchased. If L represents the labour power, and Mp the means of production, the money capital (M) is divided into two parts, of which one buys the labour power and the other the corresponding means of production. We can represent the process by means of the following formula:

$$M—C \left\{ \begin{array}{l} L \\ Mp \end{array} \right.$$

L and Mp must not only be adapted to each other in respect of quality, but also in respect of quantity. Mp must be sufficient to employ L, including such surplus-labour as may be required. For instance, if the daily value of labour power be 75 cents and if these 75 cents be the product of 5 hours' labour, according to the laws of capitalist production previously set forth, the 75 cents must be considered as the wage for more than 5 hours' labour—let us say, for 10 hours' labour. If such a contract, for example, be made with 50 workmen, the latter must collectively furnish the purchaser with 500 working-hours per day, of which 250 represent exclusively surplus-labour. The capitalist who buys the 50 labour powers must therefore buy such an amount of Mp, that the latter suffice not only for 250, but for 500 working-hours. The relation in which the money capital must be divided when purchasing L and Mp, is thus a perfectly definite one. When this has been done, the capitalist not only disposes of the amount of Mp and L necessary for the production of a useful article; but he likewise disposes of the means necessary to produce articles of greater value, *i. e.* surplus-value. His money capital has become productive capital.

We know that the purchase of labour power (M—L) is the essential feature of this process, seeing that surplus-value arises from the employment of labor power. M—Mp is only necessary in so far as it enables the labour power purchased to enter into activity. Thus although, in the process M—L, the owner of money and the owner of labour power meet each other solely in their respective capacities of buyer and seller, the capital-relation is none the less already included in this incident of circulation. As a matter of fact, the capitalist, before he can apply for the first time his money as capital, must purchase the means of production (buildings, machines, etc.) before purchasing the labour power; for as soon as the latter comes under his control, Mp must be there in order to render the utilisation of L possible. When he buys L, the capitalist is thus already the owner of Mp. The capital-relation, the class-relation between capitalist and wage-labourer thus already exists, nay, is already presumed, when the two confront each other in the process M—L; and this relation exists by reason of the fact that the conditions under which alone labour power can enter into activity, *i. e.* the necessaries of life and the means of production, are entirely outside the control of the owner of labour power. The capital-relation existing during the process of production is only rendered manifest because it already exists in the process of circulation, *i. e.* in the various fundamental economic conditions under which buyer and seller confront each other—in other words, in their class-relation.

When the process of production is terminated, a certain amount of commodities is available (C'), *e. g.* 10,000 lbs. of yarn, the value of which is greater than the value of the total amount of commodities available when the process of production commenced. The fact that the commodities produced constitute capital is manifest in this increase of value. Such commodities must now be sold. For as long as they are lying on the market, production is at a standstill. According to the rapidity with which capital is reconverted from the commodity form to the money form, will the same capital-value serve in a very unequal degree for the creation of new prod- ucts and new value. Further, the entire amount of the com- modities C' must be sold, for it is essential that no part of the lot should remain unsold. Only when the capitalist has sold all the 10,000 lbs. of yarn, has he converted the entire capital-value and surplus-value into money. After the sale, at the end of the whole process of circulation, the capital- value resumes the original form in which it entered upon that process; thus it can begin the process again as money capital, and pass through its various phases.

When the sale C'—M' is finished, the original capital- value and the added surplus-value are to be found, one next to the other, in the sum of money which appears as the final result of the whole process of circulation, and can thus be separated from each other, or not, as the owner desires. This is important for the continuation of the process of production, according as to whether the surplus-value is added to the capital in its entirety or partially, or is not added to it at all.

The process of the circulation of capital can proceed nor- mally, only as long as its various phases pass into each other without let or hindrance. On the other hand, it is in the nature of things that the process of circulation should itself determine the immobilisation of the capital in the various phases of the process, during definite time-lengths.

The process of circulation of capital manifests, in its total- ity, the intimate connection between production and circula- tion. In the first phase of its circulation, capital needs the general circulation of commodities in order to assume the form in which alone it can function in the process of produc- tion. Capital requires that general circulation just as much in the third phase, in order to cast off its commodity form, under which it would be unable to renew the process of its circula- tion: it needs it likewise in order to have the possibility of separating the process of its own circulation as capital, from the process of the circulation of the surplus-value added to it.

The circulation of money capital is thus the most one-sided, and hence striking and characteristic form in which industrial capital manifests itself; in that process the aim and motive power of industrial capital—expansion of value, making money accumulation—assert themselves most emphatically in the shape of buying in order to sell dearer. The fact that the first phase is M—C, renders manifest the origin of the component parts of the productive capital as derived from the commodities market, and also renders manifest the further fact that the capitalist process of production is conditioned by circulation, *i. e.* trade. The circular course of money capital is not only the production of commodities; it is itself brought about solely by the process of circulation, which it presupposes.

The labour power, which the capitalist buys, must as a rule be paid for by him at the end of 1 or 2 weeks. With the means of production, the case is different. In this case the dates of purchase and payment are different. Consequently a part of the money must be used to complete the process M—C whilst another part retains its money form. The necessities of circulation thus cause a storing-up of money. Seeing that all money withdrawn from circulation takes the form of treasure, the treasuring-up of money is indispensable for the regular functioning of money capital.

The storing-up of a money treasure results also in another way. In the chapter on accumulation we saw that surplus-value is always added afresh to capital, *i. e.* is applied to extending the scope of production or to creating new places where capital is carried-on. For this purpose, however, it must be of a certain size. It must be sufficient to employ a given number of workmen and to procure the means of production required by them. For the proportions in which production can be extended are not arbitrary, but are determined by technical necessities. If the surplus-value derived from one circular course of capital is not sufficient, it must be accumulated until, after many such circular courses, it has attained the requisite dimensions. Meanwhile it is immobilised in the shape of treasure, and forms in this shape potential money capital, *i. e.* money susceptible of serving as capital, but which does not yet serve as such.

If the commodities sold by our capitalist are not payable immediately, but only after a certain time, which may be short or long, that part of the surplus-product destined to be added to the capital is not turned into money, but into claims, or proprietary rights to some counter-value; the latter may perhaps already be in the possession of the buyer, perhaps only in his prospective possession.

As to whether the gold surplus-value shall be added once more immediately to the productive capital-value, depends on circumstances which are independent of its mere existence. If it is to serve as money capital in a second, independent business transaction, it must amount to the requisite minimum sum. Such a minimum sum is likewise necessary if it is to be applied to the increase of the original capital. The spinner, for instance, cannot augment the number of his spindles without simultaneously procuring the corresponding number of carding machines and roving frames, to say nothing of the increased expenses for cotton and wages necessitated by such an extension of business. As long as the surplus-value which has been turned into money does not attain this minimal amount, the circular course of capital must be repeated several times. Even modifications of details, e. g. in the spinning machinery, in so far as they render the latter more productive, require a greater outlay for spinning material, an increase of the carding machinery, etc. Thus the surplus-value will, in the meantime, be accumulated.

Once the process of production is completed, the capitalist throws his commodities into the stream of circulation, in order to sell them. These commodities possess greater value than those $(L + Mp)$ bought by the capitalist before the process of production began. He thus draws, through the sale of his products, a greater value from the process of circulation in the form of money, than he originally threw into it in the same form. But he can only do this because he throws a greater value into the stream of circulation, in the form of commodities, than he withdrew from it. In so far as we consider only the "industrial" capitalist,[1] the latter invariably

[1] By this we mean the capitalist who produces, whether in the domain of agriculture, or in that of industry or mining—in contradistinction to the merchant, banker, mere landed proprietor, etc., who do not produce.

throws a greater value in the form of commodities into circulation, than he withdraws from it. If his supply of commodity-values harmonised with his demand, his capital would obtain no increment. He must, indeed, "sell dearer than he bought." He can do this, however, only because he has meanwhile transformed in the course of the process of production, the less valuable commodities bought by him into more valuable ones. The profit yielded by his capital increases in the proportion that his supply of commodity-values exceeds his demand. He can, therefore, never aim at establishing an equilibrium between his supply and his demand; but, on the contrary, he must constantly endeavour to increase the former as much as possible beyond the latter.

Exactly the same holds good of the capitalist class in its totality. It is, of course, only question here of the demand which is requisite for production, $i. e.$ of the demand for L and Mp.

As we have already seen, the capital advanced (Cp) is divided into the part applied for buying Mp and the part applied for buying L. If we consider its value, the demand for Mp is therefore smaller than the capital advanced, and, in consequence, much smaller than the commodity-capital which is, last of all, after the process of production is completed, thrown into circulation.

The demand for L is increasingly less than the demand for Mp. (Comp. the chapter on Accumulation, ch. XX.)

In so far as the labourer converts the greater part of his wages into means of subsistence—and especially into indispensable means of subsistence—the demand of the capitalist for L is at the same time, indirectly, a demand for the articles of consumption required by the labouring class. But this demand is equal to v, and not an atom larger—at the most it is smaller, if the labourer economises on his wages ($v =$ variable capital).

Thus the total demand for commodities, on the part of the capitalist, can never be greater than Cp $= c + v$. But his supply is equal to $c + v + s$. The greater the rate of profit, $i. e.$ the greater the surplus-value relatively to capital, the more will the supply of commodities by the capitalist exceed his demand, and the less will be his demand relatively to his supply (c = constant capital, s = surplus-value).

We must not forget that his demand for Mp is always less than his capital, calculated day by day. Let us assume the existence of another capitalist, alongside of him, who supplies him with those Mp, and who, under otherwise identical circumstances, works with an equally large capital; in this case, the demand of the first capitalist for Mp will always be less, in respect of value, than the commodities-product of the second one. The fact that there is not only one capitalist, but many, does not alter the matter. Let us assume, that his capital amounts to $250, of which the constant part (c) is $200. In this case, the demand made by him on the collectivity of capitalists is equal to $200; together they furnish, on $250 of capital at equal profit rates, Mp for the value of $300. Thus his demand only covers two-thirds of their supply, whereas his own total demand is equal to but four-fifths of his own supply, considered according to the amount of the value.

Only if the capitalist were to consume the entire surplus-value, and were to continue producing with the capital in its original size, would his demand—as capitalist—be equal in value to his supply. But even then, his demand as capitalist only corresponds to four-fifths of his supply—considered according to the amount of the value; he consumes one-fifth in his capacity as non-capitalist.

But that is impossible. The capitalist must not only constitute a reserve capital in view of the variations of prices, and in order to be able to wait for the most favourable opportunities for purchase and sale; he must accumulate capital in order to extend the scope of production and to be able to utilise the latest technical progress in his undertaking.

In order to accumulate capital, he must first let a part of the surplus-value (s) in money form, which he reaped from the process of circulation, accumulate as treasure, until this treasure has attained the necessary magnitude. As long as the process of the formation of treasure lasts, the demand of the capitalist does not increase. The money is immobilised; it withdraws from the commodities market no equivalent in the shape of commodities, in return for the money which it withdrew from that market in exchange for commodities supplied.

We make abstraction here of credit. When a capitalist, for instance, deposits his money, in the measure in which it accumulates, in a bank on interest, this is also a credit operation.

The total time needed by capital for its circular course is equal to the time of its production and the time of its circulation.[1]

The time of working up is included in the time of production, but the latter is longer than the former. The process of production may render interruptions of the labour process necessary, during which the object of labour is exposed to the influence of physical processes without any further human intervention, as e. g. in the case of corn which is sown, of wine which ferments in the cellar, or of the labour material needed by numerous manufactures, such as tanneries, which is subjected to chemical processes. The capitalist must further have a stock of raw materials in hand, and it must be remembered that the implements of labour, machines, etc., consume much time in the course of the process of production without producing anything.

All this is capital which is lying idle. As far as labour is possible at this stage—e. g. in order to keep the stocks in hand in good condition—it is productive labour which creates surplus-value, seeing that a part of such labour (as is the case with all other wage-labour) is not paid for. The normal interruptions of the whole process of production produce, on the contrary, neither value nor surplus-value. Hence the efforts made to enforce night-labour.

The interruptions of labour time which the object of labour must undergo during the process of production—e. g. the drying of wood—produce neither value nor surplus-value.

Whatever be the reason for the time of production exceeding labour time, in none of these cases do the means of production (Mp) absorb labour, nor—in consequence—surplus-labour. Hence the tendency of capitalist production to shorten as much as possible the prolongation of the time of production over and above the labour time.

[1] From here on, vol. II, ch. 5 (German ed.).

Apart from the time of production, capital must pass through the time of circulation. During this time it produces neither commodities nor surplus-value. The longer the time of circulation lasts, therefore, the smaller, proportionately, is the surplus-value produced. Inversely, the more the capitalist succeeds in reducing the time of circulation, the greater will be the surplus-value. This phenomenon would appear to confirm the false idea that surplus-value is derived from circulation.

CHAPTER XVIII

COMMERCIAL ACTIVITY

(Extracted from vol. II, ch. 6, German ed.)

(A) *Purchase and Sale*

As we have assumed that commodities are bought and sold at their value, it is only question in these transactions of converting the same value from a commodity form into a money form, and *vice versa*. If commodities should not be sold at their value, the sum total of the values thus converted remains none the less unchanged; for what is *plus* on the one side of the balance-sheet is *minus* on the other side.

The process of conversion requires time and labour power, not, indeed, in order to create value, but in order to render possible the conversion of the value from one form into another. It must be observed, in this connexion, that the reciprocal attempt to obtain on this occasion a surplus quantity of value, does not alter matters. This labour, augmented by the reciprocal evil intentions, creates no more value than the labour which takes place in the course of legal proceedings augments the value of the object of litigation. If therefore, the owners of commodities are not capitalists, but independent and direct producers, the time spent on purchase and sale must be deduced from their labour time; for this reason they have always—in ancient times as in the middles ages—sought to relegate such operations to festival days.

The dimensions assumed by the turnover of commodities in the hands of the capitalists cannot, of course, transform such labour, which produces no value, into labour producing value. Such a miracle would be equally impossible if the capitalist were to confine such work to other persons.

Purchase and sale become one of the main functions of the capitalist who employs others to work for him. Seeing that he takes possession on a larger scale of the product of others, he must also sell it on a larger scale, and must, further, subsequently buy the elements of production likewise on a larger scale. Neither before nor after do purchase and sale create any value. Such an illusion is due to the existence of commercial capital, of which we shall speak later. But this much is clear from the beginning: if—by means of the division of labour—one single merchant having his own capital undertakes on behalf of many capitalists the sale of their commodities, he can thereby shorten, for them, the time required for purchase and sale. In this case he must be regarded as a machine who reduces useless expenditure of force, or who helps to shorten the time of production. But nothing in the nature of such activity is changed thereby, and this activity does not thereby become creative of value.

We will assume—seeing that we will only later consider the merchant in his capacity as capitalist, and commercial capital —that this agent for purchase and sale is an employé of the manufacturer, who buys his labour power. He lives by his activity as buyer and seller, in the same way as others do by spinning or making pills. He fulfils a necessary function. He works as well as anyone else, but the contents of his work create neither value nor a product of any sort. He himself must be reckoned among the costs of production. His usefulness does not consist in transforming unproductive into productive labour, but rather in the fact that through him the amount of labour power and labour time employed in unproductive work is reduced. We will go further. We will assume him to be a mere wage-labourer—nay, if you like a better paid one. Whatever his wages may be, he works a part of the time for nothing. He receives, perhaps, the equivalent of the produce of eight working-hours daily, and works ten hours. The 2 hours surplus-labour performed by him produce just as little value as the 8 hours of necessary labour. But the cost of circulation, as represented by him, are reduced by one-fifth. The costs of circulation of the capital belonging to the capitalist who employs him, and which must be deducted from that capitalist's income, are reduced by the non-payment of the 2 hours in question.

The time spent on this is, under all circumstances, to be reckoned among the costs of circulation; and it adds nothing to the values turned over. It is the same as if one part of the product were transformed into a machine, which would buy and sell the other part. This machine causes a deduction from the product, although it can diminish the labour power etc. consumed in the process of circulation. It does but form a part of the costs of circulation.

(B) *Bookkeeping* *future* ⟶ Computers

Working-time is not only expended in effectual buying and selling, but also in bookkeeping, which, in turn, requires working instruments, such as pens, ink, paper, desks, office expenses. In this case, the position is similar to what it is in the case of the labour of buying and selling.

As long as the individual producer of commodities merely keeps his accounts either in his head or else incidentally, outside the working-time needed for production, it is evident that this activity of his, and also the working instruments consumed by him during the process, such as paper etc., must be deducted alike from the time and from the working instruments which he is able to consume productively. Neither the scope of the functions, nor the fact that the latter are exercised independently by special bookkeepers, alter this in any way.

Already in the most ancient Indian communities there existed a bookkeeper for agriculture. Bookkeeping here became the exclusive function of an official of the community. Time, trouble, and expense are saved by this division of labour. But production, and the bookkeeping concerned with such production, remain just as distinct entities as *e. g.* the cargo on board a ship, and the bill of lading. In the person of the bookkeeper part of the labour power of the community is withdrawn from the process of production; the costs entailed by his functions are not refunded from out of his own work, but are subtracted from the total product on the community. In the long run, the position is identical in the case of the bookkeeper employed by the capitalist and in that of the book-keeper employed by the Indian community.

There is nevertheless a certain difference between the costs arising out of the process of bookkeeping and those arising out of the process of buying and selling. The latter arise solely from the fact that the product is a commodity, and would consequently disappear as soon as the process of production assumed another social form. Bookkeeping, on the contrary, in so far as it controls that process and epitomises it in an ideal manner, becomes all the more necessary in the measure in which the social scale of production develops, and in which the process of production loses its individualist character. Bookkeeping is, therefore, more necessary in the capitalist system of production than in the split-up systems of handicraft and peasant production—and still more necessary in a system of production by the community itself, than in the capitalist system. But the costs of bookkeeping diminish simultaneously with the increased concentration of the process of production.

(C) *The Cost of Money*

Those commodities which serve as money are not absorbed by the process of consumption. Here we have social labour in a form in which it serves as a mere instrument of circulation. Apart from the fact that a part of the social wealth is assigned this unproductive form, the wear and tear of money necessi-tates its being continually replaced. The costs of such replac-ing are, in the case of nations which are highly developed from a capitalist point of view, important; seeing that the amount of wealth that assumes the form of money is very large. Gold and silver as money commodities constitute, for the society, costs of circulation which have their origin solely in the social form of production. They are costs derived from the produc-tion of commodities *per se,* and are a part of the social wealth which must be sacrificed to circulation.

(D) *Costs of Storage*

If production and reproduction are to continue without interruption, a quantity of commodities (means of production) must always be available on the market, *i. e.* a provision must always be to hand. The labourer must likewise find the greater part of his means of subsistence available on the market. For this purpose buildings, stores, reservoirs, stocks of commodities are necessary—*i. e.* constant capital must be advanced; similarly, labour power must be paid for, in order to store the commodities. Commodities deteriorate, into the bargain, and are exposed to the detrimental influence of the weather. In order to protect them, additional capital is required, which must be laid out partly in instruments of labour, partly in labour power.

These costs of circulation differ from those already enumerated, in that they enter, to a certain extent, into the value of the commodities. In so far as the costs of circulation due to the storage of commodities have their origin only in the length of time necessary to transform available values from the commodity form into the money form, such costs assume the nature of those enumerated in §§ A—C. On the other hand, the value of the commodities is in this case only maintained—or increased—because the use-value, *i. e.* the product itself, is subjected to operations which permit of additional labour influencing that use-value. (Whereby it must be borne in mind that bookkeeping, buying and selling, etc., do not influence the use-value.) In this case, it is true, the use-value is not increased; on the contrary, it diminishes. But its diminution is limited, and it remains. Neither does the value existing in the commodity increase. But new labour, both incorporated and living labour, is added to it.

(E) *Transport*

It is not necessary to enter here into all the details of the costs of circulation, such as packing, sorting, etc. The general law is that none of those costs of circulation which arise merely out of a transformation of the form of a commodity, add any value to the latter. They are merely the costs entailed by changing the form of the commodity, and belong to the category of the incidental costs of production. They must be replaced from out of the surplus-product, and constitute, as regards the capitalist class as a whole, a deduction from the surplus-value or surplus-product; just as, in the case of the labourer, the time needed for the purchase of his means of subsistence, is time lost. But the costs of transport play too important a part for us not to consider them briefly here.

Commodities can circulate without moving in a physical sense; and the transport of products is likewise possible without the circulation of commodities. For instance if A sells a house to B, the commodity circulates, but does not move. Moveable commodity-values, such as cotton or iron, can remain in the same place whilst being bought and sold dozens of times by successive speculators. What really moves in this case is the property-title to the commodity, not the commodity itself. On the other hand, for instance, the transport industry played a great part in the empire of the Peruvian Incas.

Aggregates of products do not increase through being transported. Neither is the change sometimes brought about by the fact of transport in their natural qualities—if we allow for certain exceptions—in any way intended to augment their usefulness; on the contrary, it is generally an inevitable drawback. But the use-value of things is realised only in their consumption; and their consumption may render a displacement necessary. Transport thus completes the process of production. The productive capital invested in the transport thus adds value to the commodity transported—partly by transferring value from the means of transport, partly by the addition of value through the medium of the labour required for such transport. This last addition of value is—as is the case with all capitalist production—divided-up into replacing labour-wages, on the one hand, and into surplus-value, on the other.

Within every branch of production, the displacement of the object of labour, and the instruments of labour and the labour power necessitated hereby, play an important part— for instance, in the case of cotton, which is removed from the carding-room to the spinning-room; or in that of coal, which is raised from the mine to the surface. The transport of the finished product (as finished commodity) from one place of production to another, distant from it, does but manifest a similar phenomenon on a larger scale. The transport of the product from one place of production to another is succeeded by that of the finished commodity from out of the domain of production into the domain of consumption. The product is only ready for consumption when it has achieved this process.

CHAPTER XIX

COMMERCIAL CAPITAL AND THE WORK OF THE COMMERCIAL EMPLOYÉS

(Extracted from vol. III, part 1, ch. 16, 17, German ed.)

EVERY capital that produces must—as we have seen—transform the finished commodities into money and the money, in its turn, into Mp and L (means of production and labour); in other words, it must be continually buying and selling. It is, to a certain extent, relieved of these functions by merchants having an independent capital of their own.

Let us assume that a merchant possesses $15,000, and that he buys therewith 30,000 yards of linen from the linen manufacturer. He sells these 30,000 yards at a profit of, let us say, ten per cent. With the money thus obtained he again buys linen, which he again sells. He constantly repeats this operation of buying in view of subsequent reselling, without himself producing anything in the meantime.

As regards the linen manufacturer, he has been paid the value of his linen with the money of the merchant; and, circumstances remaining the same, he can once more buy, with that money, yarn, coal, labour power etc., and continue to produce.

But although the sale of the linen has taken place, as far as he is concerned, this is not the case, as far as the linen itself is concerned. The latter is still on the market, as a commodity destined to be sold. Nothing further has happened to the linen, beyond a change in the person of its owner.

Let us assume that the merchant does not succeed in selling the original 30,000 yards of linen before the manufacturer has the second 30,000 yards ready. In this case, the merchant is unable to buy a second time. Production comes to a standstill and has to be interrupted. Of course it is possible that the manufacturer has other money at his disposal, wherewith to continue the process of production. But the fact none the less remains that that process cannot, for the time being, be continued with the help of the original capital. Here we see clearly that the activity of the merchant simply consists in undertaking the sale of the commodity, which otherwise would have to be undertaken by the manufacturer himself. If, instead of an independent merchant, an employé of the manufacturer were to be exclusively entrusted with the functions of purchase and sale, this fact could not possibly be doubtful for a moment.

If the manufacturer of linen had to wait until his goods had really reached the last purchaser, *i. e.* the consumer, the process of his reproduction would be interrupted. Or else, to avoid this, he would have had to narrow the scope of his business operations and maintain a larger reserve of money. This division of his capital does not cease in consequence of the intervention of the merchant. But without the latter, the money reserve would have to be larger, and the scope of production correspondingly smaller. At the same time the manufacturer saves the time required for selling, and can utilise it for the work of supervising the process of production.

In the event of the merchant's capital not overstepping its necessary limits, we may assume:

1. that in consequence of the division of labour, the capital, occupied solely in buying and selling (and we must here reckon not only the money necessary to purchase commodities, but also the money necessary for storage, buildings, transport, commercial wage-labour, etc.), will be smaller than it would be if the manufacturer had personally to undertake the whole work of selling his commodities;

2. that because the merchant undertakes exclusively such

work, not only are the manufacturer's commodities converted sooner into money, but the commodity-capital itself finds a market more rapidly than it would in the hands of the manufacturer;

3. that—when we consider the total commercial capital in relation to the capital that produces—a rotation [1] of the commercial capital may not only represent the rotations of several capitals in a single branch, but also the rotations of a number of capitals in different branches. If the linen merchant has sold the product of the first manufacturer before the latter has another equivalent quantity of linen ready, he can meanwhile buy linen from other manufacturers, and sell it. Or, after the sale of the linen, during the interval which elapses before new linen is to hand, he may sell silk.

The same commercial capital can thus bring about successively the various rotations of the capitals invested in a given branch; and, consequently, it does not only replace the individual money reserve which every manufacturer should have. For example, after the merchant has sold the corn of a farmer, he can, with the same money, buy the corn of a second farmer and sell it; whereas the rotation of the farmer's capital, abstraction made of the time of circulation, is limited by the time of production, which lasts a year.

The more rapidly the commercial capital rotates, the smaller is the part of the total money capital which figures as commercial capital; inversely, the slower the rotation, the larger is that part.

We have seen that the acts of selling and buying create neither value nor surplus-value, but—on the contrary—place limits on the formation of value and surplus-value. Nothing is changed in this, of course, if such acts, instead of being performed by the industrial capitalist, are performed by other persons. Abstraction being thus made of all those functions which are not, properly speaking, commercial—e. g. storage, forwarding, carrying, sorting, retailing, which constitute a

[1] "Rotation" is a term employed by Marx to describe the entire movement of capital from the moment of its outlay for means of production, labour power, etc., till the moment when it is recuperated after sale of the finished commodity. (*Translator's note.*)

continuation of the process of production—and limited to its real function of buying in order to sell, commercial capital creates neither value nor surplus-value, but merely serves as the medium for transforming available commodities into money. Nevertheless it must yield the average yearly profit. If it were to yield a larger annual profit than the capital which is engaged in producing does, part of the latter would be converted into commercial capital. The contrary phenomenon would occur if it were to yield a smaller annual profit. No species of capital can change its functions more easily than commercial capital.

As commercial capital itself creates no surplus-value, it is clear that the surplus-value accruing to it in the shape of an average profit forms a part of the surplus-value created by the totality of productive capital. But the question now arises as to how commercial capital draws to itself its share of such surplus-value.

The belief that commercial profit merely consists in raising the price of commodities above their value, is an illusion.

It is evident that the tradesman can only reap his profit from the price of the commodities sold by him; and it is also evident that this profit, which he realises when selling the commodities, must be equal to the excess of the selling price over the purchase price.

It is possible that after the purchase of a commodity, and before its sale, extra costs (costs of circulation) are incurred. If this be the case, it is clear that the excess of the selling price over the purchase price does not represent profit alone. In order to facilitate our inquiry, we shall assume for the moment that no such costs are incurred.

How, then, is it possible that the tradesman sells the commodities at a higher price than he paid for them?

In the case of the capitalist who produces, we have already answered the same question. His cost price is equal to that part of his capital which is effectually consumed, c + v; to this must be added the average profit, and thus the selling price of the manufacturer is arrived at—*i. e.* what we have termed the "price of production". If we add together all the prices of production of all available commodities, then the sum will be equal to the real value of the totality of such commodities, *i. e.* will be equal to the amount of labour effec-- tively contained in them. Thus it comes about—at least at the present stage of our discussion—that the selling prices of the manufacturers are, in their totality, equal to the value of the commodities, *i. e.* to the amount of labour con- tained in the latter; their cost prices, on the other hand, are only equal to that part of such labour as is paid for.

But it is not so in the case of the dealer in commodities, or tradesman. He does not produce, but only continues the process of selling the commodities which the manufacturer [1] began. Already before the sale the manufacturer has the surplus-value in hand, in the shape of the commodities, and through the sale he merely transforms it into money. The tradesman must make his profit by selling. This only appears possible if he increases still further the manufacturer's price of production. As the totality of prices of production is equal to the total value of all commodities, it would seem that the tradespeople can only make profit by selling commodities for more than they are worth.

Such a form of additional charge is very easy to understand. But, on looking at the matter more closely, we shall find that this is only an illusion. (It is always question here *only* of the average, not of individual cases.)

Why do we assume that the tradesman can only realise a profit of, say, 10% on his goods, if he sells them at 10% above their prices of production? Because we have taken for granted that the manufacturer sells the commodities to the tradesman for their price of production. But we must bear in mind once more that the price of production is equal to the cost price $+$ the average profit. This means that we have taken for granted that the tradesman pays to the manufac- turer the price of production which would arise if the average profit were to be adjusted without any regard for commercial

[1] It will already have been observed by the reader that we substitute the word "manufacturer" for the more complicated expression "capita- list who produces". To the class of manufacturers, in this sense of the word, therefore, landed proprietors, &c., in so far as they produce, be- long.

capital! We have taken for granted that commercial capital plays no part in the formation of the general rate of profit. But this is a perfectly absurd assumption.

Let us assume the total amount of productive capital advanced during the year to be equal to 720 c + 180 v = 900 (say thousands of dollars), and let us further assume the rate of surplus-value to be equal to 100%. The product is thus equal to 720 c + 180 v + 180 s = 1080. The rate of profit for the total capital is, then, $\frac{180}{900} = 20$ per cent. This is, therefore, the average rate of profit. But we will now assume that, in addition to the 900 of capital which produces, commercial capital to the extent of 100 is required, which has the same share of profit in proportion to its size. This commercial capital is one-tenth of the total capital of 1000, and takes, therefore, one-tenth share of the total surplus-value of 180, *i. e.* it gets a profit of 18 per cent. As a consequence, the profit remaining to be divided between the other nine-tenths of the total capital is but 162, *i. e.* also 18 per cent on a capital of 900. Hence the price at which the total number of commodities produced are sold to the trade by the owners of the productive capital is equal to 720 c + 180 v + 162 s = 1062. And if the merchant adds the average profit of 18% to his capital of 100, he sells the commodities for 1062 + 18 = 1080, *i. e.* for their value, although he only makes his profit in and through the process of circulation, and only through the excess of his selling price over his price of purchase.

Thus, in the formation of the general rate of profit, commercial capital co-operates in proportion to the part played by it in the total capital. The share of the total profit due to the commercial capital is already reckoned in the average rate of profit.

The price of production, at which the productive capitalist, as such, sells, is therefore smaller than the real price of production of the commodity; or, if we consider the total amount of commodities, the prices at which the productive class of capitalists sells them, are less than their value. In the above example, the tradesman, by selling for 118 commodities which cost him 100, adds, it is true, 18% to them. But as the commodity which he purchased for 100 is worth 118, he does not, on that account, sell them above their value.

The question now arises: what is the position of the commercial wage-labourers whom the tradesman employs?

From one point of view, such a commercial employé is a wage-labourer like any other. The variable capital of the tradesman, and not that money destined for his private upkeep, serves to buy the employé's labour power. His labour power is not bought for the purpose of private service, but for the purpose of utilising the capital advanced in commerce. The value of his labour power, and consequently his wages, are therefore—as in the case of all other wage labourers—not determined by the product of his labour, but by the costs of restoring his labour power.

But the same difference must exist between him and those labourers directly employed by the capital which produces, as separates commercial from productive capital, the tradesman from the manufacturer. For since the tradesman or merchant merely serves as medium for the sale of the commodities, and produces neither value nor surplus-value, the commercial employés cannot directly produce surplus-value for him. (As in the case of the productive labourers, we assume that the wages are determined by the value of the labour power, that the tradesman, consequently, does not enrich himself by deductions from them.)

What is difficult, in the case of the commercial employés, is by no means to explain how they produce directly profit for their employer, although not directly producing surplus value. This question is already settled by the fact of our having shown whence commercial profit is derived. Just as productive capital makes profit by selling labour, incorporated in the goods, which it has never remunerated; so commercial capital makes its profit by paying to productive capital only a part of this unremunerated labour, whilst obtaining payment, when the commodities are sold, for that part also. Productive capital engenders surplus-value by directly appropriating unpaid labour; commercial capital causes part of the already available surplus-value to be transferred to itself. The quantity of his profit depends, in the case of the individual tradesman, on the quantity of capital which he can apply to buying and selling; and the larger the amount of unpaid labour of his employés, the larger that quantity will be. The function itself, through the exercise of which profit accrues to commercial capital, is for the greater part abandoned by the tradesman to his employés. The unpaid labour of the latter, although not creating surplus-value, enables the tradesman none the less to appropriate surplus-value—which is, in practice, the same thing as far as individual capitals are concerned; such unpaid labour is hence the source of profit for those capitals. Commercial transactions could otherwise never be carried out on a large scale, could never develop on a capitalistic basis. Just as the unpaid labour of the productive worker directly creates surplus-value for the latter's employer, so does the unpaid labour of the commercial employé obtain for commercial capital a share of that surplus-value.

With the commercial employé the difficulty lies, rather, in the following direction: seeing that the labour of the tradesman himself creates no value—although it obtains for him a share of already available surplus-value; what is the position in regard to his variable capital, out of which he pays the wages of his employés? Is such variable capital to be reckoned as commercial capital advanced by him? If not, this would seem to contradict the law of the mutual balancing of the rates of profit; what capitalist would advance 150 if he could only reckon 100 as capital advanced? If, on the contrary, his variable capital is to be reckoned, this would appear to be incompatible with the nature itself of commercial capital. For such capital does not obtain its profit by putting the labour of others into motion, but because it buys and sells.

If every merchant only possessed so much capital as he could cause to rotate by means of his own personal labour, a great frittering away of commercial capital would be the result; this frittering away would increase in the measure in which productive capital increases its scale of production and extends the scope of its operations. There would thus arise a growing disproportion between the two. In the measure in which capital is centralised in the process of production, it would become decentralised in the process of circulation. The productive capitalist would then be obliged to spend much time, labour, and money on purely commercial activities, seeing that instead of dealing with 100 tradespeople, he would have to deal with 1000. In this way the advantages entailed by the differentiation of commercial capital as an independent entity would be, to a large extent, lost; not only would the purely commercial costs increase, but also the other costs of circulation—*e. g.* sorting, forwarding, etc. Such would be the state of affairs so far as productive capital is concerned.

Let us now consider the commercial capital. Firstly, in regard to the purely commercial activities. More time is not required for calculating with large figures, than with small ones. It takes ten times longer to make ten purchases for $10 each, than to make a single purchase for $250. It costs ten times as many letters and stamps, ten times as much paper, to correspond with ten tradespeople in a small way of business, than it does to correspond with one large firm. The limited division of labour in commercial houses, where one employé is bookkeeper and another cashier, whilst others are respectively correspondent, buyer, salesman, traveller, etc., saves a vast amount of labour-time; so that the number of commercial workers employed in the wholesale trade is quite out of proportion to the size of the business. This is the case, because in commerce—far more than in industry—the same function, whether exercised on a large scale or a small one, requires the same amount of labour time. (For this reason, the phenomenon of concentration appears historically at an earlier date in commerce than in industry.) Then comes the expenditure of constant capital. 100 small offices are far more expensive than a single large one; similarly 100 small stores are far more expensive than one large warehouse; and so forth. The costs of transport—which, at least in the form of costs which have to be advanced, enter into the merchant's business—increase with the development of the frittering away process.

The productive capitalist would have to expend more labour and money on the commercial part of his business. The same commercial capital, distributed among numerous small tradespeople, would require—precisely on account of its being frittered away—a much larger number of labourers in order to carry out its functions; and a larger commercial capital would be necessary in order to bring about the rotation of the same commodities-capital. If we call the total commercial capital invested in the purchase and sale of commodities B, and the corresponding variable capital (advanced for the purpose of payment of the commercial employés) b, then $B + b$ is smaller than the total commercial capital B would have to be, if b did not exist, $i. e.$ if every tradesman got along without the help of any employés.

But we have not yet got over the difficulty.

The price at which the commodities are sold must suffice, firstly, to pay the average profit on $B + b$. Here, already, the reader might hesitate. We assume that the selling price is equal to the value of the commodities. We have just seen in what way the commercial capital B shares in the average profit. The latter is contained, therefore, in the price of sale. But what is the case with b? From where is the profit on the supplementary capital b, which has been advanced for the purpose of paying the employés, to be derived—over and above the profit apportioned to the commercial capital B? It would appear as if the profit on b were, in reality, constituted by an arbitrary increase in the price. But we must bear in mind that $B + b$ is smaller than B without b would be. The average profit realised with the cooperation of B is thus sufficient to yield also a profit for b.

But the selling price must, moreover, suffice, in the second place, not only to yield a profit for b, but to recuperate the sum b itself, $i. e.$ to make good the amount advanced for wages of the commercial employés. And here lies the difficulty.

If the selling price of the commodities represents nothing but the latter's value, there is—according to the stage of our examination—a sum contained in that price, out of which the cost price and the average profit of the manufacturers are paid, and further the commercial capital with its profit; and this commercial profit is large enough to yield also a profit on the sum advanced by the tradesman for wages of his employés.

But how does this sum advanced for wages—the tradesman's variable capital—come itself to be included in the selling price? Can the tradesman, merely by reason of the fact that he employs and pays employés, arbitrarily add the sums thus advanced to the selling price? Or must he pay them from out of his profit, and the latter be reduced in proportion?

That which the tradesman buys with b is—according to our assumption—only commercial work, $i. e.$ labour necessary for transforming commodities into money, and, inversely, money into commodities. Hence it is labour which transforms values, but does not create values. But if such labour be not performed, commercial capital cannot fulfil its functions; and in this case it has no share in regulating the general rate of profit, $i. e.$ it draws no dividend from out of the total profit.

Let us suppose B to be equal to 100, b to be equal to 10, and the rate of profit to be 10%. (We make abstraction of the material business costs, so as not to unnecessarily complicate the calculation. For they have nothing to do with the difficulty here confronting us. The constant capital of the tradesman is, at the most, just as large, but as a matter of fact smaller, than it would be if the manufacturer had himself to do the selling.)

If the tradesman employed nobody, and therefore had no outlay b, the work otherwise performed by the employés would none the less have to be done. The tradesman would have to do it himself. In order to buy or sell to the extent of B (100), the tradesman would give his time—and we will assume that it is the only time at his disposal. The commercial work represented by b (10) would, in this case, have to be paid out of profit, $i. e.$ presupposes the existence of another commercial capital of 100. This second B (or 100) would not become merged into the price of the commodities (as a supplement to such price); but this would be the case with the 10 per cent. Two operations would thus take place of 100 = 200, buying commodities for 200 + 20 = 220.

As commercial capital is absolutely nothing else than a differentiated part of productive capital having become independent of the latter, we will endeavour to find a solution by assuming that the differentiation of the two species of capital has not yet taken place. As a matter of fact the manufacturer also employs commercial employés in his office. Let us therefore consider, first of all, the variable capital *b* advanced for them.

This office is always very small compared with the industrial factory. It is clear that in the measure that production develops, the more numerous will the commercial activities become, which must be performed in order to permit of the turnover of the productive capital—of the sale of the product, and of the purchase of the means of production—and in order to keep account of the entire business. To such activities belong the calculation of prices, bookkeeping, financial management, correspondence, etc. The employment of commercial wage-labourers hence becomes necessary, and these persons constitute the office properly so-called. The outlay for these employés, although it takes the form of wages, differs from the variable capital expended on the wages of the productive labourers. Such outlay increases the manufacturers' expenses, the quantity of capital to be advanced, without directly augmenting the surplus-value. Like all expenditure of a like nature, the outlay in question reduces the rate of profit, seeing that the amount of capital advanced, but not the surplus-value, increases. Consequently the manufacturer seeks to keep down such expenditure—just as in the case of his expenditure for constant capital—as much as possible and to reduce it to a *minimum*. Productive capital thus adopts a different position towards its commercial employés, from that which it adopts towards its productive wage-labourers. The greater the number of these—other circumstances remaining the same—and the greater will be the amount produced, and the greater will be the quantity of surplus-value or profit. On the other hand, the more production develops, the greater the quantity of commodities produced, and which must be sold in order to realise the value and surplus-value contained in them—and the more do the office expenses increase (absolutely, if not relatively), and give rise to a sort of division of labour. The fact that such expenses are recuperated out of the profit—and thus presuppose the latter's existence—is manifested by the fact (amongst others), that concurrently with the growth of the commercial salaries, these are frequently paid—in part—by percentual participation in the profits. Not because much commercial work is done, is much value produced, but inversely—because, and if, a great quantity of values have to be calculated and turned over, much commercial work is required. It is the same with the other costs of circulation. In order to measure, weigh, pack, transport, a large quantity of commodities, that quantity must be available. The quantity of labour required for packing and forwarding, etc., depends on the quantity of commodities to be packed and forwarded; and not *vice versa*.

The commercial employé does not directly produce surplus-value. But the price of his labour power is determined by its value (*i. e.* its cost of production), whereas the exercise of that power—as in the case of all wage-labourers of all categories—is not limited by its value. Therefore his wages are by no means necessarily proportionate to the quantity of profit he helps the capitalist to realise in money. What he costs the capitalist, and what the latter gets out of him, are different magnitudes. He is worth something to the capitalist, seeing that—by means of work which is partly unpaid—he helps to reduce the costs due to the conversion of the surplus-value into money. The commercial employé properly so-called belongs to the class of better paid wage-labourer—of those whose labour is qualified labour that stands higher than average labour. Nevertheless the wages have a tendency to sink, as the capitalist system of production develops, and even relatively to the average labour. Partly, this phenomenon is due to the division of labour inside the office; this entails a one-sided development of working capacity, and such development costs—to a certain extent—the capitalist nothing, since the skill of the labourer is furthered automatically by his activity, and the more rapidly, the more one-sided that activity becomes in consequence of growing division of labour. In the second place, it is due to the fact that the preparatory education, the knowledge of commercial routine, foreign languages, etc., are constantly spreading and being acquired more rapidly, more easily, more cheaply, with every progress of science and of the educational systems, and especially in the measure in which the capitalist mode of production develops the practical tendencies of the methods of education. The spread of education permits of the recruiting of commercial employés among classes of the population formerly excluded from such professions, and used to a more primitive standard of living. In this manner the democratisation of education engenders overcrowding and sharpens competition within the commercial profession. With few exceptions, therefore, the labour power of the commercial employés diminishes in value as the capitalist system of production develops; their wages sink, whereas their capacity for labour increases.[1]

If we consider commercial work in connection with the productive capital, it is quite evident that the former cannot be a source of surplus-value. It will occur to no one to suggest that the costs entailed by the office of a factory are anything else but costs which diminish the profits to the whole extent of their amount. Apparently—but only apparently—it is different in the case of the wholesale merchant. In his case the outlay for costs of circulation appear much larger, because—apart from their own commercial offices, which are included in all factories—that part of the capital which otherwise has to be applied in this manner by the totality of manufacturers is now concentrated in the hands of individual tradesmen. But this, of course, cannot alter the nature of the thing. Costs of circulation appear to productive capital as what they are in reality, *i. e.* costs. To the tradesman they appear as the source of this profit, which—the general rate of profit being assumed *a priori*—is precisely in proportion to the amount of such costs. For commercial capital these costs of circulation are a productive investment. Therefore the commercial labour bought by such capital is directly productive for the latter.

[1] *Note by Friedrich Engels:* "How true this prophecy concerning the fate of the commercial proletariat—written in 1865—has proved to be, is clearly shown by the example of the hundreds of German clerks, who, well up in all branches of commercial work and knowing 3 or 4 languages, to-day (1894) in the City of London vainly offer their services for 25 shillings a week—a wage far less than that of a skilled machine-operator."—A lacuna of 2 pages in the manuscript left by Marx indicates that he intended discussing this subject further.

CHAPTER XX

THE INFLUENCE OF COMMERCIAL CAPITAL ON PRICES

(Extracted from vol. III, part 1, ch. 18, German ed.)

IF the price of production of 1 lb. of sugar be $5, the tradesman could for $500 buy 100 lbs. of that article. If he buys and sells this quantity in the course of a year, and if the yearly average rate of profit be 15%, he would add $75 to the sum of $500, and to the sum of $5 the price of production of $5.75. He would thus sell the lb. of sugar for $5.75. But if the price of production of 1 lb. of sugar were to fall to 25 cents the tradesman could buy for $500 2000 lbs., and sell the lb. for 28.3 cents. The yearly profit, after as before, on the capital of $500 invested in the sugar trade would be $75. Only in the one case he must sell 100 lbs., in the other 2000 lbs.

(We make abstraction here of the costs of circulation, such as storage, forwarding, etc. Only the actual buying and selling are the objects of our investigation.)

The high or low level of the price of production would have nothing to do with the rate of profit; but it would play an important, nay decisive, part in determining the size of that fraction of the selling price of every lb. of sugar which dissolves itself in commercial profit—*i. e.* the supplementary price added by the tradesman to a definite quantity of commodities

If we except the cases in which the tradesman has a commercial monopoly, and simultaneously monopolises production, as *e. g.* in former days the Dutch East India Company, then can nothing be sillier than the common belief that it depends on the tradesman to sell, at his option, a large quantity of commodities at a small profit on each one, or else a small quantity of commodities at a large profit on each one The limits to his selling price are two in number: on the one hand, the price of production of the commodity, which he does not control; on the other, the average rate of profit, which he does not control either. (It is question here only of commerce in the ordinary sense, not of speculation.)

Consequently the difference between productive and com

mercial capital is the following: the more frequently productive capital rotates, the greater the amount of profit formed by it. True, through the medium of the general rate of profit, the total profit is not distributed among the various capitals in the proportion in which they participate in the process of production, but in proportion to their size. But the greater the number of rotations of the total productive capital, the greater will be the total quantity of profit, and hence also—other circumstances remaining the same—the greater will be the rate of profit.

With commercial capital the case is different. For commercial capital the rate of profit is a given magnitude, determined on the one hand by the quantity of profit yielded by productive capital, on the other by the relative size of the total commercial capital. The number of its rotations, it is true, exerts a decisive influence on its relation to the totality of capital, since it is evident that, the more rapid the rotation of commercial capital is, the smaller its absolute size will be —and therefore the smaller will be also its relative size (proportionately to the total capital available in a society).

But—assuming the relative size of commercial capital proportionately to the totality of capital to be given—the difference in the number of rotations in the various branches of trade does not affect either the amount of the total profit due to commercial capital, or th- general rate of profit. The tradesman's profit is determined, not by the amount of his commodities-capital in rotation, but by the amount of money capital advanced by him in order to bring about this rotation. If the general yearly rate of profit be 15%, and if the tradesman advances $500—then, if his capital rotate once in the year, he will sell his commodities for $575. If his capital rotate five times in the year, he will sell the commodities (purchased for $500) five times in the course of the year for $515—*i. e.* in the whole year a commodities-capital of $2,500 for $2,575. But this amounts, after as before, to a yearly profit of 15 on a capital advanced of 100. If this were not the case, commercial capital would yield, proportionately to the number of its rotations, much larger profit than industrial capital—

which would be incompatible with the law governing the general rate of profit.

The number of rotations of commercial capital in the various branches of trade thus directly affects the selling price of the commodities. The more frequently commercial capital rotates during the year, the smaller will be the addition made to the commodities capital sold each time by it.

The same percentage of commercial profit in different branches of trade thus increases, according to the time of rotation in those branches, the selling prices of the commodities by varying percentages, calculated according to the value of such commodities. For instance, if the yearly profit be 15%: in the event of one rotation the increase will be 15%, in the event of five rotations 3%.

In the case of industrial capital, on the other hand, the time of rotation does not affect in any way the quantity of value in individual commodities, although it affects the quantity of value and surplus-values produced by a given capital in a given time, because it affects the quantity of labour exploited. This phenomenon, it is true, is concealed, and matters would seem to be different as soon as we consider the prices of production; but this is only because the prices of production of the different commodities (according to laws we have already explained) differ from their values. If we consider the process of production in its totality, *i. e.* the quantity of commodities produced by the entire industrial capital, we shall immediately find the general law confirmed.

Thus a closer scrutiny of the influence exerted, in industrial capital, by the time of rotation on the formation of value, brings us back to the general law and to the fundament of political economy—*i. e.* that the value of commodities is determined by the labour-time contained in them; in commercial capital, on the other hand, the influence exerted by the rotations on commercial profit produces certain manifestations which (without a very intensive study of the middle terms) would appear to presuppose a purely arbitrary determination of prices. Prices would seem to be determined merely by the fact that capital is resolved to make a certain quantity of profit in the year. (For instance, it wishes to make

15% profit yearly; the supplement added to the purchase price of its commodities is fixed accordingly, *e. g.* each time 3%, so that 15%, all told, shall be made during the year.) Owing to this influence exerted by the rotations it would seem as if the process of circulation *per se* determines the prices of the commodities, independently—within certain limits—of production.

Hence the notions entertained by a tradesman, a Stock Exchange speculator, or banker concerning the mechanism of the capitalist system of production, are necessarily quite wrong. The notions of the manufacturer, on the other hand, are falsified owing to the nature of the process of circulation which his capital undergoes, and owing to the equalisation of the general rate of profit. His view of the part played by competition is a wholly erroneous one. Once given the limits of value and surplus-value, and it is easy to perceive how the competition of the various capitals transforms values into prices of production and, further still, into trading prices; and how it transforms surplus-value into average profit. But without these limits it is absolutely impossible to see why competition reduces the general rate of profit to one level rather than to another, to 15% instead of to 1500%. Competition can, at the most, reduce it to a single level. But it is absolutely unable to determine this level itself.

Therefore, from the point of view of commercial capital, the rotation itself appears to determine prices.

If the same industrial capital (other circumstances, and notably its own organic composition, remaining identical) rotate four times in a year instead of twice, it produces twice as much surplus-value, and hence profit. This is manifestly clear so soon and so long as this capital possesses the monoply of the improved method of production, which enables it to accelerate the process of rotation. The difference in the time of rotation in different branches of trade manifests itself, on the contrary, in the fact that the profit yielded by the rotation of a given commodities-capital stands in inverse ratio to the number of rotations of the money capital of the tradespeople. "A large turnover and small profits"—this maxim appears, notably to the small retail tradesman, as one which he must follow on principle.

It is evident that this law holds good only for the average of the rotations made by the total commercial capital invested in a given branch. The capital belonging to A, who is in the same branch as B, may make more or less rotations than the average number. In this case, the others make less or more. This fact alters nothing in the rotation of the totality of commercial capital invested in the branch. But it has decisive importance for the individual tradesman. In this case he makes surplus profit. If competition compel him to do so, he can sell cheaper than his competitors, without his profit sinking below the average. If the conditions, which enable him to accelerate rotation, be themselves purchasable—*e. g.* the position of the building where the sales take place—he can pay an extra rent for this, *i. e.* part of his surplus profit is converted into ground-rent.

CHAPTER XXI

THE HISTORICAL DEVELOPMENT OF COMMERCIAL CAPITAL

(Extracted from vol. III, part 1, ch. 20, German ed.)

WHEN examining the question from a strictly scientific point of view, the formation of the general rate of profit appears as having its starting point in productive capital, and in the competition between the various productive capitals; and as having been, at a later period, "corrected," completed, modified by the intervention of commercial capital. But, viewed from a historical point of view, just the contrary is the case.

From what we have already said, it is evident that nothing could be more erroneous than to regard commercial capital as a species of productive capital, like mining, agriculture, cattle-breeding, manufacture, transport, etc. The simple observation that every productive capital performs exactly the same functions as commercial capital when selling its products and buying its raw materials, should alone suffice to render so primitive a conception impossible. Commercial capital is, on the contrary, but a differentiated part of productive capital, which has become independent, which constantly assumes the forms and performs the functions which are necessary to transform commodities into money (and *vice-versa*).

Up to now we have considered commercial capital from the standpoint, and within the limits, of the capitalist system of production. Not only trade itself, however, but also commercial capital, is older than the capitalist system—is, as a matter of fact, historically the oldest free form of existence of capital.

Because commercial capital is continuously and exclusively occupied with the circulation and exchange of commodities, no other conditions are necessary for its existence—apart from undeveloped forms which have their origin in direct barter—than are necessary for the simple circulation of commodities and money. Whatever be the organisation of the production which supplies commodities for sale—whether it be based on the primitive community or on slavery, or whether it be peasant production, or plebeian production, or capitalist production; whether all commodities be saleable, or only those produced in excess of the producer's own needs —such commodities must always be sold, be exchanged for others. And the medium of the sale, of the exchange, is commercial capital.

What quantity of products is brought into commerce, and consequently into the hands of the tradespeople, depends on the system of production; that quantity attains its maximum in the fully developed capitalist system of production, in which the product is, in fact, no longer anything else but a commodity, and is no longer produced as a direct means of subsistence. On the other hand, whatever be the system of production, trade gives the impulsion to produce more than the producer requires for his own individual needs, in order to exchange the surplus for treasure or means of enjoyment. There where trade once exists, therefore, it impresses on production a character tending ever more and more towards exchange-value.

However the society, for the exchange of whose commodities

the tradesman serves as intermediary, is organised, the tradesman's fortune always exists in money form, and his money invariably functions as capital, *i. e.* it functions for the purpose of making more money, or surplus-value. The motive which determines the merchant to lay out his money in bringing about the exchange of commodities, his definite aim in so doing, are—not only in the capitalist, but also in all the earlier forms of society—to make, out of money, more money. The various phases of the process of exchange M—C and C—M' appear merely as transitory incidents of the transformation of M into M', *i. e.* of money into more money. The characteristic movement of commercial capital is M—C—M' (Money—commodities—more money), and it differs from the trade between the producers themselves, characterised by C—M—C, which has as final aim the chance of use-values.

The more undeveloped production is, the less money will the producers have, and the greater will be the fortune in the form of money in the hands of the tradespeople; or else that money fortune will appear as a peculiar form of trading capital.

Thus, in all pre-capitalistic times, trade appears as the function *par excellence* of capital, as the latter's real and only aim. And all the more so, in the measure in which the process of production in itself furnished means of subsistence for the producers. At that time there was no capital other than commercial capital; whereas, as we have seen, capital, in the capitalist epoch, takes possession of production itself, and profoundly modifies its process; so that henceforth commercial capital is but a specific form or function of capital, which coexists alongside of other forms and functions.

We have thus no difficulty in understanding why commercial capital is to be found in history long before capital has taken hold of production. On the contrary, commercial capital must exist, and have attained a certain degree of development, in order that the capitalist system of production may arise—firstly, because it is a condition precedent for the concentration of money; and, secondly, because capitalist production presupposes wholesale distribution (and not distribution to the individual consumer). Capitalist production, therefore, presupposes also the existence of a tradesman, who does not buy in order to satisfy his individual wants, but in his capacity as intermediary for satisfying the wants of many. On the other hand, all development of commercial capital has the effect of impressing on the process of production a character tending ever more and more to exchange-value, *i. e.* to transform ever more and more products into commodities. But the development of commercial capital in itself is insufficient (as we shall see directly) to bring about and to explain the transition from one mode of production to another.

Within the system of capitalist production, commercial capital is deprived of its former independent existence, and becomes a specific form of capital investment in general; and the equalisation of profits reduces its rate of profit to the level of the average rate. Henceforth it functions only as the agent of productive capital. The particular social conditions which were created along with the development of commercial capital are now no longer decisive; on the contrary, there where commercial capital is still predominant, archaic conditions prevail. This holds good of different places within one and the same country—where, for instance, the purely trading towns offer us far more points for comparison with former times, than do the factory towns.[1]

The independent development, and the predominance, of commercial capital imply that capital has not yet taken hold of production. Thus the independent development of commercial capital stands in inverse ratio to the general economic development of society.

This phenomenon is especially observable in the history of the carrying trade—*e. g.* in Venice, Genoa, Holland, etc.— where the export of their own products by the countries concerned is but a subsidiary source of profit; and where profit is mainly derived from serving as intermediary for the exchange

[1] In modern English history, the commercial class properly so called and the trading towns are also politically reactionary, and allied with the landed and financial aristocracies against industrial capital. Compare, for instance, the political *role* of Liverpool with that of Manchester and Birmingham. English commercial capital and the English financial aristocracy have only recognised the complete supremacy of industrial capital since the repeal of the corn laws, etc.

of the products of communities whose trade and general economic life is still undeveloped, and from the exploitation of both producing countries.[1] Here we have commercial capital in its undiluted state, separated from the processes of production between which it serves as intermediary; and this is one of the main sources from whence its origin is derived. But this monopoly of the carrying trade—and consequently the latter itself—diminishes in the same measure in which the economic development of the nations progresses, which that monopoly exploited.—A typical example of the way in which commercial capital goes about its business in those countries in which it directly dominates production is, moreover, not only furnished by colonisation in general, but especially by the methods of the old Dutch East India Company.

At first sight, commercial profit appears impossible as long as products are sold at their value. For the law of trade is: buy cheap and sell dear; and not the exchange of equal values. The quantity in which products are exchanged is at first quite fortuitous. But if products are continuously exchanged, and therefore regularly produced in view of exchange, this state of things gradually ceases. But, at first, the fortuitous nature of the products exchanged does not cease in so far as producers and consumers are concerned; but only in regard to the intermediary between the two, *i. e.* the tradesman, who compares the money prices and pockets the difference.

The trade of the first independent, highly developed trading peoples and towns in ancient times was based, as simple carrying trade, on the lack of civilisation of the producing peoples, between whom the former served as intermediaries.

---

[1] "The inhabitants of the trading towns imported from richer countries more highly finished manufactured goods and expensive articles of luxury, and thus flattered the vanity of the large landowners, who greedily bought these things and paid for them in the shape of large quantities of raw produce from their estates. Thus, at that time, the trade of a large part of Europe consisted in exchanging the raw produce of one country for the manufactured goods of industrially more advanced countries. As soon as this taste had become general, and caused a large demand, the merchants began, with a view to saving costs, to introduce similar manufactures into their own countries." (Adam Smith, Wealth of Nations, III, ch. 3.)

In the preliminary phases of capitalist society—*i. e.* in Western Europe in the Middle Ages—trade dominates industry; the contrary is the case in modern nations. Trade naturally reacts more or less on the communities between which it is carried on; it subordinates production more and more to exchange-value, by rendering the means of enjoyment and subsistence itself dependent on sale rather than on the direct use of the product. It thereby puts an end to the conditions formerly prevailing. It increases the circulation of money. It not only seizes hold of the surplus production; it gradually invades the process of production, and renders one after another whole branches of production dependent on itself. Nevertheless, this dissolving influence depends to a large extent on the nature of the producing community.

As long as commercial capital serves as intermediary for the exchange of products between undeveloped communities, commercial profit does not only *seem* to consist of overreaching and fraud; but, as a matter of fact, it derives to a large extent its origin from these sources. When commercial capital occupies a position of unquestioned ascendency, it everywhere constitutes a system of plunder; even as its development in all trading peoples, both ancient and modern, is bound-up with extortion, piracy, slave stealing, colonial oppression. Thus it was in Carthage and Rome, and thus it was subsequently with the Venetians, Portuguese, Dutch, etc.

The development of trade and commercial capital increases everywhere the tendency of production to evolve in the direction of exchange-value; at the same time it widens the scope of production and its diversity, cosmopolitises it, develops money into world money. Trade thus exercises everywhere a more or less dissolving influence on those productive organisations which it finds already in existence, and which, in all their various forms, were mainly directed towards use-value. The extent, however, to which this process of dissolution is carried, depends in the first place on the solidity and inner structure of the former system of production. And the final result of the process—*i. e.* what sort of new system eventually replaces the old one—does not depend on trade, but on the nature of the old system itself. In the ancient world the consequence of trade and of the development of commercial capital was invariably slavery; according to what the starting-point of such development was, sometimes the mere transformation of a patriarchal system of slavery, based on the direct production of means of subsistence, into one based on the production of surplus-value. In modern times, on the contrary, the effect of the development of commercial capital is the capitalist system of production. It follows that these results themselves were also influenced by other circumstances, different from those accompanying the development itself of commercial capital.

It is in the nature of things that as soon as urban industry, as such, has been separated from agriculture, the products of the former should be, from the beginning, commodities, and that their sale should thus require the medium of trade. In so far, it is evident that trade leans for support on the development of town life, and that, on the other hand, urban development is dependent on trade. Nevertheless, how far industrial development goes hand in hand with such a process depends on entirely different circumstances. Already in the later days of the Republic commercial capital in Rome was more developed than it had ever been before in the ancient world; but there was no accompanying progress of industrial development. Whereas in Corinth and other Greek towns in Europe and Asia Minor, a highly developed industry accompanied the development of trade. On the other hand, quite contrary to the conditions of urban development, what we may call the spirit of trade and the development of commercial capital is often to be observed among nomadic peoples.

There can be no doubt—and precisely this fact has given rise to radically wrong views—that the great transformations in the 16th and 17th centuries, which in consequence of the geographic discoveries took place in trade and which greatly accelerated the development of commercial capital, constituted a decisive factor in effecting the transition from the feudal to the capitalist mode of production. The sudden extension of the world market, the diversity of the commodities circulated, the competition between the European nations for the possession of Asiatic products and American treasures, the colonial system: all these contributed in a vast measure to the bursting of the chains placed by feudalism on production. Nevertheless the modern mode of production, in its first phase—the manufacturing period—was only developed there where the conditions for such a development had been engendered during the Middle Ages. Compare, for instance, Holland with Portugal.[1] And if, in the 16th century—and in part, still, in the 17th—the sudden extension of trade and the opening-up of a new world market exerted decisive influence on the downfall of the old and the rise of the capitalist mode of production, this took place, inversely, on the basis of that capitalist mode, once it had come into being. The world market itself constitutes the foundation of this mode of production. On the other hand, the necessity of constantly increasing the scale of production, inherent to the capitalist system, causes a continuous expansion of the world market, so that, in this case, it is not trade which revolutionises industry, but industry which perpetually revolutionises trade. The supremacy of trade is now bound up with the degree of predominance of the conditions of modern industry. We need only compare, for example, England and Holland. The history of the decline of Holland as the leading trading nation is the history of the subordination of commercial capital to industrial capital. The resistance offered to the dissolving influence of trade by the inner cohesion and structure of the national, pre-capitalistic systems of production, is clearly manifested in the relations maintained by England with India and China. Here, the combination of agriculture on a small scale and domestic industry constitutes the broad basis of the mode of produc-

[1] How greatly predominant, in the development in Holland, and apart from other circumstances, the basis was which had been formed previously in the shape of fishery, manufacture, and agriculture—this fact was already pointed out by writers in the 18th century.—Contrary to the views formerly current, and according to which the extent and importance of Asiatic, ancient, and Middle Age trade were underestimated, it has become the fashion to greatly overestimate them. The best cure for this notion is to consider the English exports and imports at the beginning of the 18th century, and to compare them with those at the present time. And yet the former were incomparably larger than any of those of any older trading people.

tion; to this must be added, in India, the village community based on collective property of the soil, which community was likewise the original form of the economic organisation in China. In India, the English applied simultaneously political and economic pressure, alike as rulers and as owners of ground rent, in order to destroy these little economic communities. In this case, if English trade has been able to influence the system of production, it is only in so far as the cheaper prices of English goods succeed in eliminating the native spinning and weaving industries and thus rend the village communities asunder. Even then, this process of dissolution is a very slow and gradual one. In China, where direct political pressure is not available, the English have been even less successful. The great saving of time and labour due to the direct combination of agriculture and manufacture, offers here the stubbornest resistance to the invasion of the products of modern industry, whose prices are increased by the costs of the process of circulation which everywhere breaks through it.

The transition from the feudal mode of production takes place in a twofold manner. Either the producer himself becomes tradesman and capitalist—this is the really revolutionary manner. Or the tradesman takes direct possession of the process of production. However much this last manner of transition may, from a historical point of view, be regarded as such—e. g. as in the case of the English clothier of the 17th century, who sells the wool to, and buys the cloth from, those weavers who have remained independent—it none the less does not bring about by itself the transformation of the old mode of production; rather does it maintain the latter as the condition precedent of its own existence. For instance, up to the middle of the 19th century, in the French silk industry, as in the English stocking and lace industries, the manufacturer is only nominally manufacturer. In reality he is a mere tradesman, who let the weavers continue their work as before, each one for himself in his little workshop; and he did but exercise the functions of a tradesman for whom, as a matter of fact, they performed their labour. The same held good of the ribbon manufacture, lace-trimming and silk-weaving industries on the banks of the Rhine. This system is everywhere an impediment to the capitalist mode of production, properly so called, and disappears in the measure of the latter's development. Without transforming the mode of production, that system does but render the position of the labourer worse, turns him into a mere wage-labourer and proletarian under worse conditions than those prevailing among the labourers working directly under capital, and appropriates his surplus-labour on the basis of the old mode of production. Except for a few points of difference, the same state of affairs prevails (1865) in a section of the London furniture industry. The latter is divided up into a number of business branches quite independent of one another. One branch only manufactures chairs, another tables, a third cupboards, etc. But these various branches are themselves carried on on a more or less handicraft basis, by a master in a small way and a few apprentices. None the less is the production too extensive from these branches to be able to work direct for private individuals. Their clients are the owners of the furniture shops. On Saturdays the master goes to the latter and sells his product; whereby seller and buyer bargain over the price just as people in a pawnshop bargain over the loan to be advanced on a given pledge. These masters must sell their products weekly, if only to be able to buy raw material again for the next week, and to pay out wages. Under these circumstances they are in reality but intermediaries between the tradesman and their own workers. The tradesman is the real capitalist, who pockets the greater part of the surplus value. The position is similar to that when the transition of the branches which had formerly been handicraft-worked, or had been side-branches of rural industry, to the stage of manufacture took place. In the measure of the technical level attained by such a small workshop—there where it already employs itself such machines as admit of a handicraft organisation—the transition to modern industry takes place. Instead of by hand, the machine is propelled by steam, as this has recently (1865) happened in the English stocking industry.

The transition thus takes place in three ways. Firstly, the tradesman becomes, directly, an industrial producer; this is the case with the branches of industry which have developed out of trade—especially with the industry of luxury articles, which was imported by the tradespeople from abroad along with the raw materials and labourers, *e. g.,* in the 15th century, into Italy from Constantinople. Secondly, the tradesman makes of the small master his intermediary, or he buys direct from the self-producer; he lets the latter remain nominally independent, and does not alter his system of production. Thirdly, the industrial producer becomes a tradesman and produces wholesale for the purpose of trade.

In the Middle Ages the tradesman does but set in movement, so to speak, the commodities produced either by the members of the guilds, or by the peasantry. The tradesman becomes an industrial producer, or, rather, he lets the handicraft-worked—and especially the small rural—industry perform labour for him. On the other hand, the producer becomes trader. For instance, instead of receiving his wool little by little in small portions from the tradesman, and working with his apprentice for the latter, the clothweaver buys himself wool or yarn, and sells his cloth to the tradesman. And now the clothweaver produces for the trading world, instead of for the individual tradesman or for definite clients. The producer is himself a trader. Originally, trade was the condition precedent for transforming the guild-organised and rural domestic branches of industry, and also feudal agriculture, into capitalist undertakings. It creates the market for the product, it supplies new raw and auxiliary materials, and it thus opens out branches of production which are, from the start, founded on trade. As soon as manufacture, and still more modern industry, have developed to a certain extent, they create in turn the market, which they conquer by means of their commodities. Trade now becomes the servant of industrial production, for which the constant extension of the market is indispensable. Mass production on an ever increasing scale overflows the available market, and prompts thus to a continual widening-out of this market. This mass production is not limited by trade (in so far as the latter is but the expression of existing demand), but by the size of the functioning capital and the degree of development of the productive force of labour. The productive capitalist has the world market continually before him, and compares—and m ust compare—his own cost prices with the market prices, not only at home, but in the whole world. In the former period, this comparison falls almost entirely upon the shoulders of the merchants and thereby secures for merchants capital the supremacy over industrial capital.

CHAPTER XXII

INTEREST AND THE PROFIT DERIVED FROM INDUSTRIAL UNDERTAKINGS

(Extracted from vol. III, part 1, ch. 21, 22, 23, German ed.)

MONEY—here taken as the independent expression of a sum of value, whether the latter exist, in fact, in the form of money, or in that of commodities—can, on the basis of capitalist production, be employed as capital, and is hereby transformed from a given value into an increasing one. It enables the capitalist to get out of the labourers a definite quantity of unpaid labour, which the capitalist appropriates. In this way it obtains a new use-value, *i. e.* the use-value of making profit. In this capacity it becomes a commodity, but a commodity of a special kind.

A man who has $25 at his disposal, is able—assuming the yearly average rate of profit to be 20 per cent—to make $30 out of the original sum. If this man hands over the $25 to another man for a year, and the other man really employs them as capital, the former gives the latter the means of producing $5 profit. If the latter man pays, at the end of the year, say $1.25 to the owner of the $25—*i. e.* a part of the profit yielded by this sum—he thereby pays the use-value of the $25, the use-value of their function as capital. That part of the profit paid by him is called interest, which is thus but a special name for designating a part of the profit.

It is clear that the property of the $25 gives their owner the power to appropriate a part of the profit produced by his capital, *i. e.* the interest. If he did not give the other man the $25, the latter could not make the profit.

What does the money capitalist give the borrower, *i. e.* the industrial capitalist? What does he, in fact, sell him?

What is sold in an ordinary sale? Not the value of the commodity sold, seeing that the latter merely changes its form, and remains in another form in the hands of the seller. What is really sold by the seller, and is consequently transferred to the consumption of the buyer, is the use-value of the commodity.

What is, now, the use-value which the money capitalist sells for the time of the loan, and which he abandons to the borrower? It is precisely the capacity of producing a surplus-value, beside which the original value remains intact. In the case of all other commodities, the use-value is in the long run consumed; and thus the substance of the commodity disappears, and, with its substance, its value. The commodity we call capital, on the other hand, has a specific peculiarity: through the utilisation of its use-value, its value and use-value are not only maintained but increased.

What, now, does the industrial capitalist pay, and what is, therefore, the price of the capital lent? A part of the profit which can be produced with it.

How much of the profit must be paid as interest, and how much remains as actual profit—in other words: the so-called "price" of the capital lent—will be regulated by demand and supply, *i. e.* by competition, just like the market prices of commodities. But already here the difference is manifest. If demand and supply correspond to each other, the market price is, in the case of ordinary commodities, equal to the price of production (cost price + average profit). That is to say, their price then appears to be regulated by the inner laws of capitalist production, independently of competition. For the fluctuations of supply and demand explain nothing but the deviations of the market prices from the prices of production. And these deviations balance each other mutually, so that within certain long periods of time, the average market prices are equal to the prices of production. It is the same with wages. If demand for, and supply of, labour power correspond to each other, their effect is annulled, and wages are equal to the value of labour power.

It is different, however, in the case of the interest on money capital. Here competition does not determine the deviations from the general rule, but, on the contrary, no general rule for division exists except the one dictated by competition; because as we shall shortly see, no "natural" rate of interest exists. There is no such thing as "natural" limits of the rate of interest.

Seeing that interest is merely a part of the profit, that part which, on our assumption, must be paid by the industrial capitalist to the money capitalist, the maximum limit of the rate of interest appears as constituted by the profit itself, in which the part due to the functioning capitalist would be equal to zero. If we make abstraction of individual cases, in which interest can, in fact, be higher than the profit, but cannot, in consequence, be paid out of the latter—we could perhaps consider as maximal limit of interest the entire profit *minus* that part of it to be developed later, and which is dissolvable in wages of superintendence. The minimal limit of the interest is entirely indeterminable. It can sink to any level. But opposing forces always then enter into play, and raise it.

The average rate of interest prevailing in a country cannot be determined by means of any law. There is no such thing as a natural rate of interest in the sense of which the economists speak of a natural rate of profit and a natural rate of wages. The correspondence of demand and supply—the average rate of profit being assumed as given—here means absolutely nothing. There is absolutely no reason why the equilibrium between lender and borrower should result in a rate of interest of 3, 4 or 5 per cent, etc.

If we ask why the limits of the mean rate of interest are not to be traced to a general law, the answer is that this is due simply to the nature of interest. The latter is but a part of the average profit. How the two persons having a claim to such profit share it, is in itself purely accidental, just like the distribution of percentages of the common profit of a business company to the various co-proprietors.

Despite this, the rate of interest appears much more as a uniform, definite and palpable magnitude, than is the case with the general rate of profit.

So far as the rate of interest is determined by the rate of profit, it is invariably determined by the general rate of profit; not by the special rates of profit of particular branches of industry, and still less by the possible extra profit of individual capitalists.

True, it is exact that the rate of interest itself differs constantly according to the securities furnished by the borrowers, and according to the duration of the loan; but for each of these categories it is, at a given moment, uniform.

The mean rate of interest appears in every country, during a long period of time, as a constant magnitude, because the general rate of profit—despite the continual changes in the special rates of profit, which changes, however, balance each other—only varies in long periods of time.

As far as the constantly fluctuating market rate of interest is concerned, however, it must at every moment be regarded as a given magnitude, seeing that on the money market, all loanable capital is, in its totality, perpetually facing the active capital; thus the relation between the offer of loanable capital, on the one hand, and the demand for it, on the other, decides each time the market level of interest. This is *a forteriori* the case, the more the system of credit, owing to its development and consequent concentration, seizes hold of the loanable capital and throws it all at once, simultaneously, on to the money market. On the other hand, the general rate of profit exists always as a mere tendency, as a mutual balancing movement of the special rates of profit. The competition between the capitalists consists here in gradually withdrawing capital from those branches in which profit has for a long time remained below the average, and, inversely, in gradually supplying it to those branches in which profit is above that level; or else in gradually distributing, in varying proportions, supplementary capital among such branches. We have here a constant fluctuation of the supply and withdrawal of capital; not simultaneous operations in bulk, as is the case with the determination of the rate of interest.

The average profit does not appear as a fact which is directly given, but as the final result of the equilibrium of antagonistic fluctuations, which can only be discovered after minute investigation. It is otherwise with the rate of interest. The latter is—at least viewed locally—generally valid, generally fixed, generally known; and both the industrial and the commercial capital include it as an item in their calculations. The level of barometer and thermometer are not more exactly registered by meteorological reports, than is the rate of interest by the Stock Exchange reports—and not the rate for this or that individual capital, but for the total capital on the money market, *i. e.* for all loanable capital.

On the money market, lender and borrower are placed alone in front of one another. The commodity has but one single form, *i. e.* money. All the varying forms of capital, according to its investment in particular branches of production and circulation, disappear here. Here, capital exists in the homogeneous form of an independent value, *i. e.* of money. Here, the competition between particular branches ceases; all such branches are, in regard to capital, merged in the one branch of money borrowers; and capital itself is still indifferent to the particular manner in which it shall be employed. It is here in reality the common capital of a class, appearing in one single phenomenon of supply and demand.

It must be added that, along with the development of modern industry, money-capital—in so far as it appears on the market—is represented in an ever decreasing degree by the individual capitalist, the owner of this or that fraction of the capital available on the market; and that it appears, in an ever increasing measure, as a concentrated, organised mass, which is placed under the control of the bankers, as the representatives of the social capital, to a far greater extent than is the case with production. The consequence is that, as regards the form of the demand, the massive weight of a class confronts the loanable capital; and, as regards the supply, capital itself appears *en masse* as loan capital.

These are some of the reasons why the general rate of profit appears vague and hazy by comparison with the definite rate of interest; which, it is true, fluctuates in its amount; but, since it fluctuates equally for all borrowers, it appears always to the latter as a fixed magnitude.

How does it come about that the purely quantitative

division of profit into net profit and interest is transformed into a qualitative one? In other words, how does it come about that the capitalist also, who only employs his own, and not borrowed, capital, specially calculates a part of his gross profit as interest? And further, that all capital, whether borrowed or not, as bearing interest, be distinguished from itself as yielding net profit?

(Every quantitative division of profit is not turned into a qualitative differentiation; for instance, this is not the case with the division of profits between partners in a joint concern.)

For the productive capitalist, who works with borrowed capital, the gross profit is divided into two parts: The interest, which he must pay the lender; and the surplus obtained over and above the interest and which constitutes his own share of the profit. Now, whatever may be the amount of the gross profit, the interest is fixed by the general rate of interest, and is anticipated (sometimes by special legal agreements) before the process of production commences and before any sort of profit is made; so that the question as to how much of the profit remains for the producing capital, depends on the amount of interest. This last part of the profit appears, therefore, to the capitalist, as being necessarily derived from the employment of capital in trade or production. Contrary to interest, the still remaining part of the profit which is due to him thus assumes the form of industrial profit (or commercial, as the case may be) or the form of undertaker's profit.[1]

We have seen that the rate of profit—consequently also the gross profit—does not depend only on the surplus-value, but also on many other circumstances: on the purchase prices of the means of production, on the employment of exceptionally productive methods, on the economy of constant capital, etc.

[1] The word "undertaker" is the exact translation of the German word "Unternehmer" and of the French "entrepreneur." It was, to our knowledge, first introduced in this sense into the English vocabulary by Marshall in his *Principles of Economics*. The undertaker is the owner of an undertaking, who runs it at his own risk. Whether he himself possess the necessary working capital, or whether he has borrowed it from a financier (or money capitalist), is indifferent.—*Translator's Note*.

And, apart from the price of production, it depends on specially favourable junctures of affairs, and, in each and every business transaction, on the greater or lesser cunning and activity of the capitalist, how far the latter buys or sells over or beneath the price of production.

It would thus seem as if the interest which he pays the owner of the money capital, is due to the latter in his capacity *per se* as proprietor of capital. In contradiction herewith, the remaining part now appears as undertaker's profit, exclusively derived from the activity of the undertaker in industry or trade. From the standpoint of the capitalist, therefore, interest appears solely as the fruit yielded by capital *per se,* in so far as it does not "work"; whereas the undertaker's profit appears to him as being solely the fruit derived from the functions fulfilled by him, *i. e.* as the fruit derived from his own personal activity, as contrasted with the inactivity of the money capitalist.

A separation is thus effected between the two parts of the gross profit, as if they derived from two essentially different sources; each of them becomes "fixed," and independent of the other; and this respective "fixity" and independence must be established for the entire capitalist class and for the totality of capital. It is indifferent whether the capital employed by the active capitalist be borrowed or not. The profit on every capital, consequently also the average profit, is split up into two qualitatively different, independent parts, namely interest and undertaker's profit, both of which are determined by special laws. The capitalist who works with his own capital, and the capitalist who works with borrowed capital, divide their gross profit into interest and undertaker's profit. Interest, which, in the case of the former, is due to himself as proprietor of capital which he lends to himself; and undertaker's profit, which is due to both in their capacity as active capitalists. The capital itself is, in respect of the different kinds of profit yielded by it, split up into ownership, *i. e.* capital which remains *outside* the process of production, and which yields interest; and capital *within* the process of production, which yields the undertaker's profit.

Capital which yields interest, and interest itself, a subdivision of surplus-value, exist historically long before capitalist production and the conceptions of capital and profit implied by the latter. For this reason, the capital which produces interest is, in the public opinion, capital *par excellence*. For the same reason it was long believed that interest serves to remunerate money as such. The fact that money lent produces interest, whether it be really utilised as capital or not, confirms the belief that this form of capital is a distinct and independent one.

Interest thus appears to the capitalist as surplus-value which capital yields *per se,* and which it would yield also even if employed unproductively. This is true, in practice, for the individual capitalist. The latter has the choice between lending his capital in return for interest, or utilising it himself as productive capital. But from a general point of view, and applied to the entire social capital, such a notion is entirely wrong—although some economists have sought to make of it the basis of all profit. It is, of course, absurd to assume that the totality of capital will be employed as loan capital, without people being there to buy and utilise the means of production. If an excessive number of capitalists wished to lend their capital on interest, the result would be an immense depreciation of the value of money capital, and a corresponding decrease of the rate of interest. Many would be at once rendered unable to live on their interest, and would thus be compelled to become once more industrial capitalists. But, we repeat, it holds good of the individual capitalist. The latter thus necessarily considers—even if he works by means of his own capital —that part of his average profit which is equal to the average interest, to be the fruit of his capital as such, apart from all production. Capital bearing interest is *property-capital*, and as such is opposed to *capital as function*.

The producing (or active) capitalist bases his claim to the undertaker's profit on—and consequently derives that profit itself from—the fact that capital functions (as distinct from the ownership of capital). But, unlike the owner of the capital which bears interest, the representative of the capital in function holds no sinecure. The capitalist directs the process of production and that of circulation alike. The exploitation of productive labour cost much effort, whether the capitalist exploits it personally or entrusts the task to others. His profit as undertaker, contrary to the profit on interest, does not appear to him as the result of ownership, but of non-ownership —as the result of his activity as "labourer".

He thus imagines that his profit as undertaker, far from constituting a contrast to wage-labour and deriving from the unpaid labour of others, is itself wages, *i. e.* the wages of superintendence.

Even as interest appears as that part of the surplus-value which is engendered by capital itself, so does the undertaker's profit appear to be necessarily derived from production. The undertaker thus appears to create surplus-value, not because he works *as capitalist,* but because quite apart from his position as capitalist, he also performs work *as such.*

The idea of the undertaker's profit being wages of superintendence is further supported by the fact that a part of the profit can be isolated under the form of wages; or, rather, that a part of the wages appears as a part of the profit. This is the case with the salary of the manager of the undertaking.

The work of superintendence and management necessarily arises everywhere many persons perform labour in common for a common purpose. Such work has a double aspect.

On the one hand, in all labour performed by many persons in common, the unity of the process is ensured by a commanding will and by functions which have not in view the detail labour, but the total activity of the whole undertaking; as in the case of the orchestra conductor. This is productive labour, which must be performed everywhere a number of persons work together.

On the other hand, this work of superintendence arises necessarily in all systems of production based on the antagonism between the labourer and the owner of the means of production. The greater this antagonism, the more necessary the superintendence. Just as in despotic States the superintendence and interference of the government in general include both the performance of the common labour indispensable in all communities, and also the special functions which arise in consequence of the antagonism between the government and the people.

The ancient authors, who had slavery before their eyes, and who expose in theory what they saw in practice, describe the two aspects of the work of superintendence in absolutely the same way as do these economists for whom the capitalist system of production is eternal. Aristotle pointed out that all domination, whether political or economic, imposes on those in power the labour of government; in the economic sphere, therefore, they must understand how to suitably employ labour power. Aristotle adds that no great show can be made with work of superintendence; for which reason the master, as soon as he is rich enough, is glad to abandon the honour of carrying-out such duties to a manager or foreman.

The fact that the duties of management and superintendence are incumbent on the master in consequence of the exploitation of the labour of others, has often enough been held to justify such exploitation. And, just as often, the taking possession of the unpaid labour of others has been held to constitute a legitimate wage for such work performed by the capitalist. This argument has never been better stated than by a defender of slavery in the United States, a lawyer named O'Connor, in a speech in New-York on December 19th, 1859, the motto of which was "Justice for the South." [1] "Gentlemen," he said amidst great applause, "Nature itself has predestined the negro to this servitude. He has the necessary strength for work; but Nature, who gave him that strength, denied him the will to work and the reasoning powers indispensable for governing. Both have been denied him. And the same Nature, which denied him the will to work, gave him a master to compel him to work and to make of him, in the climate to which he is adapted, a being useful to himself and to the master who governs him. I maintain that there is no injustice in leaving the negro in the position in which Nature has placed him, and in giving him a master to rule him. We deprive him of none of his natural rights by compelling him to work in re-

---

[1] In April 1861 the Civil War between the Northern and the Southern States broke out, caused by the question of slavery, which the Southern States wished to maintain.

turn and thereby to furnish his master with an adequate compensation for the labour and talent expended by the master governing him, and in thus rendering the latter useful to himself and to society."

Like the slave, the wage-labourer must have a master in order to make him work and govern him. If we assume the relation of the governing to the governed to be eternal and immutable, and as indispensable for production, it is only natural that the wage-labourer be compelled to produce, not only his own labour wage, but also the wages of superintendence, and "thereby to furnish his master with an adequate compensation for the labour and talent expended by the master in governing him, and in thus rendering him useful to himself and to society." [1]

The work of superintendence and management, however, in so far as it originates in the domination of labour by capital, is even in the capitalist system not directly and inseparably connected with the productive functions that derive from the nature itself of labour performed in common. The wages of "epitropos" in ancient Greece, or of a *régisseur* in feudal France, are quite separate from the profit; and assume the form of labour wages for skilful work, as soon as business is done on a scale which admits of the payment of such a manager. Capitalist production itself is responsible for the fact that the work of management, henceforth entirely separated from ownership of capital, is to be found on the street. A musical conductor needs not by any means be the owner of his orchestra's instruments; nor is it a part of his functions as conductor to have anything to do with the "wages" of the other musicians. The cooperative factories prove that the capi-

---

[1] EDITOR'S NOTE.—It is worthy of remark that the founder of the Conservative Party in Prussia, Friedrich Julius Stahl (1802-1861), expressed exactly the same idea in regard to the modern proletariat. If he has to rely on himself the proletarian will go to the wall; therefore has Providence in its wisdom appointed masters for him, to whom he ought, for reasons of gratitude and in his own interest, to submit completely; the master has a right to claim remuneration for his labour of government. *Die gegenwärtigen Parteien in Staat und Kirche.* (The present parties in State and Church. Written in 1850. 20th lecture.)

talist has become superfluous as a functionary in the process of production. After each crisis in the manufacturing districts in England, we can see a number of ex-manufacturers henceforth superintending, for cheap wages, the factories formerly their own, as the managers to the new owners, who are frequently their creditors.[1]

We can see from the public statements of accounts of the cooperative factories in England, that after deduction of the salary of the manager—which, just like the wages of the other labourers, belongs to the variable capital—the profit was larger than the average, although the cooperative factories paid, in some cases, far higher interest than the private manufacturers. In all these cases the increase of profit was due to greater economy in the employment of the means of production. What interests us most, however, is the fact, that here the average profit (= interest + undertaker's profit) is manifestly and palpably a magnitude entirely independent of any salary paid for administration. As the profit was here larger than the average profit, so also was the undertaker's profit larger than usual.

The same fact can be witnessed in some capitalist undertakings, e. g. joint stock banks. Not only the salary of the manager, but also the interest due on deposits is here deducted from the gross profit; and yet a very large profit of undertaking frequently remains over.

The confusion of undertaker's profit with the wages of superintendence and administration, arose originally out of the external contrast between interest and the surplus part of profit. It was enhanced owing to the fact that profit was represented, not as surplus-value (i. e. unpaid labour), but as the wages of the capitalist himself for labour performed by him. Socialism, on the other hand, demanded that profit should be measured in practice according to what it claimed to be in theory, namely wages of superintendence. And this

[1] "In a case known to me, a bankrupt manufacturer became, after the crisis in 1868, wage-labourer of his own former labourers. After the bankruptcy, the factory was taken over by a cooperative association of the latter, who appointed the ex-proprietor as manager." (Note by Friedrich Engels.)

was very disagreeable, seeing that such wages of superintendence—like all other wages—were constantly sinking as a result of competition and the cheapening of education. With the development of cooperative societies among the workers, and of joint stock companies among the bourgeoisie, the last pretext for confounding undertaker's profit with wages of administration vanished.

In the case of joint stock companies a new swindle has developed in connection with the wages of administration; alongside of, and above, the real manager, a number of administrators and directors are appointed, for whom, as a matter of fact, administration and superintendence are but pretexts for enriching themselves at the expense of the shareholders. "The increment accruing to bankers and merchants by reason of the fact that they act as directors of 8 or 9 different companies, can be seen in the following case: the private balance-sheet of Timothy Abraham Curtis, handed in to the Courts after his insolvency, showed an annual income of £800 to £900 under the heading 'directorship.' As Curtis had been a Director of the Bank of England and of the East India Company, every joint stock company was delighted to be able to obtain his services as director." [1]—The remuneration of the directors of such companies amounts to at least a guinea [$5.00] for each weekly board meeting. The proceedings in the Court of Bankruptcy showed that these wages of superintendence are generally in inverse ratio to the real superintendence effectually exercised by such directors.

CHAPTER XXIII

CREDIT AND BANKS

(Extracted from vol. III, part 1, ch. 19, 25, 27; vol. III, part 2, ch. 29. German ed.)

THE capitalist has constantly to pay money to a large number of persons, and has also constantly to receive money in payment from a large number. The technical operations of

[1] *The City, or the Physiology of Business in London.* 1845. p. 82.

paying and receiving money are in themselves labour which produces no value and which must be reckoned among the costs of circulation. In addition, a definite part of the capital must always be available as treasure: a reserve of means of purchase and payment, unemployed capital awaiting employment in the form of money. This renders—besides receiving and paying money, and bookkeeping—a storing of the treasure necessary; which, in turn, constitutes a special kind of labour.

These purely technical processes of development, through which money has to pass—and the labour and costs which arise therefrom—are shortened by the fact that they are carried out by a particular section of agents or capitalists, on behalf of the whole capitalist class. Through the process of division of labour they become the special function of a section of capitalists, and hence (just as in the case of commercial capital) are concentrated, and take place on a large scale. Within this particular process, again, we find division of labour; which manifests itself alike in the constitution of heterogeneous branches, independent of one another; and also in the development of the workshop within each of these branches: payment and reception of money, balancing of accounts, bookkeeping, deposits, &c.

We have already shown how money originally develops in the process of barter between communities. The money trade, *i. e.* the trade in the money commodity, develops at first, therefore, out of international intercourse. As soon as different coinages exist in different countries, the merchants who buy abroad must change their local coin for the coin of the country with which they are dealing, and vice versa; or else various coins must be exchanged for uncoined silver and gold, the world money. Hence we may consider exchange as one of the main foundations of the modern trade in money.[1]

[1] "The necessity of employing everywhere the local coinage in commercial transactions, in which a settlement by means of coin was indispensable, arose from the great divergency of the coinages of the numerous princes and towns authorised to coin money, in respect of their standard of value. In order to effect cash payments, the merchants, when travelling to foreign markets, provided themselves with pure, uncoined silver and also with gold. In the same way, on starting

Out of exchange discount banks develop, in which silver or gold in their capacity as world money—now as bank or trade money—function in contradistinction to current coinage.

This exchange business, this trade in money, is one of the causes that gave rise to the development of credit. The detailed study of credit and of the instruments employed by it (credit money etc.) does not lie within our purpose. Only a few points need here be dwelt on, because they are characteristic of the capitalist system of production. We have to deal only with commercial and banking credit. The connection between their development and that of public credit will not be discussed. In chapter XVI (p. 220) we have already shown how the function of money as medium of payment develops out of the simple circulation of commodities, and how relations as between creditor and debtor are formed between the producers of, and the dealers in, commodities. "One sort of commodity requires a longer, another a shorter time for its production. Again, the production of different commodities depends on different seasons of the year. One sort of commodity may be born on its own market-place, another has to make a long journey to market. Commodity-owner No. 1 may therefore be ready to sell, before No. 2 is ready to buy. When the same transactions are continually repeated between the same persons, the conditions of sale are regulated in accordance with the conditions of production. On the other hand, the use of a given commodity, of a house for instance, is sold for a definite period. Here, it is only at the end of the term that the buyer has actually received the use-value of the commodity. He therefore buys it before he pays for it. The vendor becomes a creditor, the purchaser becomes a debtor."

With the development of trade and of the capitalist system of production, which only produces in view of circulation, the basis of credit is enlarged, elaborated, and universalised.

on their return journey, they changed the local money paid over to them into uncoined silver or gold. The exchange of uncoined precious metal for local coinage, and vice versa, was thus a widespread and lucrative form of business." (Hüllmann, *Städtewesen des Mittelalters,* Bonn 1826-29, vol. I, p. 437.)

On the whole, money here functions only as means of pay-ment, *i. e.* the commodity is not sold for cash but for a written promise to pay at a certain date. (For the sake of convenience we shall designate all such promises of payment as bills of exchange.) Until maturity, these bills themselves circulate as means of payment and form trade money (or commercial money) properly so-called.

"In every country the majority of credit transactions take place in the sphere of industry itself.... The producer of the raw material advances the latter to the manufacturer who works it up, and receives from him a promise to pay on a given day. The manufacturer, having completed his part of the work, advances in its turn the commodity on similar condi-tions to another manufacturer, who elaborates it further, and thus credit extends over an ever wider area, from one person to another as far as the consumer. The wholesale dealer ad-vances commodities to the retail tradesman, whereas the former receives advances from the manufacturer or the com-missioner. Everyone borrows with the one hand and lends with the other, sometimes money, but more often products. Thus, in the world of industry, an incessant exchange of advances takes place, which combine and clash with one another in all directions. It is precisely in the diversity and growth of these mutual advances that the development of credit resides, and here is the real source of its power." [1]

The other aspect of credit is connected with the develop-ment of the trade in money, which in capitalist production naturally keeps pace with the development of the trade in commodities. The storing of the reserve funds of the busi-ness world, the technical operations of receiving and paying out money, the international payments, and consequently the bullion trade, become concentrated in the hands of the money dealers.

"The cashier receives from the tradespeople who utilise his services, a certain sum of money, in return for which he opens them a 'credit account' in his books. They send him,

[1] Coquelin, *Le crédit et les banques dans l'industrie,* in *Revue des Deux Mondes,* 1842.

further, their claims for the sums due to them, which sums he collects and places to their credit; on the other hand, he makes payments for them conformably with their instructions, and debits their current account for the amount. For these services he demands a small remuneration, which, however, can afford adequate compensation for his work only in the measure of the extent and magnitude of his operations. If payments have to be balanced between two tradesmen working with one and the same cashier, such payments can very easily be effected by reciprocal bookings, whereas the cashiers, from day to day, adjust their reciprocal claims for them." (Vissering, *Handboek van praktische Staatshuishoudkunde*, Amsterdam, 1860, vol. I, p. 247.)

"In view of the need resulting from local conditions in Venice, where the carrying of cash is more inconvenient than it is elsewhere, the wholesale merchants of that city founded 'associations of depositors.' The members of such associations deposited certain sums under the requisite guarantees of security, control and administration; they gave their creditors payment-orders; whereupon the sum paid was debited to the debtor's account in the book kept for this purpose, and credited to the account of the creditor. The first beginnings of deposit and clearing banks." (Hüllmann, *Städtewesen des Mittelalters*, Bonn 1826-29, vol. I, p. 550.)

The administration of capital bearing interest, or money capital, develops in connection herewith into a special function of the money dealers. Borrowing and lending money becomes their speciality. They serve as intermediaries between the real lender and the borrower of money capital. Expressed in general terms, banking business, from this point of view, consists in concentrating the loanable capital in large quantities in the hands of the bankers, so that instead of the individual moneylender, the bankers appear as the representatives of the totality of moneylenders, on the one hand, facing the industrial and the commercial capitalists, on the other. They become the universal administrators of money capital. Inversely they concentrate the borrowers, in regard to the totality of moneylenders, by borrowing for the entire commercial world. In general their profit consists in borrowing at a lower rate of interest than they lend.

The banks obtain possession of the loanable capital at their disposal in various ways. At first the money capital which every producer and tradesman has in reserve, or which is paid him, is concentrated in their hands by reason of the fact that they are the cashiers of the industrial capitalists. In this way, the reserve fund of the trading world, being concentrated in common, is limited to the necessary minimum; and part of the money capital, which would otherwise lie idly in reserve is paid out in loans. Secondly, the loanable capital at the disposal of the banks is formed by the cash deposits of the money capitalists, who entrust the task of lending to them. Thirdly, as soon as the banks begin paying interest on deposits, the savings of all classes and all the money momentarily unemployed are deposited with them. Small sums, each of which is in itself unable to function as money capital, are gathered together in large quantities and thus constitute a financial power. Fourthly, incomes which are but gradually consumed, are deposited with the banks.

The loans are made by discounting the bills of exchange —*i. e.* by paying in cash before they are due the amount they represent—and by means of advances in sundry shapes: direct loans on personal credit, loans on the security of papers of all sorts bearing interest, especially of certificates of ownership of commodities, etc.

It is clear that the money capital with which the banks deal is none other than the capital in circulation of merchants and industrial undertakers; and that the operations undertaken by the banks are simply the operations of such merchants and undertakers, for which the banks serve as intermediaries.

It is equally clear that their profit is but a deduction from the surplus-value, since they only deal with values already realised—even if merely in the shape of debt claims.—Part of the technical operations connected with the circulation of money must be carried out by the tradespeople and producers themselves.

The general observations made so far by us in the course of our study of credit were the following:

I. Credit is necessary in order to create a medium whereby the rate of profit may be equalised.

II. It reduces the costs of circulation.
  1. Money is saved in three ways by the introduction of credit.
     A) Because it is henceforth not needed in a large number of transactions.
     B) Because its circulation is accelerated. On the one hand, owing to the technical methods adopted by the banks. On the other hand, owing to the acceleration of the turnover of commodities due to credit.
     C) Because paper money is substituted for gold.
  2. Credit shortens the various phases of circulation, hence also the whole process of reproduction. On the other hand, it permits of the processes of buying and selling being longer separated, and thus serves as basis for speculation.

     It reduces the reserve fund, which phenomenon can be regarded from a twofold point of view: from that of the reduction of the medium of exchange in circulation, and from that of the reduction of the amount of capital necessary in money form.

III. Formation of joint stock companies. Hereby:
  1. Immense extension of the scale of production, and foundation of undertakings which would have been impossible for any individual capital.
  2. In itself, capital rests on the cooperation of the many. In the joint stock company it directly assumes the form of social capital, in contradiction to private capital. Here we have the suppression of capital as private property within the limits of the capitalist mode of production itself.
  3. The capitalist, who, in reality, is the functioning capitalist, becomes in the joint stock company a mere director, the administrator of the capital of others; and the owners of the capital become mere money capitalists. Even if their dividends include the inter-

est and the profit of undertaking, *i. e.* the total profit, the latter is none the less obtained henceforth only in the form of interest (for the director's salary is, or is meant to be, a simple labour-wage); that is to say, it is obtained in the form of a mere remuneration due to the owner of capital. Ownership of capital is henceforth entirely separated from the latter's function in the real process of reproduction and viceversa.

This phenomenon, the result of the most complete development of capitalist production, constitutes an essential stepping-stone to the re-transformation of capital into the property of the producers—not as the private property of individual producers, but as social property. It is also the stepping-stone to the transformation of all those functions hitherto bound-up with the private ownership of capital, into social functions.

As profit, in this case, assumes purely and simply the form of interest, such undertakings are still possible if they do but pay interest.

(Additional Note by Friedrich Engels: Since Marx wrote the above, new forms of industry have been developed, by which the joint stock company has been raised to the second and third power. The time-honoured freedom of competition is at an end, and must itself admit its scandalous bankruptcy. It is bankrupt because, in every country, the magnates in any particular branch of industry unite in view of regulating production. In some cases it even came for a time to international trusts, *e. g.* between the English and the German iron industries. But even this form of socialisation of production did not suffice. The antagonism of the interests of the individual business firms caused it to be broken through too often. And thus it came about that, in some branches, in which the level attained by the process of production admitted of it, the entire production of the branch was concentrated in one single vast joint stock company under homogeneous management. In these branches, therefore, competition is replaced by monopoly, and the future expropriation by the whole society, the nation, has been most happily prepared.)

This is equivalent to the abolition of capitalist production within the capitalist system of production—a glaring anomaly which already at first sight appears as a mere transitional stage to a new form of production.

IV. Apart from the joint stock organizations, credit gives the individual capitalist—or him who plays the part of capitalist—an absolute control, within certain limits, over the capital, and consequently over the labour, of others. This capital, which a man really—or according to public opinion—possesses, becomes the basis for the superstructure of credit. This is especially true of the wholesale trade. That, which is risked by the speculating wholesale tradesman is not his own, but social property. The catchword of the origin of capital being found in saving also becomes wholly obsolete; for the tradesman in question demands precisely that others should save for him.

The cooperative factories of the working-classes are, within the old form of production, the first positive breach of that form; although they naturally manifest everywhere in their organisation the defects of the existing state of things. But, in them, the antagonism between capital and labour has been suppressed, although at first only in so far as the labourers, in their capacity of cooperators, become their own capitalists. The cooperative factories in question show us how a new mode of production develops naturally out of the old one, once a certain degree of development of the productive forces, and of the corresponding forms of production, has been reached.

The capitalist joint stock undertakings are, just like

the cooperative factories, stepping-stones leading from the capitalist to the social system of production; in the former, the antagonism has been negatively, in the latter, positively suppressed.

Bank capital consists of (1) cash, either gold or notes, (2) scrip securities.[1]   The latter, in turn, may be divided into two categories, viz:

1. Commercial papers, bills of exchange; the latter are "floating values," which become due from time to time; in the discounting of such bills (*i. e.* their payment in advance, before maturity), banking business properly so-called consists.

2. Public securities, such as treasury notes, shares of all kinds, in short scrip bearing interest, but which differ essentially from bills of exchange. Mortgages can be reckoned among such scrip.

The capital thus composed is subdivided into the invested capital of the banker himself and the deposits. In the case of banks issuing notes, the latter constitute a third subdivision.

For the present we shall leave deposits and notes out of consideration.

The form assumed by capital bearing interest causes every definite and regular income to appear as interest on capital, whether the income in question derives from capital or nct. In the same way every value-sum appears as capital as soon as it is not spent as income—*i. e.* it appears as main sum contrasting with the possible or real interest which it can bear.

The matter is simple. Let us assume the average rate of interest to be 5 per cent yearly. A sum of $125 would thus yield $6.25 every year, if transformed into capital bearing interest. Every fixed yearly income of $6.25 is thus regarded as the interest on a capital of $125. But this is a pure illusion, except in the case that the source from which the $6.25 derive is susceptible of being transferred—whatever that source it-

[1] From here on vol. III, part 2, ch. 29, German ed.

self may be, whether a mere right of ownership or debt claim, or a real means of production such as landed estate.

Let us take, for example, the public debt and labour-wages.

The State must pay its creditors every year a certain quantity of interest for the borrowed capital. The creditor cannot, in this case, give notice to his debtor to pay, but he can only sell his claim. The capital itself has been consumed, spent by the State. It exists no longer. What the creditor of the State has in hands is (1) a promissory note signed by the State for, say $25; (2) thanks to this promissory note a claim on the yearly State revenue, *i. e.* on the product of taxation, for a certain amount, say $1.25 or 5 per cent; (3) he can sell this promissory note, if he wishes, to any other person. But in all these cases the capital, which is supposed to yield the interest paid by the State, is purely illusory and fictitious capital. Not only has the sum originally lent to the State ceased to exist; but it was never intended to invest that sum as capital.

Let us now come to labour power. Labour wages are here regarded as interest, and consequently labour power is considered as the capital which yields this interest. For instance, if a year's wages amount to $250 and the rate of interest is 5 per cent, the annual labour power is equal to a capital of $5,000. The capitalist way of thinking attains here its highest pinnacle of absurdity. This foolish idea is, of course, disproved by two circumstances; firstly, the labourer must work in order to obtain his "interest"; and secondly, he cannot convert the "capital value" of his labour power into cash by transferring it.

This method of calculation is termed "capitalisation." Every regular income is capitalised by reckoning it—on the basis of the average rate of profit—as the amount which a capital lent at such a rate would yield. The last traces of any connection with the real process of the utilisation of capital are thus lost sight of; and the idea gains ground that capital undergoes, in some mysterious way, a sort of process of self-utilisation.

Even there where the promissory note—in the security —does not, as in the case of the public debt, represent absolutely fictitious capital, its capital value is purely illusory. The shares of railway, mining and shipping companies represent real capital, namely, the capital invested in those undertakings. But such capital has not a double existence—on the one hand as capital value of the shares, on the other as capital effectively invested in the undertakings. It exists only in this latter shape, and the share is nothing but a right of ownership to the surplus-value made by it.

The scrip is saleable, and consequently becomes a commodity; the movement and fixation of the latter's price are peculiar. The price of the shares of an undertaking rises in the measure in which its profits increase. If the nominal value of the share (i. e. the sum invested, which the share originally represented) be $25, and if the profit of the undertaking increases from 5 to 10 per cent, the share's value rises to $50, other circumstances remaining identical, and the rate of interest being 5 per cent. The contrary is the case if the profit diminishes. But if the utilisation of the effective capital remain the same; or if, as in the case of the public debt, no real capital be available, the price of the scrip rises or falls in inverse ratio to the rate of interest. If the latter rise from 5 to 10 per cent, a security which guarantees $1.25 interest henceforth represents but a capital of $12.50. If the rate of interest falls to $2\frac{1}{2}$ per cent, the same security represents a capital of $50. In times when the money market is depressed, these securities will fall twofold in price; firstly because the rate of interest rises, and secondly, because they will be thrown in large quantities on the market.

All such scrip represents, in fact, nothing but accumulated claims, rights of ownership to future production.

The greater part of bankers' capital is thus purely fictitious, and consists of debt claims (bills of exchange), State securities (representing former capital) and shares (drafts drawn on future increments).

With the development of the credit system, therefore, all capital appears to be doubled, or sometimes even trebled, because the claims for debts and the rights to ownership, which always represent but one and the same capital, are to be found in various hands and under various forms. A large part of the capital alleged to be available is mere phantasmagoria. This holds true, also, of the "reserve funds," in which we had thought to grasp at last something solid.

(Illustration furnished by Friedrich Engels: In November 1892 the 15 largest London banks had a reserve fund of nearly £28,000,000 all told, of which £3,000,000 at the outside was available as cash in their safes. The remainder consisted of their credit balances at the Bank of England. But the latter itself had, in the same month, always less than £16,000,000 as cash reserve.)

The bank system is, from the standpoint of formal organisation, the most artificial and highly evolved product which capitalist society is capable of producing. Hence, the immense influence exercised by an institution like the Bank of England on trade and industry, although the real movement of these latter are quite outside the sphere of activity of the former, who maintains a passive attitude towards it. True, the form of a general bookkeeping and of a general distribution of the means of production on a social scale comes hereby into existence; but only the form. We have seen that the average profit of the individual capitalist, or of every particular capital, is not determined by the surplus-labour which this capital appropriates first-hand; but by the quantity of total surplus-value appropriated by the totality of capital, and out of which each particular capital draws its dividend only as a proportional part of that totality. This social character of capital is not completely realised, until the full development of credit and banking. On the other hand, the effects of that development are more far-reaching still. The system of credit and banks places all the momentarily unemployed capital of society at the disposal of the productive and commercial capitalists, so that neither he who lends nor he who utilises that capital are its owner or its creator. The system thus suppresses the private aspect of capital and implies *per se*—but only *per se*—the suppression of capital itself. Through the medium of the banks, the repartition of capital is taken out of the hands of private capitalists and usurers, and is transformed into a special social function. But precisely on account of this, credit and banks constitute at the same time the instruments *par excellence* for impelling the capitalist system of production beyond its own natural limits; and become powerful means for producing crises and promoting fraud.

There is, finally, no doubt that credit will serve as a powerful lever during the transition from capitalist production to the system of production by social labour; but only as an element taken in conjunction with other radical transformations of the mode of production itself. On the other hand, the fallacies regarding the miraculous socialising influence of credit and banks are due to complete ignorance of the laws of capitalist production, and of the credit system which is one of the forms of that mode of production.

CHAPTER XXIV

CRISES

Editor's Introductory Note: Marx's theory of crises is so important for a comprehension of his whole teaching, that it cannot be omitted here. Unfortunately, every attempt to render this theory easily comprehensive in the same manner as the other parts of the work, that is to say by abbreviation and occasional modification of the terms of expression, has failed. In *Capital,* several hundred pages are devoted to this theory.[1] Marx has here undertaken a detailed study of the proportions in which capital and labour must be distributed in the different branches of production, if the equilibrium between production and consumption is to remain undisturbed; and further, the demonstration that, with every increase of production—increase which is continuously necessitated by capital's need for accumulation—the capitalist system destroys the equilibrium, thereby causing the crises. Marx thus shows that crises are not caused by mistakes committed by the capitalists, but are, on the contrary, an

---

[1] Cf. notably vol. II, ch. 18-21, 7-9, 13-17; vol. III, part 1, ch. 15; vol. III, part 2, ch. 30; in addition to which, observations are scattered throughout all three volumes.

inevitable result of normal activity of capital. If we wished to repeat all Marx's calculations, unending series of extremely dry arithmetical propositions would be the consequence, comprehensible only to those who, by dint of exceptional energy, could remember the innumerable details; and which, therefore, would probably be read by nobody. This, however, would be contrary to the purpose of *The People's Marx*.

We have therefore decided to go to work differently. We reproduce but a small fraction of Marx's calculations, in order to illustrate the method adopted by him. We then supplement these calculations by means of an essay written by us personally, which aims at showing and making comprehensible to the reader all that, in the present chapter, is essential.

We would add, that in his book *Finanzkapital* (Vienna, 1910 ch. 16-20, especially pp. 304-318), Rudolf Hilferding has given a good summary of Marx's arguments. Another work which in this connection may be read usefully, is the third section of chapter 12 of Franz Mehring's book *Karl Marx*, (Leipzig, 1918, pp. 378-387). The author of the section in question was Rosa Luxemburg.

* * *

If we consider the commodity product [1] supplied by society during the course of the year, we find it includes those parts which go to replace capital, and also those destined for consumption and which are, in fact, consumed by labourers and capitalists. How is the value of the capital consumed in the process of production replaced out of the annual product? And how is this interwoven with the phenomenon of the consumption of surplus-value by the capitalists and of labour-wages by the labourers?

We shall at first base our investigation on the assumption that the process of reproduction is carried-on on a simple scale, *i. e.* that this process is not extended, and is carried on as it was previously. We shall further assume that products are exchanged according to their value, and that the com-

[1] Extracted from vol. II, ch. 20, German ed.

ponent parts of productive capital do not alter their value either. In so far as prices deviate from value, this can exert no influence on the movement of the totality of the social capital. After as before, products are exchanged, on the whole, to the same amount; only the value of the share of each individual capitalist in the process, is no longer proportionate to the capital advanced, or to the surplus-value produced, by each one. But as far as other changes of value are concerned, such changes—in so far as they are of a uniform and general nature—cannot modify the relation between the respective value of the various component parts of the total annual product. On the other hand, in so far as such changes are only local and are not uniform, they can be understood only if we consider them to be deviations from relations of value which remain unchanged. But if we succeed in discovering the rules according to which one part of the annual product replaces constant, and another variable capital, a change in the value of the constant or variable capital would not modify those rules, but only the amount of the part passing over into the one or the other function.

The movement with which we are now dealing, *i. e.* the reconversion of a part of the value of the product into capital, whereas the other part is absorbed by the consumption of the capitalist and labouring classes alike, does not only replace value, but also matter; and is thus determined alike by the mutual relation of the respective values of the various component parts of the social product to one another, and by the material composition of those parts.

It must, further, be remembered that simple reproduction on a uniform scale does not in reality take place in capitalist society. On the one hand, to assume the absence of all accumulation on a capitalist basis, would be a strange hypothesis; on the other hand, the conditions of production are not absolutely identical in different years. However, in so far as accumulation takes place, simple reproduction invariably forms part of it, and can therefore be considered in itself.

The total product, consequently also the total production, of society, may be divided into two main parts, viz:

I. Means of production, *i. e.* commodities in a shape in which they must, or at least can, serve the purpose of new production (or, in other words, be absorbed by productive consumption).

II. Means of consumption, *i. e.* commodities in a shape in which they are consumed by the capitalists and labourers, (or, in other words, in which they are absorbed by individual consumption).

In each of these divisions, capital falls into two parts:

1. Variable capital. Considered from the point of view of value, this capital is equal to the value of the labour power employed in the division, consequently it is equal to the sum total of wages paid for such labour power. From the point of view of material, it consists in the active labour power itself.

2. Constant capital. The value of all the means of production employed in the division. The means of production themselves fall into two parts: fixed capital (machines, tools, buildings, cattle, etc.); and circulating constant capital (raw and auxiliary materials for production, semi-manufactured articles, etc.).

The value of the annual product produced in each of the two divisions, falls itself into two parts; one represents the constant capital (c), which has been consumed and its value transferred to the product; the other represents the supplementary value due to the year's labour. This latter part, in its turn, is subdivided; one fraction of it replaces the variable capital (v), which has been advanced; and the other is the surplus-value (s). Thus, just like the value of every individual commodity, that of the annual product of each division falls into c + v + s.

The value of c, representing the constant capital *consumed* in the process of production, is not identical with the value of the constant capital *applied* to that process. True, the materials necessary for production have been completely consumed and their value has been, in consequence, completely transferred to the product. But only a part of the fixed capital employed has been consumed and its value transferred to the product. Another part of the fixed capital (machines, buildings, etc.) still exists and functions—although we must make a deduction for wear and tear during the year. When we consider the value of the product, this part of the fixed capital, which continues to function, does not enter into our calculations. But we must also, at least provisionally, make abstraction of the value transferred, through wear and tear during the year, by fixed capital to the product—in so far as such fixed capital has not been, in the course of the year, replaced in natura. We shall discuss this point separately later on.

For the purpose of our investigation of the process of simple reproduction, we shall adopt the following formula as basis, in which

$$c = \text{constant capital}$$
$$v = \text{variable capital}$$
$$s = \text{surplus value}$$
$$\frac{s}{v} = \text{the ratio of utilisation, assumed at } 100\%,$$

i. e. it is assumed that the surplus-value is exactly equal to the outlay for labour-wages. (We may suppose the figures to represent millions of pounds sterling or dollars.)

I. Production of means of production (mp):
Capital $4000\ c + 1000\ v = 5000$
Commodity product $4000\ c + 1000\ v + 1000\ s = 6000$
existing in the form of means of production (mp).

II. Production of means of consumption (mc):
Capital $2000\ c + 500\ v = 2500$
Commodity product $2000\ c + 500\ v + 500\ s = 3000$
existing in the form of means of consumption (mc).

Hence the total annual commodity-product amounts to
I. $4000\ c + 1000\ v + 1000\ s = 6000$ means of production
II. $2000\ c + 500\ v + 500\ s = 3000$ means of consumption. Total value = 9000, from which the fixed capital which continues to exist in its natural form is excluded.

Let us now see what turnovers are necessary in this case, on the basis of simple reproduction in which the entire surplus-value is consumed. If we at first make abstraction of the money circulation which serves as medium for them, we at once get three important clues:

1. The 500 v, labour-wages, and 500 s, surplus-value of the capitalists in division II, must be spent on mc. But their value in mc amounts to 1000, which, in the hands of the capitalists of division II, replace the 500 v advanced and represent the 500 s. The labour-wages and surplus-value of division II are thus, within that division, exchanged for the product of II. Thus (500 v + 500 s) II = 1000 mc disappear from the total product.

2. The 1000 v + 1000 s of division I must likewise be spent on mc, consequently on the product of division II. They must therefore be exchanged for that part of the constant capital 2000 c still remaining over from this product. In return, division II receives a similar amount of mp, which incorporate the labour wages and the surplus-value of division I. Hence 2000 II c and (1000 v + 1000 s) I disappear from our calculation.

3. There still remain 4000 I c. These consist of mp, which can only be utilised in division I, which serve to replace its consumed constant capital, and which thus accomplish their destiny by being exchanged between the individual capitalists of division I.

(The above is for the meantime, to enable the reader to understand better what follows.)

Let us now come to the great exchange which takes place between the two divisions.

(1000 v + 1000 s) I—mp in the hands of the producers in division I—are exchanged for 2000 c II, *i. e.* for values in the natural form of mc. The capitalists of division II thus convert again their constant capital from out of the form mc into the form mp; and the latter are precisely such mp as are able to produce new mc. On the other hand, the labourers and capitalists of division I receive in this way, in exchange for their wages and surplus-value, the mc needed by them.

For this mutual turnover, however, a process of money

circulation serves as medium; the process in question renders more difficult the comprehension of the former; but it has decisive importance, for the reason that labour-wages (the variable part of capital) must perpetually reappear in money form. In all branches of business, whether in division I or division II, wages are paid in that form. In order to obtain the money, the capitalist must sell commodities.

In division I the total capital has paid 1000 (which we may designate as $1000, in order to underline the fact that it is a money value) = 1000 v to the labourers for that part of the product already existing as v part. The labourers buy for the $1000 mc from the capitalists of division II, and thus transform half the constant capital of the latter into money; the capitalists of division II, in their turn, buy with the $1000 mp from those of division I; the latter's variable capital is herewith once more converted into money, for which they can buy new labour power. The capitalists of division I have, therefore, originally advanced this money themselves.

More money is necessary, in order to exchange those mp which represent the surplus-value of the capitalists of division I, for the second half of the constant capital of division II. These sums can be advanced in different ways, but must under all circumstances be derived from the capitalists; for we have already settled our account in respect of the money thrown into the process of circulation by the labourers. A capitalist in division II can buy mp with the money capital he possesses in addition to his productive capital; or, vice-versa, a capitalist in division I can buy mc out of money reserves destined to meet his personal expenses (and not for investment as capital). Certain money reserves—whether for investment as capital or for personal expenditure—must under all circumstances be presumed available, alongside of productive capital, in the hands of the capitalists. Let us assume (for our purpose the proportion is quite indifferent) that one half of the money is advanced by the capitalists of division II for the purchase of mp, whereas the other half is spent by the capitalists of division I on mc. In this case, division II has replaced three-quarters of its constant capital *in natura* with $500 (including the $1000 derived from the labourers of division I). Division I, however, gives the $500 thus obtained back to division II in exchange for mc; and division II gets back in this way the $500 as money capital, which it owns alongside of its productive capital. In addition to this, division I gives also $500 for the purchase of mc. With these last $500 division II buys mp, and has thus replaced its entire constant capital (1000 + 500 + 500 = 2000) *in natura;* whereas division I has spent its whole surplus-value on mc. All in all, a turnover of commodities to the extent of $4000 with a money circulation of $2000 would have taken place. We only obtain this amount of money because we assumed that the entire annual product was, all at a time, turned over in a few large lots. The only thing of importance, here, is that division II exchanges its constant capital mc for mp, and also gets back the $500 advanced for the purchase of mp; and that division I regains possession in money form of its variable capital, which had the form of mp, and is thus enabled to buy new labour power, and that it likewise receives back the $500 which it had expended on the purchase of mc before having sold the surplus-value of its capital. These $500, however, flowed back, not by reason of the expenditure, but through the subsequent sale of a part of the commodity-product of the division containing half its surplus-value.

The general consequence is: so much of the money thrown by the producing capitalists into the process of circulation returns into the hands of each individual capitalist, as he has advanced for the money circulation.

There now remains only the variable capital (labour-wages) of division I. At the end of the process of production it first exists in that commodity form in which the labourers have supplied it, *i. e.* in mp. The labourers have received their wages from the capitalists of division I. But the labourers do not buy mp, this money does not return direct to the capitalists of I, but first goes to the capitalists of II, from whom the labourers buy their mc. And, only because the capitalists of II spend the money on the purchase of mp, does it return by this circuitous route into the possession of the capitalists of I.

In the case of simple reproduction, therefore, that part of the annual product of division I which represents the sum $v + s$ of division I must be equal to the constant capital of division II, or to that part of the total product of division II which represents the latter's constant capital. I $(v + s)$ $= II c$.

It still remains for us to study the component parts $v + s$ of the value of the product of division II. With the labour-wages received from the capitalists of division II, the labourers of this division evidently buy back a part of their own produce. Hereby the capitalists of division II re-transform the money capital advanced by them for wages, into money form. It is just the same as if they had merely paid their labourers in stamps.

Division II of production consists of the most heterogeneous branches of industry, which can, however, be grouped in two main subdivisions:

A) Means of consumption, which are needed by the labourers, and which, in so far as they are necessary means of subsistence, also constitute a part of the consumption of the capitalists. For our purpose we may conveniently resume this whole subdivision as the subdivision of *necessary* means of consumption. It is indifferent whether any given product, such as *e. g.* tobacco, be physiologically necessary or not; it suffices, that it is habitually consumed by the labourers.

B) *Luxuries* for consumption, *i. e.* those means of consumption which are consumed exclusively by the capitalists, and which, therefore, can only be exchanged for surplus-value.

In the case of the *necessary* mc, it is clear, that the wages advanced in money form in the course of their production must return direct to those capitalists of division II who produce such necessary means of subsistence (*i. e.* to the capitalists of II A). The means of circulation are here directly furnished by the money which the labourers spend. It is different with subdivision II B. It is here a question of articles of luxury, which are not bought by the labourers. If the wages advanced for the production of those articles are to return again in money form to the capitalists, this cannot be effected directly; an intermediary is required. On calculating more closely we obtain a formula very similar to that obtained when the surplus-value of division I (mp) is exchanged for mc; and which shows that a similar proportion between the production of necessary means of subsistence and that of luxuries is required.

Assuming simple reproduction, we come necessarily to the following result:

1. That part of the yearly product, which, in the form of mp, represents newly created value $(v + s)$, must be equal to the constant capital of the other part existing in the form of mc. If the former were smaller than II c, II could not entirely reconvert its constant capital into mp, and could not, therefore, continue producing on the old scale. If, on the other hand, it were larger, a surplus would remain unutilised.

2. The wages of the labourers engaged in producing luxuries must be smaller than the surplus-value of those capitalists who produce necessary means of subsistence.[1]

2. The Theory of Crises [2]

BY JULIAN BORCHARDT

IN view of the fundamental divergency between the bourgeois and the socialist economic systems, opinions regarding the phenomena of crises differ widely on almost all points. But it is a matter of general agreement that the crisis constitutes a grave disturbance of the equilibrium between production and consumption. As Paul Mombert writes: [3] "A

---

[1] We break off here—conformably with what we said in the introductory note to this chapter — Marx's exposition of the subject, and we would refer the reader to the essay which follows entitled *The Essence of Marx's Theory of Crises.*

[2] An explanation of chapter XXIV.

[3] Wirtshaftskrisen (Economic Crises), Karlsruhe, 1913, p. 1.

state of things whereby supply and demand balance each other on the commodities market, in which consequently a complete equilibrium between production and consumption exists, in which the commodities produced find buyers with just as little difficulty as the demand for commodities can be satisfied—this appears as the economic ideal. As a matter of fact the connection between producer and consumer is to-day established by means of so numerous and often complicated intermediaries, that the fundamental truth, that production exists in view of consumption, and that commodities are produced to satisfy the need for them, is easily overlooked. The natural consequence of this fundamental truth is that an equilibrium must be sought, *i. e.* as far as possible so much of each commodity must be produced as is needed by the consumers—neither more nor less. If this is not the case, either too many or too few commodities will be produced, or else commodities other than those required; and the result will be a disturbance of the market, which will make itself felt in proportion to its extent. We do not require a special training in political economy in order to perceive that, in times of crisis, on the one hand an immense amount of unsaleable commodities is lying piled up; whereas on the other hand, among the mass of consumers, a dearth of commodities prevails at the same time. True, it cannot without further ado be maintained that the discrepancy between production and consumption is the fault of either the producers or the consumers. It may be that the commodities produced correspond, both quantitatively and qualitatively, to the needs of consumption. But the very complicated apparatus which to-day conveys the commodities from the producers to the consumers, can be out of order; with the consequence that, on the one hand, commodities remain unsaleable, which, on the other hand, are urgently needed. At any rate, it is certain that, whatever be its reasons, the crisis consists in a disturbance of the equilibrium between production and consumption."

The question rises: was this always the case? Or was there a time in which no such disturbance occurred—nay, may even have been impossible. A precise answer to this

question is not possible, for our knowledge of the economic
life of primitive peoples is much smaller than might be supposed after reading certain graphic descriptions. But it is
reasonable to assume that among small hordes of savages,
who only seek to satisfy immediate wants, it is difficult to
produce more or less than is necessary for such a purpose.
If we come to the ancient Germanic tribes in the time of
Augustus and Hermann, we find that Steinhausen (Ger-
manische Kultur in der Urzeit, pp. 144, sqq.) writes concerning them: "As is the case with all peoples living in a
state of nature, labour knows but one motive—imperative
need due to scarcity. Regular labour does not exist . . . The
activity resulting from the search for food, or from the necessities of habitation and the satisfying of other elementary
wants, is at first regarded only in a limited measure as
labour. . . . Each household procures and produces itself
everything necessary." Let us imagine such a primitive Germanic tribe, perhaps consisting of only a few dozen members,
which roams about in the forest, hunts, searches for roots
and fruit, and robs other tribes; and we see at once that the
idea of these people "producing" more or less than they
immediately want, is untenable.

But this idea is difficult to conceive of in much higher
phases of civilisation as long as "self-production," *i. e.* production in view of one's own needs, is the predominant form.
This form of production does not always retain the primitive
characteristics of which we have just spoken. Economic
activity becomes regulated. But let us take a tribe of a few
hundred or even a few thousand members, which carries-on
regularly cattle-breeding and agriculture as well as hunting
and warfare; as long as "every household procures and produces itself everything necessary" the needs of each individual are well known. And it is evident that the entire
productive activity will be solely directed to satisfying these
known needs. The same applies to the communal production
of such small tribes. Of course excessive production (or
"overproduction") can take place in consequence of an unusually good harvest or of unusually large booty being captured in a raid. But in these cases the difficulty of disposing

of the surplus products should not be noticeable. And thus we may, as a matter of fact, assume that during all the centuries in which "self-production" was predominant, *i. e.* production in view of one's own needs, the equilibrium between production and consumption existed, seeing that production had to be based exclusively on the needs of the consumers.

But, however long it may have lasted, the period of self-production none the less passed away. The constant growth of population, and the accompanying increase of the latter's requirements, led to the division of labour and to the production of commodities. Let us take the case of the earlier or later Middle Ages, when the town dwellers lived, if not exclusively, at all events mainly, by their handicraft. These inhabitants of the towns in the Middle Ages were all of them peasants. Either within or without the city walls, they owned their meadows on which they let their cattle graze. But, in addition, they had their respective handicrafts, and these provided them with an ever increasing share of their food. If, now, a shoemaker continually made shoes, a tailor clothes, a weaver cloth, etc. it was perfectly clear that he did not aim at satisfying his own requirements, but those of others. The finished products had to be sold, and were from the very beginning destined for sale. Commodities were produced.

Herewith arises the possibility of a rupture of the equilibrium between production and consumption. The direct connection between them is suppressed. For it must be noted that the sale of one's own products, at least in the case of the Germans, did not originate directly in the needs of the consumers, but in the increase in the volume of production. (As for the products of foreign countries, these were since the earliest times imported and sold by foreign tradespeople.) The large landed estates, which arose under the Frankish dynasty (between about 500 and 900) brought together, on one vast property and under the command of a single master, considerable numbers of people; and they called into existence a labour organisation for their own systematic cultivation—a widely differentiated organisation of officials, warriors, administrators, peasants and handicraftsmen. Here, then, is the origin of handicraft to be found, and only here could it originate. On a small peasant holding, where perhaps less than a dozen persons lived together, it could occur to nobody to busy himself exclusively, for instance, with making clothes for so few people; he would not have had enough work to fill-up his time. But on the large estates, where it was necessary to provide hundreds of persons with food, clothing, etc. labour was at first split-up in such a way that one man made only clothes, another only utensils, etc. To this division of labour must be attributed precisely the ever growing increase of productiveness. Production increased constantly, until it finally exceeded the needs of masters and dependents alike. The sale of such excess produce began; and it is interesting to see how, in German history, the development of trade gradually separated the handicraftsman from the estate, caused him to settle down in the market centres, and thus led to the foundation and extension of urban communities.

Nevertheless, we know nothing of any commercial crises during the Middle Ages, that is to say of serious ruptures of the equilibrium between consumption and production. Or, at any rate, we know only of such as had their origin in external causes, and especially in war; and which were due to the fact that production was insufficient to meet the demands of the consumers. But we do not read of any which, as is the case to-day, had their origin in internal causes, and derived from "overproduction." And this is perfectly explicable. The primitive handicraftsman, in the Middle Ages, worked in reality only for his own immediate neighbourhood. But he knew beforehand exactly his neighbours' wants, and was able to regulate his production accordingly. For instance, the shoemaker at first only made boots to order; or such boots as he was quite sure of selling immediately. Then came the trading and handicraft guilds, which exactly portioned out the market between their members. True, such primitive conditions did not last. Traffic and trade were developed, not only between communities, but also between different countries. Of course, with every such extension, the possibility of a rupture of equilibrium increased. It was not possible to foresee the extent of the requirements in a distant town, and especially in foreign countries, with the same accuracy as those in one's own neighbourhood; and hence it was not possible to adjust production to them with the same exactitude. But none the less did the connections between production and consumption still remain clear, uncomplicated, and visible at a glance. As we have said, we know nothing of any serious disturbances.

We may, therefore, take it to be proved that during the period of self-production the equilibrium between production and consumption was, so to speak, self-evident; production was determined by the needs of the consumers. These needs then caused the division of labour, and thus created the possibility of a rupture of the equilibrium. That disturbing factor was, however, necessary, in order to engender the forces which were alone in a position to satisfy the increased requirements.

From the simple production of commodities, the process of evolution leads up to the dawn of the capitalistic era. What does the difference between capitalism and the simple production of commodities consist of? From an external point of view, in the lack of independence of the producer. The handicraftsman is his own master, who works for his own account; the wage-labourer is in the employ of the capitalist. Viewed from inside, a more essential difference is seen to reside in the fact that the organisation of labour is, in the capitalist system, more complicated. In so far as the handicraftsman of the Middle Ages is assisted by journeymen and apprentices, he is obliged to teach them the handicraft; each of them must learn everything connected with the latter. The capitalist, on the other hand, brings together from the outset, in his workshop, a number of labourers for the purpose of producing as many commodities as possible. The instruction imparted to each individual labourer interests him only in so far as such instruction enables the total number employed to produce more. But it is soon manifest that this purpose is best served by not imparting to the individual too varied and manysided instruction; but, rather, by giving him a definite partial operation to perform, to which he must intensively accustom himself. Then, by means of the systematic cooperation of all, the production is increased. In this way, manufacture arises.

Owing to this systematic cooperation, however, a new factor enters into the process of production, which was previously absent from it. The quantity of products to be turned out is henceforth no longer determined by the sole requirements of the consumers; but depends also on the necessities of production itself. For instance, in a type manufactory in former times, one founder could cast 2000 types an hour, whereas a breaker could break up 4000 and a rubber could polish 8000. (Comp. Marx, *Capital*, vol. 1, p. 338, English ed.[1]) Consequently a column consisting of one rubber, two breakers, and four founders, had to work together. This cooperation, this mutual dependence on one another, requires also that 8000 types be manufactured per hour, and not less; for otherwise, part of the labourers would not be fully employed. Let us assume that only 6000 had to be manufactured; in this case, one of the founders would have to be discharged; but the rubber and the two breakers would have to be kept, although they would necessarily remain idle part of the time, and thus inflict loss on the capitalist. The result is, that the capitalist must see that he finds a market for 8000 types an hour; otherwise he is unable to fully utilise his apparatus for production, which costs him money and cannot be reduced in size.

We see, therefore, how the connection between production and consumption is progressively dissolved. Already in the early days of the capitalistic era, of which we are now speaking, the capitalists see themselves compelled to increase the quantity of their production without any regard for the wants of the consumers. The aim of production is, so to speak, henceforth within itself. Originally, of course, the increase of production was due to the increasing requirements of the consumers, and the new mechanism of production was created in view of satisfying this growing demand. Once in existence the new mechanism leads an independent

[1] This abridged edition, p. 78.

life, and has to function with absolute disregard to the question as to whether its activity merely satisfies the requirements of the consumers, or whether it exceeds them.

Thus, for the first time, excessive production is rendered possible. Such "overproduction" is here to be understood in the rational sense of the word, as implying production over and above the requirements of the consumers. The connection between producer and consumer no longer exists, the equilibrium fluctuates. But we repeat that this development was absolutely necessary in order to engender the forces capable of satisfying the increased requirements.

The tendencies of the rupture of equilibrium between production and consumption—rupture caused, as we have seen, by the respective necessities of both—are clearly manifest, and are pushed to their extreme consequencs, in our modern capitalist society. There can here be no question of equilibrium. On the one hand, the productive apparatus is immensely vaster, and produces immense quantities of commodities; consequently it is far less able to adapt itself to the needs of the consumers, than even the manufacturing system was. For instance, if the demand for steel increase to a point at which the existing means of production can no longer satisfy it, it is impossible, in order to meet the increased demand, to build a small steel works; the latter must, under all circumstances, be large, for only on that condition can it pay. But such a large steel works produces at once a surplus quantity far greater than the quantity corresponding to the increased demand. (Cf. Hilferding, *Finanzkapital*, p. 327.) On the other hand, the labouring class, under the domination of capitalism, receives only a part of the values which the former produces; the difference, therefore, between what the labourers *are able* to consume, and what they *should* consume in order that all commodities produced be disposed of, constantly increases owing to the continuation of the developmental process in question, which is continually augmenting the production. Finally we must note that, along with the growth of production, not only does this process become more extensive, but likewise more complicated, and consequently far more susceptible to disturbance.

In order to illustrate this truth, we must once more enter into some detail.

When primitive man, living in a virgin forest, feels a want of any sort, let us say a want of food, he sets out to hunt; or else he gathers roots and fruit; and he appeases his hunger with what he kills or finds. To-day, if a man's hunger is to be appeased, a number of intermediary factors come into play. In order to produce the bread on the table before us, the baker had to perform work. But, for this, he requires an oven, together with the necessary apparatus; and also the house in which they are placed. He buys flour from the miller, who grinds the corn in his mill. In order to construct ovens and mills, and the machinery pertaining to them, factories are indispensable; and these factories, in turn, procure iron, timber, coal, in more or less worked-up form from big undertakings, such as mines, etc. In other words, the requirements of modern civilised humanity are not satisfied directly, but very indirectly. The supply of bread (and, indeed, of every article of consumption) to the consumer, is but the final link in a long chain consisting chiefly of supplies of means of production by one producer to another. These circuits were necessary in order to bring the abundance of production to its present high level. If a rupture of the equilibrium between production and consumption is to be prevented, not only must the baker furnish exactly the amount of bread needed by the consumers; but also the factories must supply the precise number of ovens necessary for the purpose of baking, the mines the precise amount of coal, iron, etc. In other words, an exact equilibrium must exist between all the various branches of production. But this is impossible for the reason already stated; namely, because the process of production, in order to develop the productive forces, must obey its own laws, which derive from its own organisation; and, therefore, it cannot accommodate itself to the requirements of the consumers. How rigorously exact the equilibrium between the different branches must be, was shown by Marx in the celebrated formulas contained in the second volume of *Capital,* of which Hilferding gives a good summary in his *Finanzkapital* (pp.

297 sqq.). We will try by means of a single example to briefly illustrate the meaning of the problem.

If, for the sake of simplicity, we assume that the entire process of production shall only be continued on the same scale as heretofore, *i. e.* that it shall not be extended, then must the capitalists be in possession of the necessary means of production and subsistence, not in money form, but *in natura*. For money cannot be used by the labourers as food, it cannot weave yarn or melt iron. Consequently, the total available quantity of means of subsistence and production must be distributed among the different branches in such a way, that each of them be in a position to continue producing. If there be anywhere the slightest disharmony, a disturbance must be the result. In what proportion must the distribution be effected?

If, for instance, the capitalists who produce means of consumption (mc) are at the end of the year in possession of 3000 mc *in natura*, they must feed their labourers and themselves with them during the coming year; and, in addition, so much must remain over, as can be exchanged for the necessary means of production (mp). Let us assume they need 500 for their workmen, 500 for themselves, whereas they buy mp for the remaining 2000 mc.

Through this last transaction, the capitalists who produce mp come into the possession of 2000 mc *in natura*, which they can utilise during the following year for feeding their workmen and themselves. Consequently, the proportion being the same as in the group mc, they will give their workmen 1000 and retain 1000 for themselves. If, now, the capitalists of the group mp are to continue producing, they must have so much mp over from their former production, as will suffice for the employment of the number of labourers who are fed for a year with 1000 mc. Assuming the proportional figures to be the same, the quantity of such mp is 4000. In other words; if the production of the group mc requires 2000 mp + 500 labour-wages + 500 surplus-value for the capitalists; in order to maintain the equilibrium, the group mp must have at its disposal for the purpose of production, 4000 mp + 1000 labour-wages + 1000 surplus-value. This is the meaning of the celebrated formula of Marx:

$$\text{I Mp } 4000c + 1000v + 1000s = 6000$$
$$\text{II Mc } 2000c + 500v + 500s = 3000$$

in which s = surplus-value, v (variable capital) = labour-wages, and c (constant capital) = means of production. A single glance at this formula suffices to show us that, under the complicated circumstances of capitalist production, such a subtle equilibrium is quite impossible. And yet we have, up to now, only resumed matters very summarily. We have placed all the capitalists who produce mp in a single group, and also all those who produce mc. But it is evident that the equilibrium must exist within much more intricate sub-divisions of these groups. For instance, those capitalists who manufacture baking ovens must have at their disposal exactly the quantity of mc and of mp adapted to their branch of production as is determined by the requirements of the bakeries. Besides which, we have proceeded on the assumption that the process of production is continued on the same scale, *i. e.* that it is not extended; and this never happens in reality. But the constant extension of the process renders the conditions of equilibrium still more subtle and complicated. Neither have we taken into consideration the different categories of mp, *i. e.* the so-called fixed and circulating capital; which again, complicates the conditions necessary for effecting an equilibrium. And, finally, we have not taken into consideration the fact that all exchanges of mp for mc, of mp for mp, of mc for mc, of labour-wages for food, etc. take place through the medium of money; and that new disturbing factors are called into existence by the employment of money.

Thus it is certain that even an approximate equilibrium between production and consumption cannot be realised in capitalist society; and that, in consequence, crises are inevitable. But at the same time we see how necessary such disturbances are, in view of causing that development of the productive forces by means of which alone the constantly increasing requirements of the consumers can be satisfied.

The only question still remaining is: can, in the future, a solution of these antagonisms, their reconciliation in a higher synthesis, be expected—and, if so, how can it be brought about?

The answer is given with classical clearness by Engels in the pamphlet, published after his death, entitled *Principles of Communism* (pp. 18-21). The immense development of the productive forces which we owe to capitalism was, at the same time, the cause of the complete, and at first sight apparently irremediable, rupture of the equilibrium between production and consumption. Crises are the inevitable consequence of the fact that the productive forces, in order to develop, can have no regard for the requirements either of the consumers or of other branches of production. Production must continue, whether a market be available or not, in order to prevent the depreciation of the value of the vast productive apparatus. Under these circumstances, periodically recurring catastrophes are inevitable. But, at the same time, the increased forces of production create quantities of commodities which are ever becoming more colossal; and, moreover, they give the possibility of producing still vaster quantities in the future. Thus, the entire meaning of the economic problem has been changed, nay inverted. In past ages the problem to be solved was: how can the requirements of the consumers be satisfied by production? To-day, on the contrary, it is: how can the immense quantities of commodities, which are easily produced, be rendered accessible to the consumers, so as to be effectively consumed? This is the great problem to be solved in a future which is no longer distant. For it is to be feared that the economic structure of modern society will not be able to withstand for long the immense perturbations to which it is continually exposed. Once we are convinced that the solution of the problem cannot and will not be effected on the lines on which alone it has hitherto been sought, namely by means of the limitation of production; that, on the contrary, the problem can only be solved by means of the increase of consumption, so that all the commodities produced now and later may be effectively consumed; once these facts are clear to us, boundless and joyful prospects are opened-up. We can then foresee the advent of social conditions under which everyone will be relieved of the burden of material difficulty and distress; and under which, in consequence, mankind will be able, because its economic existence is assured, to devote itself to new and higher tasks. In this society of the future, personal freedom and the well-being of all without exception will, for the first time in history, become realities, and the individual will, at the same time, be able to develop fully his personal aptitudes and capacities.

PART III

ıHE METHOD AND THE CALL TO ACTION

1. *The Communist Manifesto*

MANIFESTO OF THE COMMUNIST PARTY

PREFACE

THE "Manifesto" was published as the platform of the "Communist League," a workingmen's association, first exclusively German, later on international, and, under the political conditions of the Continent before 1848, unavoidably a secret society. At a Congress of the League, held in London in November, 1847, Marx and Engels were commissioned to prepare for publication a complete theoretical and practical party programme. Drawn up in German, in January, 1848, the manuscript was sent to the printer in London a few weeks before the French revolution of February 24th. A French translation was brought out in Paris shortly before the insurrection of June, 1848. The first English translation, by Miss Helen Macfarlane, appeared in George Julian Harney's "Red Republican," London, 1850. A Danish and a Polish edition had also been published.

The defeat of the Parisian insurrection of June, 1848— the first great battle between Proletariat and Bourgeoisie— drove again into the background, for a time, the social and political aspirations of the European working class. Thenceforth the struggle for supremacy was again, as it had been before the revolution of February, solely between different sections of the propertied class; the working class was reduced to a fight for political elbow-room, and to the position of extreme wing of the middle-class Radicals. Wherever independent proletarian movements continued to show signs of life they were ruthlessly hunted down. Thus the Prussiaɴ police hunted out the Central Board of the Communist League, then located in Cologne. The members were arrested, and, after eighteen months' imprisonment, they were tried in October, 1852. This celebrated "Cologne Communist trial" lasted from October 4th till November 12th; seven of the prisoners were sentenced to terms of imprisonment in a fortress, varying from three to six years. Immediately after the sentence the League was formally dissolved by the remaining members. As to the "Manifesto," it seemed to be thenceforth doomed to oblivion.

When the European working class had recovered sufficient strength for another attack on the ruling classes, the International Working Men's Association sprang up. But this association, formed with the express aim of welding into one body the whole militant proletariat of Europe and America, could not at once proclaim the principles laid down in the "Manifesto." The International was bound to have a programme broad enough to be acceptable to the English Trades' Union, to the followers of Proudhon in France, Belgium, Italy and Spain, and to the Lassalleans [1] in Germany. Marx, who drew up this programme to the satisfaction of all parties, trusted entirely to the intellectual development of the working-class, which was sure to result from combined action and mutual discussion. The very events and vicissitudes of the struggle against Capital, the defeats even more than the victories, could not help bringing home to men's minds the insufficiency of their various favorite nostrums, and preparing the way for a more complete insight into the true conditions of working-class emancipation. And Marx was right. The International, on its breaking up in 1874, left the workers quite different men from what it had found them in 1864. Proudhonism in France, Lassalleanism in Germany, were dying out, and even the conservative English Trades' Unions, though most of them had long since severed their connection with the International, were gradually advancing towards

[1] Lassalle personally, to us, always acknowledged himself to be a disciple of Marx, and, as such, stood on the ground of the "Manifesto." But in his public agitation, 1860-64, he did not go beyond demanding co-operative workshops supported by State credit.

that point at which, last year at Swansea, their President could say in their name, "Continental Socialism has lost its terrors for us." In fact, the principles of the "Manifesto" had made considerable headway among the working men of all countries.

The Manifesto itself thus came to the front again. The German text had been since 1850, reprinted several times in Switzerland, England and America. In 1872 it was translated into English in New York, where the translation was published in "Woodhull and Claflin's Weekly." From this English version a French one was made in "Le Socialiste" of New York. Since then at least two more English translations, more or less mutilated, have been brought out in America, and one of them has been reprinted in England. The first Russian translation, made by Bakounine, was published at Herzen's "Kolokol" office in Geneva, about 1863; a second one, by the heroic Vera Zasulitch, also in Geneva, 1882. A new Danish edition is to be found in "Socialdemokratisk Bibliothek," Copenhagen, 1885; a fresh French translation in "Le Socialiste," Paris, 1886. From this latter a Spanish version was prepared and published in Madrid, 1886. The German reprints are not to be counted; there have been twelve altogether, at the least. An Armenian translation, which was to be published in Constantinople some months ago, did not see the light, I am told, because the publisher was afraid of bringing out a book with the name of Marx on it, while the translator declined to call it his own production. Of further translation into other languages I have heard, but have not seen them. Thus the history of the Manifesto reflects, to a great extent, the history of the modern working-class movement; at present it is undoubtedly the most widespread, the most international production of all Socialist Literature, the common platform acknowledged by millions of working men from Siberia to California.

Yet, when it was written we could not have called it a Socialist Manifesto. By Socialists, in 1847, were understood, on the one hand, the adherents of the various Utopian systems; (Owenites in England, Fourierists in France, both of them already reduced to the position of mere sects, and gradually dying out); on the other hand, the most multifarious social quacks, who, by all manners of tinkering, professed to redress, without any danger to capital and profit, all sorts of social grievances; in both cases men outside the working class movement, and looking rather to the "educated" classes for support. Whatever portion of the working class had become convinced of the insufficiency of mere political revolutions, and had proclaimed the necessity of a total social change, that portion, then called itself Communist. It was a crude, rough-hewn, purely instinctive sort of Communism; still, it touched the cardinal point and was powerful enough among the working class to produce the Utopian Communism, in France, of Cabet, and in Germany, of Weitling. Thus, Socialism was, in 1847, a middle-class movement, Communism a working-class movement. Socialism was, on the Continent at least, "respectable"; Communism was the very opposite. And as our notion, from the very beginning, was that "the emancipation of the working class must be the act of the working class itself," there could be no doubt as to which of the two names we must take. Moreover, we have ever since been far from repudiating it.

The "Manifesto" being our joint production, I consider myself bound to state that the fundamental proposition which forms its nucleus belongs to Marx. That proposition is: that in every historical epoch the prevailing mode of economic production and exchange, and the social organization necessarily following from it, form the basis upon which is built up, and from which alone can be explained, the political and intellectual history of that epoch; that consequently the whole history of mankind (since the dissolution of primitive tribal society, holding land in common ownership) has been a history of class struggles, contests between exploiting and exploited, ruling and oppressed classes; that the history of these class struggles forms a series of evolution in which, now-a-days, a stage has been reached where the exploited and oppressed class (the proletariat) cannot attain its emancipation from the sway of the exploiting and ruling class (the bourgeoisie) without, at the same time, and once and for all, emancipating society at large from all exploitation, oppression, class-distinction and class-struggles.

This proposition which, in my opinion, is destined to do for history what Darwin's theory has done for biology, we, both of us, had been gradually approaching for years before 1845. How far I had independently progressed towards it is best shown by my "Condition of the Working Class in England." [1] But when I again met Marx at Brussels, in spring, 1845, he had it ready worked out, and put it before me in terms almost as clear as those in which I have stated it here.

From our joint preface to the German edition of 1872, I quote the following:

"However much the state of things may have altered during the last 25 years, the general principles laid down in this Manifesto are, on the whole, as correct to-day as ever. Here and there some detail might be improved. The practical application of the principles will depend, as the manifesto itself states, everywhere and at all times, on the historical conditions for the time being existing, and, for that reason, no special stress is laid on the revolutionary measures proposed at the end of Section II. That passage would, in many respects, be very differently worded to-day. In view of the gigantic strides of Modern Industry since 1848, and of the accompanying improved and extended organization of the working-class, in view of the practical experience gained, first in the February revolution, and then, still more, in the Paris Commune, where the proletariat for the first time held political power for two whole months, this programme has in some details became antiquated. One thing especially was proved by the Commune, viz., that "the working class cannot simply lay hold of the ready-made State machinery and wield it for its own purposes." (See "The Civil War in France; Address of the General Council of the International Working Men's Association," London, Truelove, 1871, p. 15, where this point is further developed.) Further, it is self-evident that the criticism of socialist literature is deficient in relation to the

[1] The Condition of the Working Class in England in 1844. By Friedrich Engels. Translated by Florence K. Wischnewetzky—London, Swan, Sonnenschein & Co.

present time, because it comes down only to 1847; also, that the remarks on the relation of the Communists to the various opposition-parties (Section IV.), although in principle still correct, yet in practice are antiquated, because the political situation has been entirely changed, and the progress of history has swept from off the earth the greater portion of the political parties there enumerated.

But then, the Manifesto has become a historical document which we have no longer any right to alter.

The present translation is by Mr. Samuel Moore, the translator of the greater portion of Marx's "Capital." We have revised it in common, and I have added a few notes explanatory of historical allusions.

FRIEDRICH ENGELS.

London, 30th January, 1888.

MANIFESTO OF THE COMMUNIST PARTY

A SPECTRE is haunting Europe—the spectre of Communism. All the Powers of old Europe have entered into a holy alliance to exorcise this spectre; Pope and Czar, Metternich and Guizot, French Radicals and German police-spies.

Where is the party in opposition that has not been decried as communistic by its opponents in power? Where the Opposition that has not hurled back the branding reproach of Communism against the more advanced opposition parties, as well as against its reactionary adversaries?

Two things result from this fact.

I. Communism is already acknowledged by all European Powers to be itself a Power.

II. It is high time that Communists should openly, in the face of the whole world, publish their views, their aims, their tendencies, and meet this nursery tale of the spectre of Communism with a Manifesto of the party itself.

To this end, Communists of various nationalities have assembled in London and sketched the following Manifesto, to be published in the English, French, German, Italian, Flemish and Danish languages.

I

BOURGEOIS AND PROLETARIANS [1]

The history of all hitherto existing society [2] is the history of class struggles.

Freeman and slave, patrician and plebeian, lord and serf, guild-master [3] and journeyman, in a word, oppressor and oppressed, stood in constant opposition to one another, carried on uninterrupted, now hidden, now open fight, a fight that each time ended, either in a revolutionary re-constitution of society at large, or in the common ruin of the contending classes.

In the earlier epochs of history we find almost everywhere a complicated arrangement of society into various orders, a manifold gradation of social rank. In ancient Rome we have patricians, knights, plebeians, slaves; in the middle ages, feudal lords, vassals, guild-masters, journeymen, apprentices, serfs; in almost all of these classes, again, subordinate gradations.

---

[1] By bourgeoisie is meant the class of modern Capitalists, owners of the means of social production and employers of wage-labor. By proletariat, the class of modern wage laborers who, having no means of production of their own, are reduced to selling their labor-power in order to live.

[2] That is, all written history. In 1847, the pre-history of society, the social organization existing previous to recorded history, was all but unknown. Since then Haxthausen discovered common ownership of land in Russia, Maurer proved it to be the social foundation from which all Teutonic races started in history, and bye and bye village communities were found to be, or to have been, the primitive form of society everywhere from India to Ireland. The inner organization of this primitive Communistic society was laid bare, in its typical form, by Morgan's crowning discovery of the true nature of the gens and its relation to the tribe. With the dissolution of these primeval communities society begins to be differentiated into separate and finally antagonistic classes. I have attempted to retrace this process of dissolution in: "Der Ursprung der Familie, des Privateigenthums und des Staats," 2nd edit., Stuttgart, 1886.

[3] Guild-master, that is, a full member of a guild, a master within, not a head.

The modern bourgeois society that has sprouted from the ruins of feudal society, has not done away with class antagonisms. It has but established new classes, new conditions of oppression, new forms of struggle in place of the old ones.

Our epoch, the epoch of the bourgeoisie, possesses, however, this distinctive feature; it has simplified the class antagonisms. Society as a whole is more and more splitting up into two great hostile camps, into two great classes directly facing each other: Bourgeoisie and Proletariat.

From the serfs of the middle ages sprang the chartered burghers of the earliest towns. From these burgesses the first elements of the bourgeoisie were developed.

The discovery of America, the rounding of the Cape, opened up fresh ground for the rising bourgeoisie. The East Indian and Chinese markets, the colonization of America, trade with the colonies, the increase in the means of exchange and in commodities generally, gave to commerce, to navigation, to industry, an impulse never before known, and thereby, to the revolutionary element in the tottering feudal society, a rapid development.

The feudal system of industry, under which industrial production was monopolized by closed guilds, now no longer sufficed for the growing wants of the new market. The manufacturing system took its place. The guild-masters were pushed on one side by the manufacturing middle-class: division of labor between the different corporate guilds vanished in the face of division of labor in each single workshop.

Meantime the markets kept ever growing, the demand ever rising. Even manufacture no longer sufficed. Thereupon, steam and machinery revolutionized industrial production. The place of manufacture was taken by the giant, Modern Industry, the place of the industrial middle-class, by industrial millionaires, the leaders of whole industrial armies, the modern bourgeois.

Modern industry has established the world market, for which the discovery of America paved the way. This market has given an immense development to commerce, to navigation, to communication by land. This development has, in its turn, reacted on the extension of industry; and in proportion as industry, commerce, navigation, railways extended, in the same proportion the bourgeoisie developed, increased its capital, and pushed into the background every class handed down from the Middle Ages.

We see, therefore, how the modern bourgeoisie is itself the product of a long course of development, of a series of revolutions in the modes of production and of exchange.

Each step in the development of the bourgeoisie was accompanied by a corresponding political advance of that class An oppressed class under the sway of the feudal nobility, an armed and self-governing association in the mediaeval commune,[1] here independent urban republic (as in Italy and Germany), there taxable "third estate" of the monarchy (as in France), afterwards, in the period of manufacture proper, serving either the semi-feudal or the absolute monarchy as a counterpoise against nobility, and, in fact, corner stone of the great monarchies in general, the bourgeoisie has at last, since the establishment of Modern Industry and of the world-market, conquered for itself, in the modern representative State, exclusive political sway. The executive of the modern State is but a committee for managing the common affairs of the whole bourgeoisie.

The bourgeoisie, historically, has played a most revolutionary part.

The bourgeoisie, wherever it has got the upper hand, has put an end to all feudal, patriarchal, idyllic relations. It has pitilessly torn asunder the motley feudal ties that bound man to his "natural superiors," and has left no other nexus between man and man than naked self-interest, than callous "cash payment." It has drowned the most heavenly ecstasies of religious fervor, of chivalrous enthusiasm, of Philistine sentimentalism, in the icy water of egotistical calculation. It has resolved personal worth into exchange value, and in place

[1] "Commune" was the name taken in France by the nascent towns even before they had conquered from their feudal lords and masters, local self-government and political rights as "the Third Estate." Generally speaking, for economical development of the bourgeoisie, England is here taken as the typical country, for its political development, France.

of the numberless indefeasible chartered freedoms, has set up that single, unconscionable freedom—Free Trade. In one word, for exploitation, veiled by religious and political illusions, it has substituted naked, shameless, direct, brutal exploitation.

The bourgeoisie has stripped of its halo every occupation hitherto honored and looked up to with reverent awe. It has converted the physician, the lawyer, the priest, the poet, the man of science, into its paid wage laborers.

The bourgeoisie has torn away from the family its sentimental veil, and has reduced the family relation to a mere money relation.

The bourgeoisie has disclosed how it came to pass that the brutal display of vigor in the Middle Ages, which reactionists so much admire, found its fitting complement in the most slothful indolence. It has been the first to show what man's activity can bring about. It has accomplished wonders far surpassing Egyptian pyramids, Roman aqueducts and Gothic cathedrals; it has conducted expeditions that put in the shade all former Exoduses of nations and crusades.

The bourgeoisie cannot exist without constantly revolutionizing the instruments of production, and thereby the relations of production, and with them the whole relations of society. Conservation of the old modes of production in unaltered form was, on the contrary, the first condition of existence for all earlier industrial classes. Constant revolutionizing of production, uninterrupted disturbance of all social conditions, everlasting uncertainty and agitation distinguish the bourgeois epoch from all earlier ones. All fixed, fast frozen relations, with their train of ancient and venerable prejudices and opinions, are swept away, all new formed ones become antiquated before they can ossify. All that is solid melts into the air, all that is holy is profaned, and man is at last compelled to face with sober senses, his real conditions of life, and his relations with his kind.

The need of a constantly expanding market for its products chases the bourgeoisie over the whole surface of the globe. It must nestle everywhere, settle everywhere, establish connections everywhere.

The bourgeoisie has through its exploitation of the world-market given a cosmopolitan character to production and consumption in every country. To the great chagrin of reactionists, it has drawn from under the feet of industry the national ground on which it stood. All old-established national industries have been destroyed or are daily being destroyed. They are dislodged by new industries, whose introduction becomes a life and death question for all civilized nations, by industries that no longer work up indigenous raw material, but raw material drawn from the remotest zones; industries whose products are consumed, not only at home, but in every quarter of the globe. In place of the old wants, satisfied by the productions of the country, we find new wants, requiring for their satisfaction the products of distant lands and climes. In place of the old local and national seclusion and self-sufficiency, we have intercourse in every direction, universal interdependence of nations. And as in material, so also in intellectual production. The intellectual creations of individual nations become common property. National onesidedness and narrowmindedness become more and more impossible, and from the numerous national and local literatures there arises a world-literature.

The bourgeoisie, by the rapid improvement of all instruments of production, by the immensely facilitated means of communication, draws all, even the most barbarian nations into civilization. The cheap prices of its commodities are the heavy artillery with which it batters down all Chinese walls, with which it forces the barbarians' intensely obstinate hatred of foreigners to capitulate. It compels all nations, on pain of extinction, to adopt the bourgeois mode of production; it compels them to introduce what it calls civilization into their midst, *i. e.*, to become bourgeois themselves. In a word, it creates a world after its own image.

The bourgeoisie has subjected the country to the rule of the towns. It has created enormous cities, has greatly increased the urban population as compared with the rural, and has thus rescued a considerable part of the population from the idiocy of rural life. Just as it has made the country dependent on the towns, so it has made barbarian and semi-barbarian countries dependent on civilized ones, nations of peasants on nations of bourgeois, the East on the West.

The bourgeoisie keeps more and more doing away with the scattered state of the population, of the means of production, and of property. It has agglomerated population, centralized means of production, and has concentrated property in a few hands. The necessary consequence of this was political centralization. Independent, or but loosely connected provinces, with separate interests, laws, governments, and systems of taxation, became lumped together in one nation, with one government, one code of laws, one national class interest, one frontier and one customs tariff.

The bourgeoisie, during its rule of scarce one hundred years, has created more massive and more colossal productive forces than have all preceding generations together. Subjection of Nature's forces to man, machinery, application of chemistry to industry and agriculture, steam-navigation, railways, electric telegraphs, clearing of whole continents for cultivation, canalization of rivers, whole populations conjured out of the ground—what earlier century had even a presentiment that such productive forces slumbered in the lap of social labor?

We see then: the means of production and of exchange on whose foundation the bourgeoisie built itself up, were generated in feudal society. At a certain stage in the development of these means of production and of exchange, the conditions under which feudal society produced and exchanged, the feudal organization of agriculture and manufacturing industry, in one word, the feudal relations of property became no longer compatible with the already developed productive forces; they became so many fetters. They had to burst asunder; they were burst asunder.

Into their places stepped free competition, accompanied by social and political constitution adapted to it, and by economical and political sway of the bourgeois class.

A similar movement is going on before our own eyes. Modern bourgeois society with its relations of production, of exchange and of property, a society that has conjured up such gigantic means of production and of exchange, is like the sorcerer, who is no longer able to control the powers of the nether world whom he has called up by his spells. For many a decade past, the history of industry and commerce is but the history of the revolt of modern productive forces against modern conditions of production, against the property relations that are the conditions for the existence of the bourgeoisie and of its rule. It is enough to mention the commercial crises that by their periodical return put on its trial, each time more threateningly, the existence of the entire bourgeois society. In these crises a great part not only of the existing products, but also of the previously created productive forces, are periodically destroyed. In these crises there breaks out an epidemic that, in all earlier epochs, would have seemed an absurdity—the epidemic of overproduction. Society suddenly finds itself put back into a state of momentary barbarism; it appears as if a famine, a universal war of devastation, had cut off the supply of every means of subsistence; industry and commerce seem to be destroyed; and why? Because there is too much civilization, too much means of subsistence, too much industry, too much commerce. The productive forces at the disposal of society no longer tend to further the development of the conditions of the bourgeois property; on the contrary, they have become too powerful for these conditions by which they are fettered, and as soon as they overcome these fetters they bring disorder into the whole of bourgeois society, endanger the existence of bourgeois property. The conditions of bourgeois society are too narrow to comprise the wealth created by them. And how does the bourgeoisie get over these crises? On the one hand by enforced destruction of a mass of productive forces; on the other, by the conquest of new markets, and by the more thorough exploitation of the old ones. That is to say, by paving the way for more extensive and more destructive crises, and by diminishing the means whereby crises are prevented.

The weapons with which the bourgeoisie felled feudalism to the ground are now turned against the bourgeoisie itself.

But not only has the bourgeoisie forged the weapons that bring death to itself; it has also called into existence the men who are to wield those weapons—the modern working-class—the proletarians.

In proportion as the bourgeoisie, *i. e.*, capital, is developed, in the same proportion is the proletariat, the modern working-class, developed, a class of laborers who live only so long as they find work, and who find work only so long as their labor increases capital. These laborers, who must sell themselves piecemeal, are a commodity, like every other article of commerce, and are consequently exposed to all the vicissitudes of competition, to all the fluctuations of the market.

Owing to the extensive use of machinery and to division of labor, the work of the proletarians has lost all individual character, and, consequently, all charm for the workman. He becomes an appendage of the machine, and it is only the most simple, most monotonous and most easily acquired knack that is required of him. Hence, the cost of production of a workman is restricted almost entirely to the means of subsistence that he requires for his maintenance, and for the propagation of his race. But the price of a commodity, and also of labor, is equal to its cost of production. In proportion, therefore, as the repulsiveness of the work increases the wage decreases. Nay more, in proportion as the use of machinery and division of labor increases, in the same proportion the burden of toil increases, whether by prolongation of the working hours, by increase of the work enacted in a given time, or by increased speed of the machinery, etc.

Modern industry has converted the little workshop of the patriarchal master into the great factory of the industrial capitalist. Masses of laborers, crowded into factories, are organized like soldiers. As privates of the industrial army they are placed under the command of a perfect hierarchy of officers and sergeants. Not only are they the slaves of the bourgeois class and of the bourgeois state, they are daily and hourly enslaved by the machine, by the overlooker, and, above all, by the individual bourgeois manufacturer himself. The more openly this despotism proclaims gain to be its end and aim, the more petty, the more hateful and the more embittering it is.

The less the skill and exertion or strength implied in manual labor, in other words, the more modern industry becomes developed, the more is the labor of men superseded by that of women. Differences of age and sex have no longer any distinctive social validity for the working class. All are instruments of labor, more or less expensive to use, according to their age and sex.

No sooner is the exploitation of the laborer by the manufacturer, so far at an end, that he receives his wages in cash, than he is set upon by the other portions of the bourgeoisie, the landlord, the shopkeeper, the pawnbroker, etc.

The lower strata of the middle class—the small tradespeople, shopkeepers and retired tradesmen generally, the handicraftsmen and peasants—all these sink gradually into the proletariat, partly because their diminutive capital does not suffice for the scale on which Modern Industry is carried on, and is swamped in the competition with the large capitalists, partly because their specialized skill is rendered worthless by new methods of production. Thus the proletariat is recruited from all classes of the population.

The proletariat goes through various stages of development. With its birth begins its struggle with the bourgeoisie. At first the contest is carried on by individual laborers, then by the workpeople of a factory, then by the operatives of one trade, in one locality, against the individual bourgeois who directly exploits them. They direct their attacks not against the bourgeois conditions of production, but against the instruments of production themselves; they destroy imported wares that compete with their labor, they smash to pieces machinery, they set factories ablaze, they seek to restore by force the vanished status of the workman of the Middle Ages.

At this stage the laborers still form an incoherent mass scattered over the whole country, and broken up by their mutual competition. If anywhere they unite to form more compact bodies, this is not yet the consequence of their own active union, but of the union of the bourgeoisie, which class, in order to attain its own political ends, is compelled to set the whole proletariat in motion, and is moreover yet,

for a time, able to do so. At this stage, therefore, the proletarians do not fight their enemies, but the enemies of their
enemies, the remnants of absolute monarchy, the landowners,
the non-industrial bourgeois, the petty bourgeoisie. Thus the
whole historical movement is concentrated in the hands of
the bourgeoisie, every victory so obtained is a victory for the
bourgeoisie.

But with the development of industry the proletariat not
only increases in number; it becomes concentrated in greater
masses, its strength grows and it feels that strength more.
The various interests and conditions of life within the ranks
of the proletariat are more and more equalized, in proportion as machinery obliterates all distinctions of labor, and
nearly everywhere reduces wages to the same low level. The
growing competition among the bourgeois, and the resulting
commercial crisis, make the wages of the workers even more
fluctuating. The unceasing improvement of machinery, ever
more rapidly developing, makes their livelihood more and
more precarious; the collisions between individual workmen and individual bourgeois take more and more the character of collisions between two classes. Thereupon the workers begin to form combinations (Trades' Unions) against
the bourgeois; they club together in order to keep up the
rate of wages; they found permanent associations in order
to make provision beforehand for these occasional revolts.
Here and there the contest breaks out into riots.

Now and then the workers are victorious, but only for a
time. The real fruit of their battle lies not in the immediate result but in the ever-expanding union of workers. This
union is helped on by the improved means of communication
that are created by modern industry, and that places the
workers of different localities in contact with one another. It
was just this contact that was needed to centralize the numerous local struggles, all of the same character, into one national
struggle between classes. But every class struggle is a political
struggle. And that union, to attain which the burghers of
the Middle Ages with their miserable highways, required centuries, the modern proletarians, thanks to railways, achieve
in a few years.

This organization of the proletarians into a class, and consequently into a political party, is continually being upset again by the competition between the workers themselves. But it ever rises up again, stronger, firmer, mightier. It compels legislative recognition of particular interests of the workers by taking advantage of the divisions among the bourgeoisie itself. Thus the ten hours' bill in England was carried.

Altogether collisions between the classes of the old society further, in many ways, the course of development of the proletariat. The bourgeoisie finds itself involved in a constant battle. At first with the aristocracy; later on, with those portions of the bourgeoisie itself whose interests have become antagonistic to the progress of industry; at all times, with the bourgeoisie of foreign countries. In all these battles it sees itself compelled to appeal to the proletariat, to ask for its help, and thus, to drag it into the political arena. The bourgeoisie itself, therefore, supplies the proletariat with its own elements of political and general education; in other words, it furnishes the proletariat with weapons for fighting the bourgeoisie.

Further, as we have already seen, entire sections of the ruling classes are, by the advance of industry, precipitated into the proletariat, or are at least threatened in their conditions of existence. These also supply the proletariat with fresh elements of enlightenment and progress.

Finally, in times when the class-struggle nears the decisive hour, the process of dissolution going on within the ruling class—in fact, within the whole range of an old society—assumes such a violent, glaring character that a small section of the ruling class cuts itself adrift and joins the revolutionary class, the class that holds the future in its hands. Just as, therefore, at an earlier period, a section of the nobility went over to the bourgeoisie, so now a portion of the bourgeoisie goes over to the proletariat, and in particular, a portion of the bourgeois ideologists, who have raised themselves to the level of comprehending theoretically the historical movements as a whole.

Of all the classes that stand face to face with the bourgeoisie to-day the proletariat alone is a really revolutionary class. The other classes decay and finally disappear in the face of modern industry; the proletariat is its special and essential product.

The lower middle class, the small manufacturer, the shop-keeper, the artisan, the peasant, all these fight against the bourgeoisie, to save from extinction their existence as fractions of the middle class. They are therefore not revolutionary, but conservative. Nay, more; they are reactionary, for they try to roll back the wheel of history. If by chance they are revolutionary, they are so only in view of their impending transfer into the proletariat; they thus defend not their present, but their future interests; they desert their own standpoint to place themselves at that of the proletariat.

The "dangerous class," the social scum, that passively rotting mass thrown off by the lowest layers of old society, may, here and there, be swept into the movement by a proletarian revolution; its conditions of life, however, prepare it far more for the part of a bribed tool of reactionary intrigue.

In the conditions of the proletariat, those of the old society at large are already virtually swamped. The proletarian is without property; his relation to his wife and children has no longer anything in common with the bourgeois family relations; modern industrial labor, modern subjection to capital, the same in England as in France, in America as in Germany, has stripped him of every trace of national character. Law, morality, religion, are to him so many bourgeois prejudices, behind which lurk in ambush just as many bourgeois interests.

All the preceding classes that got the upper hand sought to fortify their already acquired status by subjecting society at large to their conditions of appropriation. The proletarians cannot become masters of the productive forces of society, except by abolishing their own previous mode of appropriation, and thereby also every other previous mode of appropriation. They have nothing of their own to secure and to fortify; their mission is to destroy all previous securities for and insurances of individual property.

All previous historical movements were movements of

minorities, or in the interest of minorities. The proletarian movement is the self-conscious, independent movement of the immense majority. The proletariat, the lowest stratum of our present society, cannot stir, cannot raise itself up without the whole superincumbent strata of official society being sprung into the air.

Though not in substance, yet in form, the struggle of the proletariat with the bourgeoisie is at first a national struggle. The proletariat of each country must, of course, first of all settle matters with its own bourgeoisie.

In depicting the most general phases of the development of the proletariat, we traced the more or less veiled civil war, raging within existing society, up to the point where that war breaks out into open revolution, and where the violent overthrow of the bourgeoisie, lays the foundations for the sway of the proletariat.

Hitherto every form of society has been based, as we have already seen, on the antagonism of oppressing and oppressed classes. But in order to oppress a class, certain conditions must be assured to it under which it can, at least, continue its slavish existence. The serf, in the period of serfdom, raised himself to membership in the commune, just as the petty bourgeois, under the yoke of feudal absolutism managed to develop into a bourgeois. The modern laborer, on the contrary, instead of rising with the progress of industry, sinks deeper and deeper below the conditions of existence of his own class. He becomes a pauper, and pauperism develops more rapidly than population and wealth. And here it becomes evident that the bourgeoisie is unfit any longer to be the ruling class in society, and to impose its conditions of existence upon society as an over-riding law. It is unfit to rule, because it is incompetent to assure an existence to its slave within his slavery, because it cannot help letting him sink into such a state that it has to feed him, instead of being fed by him. Society can no longer live under this bourgeoisie; in other words, its existence is no longer compatible with society.

The essential condition for the existence, and for the sway of the bourgeois class, is the formation and augmentation of capital; the condition for capital is wage labor. Wage labor rests exclusively on competition between the laborers. The advance of industry, whose involuntary promoter is the bourgeoisie, replaces the isolation of the laborers, due to competition, by their involuntary combination, due to association. The development of Modern Industry, therefore, cuts from under its feet the very foundation on which the bourgeoisie produces and appropriates products. What the bourgeoisie therefore produces, above all, are its own grave diggers. Its fall and the victory of the proletariat are equally inevitable.

II

PROLETARIANS AND COMMUNISTS

In what relation do the Communists stand to the proletarians as a whole?

The Communists do not form a separate party opposed to other working-class parties.

They have no interests separate and apart from those of the proletariat as a whole.

They do not set up any sectarian principles of their own, by which to shape and mould the proletarian movement.

The Communists are distinguished from the other working class parties by this only: 1. In the national struggles of the proletarians of the different countries, they point out and bring to the front the common interests of the entire proletariat, independently of all nationality. 2. In the various stages of development which the struggle of the working class against the bourgeoisie has to pass through, they always and everywhere represent the interests of the movement as a whole.

The Communists, therefore, are on the one hand practically the most advanced and resolute section of the working class parties of every country, that section which pushes forward all others; on the other hand, theoretically, they have over the great mass of the proletariat the advantage of clearly understanding the line of march, the conditions, and the ultimate general results of the proletarian movement.

The immediate aim of the Communists is the same as that of all the other proletarian parties: formation of the proletariat into a class, overthrow of the bourgeois of supremacy, conquest of political power by the proletariat.

The theoretical conclusions of the Communists are in no way based on ideas or principles that have been invented or discovered by this or that would-be universal reformer.

They merely express, in general terms, actual relations springing from an existing class struggle, from a historical movement going on under our very eyes. The abolition of existing property relations is not at all a distinctive feature of Communism.

All property relations in the past have continually been subject to historical change consequent upon the change in historical conditions.

The French Revolution, for example, abolished feudal property in favor of bourgeois property.

The distinguishing feature of Communism is not the abolition of property generally, but the abolition of bourgeois property. But modern bourgeois private property is the final and most complete expression of the system of producing and appropriating products, that is based on class antagonism, on the exploitation of the many by the few.

In this sense, the theory of the Communists may be summed up in the single sentence: Abolition of private property.

We Communists have been reproached with the desire of abolishing the right of personally acquiring property as the fruit of a man's own labor, which property is alleged to be the groundwork of all personal freedom, activity and independence.

Hard won, self-acquired, self-earned property! Do you mean the property of the petty artisan and of the small peasant, a form of property that preceded the bourgeois form? There is no need to abolish that; the development of industry has to a great extent already destroyed it, and is still destroying it daily.

Or do you mean modern bourgeois private property?

But does wage labor create any property for the laborer?

Not a bit. It creates capital, *i. e.*, that kind of property which exploits wage labor, and which cannot increase except upon condition of getting a new supply of wage labor for fresh exploitation. Property, in its present form, is based on the antagonism of capital and wage labor. Let us examine both sides of this antagonism.

To be a capitalist is to have not only a purely personal, but a social status in production. Capital is a collective product, and only by the united action of many members, nay, in the last resort, only by the united action of all members of society, can it be set in motion.

Capital is therefore not a personal, it is a social power.

When, therefore, capital is converted into common property, into the property of all members of society, personal property is not thereby transformed into social property. It is only the social character of the property that is changed. It loses its class character.

Let us now take wage labor.

The average price of wage labor is the minimum wage, *i. e.*, that quantum of the means of subsistence which is absolutely requisite to keep the laborer in bare existence as a laborer. What, therefore, the wage laborer appropriates by means of his labor, merely suffices to prolong and reproduce a bare existence. We by no means intend to abolish this personal appropriation of the products of labor, an appropriation that is made for the maintenance and reproduction of human life, and that leaves no surplus wherewith to command the labor of others. All that we want to do away with is the miserable character of this appropriation, under which the laborer lives merely to increase capital and is allowed to live only in so far as the interests of the ruling class require it.

In bourgeois society, living labor is but a means to increase accumulated labor. In Communist society accumulated labor is but a means to widen, to enrich, to promote the existence of the laborer.

In bourgeois society, therefore, the past dominates the present; in communist society the present dominates the past. In bourgeois society, capital is independent and has individuality, while the living person is dependent and has no individuality.

And the abolition of this state of things is called by the bourgeois abolition of individuality and freedom! And rightly so. The abolition of bourgeois individuality, bourgeois independence and bourgeois freedom is undoubtedly aimed at.

By freedom is meant, under the present bourgeois conditions of production, free trade, free selling and buying.

But if selling and buying disappears, free selling and buying disappears also. This talk about free selling and buying, and all the other "brave words" of our bourgeoisie about freedom in general have a meaning, if any, only in contrast with restricted selling and buying, with the fettered traders of the Middle Ages, but have no meaning when opposed to the Communistic abolition of buying and selling, of the bourgeois conditions of production, and of the bourgeoisie itself.

You are horrified at our intending to do away with private property. But in your existing society private property is already done away with for nine-tenths of the population; its existence for the few is solely due to its non-existence in the hands of those nine-tenths. You reproach us, therefore, with intending to do away with a form of property, the necessary condition for whose existence is the non-existence of any property for the immense majority of society.

In one word, you reproach us with intending to do away with your property. Precisely so: that is just what we intend.

From the moment when labor can no longer be converted into capital, money, or rent, into a social power capable of being monopolized, i. e., from the moment when individual property can no longer be transformed into bourgeois property, into capital, from that moment, you say, individuality vanishes.

You must, therefore, confess that by "individual" you mean no other person than the bourgeois, than the middle-class owner of property. This person must, indeed, be swept out of the way and made impossible.

Communism deprives no man of the power to appropriate the products of society: all that it does is to deprive him of the power to subjugate the labor of others by means of such appropriation.

It has been objected that upon the abolition of private property all work will cease and universal laziness will overtake us.

According to this, bourgeois society ought long ago to have gone to the dogs through sheer idleness; for those of its members who work acquire nothing, and those who acquire anything do not work. The whole of this objection is but another expression of the tautology: that there can no longer be any wage labor when there is no longer any capital.

All objections urged against the Communistic mode of producing and appropriating material products have, in the same way, been urged against the Communistic modes of producing and appropriating intellectual products. Just as, to the bourgeois, the disappearance of class property is the disappearance of production itself, so the disappearance of class culture is to him identical with the disappearance of all culture.

That culture, the loss of which he laments, is, for the enormous majority, a mere training to act as a machine.

But don't wrangle with us so long as you apply, to our intended abolition of bourgeois property, the standard of your bourgeois notions of freedom, culture, law, etc. Your very ideas are but the outgrowth of the conditions of your bourgeois production and bourgeois property, just as your jurisprudence is but the will of your class made into a law for all, a will whose essential character and direction are determined by the economical conditions of existence of your class.

The selfish misconception that induces you to transform into eternal laws of nature and of reason the social forms springing from your present mode of production and form of property—historical relations that rise and disappear in the progress of production—this misconception you share with every ruling class that has preceded you. What you see clearly in the case of ancient property, what you admit in the case of feudal property, you are of course forbidden to admit in the case of your own bourgeois form of property.

Abolition of the family! Even the most radical flare up at this infamous proposal of the Communists.

On what foundation is the present family, the bourgeois family, based? On capital, on private gain. In its completely developed form this family exists only among the bourgeoisie. But this state of things finds its complement in the practical absence of the family among the proletarians, and in public prostitution.

The bourgeois family will vanish as a matter of course when its complement vanishes, and both will vanish with the vanishing of capital.

Do you charge us with wanting to stop the exploitation of children by their parents? To this crime we plead guilty.

But, you will say, we destroy the most hallowed of relations when we replace home education by social.

And your education! Is not that also social, and determined by the social conditions under which you educate; by the intervention, direct or indirect, of society by means of schools, etc.? The Communists have not invented the intervention of society in education; they do but seek to alter the character of that intervention, and to rescue education from the influence of the ruling class.

The bourgeois clap-trap about the family and education, about the hallowed correlation of parent and child, become all the more disgusting, the more, by the action of Modern Industry, all family ties among the proletarians are torn asunder and their children transformed into simple articles of commerce and instruments of labor.

But you communists would introduce community of women, screams the whole bourgeoisie chorus.

The bourgeois sees in his wife a mere instrument of production. He hears that the instruments of production are to be exploited in common, and, naturally, can come to no other conclusion, than that the lot of being common to all will likewise fall to the women.

He has not even a suspicion that the real point aimed at is to do away with the status of women as mere instruments of production.

For the rest, nothing is more ridiculous than the virtuous indignation of our bourgeois at the community of women which, they pretend, is to be openly and officially established by the Communists. The Communists have no need to introduce community of women; it has existed almost from time immemorial.

Our bourgeois, not content with having the wives and daughters of their proletarians at their disposal, not to speak of common prostitutes, take the greatest pleasure in seducing each others' wives.

Bourgeois marriage is in reality a system of wives in common, and thus, at the most, what the Communists might possibly be reproached with, is that they desire to introduce, in substitution for a hypocritically concealed, an openly legalized community of women. For the rest, it is self-evident that the abolition of the present system of production must bring with it the abolition of the community of women springing from that system, *i. e.*, of prostitution both public and private.

The Communists are further reproached with desiring to abolish countries and nationalities.

The working men have no country. We cannot take from them what they don't possess. Since the proletariat must first of all acquire political supremacy, must rise to be the leading class of the nation, must constitute itself the nation, it is, so far, itself national, though not in the bourgeois sense of the word.

National differences and antagonisms between peoples are daily more and more vanishing, owing to the development of the bourgeoisie, to freedom of commerce, to the world-market, to uniformity in the mode of production and in the conditions of life corresponding thereto.

The supremacy of the proletariat will cause them to vanish still faster. United action, of the leading civilized countries at least, is one of the first conditions for the emancipation of the proletariat.

In proportion as the exploitation of one individual by another is put an end to, the exploitation of one nation by another will also be put an end to. In proportion as the antagonism between classes within the nation vanishes, the hostility of one nation to another will come to an end.

The charges against Communism made from a religious,

a philosophical, and generally, from an ideological standpoint, are not deserving of serious examination.

Does it require deep intuition to comprehend that man's ideas, views and conceptions, in one word, man's consciousness, changes with every change in the conditions of his material existence, in his social relations and in his social life?

What else does the history of ideas prove than that intellectual production changes in character in proportion as material production is changed? The ruling ideas of each age have ever been the ideas of its ruling class.

When people speak of ideas that revolutionize society they do but express the fact that within the old society the elements of a new one have been created, and that the dissolution of the old ideas keeps even pace with the dissolution of the old conditions of existence.

When the ancient world was in its last throes the ancient religions were overcome by Christianity. When Christian ideas succumbed in the 18th century to rationalist ideas, feudal society fought its death-battle with the then revolutionary bourgeoisie. The ideas of religious liberty and freedom of conscience merely gave expression to the sway of free competition within the domain of knowledge.

"Undoubtedly," it will be said, "religious, moral, philosophical and judicial ideas have been modified in the course of historical development. But religion, morality, philosophy, political science, and law, constantly survived this change.

"There are, besides, eternal truths, such as Freedom, Justice, etc., that are common to all states of society. But Communism abolishes eternal truths, it abolishes all religion and all morality, instead of constituting them on a new basis; it therefore acts in contradiction to all past historical experience."

What does this accusation reduce itself to? The history of all past society has consisted in the development of class antagonisms, antagonisms that assumed different forms at different epochs.

But whatever form they may have taken, one fact is common to all past ages, viz., the exploitation of one part of society by the other. No wonder, then, that the social consciousness of past ages, despite all the multiplicity and variety it displays, moves within certain common forms, or general ideas, which cannot completely vanish except with the total disappearance of class antagonisms.

The Communist revolution is the most radical rupture with traditional property relations; no wonder that its development involves the most radical rupture with traditional ideas.

But let us have done with the bourgeois objections to Communism.

We have seen above that the first step in the revolution by the working class is to raise the proletariat to the position of ruling class, to win the battle of democracy.

The proletariat will use its political supremacy to wrest, by degrees, all capital from the bourgeoisie, to centralize all instruments of production in the hands of the State, *i. e.*, of the proletariat organized as a ruling class; and to increase the total productive forces as rapidly as possible.

Of course, in the beginning, this cannot be effected except by means of despotic inroads on the rights of property, and on the conditions of bourgeois production; by means of measures, therefore, which appear economically insufficient and untenable, but which in the course of the movement outstrip themselves, necessitate further inroads upon the old social order, and are unavoidable as a means of entirely revolutionizing the mode of production.

These measures will of course be different in different countries.

Nevertheless in the most advanced countries the following will be pretty generally applicable:

1. Abolition of property in land and application of all rents of land to public purposes.

2. A heavy progressive or graduated income tax.

3. Abolition of all right of inheritance.

4. Confiscation of the property of all emigrants and rebels.

5. Centralization of credit in the hands of the State, by means of a national bank with State capital and an exclusive monopoly.

6. Centralization of the means of communication and transport in the hands of the State.

7. Extension of factories and instruments of production owned by the State; the bringing into cultivation of waste lands, and the improvement of the soil generally in accordance with a common plan.

8. Equal liability of all to labor. Establishment of industrial armies, especially for agriculture.

9. Combination of agriculture with manufacturing industries; gradual abolition of the distinction between town and country by a more equable distribution of the population over the country.

10. Free education for all children in public schools. Abolition of children's factory labor in its present form. Combination of education with industrial production, etc., etc.

When, in the course of development, class distinctions have disappeared, and all production has been concentrated in the hands of a vast association of the whole nation, the public power will lose its political character. Political power, properly so called, is merely the organized power of one class for oppressing another. If the proletariat during its contest with the bourgeoisie is compelled, by the force of circumstances, to organize itself as a class, if, by means of a revolution, it makes itself the ruling class, and, as such, sweeps away by force the old conditions of production, then it will, along with these conditions, have swept away the conditions for the existence of class antagonism, and of classes generally, and will thereby have abolished its own supremacy as a class.

In place of the old bourgeois society, with its classes and class antagonisms, we shall have an association in which the free development of each is the condition for the free development of all.

III

SOCIALIST AND COMMUNIST LITERATURE

1. *Reactionary Socialism*

(A) *Feudal Socialism*

OWING to their historical position, it became the vocation of the aristocracies of France and England to write pamphlets against modern bourgeois society. In the French revolution of July, 1830, and in the English reform agitation, these aristocracies again succumbed to the hateful upstart. Thenceforth, a serious political contest was altogether out of the question. A literary battle alone remained possible. But even in the domain of literature the old cries of the restoration period [1] had become impossible.

In order to arouse sympathy the aristocracy were obliged to lose sight, apparently, of their own interests and to formulate their indictment against the bourgeoisie in the interest of the exploited working class alone. Thus the aristocrats took their revenge by singing lampoons on their new master, and whispering in his ears sinister prophecies of coming catastrophe.

In this way arose feudal socialism: half lamentation, half lampoon; half echo of the past, half menace of the future; at times, by its bitter, witty and incisive criticism, striking the bourgeoisie to the very hearts' core, but always ludicrous in its effect, through total incapacity to comprehend the march of modern history.

The aristocracy, in order to rally the people to them, waved the proletarian alms-bag in front of a banner. But the people, so often as it joined them, saw on their hindquarters the old feudal coat of arms, and deserted with loud and irreverent laughter.

One section of the French Legitimists, and "Young England," exhibited this spectacle.

In pointing out that their mode of exploitation was different to that of the bourgeoisie, the feudalists forget that they exploited under circumstances and conditions that were quite different, and that are now antiquated. In showing that, under their rule, the modern proletariat never existed, they forget that the modern bourgeoisie is the necessary offspring of their own form of society.

For the rest, so little do they conceal the reactionary character of their criticism that their chief accusation against the bourgeoisie amounts to this, that under the bourgeois régime

[1] Not the English Restoration, 1660 to 1689, but the French Restoration, 1814 to 1830.

a class is being developed which is destined to cut up root and branch the old order of society.

What they upbraid the bourgeoisie with is not so much that it creates a proletariat, as that it creates a revolutionary proletariat.

In political practice, therefore, they join in all coercive measures against the working-class; and in ordinary life, despite their high-falutin phrases, they stoop to pick up the golden apples dropped from the trees of industry, and to barter truth, love and honor for traffic in wool, beetroot-sugar and potato spirit.[1]

As the parson has ever gone hand in hand with the landlord, so has Clerical Socialism with Feudal Socialism.

Nothing is easier than to give Christian asceticism a Socialist tinge. Has not Christianity declaimed against private property, against marriage, against the State? Has it not preached, in the place of these, charity and poverty, celibacy and mortification of the flesh, monastic life and Mother Church? Christian Socialism is but the Holy water with which the priest consecrates the heartburnings of the aristocrat.

(B) *Petty Bourgeois Socialism*

The feudal aristocracy was not the only class that was ruined by the bourgeoisie, not the only class whose conditions of existence pined and perished in the atmosphere of modern bourgeois society. The medieval burgesses and the small peasant bourgeoisie were the precursors of the modern bourgeoisie. In those countries which are but little developed, industrially and commercially, these two classes still vegetate side by side with the rising bourgeoisie.

In countries where modern civilization has become fully developed, a new class of petty bourgeois has been formed,

[1] This applies chiefly to Germany, where the landed aristocracy and squirearchy have large portions of their estates cultivated for their own account by stewards, and are, moreover, extensive beetroot-sugar manufacturers and distillers of potato spirits. The wealthier British aristocracy are, as yet, rather above that; but they, too, know how to make up for declining rents by lending their names to floaters of more or less shady joint-stock companies.

fluctuating between proletariat and bourgeoisie, and ever renewing itself as a supplementary part of bourgeois society. The individual members of this class, however, are being constantly hurled down into the proletariat by the action of competition, and, as modern industry develops, they even see the moment approaching when they will completely disappear as an independent section of modern society, to be replaced, in manufactures, agriculture and commerce, by overlookers, bailiffs and shopmen.

In countries like France, where the peasants constitute far more than half of the population, it was natural that writers who sided with the proletariat against the bourgeoisie should use, in their criticism of the bourgeois régime, the standard of the peasant and petty bourgeois, and from the standpoint of these intermediate classes should take up the cudgels for the working class. Thus arose petty bourgeois Socialism. Sismondi was the head of this school, not only in France, but also in England.

This school of socialism dissected with great acuteness the contradictions in the conditions of modern production. It laid bare the hypocritical apologies of economists. It proved incontrovertibly the disastrous effects of machinery and division of labor; the concentration of capital and land in a few hands; overproduction and crises; it pointed out the inevitable ruin of the petty bourgeois and peasant, the misery of the proletariat, the anarchy in production, the crying inequalities in the distribution of wealth, the industrial war of extermination between nations, the dissolution of old moral bonds, of the old family relations, of the old nationalities.

In its positive aims, however, his form of Socialism aspires either to restoring the old means of production and of exchange, and with them the old property relations and the old society, or to cramping the modern means of production and of exchange, within the framework of the old property relations that have been, and were bound to be, exploded by those means. In either case it is both reactionary and Utopian.

Its last words are: corporate guilds for manufacture; patriarchal relations in agriculture.

Ultimately, when stubborn historical facts had dispersed

all intoxicating effects of self-deception, this form of Socialism ended in a miserable fit of the blues.

The Socialist and Communist literature of France, a literature that originated under the pressure of a bourgeoisie in power, and that was the expression of the struggle against this power, was introduced into Germany at a time when the bourgeoisie in that country had just begun its contest with feudal absolutism.

German philosophers, would-be philosophers and *beaux esprits* eagerly seized on this literature, only forgetting that, when these writings emigrated from France into Germany, French social conditions had not emigrated along with them. In contact with German social conditions this French literature lost its immediate practical significance and assumed a purely literary aspect. Thus, to the German philosophers of the Eighteenth Century the demands of the first French Revolution were nothing more than the demands of "Practical Reason" in general, and the utterance of the will of the revolutionary French bourgeoisie signified in their eyes the laws of pure Will, of Will as it was bound to be, of true human Will generally.

The work of the German literati consisted solely in bringing the new French ideas into harmony with their ancient philosophical conscience, or, rather, in annexing the French ideas without deserting their own philosophic point of view.

This annexation took place in the same way in which a foreign language is appropriated, namely, by translation.

It is well known how the monks wrote silly lives of Catholic Saints over the manuscripts on which the classical works of ancient heathendom had been written. The German literati reversed this process with the profane French literature. They wrote their philosophical nonsense beneath the French original. For instance, beneath the French criticism of the economic functions of money they wrote "Alienation of Humanity," and beneath the French criticism of the bourgeois State they wrote "Dethronement of the Category of the General," and so forth.

The introduction of these philosophical phrases at the back of the French historical criticisms they dubbed "Philosophy of Action," "True Socialism," "German Science of Socialism," "Philosophical Foundation of Socialism," and so on.

The French Socialist and Communist literature was thus completely emasculated. And, since it ceased in the hands of the German to express the struggle of one class with the other, he felt conscious of having overcome "French one-sidedness" and of representing, not true requirements, but the requirements of Truth, not the interests of the proletariat, but the interests of Human Nature, of Man in general, who belongs to no class, has no reality, who exists only in the misty realm of philosophical phantasy.

This German Socialism, which took its school-boy task so seriously and solemnly, and extolled its poor stock-in-trade in such mountebank fashion, meanwhile gradually lost its pedantic innocence.

The fight of the German, and especially of the Prussian, bourgeoisie against feudal aristocracy and absolute monarchy, in other words, the liberal movement, became more earnest.

By this, the long-wished-for opportunity was offered to "True Socialism" of confronting the political movement with the socialist demands, of hurling the traditional anathemas against liberalism, against representative government, against bourgeois competition, bourgeois freedom of the press, bourgeois legislation, bourgeois liberty and equality, and of preaching to the masses that they had nothing to gain and everything to lose by this bourgeois movement. German Socialism forgot, in the nick of time, that the French criticism, whose silly echo it was, presupposed the existence of modern bourgeois society, with its corresponding economic conditions of existence, and the political constitution adapted thereto, the very things whose attainment was the object of the pending struggle in Germany.

To the absolute governments, with their following of parsons, professors, country squires and officials, it served as a welcome scarecrow against the threatening bourgeoisie.

It was a sweet finish after the bitter pills of floggings and bullets with which these same governments, just at that time, dosed the German working class risings.

While this "True" Socialism thus served the governments

as a weapon for fighting the German bourgeoisie, it at the same time directly represented a reactionary interest, the interest of the German Philistines. In Germany the petty bourgeois class, a relic of the 16th century, and since then constantly cropping up again under various form, is the real social basis of the existing state of things.

To preserve this class is to preserve the existing state of things in Germany. The industrial and political supremacy of the bourgeoisie threatens it with certain destruction; on the one hand, from the concentration of capital; on the other, from the rise of a revolutionary proletariat. "True" Socialism appeared to kill these two birds with one stone. It spread like an epidemic.

The robe of speculative cobwebs, embroidered with flowers of rhetoric, steeped in the dew of sickly sentiment, this transcendental robe in which the German Socialists wrapped their sorry "eternal truths," all skin and bone, served to wonderfully increase the sale of their goods amongst such a public.

And on its part, German Socialism recognized more and more its own calling as the bombastic representative of the petty bourgeois Philistine.

It proclaimed the German nation to be the model nation, and the German petty Philistine to be the typical man. To every villainous meanness of this model man it gave a hidden, higher, socialistic interpretation, the exact contrary of its true character. It went to the extreme length of directly opposing the "brutally destructive" tendency of Communism, and of proclaiming its supreme and impartial contempt of all class struggle. With very few exceptions, all the so-called Socialist and Communist publications that now (1847) circulate in Germany belong to the domain of this foul and enervating literature.

2. Conservative or Bourgeois Socialism

A part of the bourgeoisie is desirous of redressing social grievances, in order to secure the continued existence of bourgeois society.

To this section belong economists, philanthropists, humanitarians, improvers of the condition of the working class, organizers of charity, members of societies for the prevention of cruelty to animals temperance fanatics, hole and corner reformers of every imaginable kind. This form of Socialism has, moreover, been worked out into complete systems.

We may cite Proudhon's "Philosophie de la Misère" as an example of this form.

The socialistic bourgeois want all the advantages of modern social conditions without the struggles and dangers necessarily resulting therefrom. They desire the existing state of society minus its revolutionary and disintegrating elements. They wish for a bourgeoisie without a proletariat. The bourgeoisie naturally conceives the world in which it is supreme to be the best; and bourgeois Socialism develops this comfortable conception into various more or less complete systems. In requiring the proletariat to carry out such a system, and thereby to march straightway into the social New Jerusalem, it but requires in reality that the proletariat should remain within the bounds of existing society, but should cast away all its hateful ideas concerning the bourgeoisie.

A second and more practical, but less systematic, form of this socialism sought to depreciate every revolutionary movement in the eyes of the working class by showing that no mere political reform, but only a change in the material conditions of existence, in economical relations, could be of any advantage to them. By changes in the material conditions of existence this form of Socialism, however, by no means signifies abolition of the bourgeois relations of production, an abolition that can be effected only by a revolution, but administrative reforms, based on the continued existence of these relations; reforms, therefore, that in no respect affect the relations between capital and labor, but, at the best, lessen the cost, and simplify the administrative work, of bourgeois government.

Bourgeois Socialism attains adequate expression when, and only when, it becomes a mere figure of speech.

Free trade: for the benefit of the working class. Protective duties: for the benefit of the working class. Prison reform: for the benefit of the working class. This is the last word and the only seriously meant word of bourgeois Socialism.

It is summed up in the phrase: the bourgeois is a bourgeois—for the benefit of the working class.

3. *Critical-Utopian Socialism and Communism*

We do not here refer to that literature which, in every great modern revolution, has always given voice to the demands of the proletariat: such as the writings of Babeuf and others.

The first direct attempts of the proletariat to attain its own ends, made in times of universal excitement, when feudal society was being overthrown, these attempts necessarily failed, owing to the then undeveloped state of the proletariat, as well as to the absence of the economic conditions for its emancipation, conditions that had yet to be produced, and could be produced by the impending bourgeois epoch alone. The revolutionary literature that accompanied these first movements of the proletariat had necessarily a reactionary character. It inculcated universal asceticism and social leveling in its crudest form.

The Socialist and Communist systems properly so called, those of St. Simon, Fourier, Owen and others, spring into existence in the early undeveloped period, described above, of the struggle between proletariat and bourgeoisie (see Section I. Bourgeois and Proletarians).

The founders of these systems see, indeed, the class antagonisms, as well as the action of the decomposing elements in the prevailing form of society. But the proletariat, as yet in its infancy, offers to them the spectacle of a class without any historical initiative or any independent political movement.

Since the development of class antagonism keeps even pace with the development of industry, the economic situation, as they find it, does not as yet offer to them the material conditions for the emancipation of the proletariat. They therefore search after a new social science, after new social laws, that are to create these conditions.

Historical action is to yield to their personal inventive action, historically created conditions of emancipation to fantastic ones, and the gradual, spontaneous class organization of the proletariat to an organization of society specially contrived by these inventors. Future history resolves itself, in their eyes, into the propaganda and the practical carrying out of their social plans.

In the formation of their plans they are conscious of caring chiefly for the interests of the working-class, as being the most suffering class. Only from the point of view of being the most suffering class does the proletariat exist for them.

The undeveloped state of the class struggle, as well as their own surroundings, cause Socialists of this kind to consider themselves far superior to all class antagonisms. They want to improve the condition of every member of society, even that of the most favored. Hence, they habitually appeal to society at large, without distinction of class; nay, by preference, to the ruling class. For how can people, when once they understand their system, fail to see in it the best possible plan of the best possible state of society?

Hence, they reject all political, and especially all revolutionary action; they wish to attain their ends by peaceful means, and endeavor, by small experiments, necessarily doomed to failure, and by the force of example to pave the way for the new social Gospel.

Such fantastic pictures of future society, painted at a time when the proletariat is still in a very undeveloped state and has but a fantastic conception of its own position, correspond with the first instinctive yearnings of that class for a general reconstruction of society.

But these Socialist and Communist publications contain also a critical element. They attack every principle of existing society. Hence they are full of the most valuable materials for the enlightenment of the working class. The practical measures proposed in them, such as the abolition of the distinction between town and country, of the family, of the carrying on of industries for the account of private individuals, and of the wage system, the proclamation of social harmony, the conversion of the functions of the State into a mere superintendence of production, all these proposals point solely to the disappearance of class-antagonisms which were at that time only just cropping up, and which, in these publications, are recognized under the earliest, indistinct and undefined forms only. These proposals, therefore, are of a purely Utopian character.

The Significance of Critical-Utopian Socialism and Communism bears an inverse relation to historical development. In proportion as the modern class struggle develops and takes definite shape, this fantastic standing apart from the contest, these fantastic attacks on it lose all practical value and all theoretical justification. Therefore, although the originators of these systems were in many respects revolutionary, their disciples have in every case formed mere reactionary sects. They hold fast by the original views of their masters, in opposition to the progressive historical development of the proletariat. They, therefore, endeavor, and that consistently, to deaden the class struggle and to reconcile the class antagonisms. They still dream of experimental realization of their social Utopias, of founding isolated "Phalanstères," of establishing "Home Colonies," of setting up a "Little Icaria" [1]— duodecimo editions of the New Jerusalem, and to realize all these castles in the air they are compelled to appeal to the feelings and purses of the bourgeois. By degree they sank into the category of the reactionary conservative Socialists depicted above, differing from these only by more systematic pedantry, and by their fanatical and superstitious belief in the miraculous effects of their social science.

They, therefore, violently oppose all political action on the part of the working class; such action, according to them, can only result from blind unbelief in the new Gospel.

The Owenites in England, and the Fourierists in France, respectively oppose the Chartists and the "Réformistes."

---

[1] Phalanstères were Socialist colonies on the plan of Charles Fourier. Icaria was the name given by Cabet to his Utopia and, later on, to his American Communist colony.

IV. POSITION OF THE COMMUNISTS IN RELATION TO THE
VARIOUS EXISTING OPPOSITION PARTIES

SECTION II has made clear the relations of the Communists
to the existing working class parties, such as the Chartists
in England and the Agrarian Reforms in America.

The Communist fight for the attainment of the immediate
aims, for the enforcement of the momentary interests of the
working class; but in the movement of the present they also
represent and take care of the future of that movement. In
France the Communists ally themselves with the Social-
Democrats [1] against the conservative and radical bourgeoisie,
reserving, however, the right to take up a critical position in
regard to phrases and illusions traditionally handed down
from the great Revolution.

In Switzerland they support the Radicals, without losing
sight of the fact that this party consists of antagonisic elements, partly of Democratic Socialists, in the French sense,
partly of radical bourgeois.

In Poland they support the party that insists on an agrarian
revolution, as the prime condition for national emancipation,
that party which fomented the insurrection of Cracow in 1846.

In Germany they fight with the bourgeoisie whenever it
acts in a revolutionary way, against the absolute monarchy,
the feudal squirearchy, and the petty bourgeoisie.

But they never cease for a single instant to instill into the
working class the clearest possible recognition of the hostile
antagonism between bourgeoisie and proletariat, in order
that the German workers may straightway use, as so many
weapons against the bourgeoisie, the social and political conditions that the bourgeoisie must necessarily introduce along
with its supremacy, and in order that, after the fall of the
reactionary classes in Germany, the fight against the bourgeoisie itself may immediately begin.

[1] The party then represented in parliament by Ledru-Rollin, in literature by Louis Blanc, in the daily press by the Réforme. The name
of Social Democracy signified, with these its inventors, a section of the
Democratic or Republican party more or less tinged with Socialism.

The Communists turn their attention chiefly to Germany, because that country is on the eve of a bourgeois revolution, that is bound to be carried out under more advanced conditions of European civilization, and with a more developed proletariat, than that of England was in the seventeenth and of France in the eighteenth century, and because the bourgeois revolution in Germany will be but the prelude to an immediately following proletarian revolution.

In short, the Communists everywhere support every revolutionary movement against the existing social and political order of things.

In all these movements they bring to the front, as the leading question in each, the property question, no matter what its degree of development at the time.

Finally, they labor everywhere for the union and agreement of the democratic parties of all countries.

The Communists disdain to conceal their views and aims. They openly declare that their ends can be attained only by the forcible overthrow of all existing social conditions. Let the ruling classes tremble at a Communistic revolution. The proletarians have nothing to lose but their chains. They have a world to win.

Working men of all countries, unite!

2. *From the "Criticism of The Gotha Program."*

Between the capitalist and the Communist society lies the period of the revolutionary transformation of the one into the other. To this corresponds a political transition period in which the state can be nothing else but *the revolutionary dictatorship of the proletariat.*

3. *Address of the Central Authority to the Communist League, April, 1850.*

Brethren!

In the two years of revolution, 1848-1849, the League stood the test in two ways: first in the fact that its members energetically participated in the movement in every locality, that in the press, on the barricades and on the battlefields they were in the front ranks of of the proletariat, the only resolutely revolutionary class. The League further stood the test in this, that its conception of the movement, as set down in the circular letter of the Congress and the Central Authority of 1847 and in the *Communist Manifesto,* has proven the sole correct one, the expectations expressed in those documents have been wholly confirmed, and the conception of the present state of society, formerly propagated by the League only in secret, is now on everybody's lips and is openly preached in the market-place. During the same time, however, the formerly strong organization of the League became considerably relaxed. A good share of the members directly involved in the revolutionary movement believed that the time for secret societies was past and that public activity alone was enough. Various districts and communities allowed their connections with the Central Authority to slacken and gradually die away. Thus while the democratic party, the party of the petty bourgeoisie, was better and better organizing in Germany, the workers' party lost its only firm hold, remained organized at best in a few localities and for local purposes, and thus in the general movement came completely under the sway and direction of the petty bourgeois democrats. An end must be put to this state of affairs; the independence of the workers must be reëstablished. The Central Authority understood the necessity of this, and therefore as far back as the winter of 1848-1849 sent an emissary, Josef Moll, to Germany to reorganize the League. Moll's mission remained, however, without lasting effect, partly because the German workers had not then had enough experience, partly because it was interrupted by the insurrection of last May. Moll himself seized a musket, entered the Baden-Palatinate army and on July 19 fell in the battle on the Murg. The League lost in him one of its oldest, most active and most reliable members, who had been active in all the Congresses and Central Authorities and had before that time fulfilled with great success a number of missions. After the defeat of the revolutionary parties of Germany and France in July, 1849, almost all the members of the Central Authority met again in London, supplemented their ranks with new revolutionary forces and took up with renewed zeal the work of reorganizing the League.

This reorganization can be accomplished only with the aid of an emissary, and the Central Authority considers it highly important for the emissary to depart precisely at this moment when a new revolution is imminent, when the workers' party must therefore come forward as organizedly, unanimously and independently as possible, if it is not once more to be exploited and taken in tow by the bourgeoisie as in 1848.

We told you, brethren, as early as 1848 that the German liberal bourgeoisie would soon come to power and would immediately employ its new-gained might against the workers. You have seen how this was fulfilled. It was in actual fact the bourgeoisie who, after the movement of March, 1848, immediately seized possession of the state power and promptly employed this might to drive back the workers, its allies in the struggle, to their former state of oppression. While the bourgeoisie was unable to carry this through without uniting with the feudal party that had been swept aside in March, even without once more ceding dominance in the final account to this feudal, absolutist party, it nevertheless assured itself of conditions which in the long run, thanks to the financial straits of the government, would play the power into its hands and guarantee all its interests, if only it were possible for the revolutionary movement to subside right now into a so-called peaceful evolution. The bourgeoisie would not even be compelled, in order to assure its domination, to make itself odious by violent punitive measures against the people, since all these high-handed measures have already been taken by the feudal counter-revolution. But the development will not take this peaceful course. The revolution which will accelerate it is on the contrary imminent—whether it is to be called forth by an independent uprising of the French proletariat or by an invasion of the Holy Alliance against the revolutionary Babel.

And the rôle played by the German liberal bourgeoisie towards the people in 1848, that treacherous rôle will be taken over in the approaching revolution by the democratic petty bourgeoisie, who now take the same stand in the opposition, as that taken by the liberal bourgeoisie before 1848. This party, the democratic party, which is far more dangerous to the workers than the previous liberal party, consists of three elements.

1. The most progressive sections of the big bourgeoisie whose aim is the immediate and complete overthrow of feudalism and absolutism. This faction is represented by the former Berlin coalitioners, by the tax-refusers.

2. The democratic-constitutional petty bourgeoisie, whose main object during the preceding movement was the establishment of a more or less democratic federal state, such as that tried for by their representatives, the left wing of the Frankfort Assembly and later the Stuttgart Parliament, and by themselves in the campaign for the federal constitution.

3. The republican petty bourgeoisie, whose ideal is a German federative republic on the style of Switzerland, and who now call themselves Red and Social Democratic because they entertain the pious wish to remove the pressure of large capital upon small, of the great bourgeoisie upon the petty. The representatives of this faction were the members of the Democratic Congresses and Committees, the directors of the Democratic Unions, the editors of the Democratic newspapers.

Now, after their defeat, all these factions call themselves Republicans or Red, just as the Republican petty bourgeoisie in France now call themselves Socialists. Wherever they still find a chance to pursue their aims by constitutional means— as in Württemberg, Bavaria, etc.—they seize the opportunity to preserve their old phrases and reveal in action that they have not changed in the least. It is evident, moreover, that the changed name of this party does not in the slightest degree alter its attitude toward the workers, but merely proves that it must now confront a bourgeoisie united with absolutism and support itself upon the proletariat.

The petty bourgeois democratic party in Germany is very powerful, it embraces not merely a large majority of the bourgeois inhabitants of the towns, the small industrial merchants and employers; it counts among its followers also the peasants and the agricultural proletariat, in so far as these latter have not yet found a point of support in the independent proletariat of the towns.

The attitude of the revolutionary workers' party to the

petty bourgeois democracy is as follows: the party marches with it against the faction whose overthrow it seeks, but opposes it in every measure on which it seeks to get a foothold for itself.

The democratic petty bourgeois, far from desiring to overturn the whole of society for the revolutionary proletarian, strives for a change in social conditions which will make the existing society as endurable and comfortable as possible for him. He therefore demands above all a reduction of state expenditures by cutting down the bureaucracy, and a shifting of the main burden of taxation upon the large landowners and bourgeoisie. He demands further a removal of the pressure of big capital upon small by means of public credit institutions and laws against usury, making it possible for him and for the peasants to get loans on favorable terms from the state instead of from the capitalists; and further an establishment of bourgeois property relations on the land through the complete elimination of feudalism. To achieve all this, he requires a democratic—whether constitutional or republican—state constitution which will give a majority to him and his allies, the peasants, and a democratic municipal constitution which will hand over to him the direct control of municipal property and a whole series of functions which are now exercised by the bureaucrats.

The rule and rapid augmentation of capital is further to be counteracted in part by a limitation on inheritance, in part by assigning as many undertakings as possible to the state. As to the workers, they are above all to remain wage-workers as before; only the democratic petty bourgeoisie wants a better wage for the workers and a more secure existence, and hopes to procure them through partial interference from the state and through welfare measures. In short it hopes to bribe the workers with a more or less concealed charity and to break their revolutionary strength by making their position more bearable for the moment. The demands of the petty bourgeois democracy here summarized are not advocated simultaneously by all of its factions, and in their totality are cherished by a very small number as a definite aim. The further certain individuals or factions among them go, however, the more of these demands they will take over. And the few who do see in the above their own program will believe they have here put forward the utmost that is to be demanded of the revolution. But these demands can in no way satisfy the party of the proletariat. While the democratic petty bourgeois wants to bring the revolution to an end as quickly as possible, and with the settlement at most of the above claims, it is our interest and our task to make the revolution permanent, until all the more or less possessing classes are driven from power, until the proletariat has conquered the state power and the association of proletarians, not only in one country but in all the dominant countries of the world, has advanced so far that competition with the proletariat in these countries has ceased, and at least the decisive productive forces are concentrated in the hands of the proletarians. For us it cannot be a question of changing private property but only of its destruction, not of glossing over class antagonisms but of abolishing classes, not of bettering the existing society but of founding a new one. That the petty bourgeois democracy, in the course of the further development of the revolution, will momentarily acquire a preponderant influence in Germany—of that there is no doubt. The question therefore arises, what shall be the attitude towards it of the proletariat and especially of the League:

1. During the duration of the present conditions in which the petty bourgeois democrats likewise are oppressed?

2. In the coming revolutionary struggle which will give them the ascendancy?

3. After this struggle, during the period of their ascendancy over the overthrown classes and the proletariat?

1. At the present moment, when the democratic petty bourgeoisie are everywhere oppressed, they exhort the proletariat to a common unity and conciliation, they extend a hand to the proletariat and strive to establish a big opposition party, which shall embrace all shadings to be found in the ranks of the democratic party. That is, they strive to involve the workers with them in a single party organization in which those general social democratic phrases, behind which are concealed their special interests, shall predominate, and in which for the sake of peace the specific demands of the proletariat shall

not be brought forward. Such a fusion would turn out exclusively to their benefit and wholly to the detriment of the
proletariat. The proletariat would lose its whole independent,
dearly-bought position, and sink once more to the position of
an appendage of the official bourgeois democracy. This fusion
must therefore be most resolutely rejected. Instead of stoop-
ing once more to serve the bourgeois democrats as an applaud-
ing chorus, the workers, and especially the League, must strive
to establish, by the side of the official democrats, an independent organization, both secret and public, of the workers' party
and to make every municipality the central point and nucleus
of workmen's associations in which the attitude and interests
of the proletariat shall be discussed independently of bourgeois influences. Just how serious the bourgeois democrats
are with their proposal of an alliance in which the proletarians
shall stand side by side with them with equal rights and
powers, is shown, for example, by the Breslau democrats who,
in their organ, the *Neuen Oderzeitung,* are carrying on a rabid
persecution of the independently organized workers, whom
they style socialists.

In the event of a struggle against a common foe there is
no need of any special fusion. As soon as such a foe is to be
directly fought, the interests of both parties coincide for the
moment, and as in the past so in the future this union, intended
for the moment only, will form of its own accord. It goes without saying that in the impending bloody conflicts just as in
all past ones, the workers, by their courage, their resoluteness
and their self-sacrifice will play the main part in winning the
victory. As heretofore, so in this struggle the mass of the
petty bourgeoisie will maintain as long as possible an attitude
of temporizing, irresolution and inactivity, and then as soon
as the victory is decided take it in charge, summon the workers to be peaceful and return to work in order to avert so-called
excesses, and so cut off the proletariat from the fruits of the
victory. It does not lie in the power of the workers to prevent
the petty bourgeois democrats from doing this, but it does lie
in their power to render their ascendancy over the armed proletariat difficult, and to dictate to them such terms that the
rule of the bourgeois democrats shall bear within it from the
beginning the germ of its destruction, and its displacement

later by the rule of the proletariat become considerably easier. Above all things, during the conflict and right after the battle, the workers must to the fullest extent possible work against the bourgeois measures of pacification, and compel the democrats to carry into action their present terroristic phrases. They must work to prevent the immediate revolutionary excitement from being promptly suppressed after the victory. They must keep it going as long as possible. Far from setting themselves against so-called excesses, examples of popular revenge against hated individuals or public buildings with only hateful memories attached to them, they must not only tolerate these examples but take in hand their very leadership. During the struggle and after the struggle the workers must at every opportunity put forth their own demands alongside those of the bourgeois democrats. They must demand guarantees for the workers the moment the democratic citizens set about taking over the government. They must if necessary extort these guarantees, and in general see to it that the new rulers pledge themselves to every conceivable concession and promise—the surest way to compromise them. In general they must restrain in every way to the extent of their power the jubilation and enthusiasm for the new order which follows every victorious street battle, by a calm and cold-blooded conception of the situation and by an open distrust of the new government. Side by side with the new official governments, they must simultaneously set up their own revolutionary workers' governments, whether in the form of municipal committees, municipal councils or workers' clubs or workers' committees, so that the bourgeois democratic governments not only immediately lose the support of the workers, but find themselves from the very beginning supervised and threatened by authorities behind which stand the whole mass of the workers. In a word: from the first moment of victory our distrust must no longer be directed against the vanquished reactionary party, but against our previous allies, against the party which seeks to exploit the common victory for itself alone.

2. But in order to be able energetically and threateningly to oppose this party, whose betrayal of the workers will begin

with the first hour of victory, the workers must be armed and organized. The arming of the whole proletariat with muskets, rifles, cannon and ammunition must be carried out at once, and the revival of the old bourgeois militia, directed against the workers, resisted. Where this cannot be effected, the workers must endeavor to organize themselves independently as a proletarian guard with chiefs and a general staff elected by themselves, and put themselves under orders not of the state but of the revolutionary municipal councils established by the workers. Where workers are employed in state service, they must arm and organize in a separate corps or as a part of the proletarian guard with chiefs elected by themselves. Arms and munitions must not be given up under any pretext; every attempt at disarmament must if necessary be thwarted with force. Destruction of the influence of the bourgeis democrats upon the workers, immediate independent and armed organization of the workers, creation of the most difficult and compromising possible conditions for the momentarily unavoidable rule of the bourgeois democracy—these are the main points which the proletariat, and consequently the League, must have in mind during and after the coming uprising.

3. As soon as the new governments have to some extent consolidated themselves, their struggle against the workers will promptly begin. And here in order to oppose the democratic petty bourgeoisie with power, it is necessary above all that the workers be independently organized and centralized into clubs. The Central Authority, as soon as possible after the overthrow of the existing governments, will proceed to Germany, immediately convene a congress and place before it the necessary proposals for a centralization of the workers' clubs under a direction located at the focus of the movement. The rapid organization of at least a provincial union of the workers' clubs is a very important point in strengthening and developing the workers' party; the next result of the overthrow of the existing government will be the election of a National Representation. Here the proletariat must see to it:

1. That no worker shall be excluded, no matter what the

pretext, by any chicanery of the local authorities or government commissioners.

2. That everywhere beside the bourgeois democratic candidates, worker candidates shall be put forward, to be members of the League where possible and their campaigns to be pushed by every means possible. Even in those places where there is no prospect at all for their election, the workers must put forward their own candidates in order to preserve their independence, count their forces, and bring before the public their revolutionary position and party standpoint. Here they must not let themselves be taken in by the phrases of the democrats—as for example that this will split the democratic party and give the reaction a chance to win. All these phrases come to nothing in the last analysis but a swindle upon the proletariat. The advances which the proletarian party will make through such independent action are infinitely more important than the disadvantage which might be caused by the presence of a few reactionaries in the Representation. Were the democracy to come out against the reaction right at the outset with determination and terrorism, the influence of the latter in the elections would be destroyed in advance.

The first point on which the bourgeois democrats will come into conflict with the workers will be the abolition of feudalism. Just as in the first French revolution, the petty bourgeois will give the feudal landed estates to the peasants as free property—that is, will try to leave the agricultural proletariat as it is, and create a petty bourgeois peasant class which will pass through that same cycle of impoverishment and indebtedness which today still holds the French peasant in its grip.

In the interest of the agricultural proletariat as well as their own interest the workers must oppose this plan. They must demand that the confiscated property remain public property and be converted into workers' settlements to be cultivated by the associated agricultural proletariat with all the advantages of large-scale agriculture. By this means the principle of common property will at once get a firm foundation in the midst of the shaky bourgeois property relations. Just as the democrats combine with the peasants, the workers must combine with the agricultural proletariat. The democrats will furthermore either work directly for a federative republic or at least, if they cannot avoid the republic one and indivisible, strive to cripple the central government by giving the greatest possible autonomy and independence to the municipalities and provinces. The workers must strive against this plan not only for a German republic one and indivisible, but within it for a most decided centralization of power in the hands of the state government. They must not let themselves be misled by democratic talk about freedom of municipalities, self-government, etc. In a country like Germany, where so many relics of the Middle Ages are still to be swept out, where so much local and provincial obstinacy has to be overcome, it is not to be tolerated under any circumstances that every village, every town, every province should put a new obstacle in the path of the revolutionary activity which can emanate in full strength only from the center.—It is not to be tolerated that the present situation renew itself, in which the Germans have to wage a special battle for the very same step forward in each town and each province. Least of all can it be tolerated that a form of property which is still inferior to modern private property and must necessarily everywhere dissolve into it, municipal property, with the disputes between poor and rich communities entailed by it, as well as the municipal franchise existing side by side with the state franchise and involving the same chicanery against the workers—should be perpetuated by means of a so-called free municipal constitution. As in France in 1793, today in Germany the carrying through of the strictest centralization is the task of the genuinely revolutionary party.[1]

---

[1] It should be remembered today that this passage is based upon a misunderstanding. In those days it was regarded as settled—thanks to the Bonapartist and liberal falsifiers of history—that the centralized French administrative machine introduced by the Great Revolution, and particularly by the Convention, as an indispensable and decisive weapon in vanquishing the royalist and federalist reaction and the foreign foe, had been maintained. But it is now a well-known fact that during the whole revolution, up to the 18th Brumaire, the entire government of the departments, wards and municipalities consisted of authorities elected by those governed, who conducted themselves with complete freedom within the system of state law; that it was

We have seen how in the coming movement the democrats will come to power, how they will be compelled to propose more or less socialistic measures. It will be asked, what measures shall the workers propose in opposition? The workers naturally cannot as yet, at the commencement of the movement, propose any directly communistic measures. They can however:

1. Compel the democrats to entrench upon the old social order on as many sides as possible, obstruct the regularity of its course and compromise themselves, besides concentrating as many as possible of the productive forces, means of transportation, factories, railways, etc., in the hands of the state.

2. They must push to extreme lengths the proposals of the democrats, which will in no case be revolutionary but only reformist, converting them into direct attacks upon private property. For example, when the petty bourgeoisie propose to buy up the railways and factories, the workers must demand that these railways and factories, as the property of the reactionaries, be confiscated by the state simply and without compensation. If the democrats propose proportional, the workers must demand progressive taxation; if the democrats themselves move for a moderated progressive taxation, the workers must insist upon a tax whose rates are so steeply graduated as to bring ruin to big capital; if the democrats demand a regulation of the state debts, the workers must demand state bankruptcy. The demands of the workers will thus everywhere have to be guided by the concessions and measures of the democrats.

just this provincial and local self-government, similar to the American, which became the strongest lever of the revolution—so much so that Napoleon, immediately after his *coup d'état* of the 18th Brumaire, made haste to replace it with the still existing prefect-management, which was thus a pure instrument of reaction from the very beginning. But just as little as local and provincial self-government contradicts political, national centralization, so little does it need to involve that narrow cantonal and communal selfishness so repulsive to us in Switzerland, and which in 1849 all the South German federative-republicans wished to make the rule in Germany. (Annotation by Friedrich Engels to the Zurich edition of 1885.)

Should the German workers be unable to attain the power and the fulfillment of their class interests without going through a whole long revolutionary development, they have at least this time the certainty that the first act of this imminent revolutionary drama will coincide with the direct victory of their own class in France and be thereby greatly accelerated.

But they themselves must do the most for their own ultimate victory, by enlightening themselves about their class interests, by adopting as quickly as possible an independent party position and by refusing for a single instant to be diverted by the hypocritical phrases of the democratic petty bourgeoisie from the independent organization of the party of the proletariat. Their battle cry must be: The Permanent Revolution.

London, in March 1850.

4. *The Civil War in France.*

INTRODUCTION TO THE GERMAN EDITION

The invitation to prepare another edition of the address of the General Council of the International Workingmen's Association concerning the Civil War in France, and to preface it with an introduction, came to me quite unexpectedly. I can only, therefore, take up the most essential points and touch upon them very briefly.

I prefix the two shorter addresses of the General Council [1] to the longer pamphlet on the Franco-Prussian War. Firstly, because in the pamphlet on the Civil War reference is made to the second address, which itself would not be intelligible without the first. Secondly, because these two addresses, which are also the work of Marx, are, not less than the *Civil War*, excellent specimens of the marvelous gift of the author, first exhibited in the *Eighteenth Brumaire of Louis Bonaparte*, of apprehending clearly the character, the import, and the inevitable consequences of great historical events, at the very time when these events are still unfolding themselves, or have only just taken place. And lastly because, as I write, the Ger-

[1] Omitted from this volume. [M.E.]

man people are still suffering from the evils consequent upon the events here considered, as clearly foreseen and foretold by Marx.

Has it not, indeed, come to a fulfilment, as predicted in the first address, that should Germany's war of defense against Louis Bonaparte degenerate into a war of conquest against the French nation, all the calamities that befell the German people after the so-called wars of liberation would revisit them "with accumulated intensity"? Have we not had twenty years more of Bismarckian rule, and in place of the former persecution of the "demagogues" have we not had the "exceptional law" and the hounding of socialists, with the same police tyranny and the same revolting interpretation of legal texts?

And has it not come literally true, that the annexation of Alsace-Lorraine would "drive France into the arms of Russia," and that after this annexation Germany would either become the acknowledged vassal of Russia, or would have, after a short respite, to arm herself for a new war? And what a war? A "race war of the Germans against the coalesced Slavs and Latins"! Is it not a fact, that the annexation of the French provinces has driven France into the arms of Russia? Has not Bismarck for twenty years courted in vain the favor of the Czar, and lowered himself before him with even meaner servility than little Prussia, before she became the "first great power of Europe," had been accustomed to display at the feet of "Holy Russia"? And does not the "Damocles sword" overhang us of a war, on the first day of which all written treaties will be blown unto the wind like chaff; of a war as to which nothing is certain but the absolute uncertainty of its issue; of a race war which will expose all Europe to the devastation of fifteen or twenty millions of armed men, and which only hangs fire at present for the reason that even the strongest of the great military states shrinks before the absolute uncertainty of the final result?

All the more, therefore, is it our duty to render accessible to the German workingmen these brilliant but half-forgotten documents, which attest to the far-sightedness of the International's proletarian policy in connection with the events of 1870.

What applies to these two addresses, applies also to the one entitled *The Civil War in France*. On the 28th of May, the last of the combatants of the Commune were crushed by superior numbers on the heights of Belleville, and not more than two days passed, before Marx, on the 30th, read to the General Council of the International the pamphlet in question, in which the historical significance of the Paris Commune is presented briefly, but in words so powerful, so incisive, and above all, so true, that there is no equal to it in the whole range of the extensive literature on the subject.

Thanks to the economic and political development of France since 1789, Paris has for fifty years been placed in such a position that no revolution could there break out without assuming a proletarian character, in such wise that the proletariat, which had bought the victory with its blood, would immediately thereafter put forward its own demands. These demands were more or less indefinite, and even confused, in accordance with the particular degree of development to which the Paris workmen had attained at the time; but the upshot of them all was the abolition of the class contrast between capitalist and laborer. How this was to be done, 'tis true nobody knew. But the demand itself, however indefinite its form, was a danger for the existing order of society; the workmen who made it were still armed; if the bourgeoisie at the head of the State would maintain their political supremacy, they were bound to disarm the workmen. Accordingly, after every revolution made victorious with the arms of the workers, there arose a new struggle which ended with the defeat of the workers.

This happened for the first time in 1848. The Liberal bourgeoisie of the Parliamentary opposition held reform banquets in favor of an electoral change which should assure domination to their party. In their struggles with the Government driven to appeal ever more to the people, they were obliged to admit to the front rank the Radical and Republican elements of the small middle class as well as of the wealthier bourgeoisie. But behind these stood the revolutionary workmen; and the latter had, since 1830, acquired for themselves a far greater sense of political independence than even the Republicans among the middle classes suspected. In the moment of crisis between Government and Opposition, the workmen inaugurated the battle in the streets; Louis Philippe disappeared, and with him the electoral reform. In its stead arose the Republic, and moreover, a republic designated by the victorious workmen themselves as the "Social Republic." As to what was to be understood by this "social" republic, nobody was quite clear, not even the workmen themselves. But they now had weapons, and wielded power in the State. So soon, therefore, as the bourgeois Republicans, who were at the head of affairs, began to feel somewhat firm ground under their feet, their first object was to disarm the workmen. To effect this, the bourgeoisie drove them to insurrection in June, 1848, by the direct breach of pledges, by scornful and defiant treatment, and by the attempt to banish the unemployed into a distant province. The Government had taken care to have an overwhelming repressive force at hand. After five days of heroic struggle, the workmen succumbed, and now followed a massacre of the defenseless prisoners, the like of which had not been seen since the days of the Civil Wars which ushered in the downfall of the Roman Republic. It was the first time that the bourgeoisie showed to what a mad ferocity of vengeance it can be stirred up, so soon as the proletariat dares to stand up against it as a separate class with its own interests and demands. And yet 1848 was child's play compared with their fury in 1871.

But Nemesis straightway followed. If the proletariat could not as yet rule France, the bourgeoisie could not do so any more. At least, not at that time, when it was in its majority monarchical, and moreover split into three dynastic parties besides one Republican party. The internal dissensions of the bourgeoisie allowed the adventurer Louis Bonaparte to filch all positions of influence—army, police, administrative machinery—and, on December 2, 1851, to blow up the last stronghold of the bourgeoisie, the National Assembly. The Second Empire followed. It brought about the exploitation of France by a band of political and financial adventurers, but at the same time an industrial development such as had not been possible under the narrow and timid system of Louis Philippe, when France was under the exclusive domination of a mere fraction of the wealthier bourgeoisie. Louis Bonaparte took from the capitalists their political power, under the pretense, on the one hand, of protecting them against the workers, and on the other hand of protecting the workers against them; but, in return for this, his Government favored speculation and industrial activity, in short, the rise and enrichment of the whole of the capitalist class in a hitherto unheard of degree. Corruption and wholesale robbery, it is true, developed to a still greater extent at the Imperial Court and among its hangers-on, who exacted no trifling percentage of the new wealth accumulated by the bourgeoisie.

But the Second Empire—that meant also the appeal to French Chauvinism, which implied the demand for the reacquisition of the frontier of the First Empire lost in 1814, at the very least that of the First Republic. A French Empire, within the boundaries of the old Monarchy, not to say the still more circumscribed ones of 1815, was impossible for long. Hence the necessity of occasional wars and extensions of frontier; but no extension of frontier so dazzles the imagination of French Chauvinists, as that beyond the German left bank of the Rhine. One square mile on the Rhine was worth more to them than ten in the Alps or elsewhere. Given the Second Empire, the demand for the reacquisition of the left bank of the Rhine, either in the lump or piecemeal, was only a question of time. This time came with the Austro-Prussian War of 1866; but Bonaparte was juggled out of the expected territorial indemnity through Bismarck and his own all-too cunning policy of hesitation. There remained nothing for Bonaparte but war—a war which broke out in 1870 and drove him first to Sedan and thence to Wilhelmshöhe.

The necessary consequence was the Paris revolution of the 4th of September, 1870. The Empire collapsed like a house of cards, the Republic was again proclaimed. But the enemy stood before the gates. The armies of the Empire were either hopelessly shut up in Metz or prisoners in Germany. In this extremity the people allowed the Parisian deputies of the former parliament (*Corps Législatif*) to set themselves up as the "Government of National Defense." This was the more readily conceded because, for the purpose of defense, all Parisians capable of bearing arms had been armed and were enrolled in the National Guard, of which the workmen now constituted the great majority. But the antagonism between the Government, composed almost exclusively of bourgeois, and the armed proletariat, broke out soon. On the 31st of October the working class battalions stormed the Hôtel de Ville (City Hall), and took some of the members of the Government prisoners. Treachery, direct breach of faith on the part of the Government, and the intervention of some middle-class battalions freed them again, and in order not to provoke civil war inside a town besieged by a foreign power, the existing Government was permitted to remain in office.

Finally, on the 28th of January, 1871, Paris, starved out, capitulated, but with honors hitherto unheard of in military history. The forts were surrendered, the line of fortifications disarmed, the weapons of the line and of the *Garde Mobile* were handed over to the Germans, and the men themselves were regarded as prisoners of war. But the National Guard retained its weapons and cannon, and only entered into a truce with the conquerors. The latter did not venture upon a triumphal entry into Paris. Only a small portion of Paris, for the most part consisting of public parks, did they attempt to occupy, and even this only for a few days. And during the whole time they, who had kept Paris in a state of siege for 131 days, found themselves in their turn surrounded by armed Parisian workmen, who carefully watched lest any "Prussian" should overstep the narrow limits of the quarter reserved for the foreign conqueror. Such respect the Parisian workmen extorted from that army, before which all the armies of the Empire successively had laid down their weapons; and the Prussian Junkers, who had come thither in order to take revenge on the hotbed of revolution, were compelled to stand and deferentially salute this very armed revolution.

During the war the Parisian workmen had confined themselves to demanding the energetic continuance of the struggle.

But now, peace having been established after the capitulation of Paris, Thiers, the new head of the Government, could not help seeing that the rule of the propertied classes—of the great landlords and capitalists—was in continual danger so long as the Parisian workmen retained their arms. His first work accordingly was the attempt to disarm them. On the 18th of March he sent some troops to the line with the order to steal the artillery belonging to the National Guard, which had been manufactured and paid for by public subscription during the siege of Paris. The attempt miscarried. Paris instantly rose in arms like one man, and war was declared between Paris and the French Government sitting at Versailles. On the 26th of March the Paris Commune was elected, and proclaimed on the 28th. The Central Committee of the National Guard, which had hitherto carried on the Government, decreed the abolition of the scandalous Parisian "guardians of morality," and then abdicated its functions into the hands of the Commune. On the 30th the Commune abolished the conscription and the standing army, and declared the National Guard, to which all citizens capable of bearing arms were to belong, to be the only force with the right to bear arms; it remitted all rents of dwellings from October, 1870, to April, 1871, such rent as had already been paid to be deducted from future payments; and stopped all sales of pledges in the city's pawnshop. The same day the foreigners elected to the Commune were confirmed in their functions, since "the flag of the Commune is that of the Universal Republic." On the 1st of April it was decided that the highest salary of a functionary of the Commune, whether a member or otherwise, was not to exceed 6,000 francs ($1,200) a year. On the following day was decreed the separation of Church and State, the abolition of all State payments for religious purposes, and the transformation of all ecclesiastical wealth into national property. As a consequence of this, all religious symbols, dogmas, prayers—in short, "all things appertaining to the sphere of the individual conscience"—were on the 8th of April ordered to be banished from the schools, an order which was carried out as soon as possible. On the 5th, in retaliation for the daily murder of communards captured by the

Versailles troops, there was enacted a decree for the arrest of hostages, but it was never carried out. On the 6th, the guillotine was fetched out by the 137th battalion of the National Guard, and publicly burnt amid loud popular applause. On the 12th, the Commune ordered the triumphal column on the Place Vendôme, which had been constructed by Napoleon I after the war of 1809 out of captured cannon, to be overthrown, as it was a symbol of *chauvinism* and mutual hatred among the nations. This was accomplished on the 16th of May. On the 16th of April, the Commune issued an order for a statistical account of all factories and workshops which had been closed by the employers; for the elaboration of plans for their management by the workingmen hitherto engaged in them, who were to be formed into coöperative societies for the purpose; and, also, for the federation of these ṣocieties into one great coöperative organization. On the 20th, it abolished the night work of bakers, as also the register-offices for procuring employment, which, since the Second Empire, had been the monopoly of certain police-appointed scoundrels, exploiters of the worst kind. The matter was henceforward placed in the hands of the mayoralties of the twenty arrondissements of Paris. On the 30th of April it decreed the abolition of pawnshops, as being incompatible with the right of workmen to their tools and to credit. On the 5th of May it ordered the destruction of the chapel erected in expiation of the execution of Louis XVI.

Thus, since the 18th of March, the class character of the Parisian movement, hitherto thrust into the background by the struggle against the foreign invasion, came clearly and emphatically to the fore. As in the Commune there sat almost exclusively workmen, or the recognized representatives of workmen, its decisions naturally bore a distinctively proletarian character. It either decreed reforms which the Republican bourgeoisie had omitted to carry out from pure cowardice, but which formed a necessary foundation for the free action of the working class, as, for instance, the carrying out of the principle that religion, *as far as the State is concerned,* is a purely private matter; or it adopted measures directly in the interest of the working class, and in a few cases even cutting deeply into the life tissue of the old order of society. But in a besieged city all this could not be carried beyond the first stages of realization. And from the beginning of May onwards the struggle against the ever increasing masses of the army of the Versailles Government claimed exclusive attention and energy.

On the 7th of April the Versaillese had seized the bridge over the Seine at Neuilly on the west side of Paris; on the other hand, on the 11th, they were beaten back with much loss by General Eudes in an attack they made on the south side. Paris was continually bombarded by the very people who had stigmatized the bombardment of the same city by the Prussians as a sacrilegious outrage. These very people went on their knees to the Prussian Government to implore the speedy return of the French military prisoners taken at Sedan and Metz, who were to reconquer Paris for them. The gradual arrival of these troops gave a decisive superiority to the Versaillese from the beginning of May onward. This showed itself even as early as the 23d of April, when Thiers broke off the negotiations with the Commune respecting the latter's offer to exchange the Archbishop of Paris and a number of other priests retained in Paris as hostages, against Blanqui alone, who had been twice elected to the Commune, but who remained a prisoner at Clairvaux. It showed itself still more clearly in the altered language of Thiers; hitherto hesitating and ambiguous, he now suddenly became insulting, threatening, and brutal. On the south side the Versaillese took, on the 3d of May, the redoubt of Moulin Saquet; on the 9th, the fort of Issy was reduced to a heap of ruins by the cannonade; on the 14th, that of Vanves. On the west side they gradually advanced, seizing the numerous buildings and villages which extended to the outer line of fortifications, up to the *enceinte* itself; on the 21st, they succeeded, owing to treachery and the carelessness of the National Guard posted at that point, in entering the city. The Prussians, who occupied the northern and eastern forts, allowed the Versaillese to press forward into the territory in the north of the city, which the conditions of peace had closed to them, and thence to inaugurate a formidable attack over a long line, which the Parisians, believing them to be covered by the terms of the truce, had in consequence only weakly occupied. The result of this was that the resistance in the western parts of Paris, the wealthier parts of the city, was only feeble; it became tougher and more severe as the attacking troops approached the eastern half, the working class parts of the city. Only after an eight days' struggle did the last defenders of the Commune succumb on the heights of Belleville and Menilmontant. And now the murder of defenseless men, women, and children, which had raged the whole week through in ever-increasing proportions, reached its highest point! The breechloader no longer killed fast enough; the conquered were slaughtered in hundreds with the mitrailleuses; "the wall of the Federals" in the Père la Chaise cemetery, where the last massacre took place, remains to-day a dumb but eloquent witness to the frenzy of crime of which the governing classes are capable as soon as the proletariat dares to stand up for its rights. Then, as the slaughter of all was seen to be impossible, came the arrests *en masse,* the shooting down of arbitrarily selected prisoners as victims for sacrifice, and the transference of the remainder into great camps, where they awaited the mercy of the courts-martial. The Prussian troops, who were encamped to the northeast of Paris, received the order to allow no fugitives to pass. Nevertheless, the officers often shut their eyes when the soldiers obeyed the call of humanity rather than that command. Especially does the Saxon Army Corps deserve the credit of having acted very humanely and having let through many whose character as combatants of the Commune was obvious.

Looking back to-day, after twenty years, upon the acts and historical significance of the Paris Commune, it appears to us that the information contained in the pages of the *Civil War in France* may usefully be supplemented here by some special considerations.

The members of the Commune were divided into a majority of Blanquists, who had also predominated in the central committee of the National Guard, and a minority, which consisted for the most part of members of the International Workingmen's Association, who were adherents of the Proudhonian School of Socialism. The great mass of the Blanquists at that time were socialists only because of their revolutionary proletarian instinct. A few only had attained to greater clearness of principle owing to Vaillant, who was acquainted with German scientific socialism. Thus we can understand why, in the economic field, many things were left undone which, according to our present conceptions, should have been done by the Commune. The most difficult thing to understand is, indeed, the sacred respect with which the Commune reverently stopped before the portals of the Bank of France. This was also a portentous political error. The Bank in the hands of the Commune—that was worth more than ten thousand hostages. It would have meant the pressure of the entire French bourgeoisie upon the Versailles Government in the interest of peace with the Commune. But what is still more wonderful, is the number of correct things done by the Commune, in spite of its make-up of Blanquists and Proudhonists. Of course, the Proudhonists are responsible for the economic decrees of the Commune, for those that are praiseworthy as well as for those that are not, while the Blanquists are responsible for the political acts of commission and omission. And in both cases the irony of history would have it—as is usual when doctrinaires take the helm of the State—that both the ones and the others did the reverse of that which the doctrines of their school prescribed.

Proudhon, the socialist of the small farmer and petty tradesman, hated association most heartily. According to him, it does more harm than good; it is naturally unfruitful, even detrimental, because it curtails the worker's freedom; it is pure dogma, unproductive and troublesome, destructive of the freedom of the worker as well as the saving of labor; its disadvantages multiply faster than its advantages; while competition, division of labor, private property, are economic springs of greater power. Only in exceptional cases—these are Proudhon's own words—of great industries and great business corporations, the railroads, for instance, is the association of the workers good and proper.[1]

And yet, even in Paris, the center of the artistic trades, production on a large scale had so far ceased to be an exception in 1871 that the most important decree of the Commune had for its object the organization of great industries and even of manufacture; and this organization was to comprise not only the association of the workers in each factory but also the union of all these coöperative associations into one great federation: in short, an organization of such a character that, as Marx very correctly states in the *Civil War,* it must have ultimately ended in communism, that is, in the very opposite of the Proudhonistic theory. For this reason, the Commune was the grave of the Proudhonist School of Socialism. This school no longer exists among the French workers; and among the Possibilists no less than among the Marxists, there now rules undisputedly the Marxian theory. To-day Proudhonists are found only among the "radical" bourgeoisie.

The Blanquists fared no better. Brought up in the school of conspiracy, held together by the rigid discipline essential to it, they started from the conception that a comparatively small number of resolute, well organized men would be able not only to grasp the helm of State at a favorable moment, but also, through the display of great energy and reckless daring, to hold it as long as required, that is, until they had succeeded in carrying the masses of the people into the revolutionary current and ranging them around the small leading band. To accomplish this, what was necessary, above all else, was the most stringent, dictatorial centralization of all power in the hands of the new revolutionary government. And what did the Commune do, which in the majority consisted of these very Blanquists? In all its proclamations to the French people in the provinces, it called upon them for a free federation of all French communes with Paris, for a national organization, which for the first time was to be the real creation of the nation. The army, the political police,

[1] See *Idée générale de la Révolution,* 3me étude.

the bureaucracy, all those agencies of oppression in a centralized government, which Napoleon had created in 1798, and which since then every new government had gladly used and kept up as ready weapons against its enemies, were to be abolished everywhere, as they had been abolished in Paris.

From the very outset the Commune had to recognize that the working class, having once attained supremacy in the State, could not work with the old machinery of government; that this working class, if it was not to lose the position which it had just conquered, had, on the one hand, to abolish all the old machinery of oppression that had hitherto been utilized against itself, and, on the other hand, to secure itself against its own representatives and officers by declaring them to be removable, without exception and at all times. In what did the chief characteristic of the old State consist? Society had created for itself definite organs, originally by simple division of labor, for the provision of its common interests. But these organs, at the head of which is the power of the State, had in the course of time, and in the service of their own separate interests, transformed themselves from the servants of society into its masters. And this is true not only of the hereditary monarchy, but also of the democratic republic. Nowhere do the "politicians" form a more distinct and more powerful subdivision of the nation than in the United States. Here both the great parties, to which the predominance alternately falls, are in their turn ruled by people who make a business of politics, who speculate upon seats in the legislative bodies of the Union and the separate States, or who live by agitation for their party and are rewarded with offices after its victory. It is well known how the Americans have tried for thirty years past to throw off this yoke, which has become intolerable, and how, notwithstanding, they sink ever deeper into the mire of corruption. It is just in the United States that we can most clearly see the process through which the State acquires a position of independent power over against the society, for which it was originally designed as a mere tool. There exists here no dynasty, no aristocracy, no standing army with the exception of a few men to guard against the Indians, no bureaucracy permanently installed and pensioned. Nevertheless, we have here two great rings of political speculators, that alternately take possession of the power of State and exploit it with the most corrupt means and to the most corrupt purposes. And the nation is powerless against these men, who nominally are its servants, but in reality are its two overruling and plundering hordes of politicians.

Against this transformation of the State and the State's organs from the servants of society into its rulers—a transformation which has been inevitable in all hitherto existing States—the Commune adopted two unfailing remedies. In the first place it filled all positions of administration, justice, and instruction, through election by universal suffrage, the elected being at all times subject to recall by their constituents. And secondly, it paid for all services, high or low, only the same pay that other workers received. The highest salary that it ever paid was six thousand francs. Thus a check was put to all place-hunting and career-making, even without the imperative mandate under which delegates to the representative bodies were placed, quite superfluously.

This disruption of the power formerly possessed by the State, and its replacement by a new power that was truly democratic, is described in detail in the third chapter of the *Civil War*. But it was necessary to enter here once more upon some of its features, because in Germany the superstition concerning the State has been transmitted from philosophy into the general consciousness of the bourgeoisie, and even of many workers. According to the conception of philosophy, the State is the "realization of the Idea," or the philosophic equivalent of the Kingdom of God upon earth —the sphere in which eternal truth and righteousness are, or ought to be, realized. There follows from this a superstitious reverence for the State and all its adjuncts, a superstition that is all the more natural, since from our very childhood we have grown up in the idea that the affairs and interests common to the whole of society could not be provided for in any other way than had been the practice hitherto, namely, through the State and its highly paid functionaries. And people imagine they taken a very bold step, when they have once freed themselves from the belief in monarchy and swear now by the democratic republic. But in reality the State is nothing else than a machine for the oppression of one class by another class, and that no less so in the democratic republic than under the monarchy. At the very best it is an inheritance of evil, bound to be transmitted to the proletariat when it has become victorious in its struggle for class supremacy, and the worst features of which it will have to lop off at once, as the Commune did, until a new race, grown up under new, free social conditions, will be in a position to shake off from itself this State rubbish in its entirety.

The German philistine has lately been thrown once again into wholesome paroxysms by the expression "dictatorship of the Proletariat." Well, gentle sirs, would you like to know how this dictatorship looks? Then look at the Paris Commune. That was the dictatorship of the proletariat.

FREDERICK ENGELS.

*London, on the 20th anniversary of the
Commune, March 18, 1871.*

THE CIVIL WAR IN FRANCE

CHAPTER I

THE NATIONAL DEFENSE

On the 4th of September, 1870, when the workingmen of Paris proclaimed the Republic, which was almost instantaneously acclaimed throughout France, without a single voice of dissent, a cabal of place-hunting barristers, with Thiers for their statesman and Trochu for their general, took hold of the Hôtel de Ville. At that time they were imbued with so fanatical a faith in the mission of Paris to represent France in all epochs of historical crises, that, to legitimatize their usurped titles as governors of France, they thought it quite sufficient to produce their lapsed mandates as representatives of Paris. In our second address on the late war, five days after the rise of these men, we told you who they were. Yet, in the turmoil of surprise, with the real leaders of the working class still shut up in Bonapartist prisons and the Prussians already marching upon Paris, Paris bore with their assumption of power, on the express condition that it was to be wielded for the single purpose of national defense. Paris, however, was not to be defended without arming its working class, organizing them into an effective force, and training their ranks by the war itself. But Paris armed was the Revolution armed. A victory of Paris over the Prussian aggressor would have been a victory of the French workman over the French capitalist and his State parasites. In this conflict between national duty and class interest, the Government of National Defense did not hesitate one moment to turn into a Government of National Defection.

The first step they took was to send Thiers on a roving tour to all the Courts of Europe, there to beg mediation by offering the barter of the Republic for a king. Four months after the commencement of the siege, when they thought the opportune moment had come for breaking the first word of capitulation, Trochu, in the presence of Jules Favre and others of his colleagues, addressed the assembled mayors of Paris in these terms:

"The first question put to me by my colleagues on the very evening of the 4th of September was this: Paris, can it, with any chance of success stand a siege by the Prussian army? I did not hesitate to answer in the negative. Some of my colleagues here present will warrant the truth of my words and the persistence of my opinion. I told them, in these very terms, that, under the existing state of things, the attempt of Paris to hold out a siege by the Prussian army would be folly. Without doubt, I added, it would be an heroic folly, but that would be all. . . . The events [managed by himself] have not given the lie to my prevision." This nice little speech of Trochu was afterwards published by M. Corban, one of the mayors present.

Thus, on the very evening of the proclamation of the Republic, Trochu's "plan" was known to his colleagues to be the capitulation of Paris. If national defense had been more than a pretext for the personal government of Thiers, Favre & Co., the upstarts of the 4th of September, would have abdicated on the 5th—would have initiated the Paris people into Trochu's "plan," and called upon them to surrender at once, or to take their own fate into their own hands. Instead of this, the infamous impostors resolved upon curing the heroic folly of Paris by a regimen of famine and broken heads, and to dupe her in the meanwhile by ranting manifestoes, holding forth that Trochu, "the Governor of Paris, will never capitulate," and Jules Favre, the Foreign Minister, will "not cede an inch of our territory, nor a stone of our fortresses." In a letter to Gambetta, that very same Jules Favre avows that what they were "defending" against were not the Prussian soldiers, but the workingmen of Paris. During the whole continuance of the siege the Bonapartist cut-throats, whom Trochu had wisely intrusted with the command of the Paris army, exchanged, in their intimate correspondence, ribald jokes at the well-understood mockery of defense.[1] The mask of imposture was at last dropped on

[1] See, for instance, the correspondence of Alphonse Simon Guiod, supreme commander of the artillery of the Army of Defense of Paris

the 28th of January, 1871. With the true heroism of utter self-debasement, the Government of National Defense, in their capitulation, came out as the Government of France by Bismarck's permission—a part so base that Louis Bonaparte himself had, at Sedan, shrunk from accepting it. After the events of the 18th of March, on their wild flight to Versailles, the *capitulards* left in the hands of Paris the documentary evidence of their treason, to destroy which, as the Commune says in its manifesto to the provinces, "those men would not recoil from battering Paris into a heap of ruins washed by a sea of blood."

To be eagerly bent upon such a consummation, some of the leading members of the Government of Defense had, besides, most peculiar reasons of their own.

Shortly after the conclusion of the armistice, M. Millière, one of the representatives of Paris to the National Assembly, now shot by express order of Jules Favre, published a series of authentic legal documents in proof that Jules Favre, living in concubinage with the wife of a drunkard resident at Algiers, had, by a most daring concoction of forgeries, spread over many years, contrived to grasp in the name of the children of his adultery, a large succession, which made him a rich man, and that, in a lawsuit undertaken by the legitimate heirs, he only escaped exposure by the connivance of the Bonapartist tribunals. As these dry legal documents were not to be got rid of by any amount of rhetorical horsepower, Jules Favre, for the first time in his life, held his tongue, quietly awaiting the outbreak of the civil war, in order, then, frantically to denounce the people of Paris as a band of escaped convicts in utter revolt against family, religion, order, and property. This same forger had hardly got into power, after the 4th of September, when he sympathetically let loose upon society Pic and Taillefer, convicted, even under the Empire, of forgery, in the scandalous affair of the *Étendard*. One of these men, Taillefer, having dared to return to Paris under the Commune, was at once reinstated

and Grand Cross of the Legion of Honor, to Suzanne, general of division of artillery, a correspondence published by the *Journal Officiel* of the Commune.

in prison; and then Jules Favre exclaimed, from the tribune of the National Assembly, that Paris was setting free all her jailbirds!

Ernest Picard, the Joe Miller of the Government of National Defense, who appointed himself Home Minister of the Republic after having in vain striven to become the Home Minister of the Empire, is the brother of one Arthur Picard, an individual expelled from the Paris Bourse as a blackleg,[1] and convicted, on his own confession, of a theft of 300,000 francs, while manager of one of the branches of the *Société Générale*, rue Palestro, No. 5.[2] This Arthur Picard was made by Ernest Picard the editor of his paper, *l'Électeur Libre*. While the common run of stockjobbers were led astray by the official lies of the Home Office paper, Arthur was running backwards and forwards between the Home Office and the Bourse, there to discount the disasters of the French army. The whole financial correspondence of that worthy pair of brothers fell into the hands of the Commune.

Jules Ferry, a penniless barrister before the 4th of September, contrived, as the mayor of Paris during the siege, to job a fortune out of famine. The day on which he would have to give an account of his maladministration would be the day of his conviction.

These men, then, could find, in the ruins of Paris only, their tickets-of-leave: they were the very men Bismarck wanted. With the help of some shuffling of cards, Thiers, hitherto the secret prompter of the Government, now appeared at its head, with the ticket-of-leave men for his Ministers.

Thiers, that monstrous gnome, has charmed the French bourgeoisie for almost half a century, because he is the most consummate intellectual expression of their own class-corruption. Before he became a statesman he had already proved his lying powers as an historian. The chronicle of his public life is the record of the misfortunes of France. Banded, before 1830, with the Republicans, he slipped into office under Louis Philippe by betraying his protector Lafitte,

---

[1] See report of the Prefecture of Police, dated July 13th, 1867.
[2] See report of the Prefecture of Police, dated December 11th, 1868

ingratiating himself with the king by exciting mob-riots
against the clergy, during which the Church of Saint Ger-
main l'Auxerrois and the Archbishop's palace were plundered,
and by acting the minister-spy upon, and the jail-accoucheur
of, the Duchess de Berri. The massacre of the Republicans in
the rue Transnonain, and the subsequent infamous laws of
September against the press and the right of association, were
his work. Reappearing as the chief of the Cabinet in March,
1840, he astonished France with his plan of fortifying Paris.
To the Republicans, who denounced this plan as a sinister
plot against the liberty of Paris, he replied from the tribune
of the Chamber of Deputies:

"What! to fancy that any works of fortification could
ever endanger liberty! And first of all you calumniate any
possible Government in supposing that it could some day
attempt to maintain itself by bombarding the capital. . . . But
that Government would be a hundred times more impossible
after its victory than before." Indeed, no Government would
ever have dared to bombard Paris from the forts, but that
Government which had previously surrendered these forts to
the Prussians.

When King Bomba tried his hand at Palermo, in January,
1848, Thiers, then long since out of office, again rose in the
Chamber of Deputies: "You know, gentlemen, what is happening at Palermo. You, all of you, shake with horror [in the
parliamentary sense] on hearing that during forty-eight
hours a large town has been bombarded—by whom? Was it
by a foreign enemy exercising the rights of war? No, gentlemen, it was by its own Government. And why? Because that
unfortunate town demanded its rights. Well, then, for the demand of its rights it has got forty-eight hours of bombardment. . . . Allow me to appeal to the opinion of Europe. It is
doing a service to mankind to arise, and to speak out from
this tribune—the greatest, perhaps, in Europe—some re-
sounding words [mere words, indeed] of indignation against
such acts. . . . When the Regent Espartero, who had rendered
services to his country [which M. Thiers never did], in-

tended bombarding Barcelona, in order to suppress its insurrection, there arose from all parts of the world a general outcry of indignation."

Eighteen months afterwards, M. Thiers was amongst the fiercest defenders of the bombardment of Rome by a French army. In fact, the fault of King Bomba seems to have consisted in this only, that he limited his bombardment to forty-eight hours.

A few days before the Revolution of February, fretting at the long exile from place and pelf to which Guizot had condemned him, and sniffing in the air the scent of an approaching popular commotion, Thiers, in that pseudo-heroic style which won him the nickname of *Mirabeaumouche,* declared to the Chamber of Deputies: "I am of the party of Revolution, not only in France, but in Europe. I wish the government of the Revolution to remain in the hands of moderate men ... but if that government should fall into the hands of ardent minds, even into those of Radicals, I shall, for all that, not desert my cause. I shall always be of the party of the Revolution." The Revolution of February came. Instead of displacing the Guizot Cabinet by the Thiers Cabinet, as the little man had dreamt, it superseded Louis Philippe by the Republic. On the first day of the popular victory he carefully hid himself, forgetting that the contempt of the workingmen screened him from their hatred. Still, with his legendary courage, he continued to shy the public stage, until the June massacre had cleared it for his sort of action. Then he became the leading mind of the "Party of Order" and its Parliamentary Republic, that anonymous interregnum, in which all the rival factions of the ruling class conspired together to crush the people, and conspired against each other to restore each of them its own monarchy. Then, as now, Thiers denounced the Republicans as the only obstacle to the consolidation of the Republic; then, as now, he spoke to the Republic as the hangman spoke to Don Carlos: "I shall assassinate thee, but for thine own good." Now, as then, he will have to exclaim on the day after his victory: *L'Empire est fait*—the Empire is consummated. Despite his hypocritical homilies about necessary liberties and his personal grudge against Louis Bonaparte, who had made a dupe of him and kicked out parliamentarism—and outside of its factitious atmosphere the little man is conscious of withering into nothingness—he had a hand in all the infamies of the Second Empire, from the occupation of Rome by French troops to the war with Prussia; a war which he incited by his fierce invective against German unity, not as a cloak of Prussian despotism, but as an encroachment upon the vested right of France in German disunion. Fond of brandishing, with his dwarfish arms, in the face of Europe the sword of the First Napoleon, whose historical shoeblack he had become, his foreign policy always culminated in the utter humiliation of France, from the London convention of 1841 to the Paris capitulation of 1871, and the present civil war, when he hounds on the prisoners of Sedan and Metz against Paris by special permission of Bismarck. Despite his versatility of talent and shiftiness of purpose, this man has his whole lifetime been wedded to the most fossil routine. It is self-evident that to him the deeper undercurrents of modern society remained forever hidden; but even the most palpable changes on its surface were abhorrent to a brain all the vitality of which had fled to the tongue. Thus he never tired of denouncing as a sacrilege any deviation from the old French protective system. When a minister of Louis Philippe, he railed at railways as a wild chimera; and when in opposition under Louis Bonaparte, he branded as a profanation every attempt to reform the rotten French army system. Never in his long political career has he been guilty of a single —even the smallest—measure of any practical use.

Thiers was consistent only in his greed for wealth and his hatred of the men that produce it. Having entered his first ministry under Louis Philippe poor as Job, he left it a millionaire. His last ministry under the same king (of the 1st of March, 1840), exposed him to public taunts of peculation in the Chamber of Deputies, to which he was content to reply by tears—a commodity he deals in as freely as Jules Favre, or any other crocodile. At Bordeaux his first measure for saving France from impending financial ruin was to en-

dow himself with three millions a year, the first and the last
word of the "Economical Republic," the vista of which he
had opened to his Paris electors in 1869. One of his former
colleagues of the Chamber of Deputies of 1830, himself a
capitalist and, nevertheless, a devoted member of the Paris
Commune, M. Beslay, lately addressed Thiers thus in a
public placard: "The enslavement of labor by capital has always been the cornerstone of your policy, and from the very
day you saw the Republic of Labor installed at the Hôtel
de Ville, you have never ceased to cry out to France: 'These
are criminals!' " A master in small state roguery, a virtuoso
in perjury and treason, a craftsman in all the petty stratagems,
cunning devices, and base perfidies of parliamentary party-
warfare; never scrupling, when out of office, to fan a revolution, and to stifle it in blood when at the helm of the State;
with class prejudices standing him in the place of ideas, and
vanity in the place of a heart; his private life as infamous
as his public life is odious—even now, when playing the part
of a French Sulla, he cannot help setting off the abomination
of his deeds by the ridicule of his ostentation.

The capitulation of Paris, by surrendering to Prussia not
only Paris, but all France, closed the long-continued intrigues
of treason with the enemy, which the usurpers of the 4th of
September had begun, as Trochu himself said, on that very
same day. On the other hand, it initiated the civil war they
were now to wage with the assistance of Prussia, against the
Republic and Paris. The trap was laid in the very terms of
the capitulation. At that time above one-third of the territory was in the hands of the enemy, the capital was cut off
from the provinces, all communications were disorganized. To
elect under such circumstances a real representation of France
was impossible, unless ample time were given for preparation. In view of this, the capitulation stipulated that a National Assembly must be elected within eight days; so that
in many parts of France the news of the impending election
arrived on its eve only. This Assembly, moreover, was, by an
express clause of the capitulation, to be elected for the sole
purpose of deciding on peace or war, and, eventually, to
conclude a treaty of peace. The population could not but

feel that the terms of the armistice rendered the continuation of the war impossible, and that for sanctioning the peace imposed by Bismarck, the worst men in France were the best. But not content with these precautions, Thiers, even before the secret of the armistice had been broached to Paris, set out for an electioneering tour through the provinces, there to galvanize back into life the Legitimist party, which now, along with the Orleanists, had to take the place of the then impossible Bonapartists. He was not afraid of them. Impossible as a government of modern France, and, therefore, contemptible as rivals, what party were more eligible as tools of counter-revolution than the party whose action, in the words of Thiers himself (Chamber of Deputies, January 5, 1833), "had always been confined to the three resources of foreign invasion, civil war, and anarchy"? They verily believed in the advent of their long-expected retrospective millennium. There were the heels of foreign invasion trampling upon France; there was the downfall of an Empire, and the captivity of a Bonaparte; and there they were themselves. The wheel of history has evidently rolled back to stop at the *Chambre introuvable* of 1816. In the assemblies of the Republic, 1848 to '51, they had been represented by their educated and trained parliamentary champions; it was the rank-and-file of the party which now rushed in—all the Pourceaugnacs of France.

As soon as this Assembly of "Rurals" had met at Bordeaux, Thiers made it clear to them that the peace preliminaries must be assented to at once, without even the honors of a parliamentary debate, as the only condition on which Prussia would permit them to open the war against the Republic and Paris, its stronghold. The counter-revolution had, in fact, no time to lose. The Second Empire had more than doubled the national debt and plunged all the large towns into heavy municipal debts. The war had fearfully swelled the liabilities, and mercilessly ravaged the resources of the nation. To complete the ruin, the Prussian Shylock was there with his bond for the keep of half a million of his soldiers on French soil, his indemnity of five milliards and interest at 5 per cent. on the unpaid instalments thereof. Who was to pay the bill? It was only by the violent overthrow of the Republic that the appropriators of wealth could hope to shift on to the shoulders of its producers the cost of a war which they, the appropriators, had themselves originated. Thus, the immense ruin of France spurred on these patriotic representatives of land and capital, under the very eyes and patronage of the invader, to graft upon the foreign war a civil war—a slaveholders' rebellion.

There stood in the way of this conspiracy one great obstacle —Paris. To disarm Paris was the first condition of success. Paris was therefore summoned by Thiers to surrender its arms. Then Paris was exasperated by the frantic anti-republican demonstrations of the "Rural" Assembly and by Thiers' own equivocations about the legal status of the Republic; by the threat to decapitate and decapitalize Paris; the appointment of Orleanist ambassadors; Dufaure's laws on over-due commercial bills and house rents, inflicting ruin on the commerce and industry of Paris; Pouyer-Quertier's tax of *two* centimes upon every copy of every imaginable publication; the sentences of death against Blanqui and Flourens; the suppression of the Republican journals; the transfer of the National Assembly to Versailles; the renewal of the state of siege declared by Palikao, and expired on the 4th of September; the appointment of Vinoy, the *Décembriseur,* as governor of Paris—of Valentin, the Imperialist gendarme, as its prefect of police—and of D'Aurelles de Paladine, the Jesuit general, as the commander-in-chief of its National Guard.

And now we have to address a question to M. Thiers and the men of national defense, his understrappers. It is known that, through the agency of M. Pouyer-Quertier, his finance minister, Thiers had contracted a loan of two milliards, to be paid down at once. Now, is it true or not—

1. That the business was so managed that a consideration of several millions was secured for the private benefit of Thiers, Jules Favre, Ernest Picard, Pouyer-Quertier, and Jules Simon? and—

2. That no money was to be paid down until after the "pacification" of Paris?

At all events, there must have been something very pressing in the matter, for Thiers and Jules Favre, in the name of the majority of the Bordeaux Assembly, unblushingly solicited the immediate occupation of Paris by Prussian troops. Such, however, was not the game of Bismarck, as he sneeringly, and in public, told the admiring Frankfort Philistines on his return to Germany.

CHAPTER II

THE EIGHTEENTH OF MARCH

ARMED Paris was the only serious obstacle in the way of counter-revolutionary conspiracy. Paris was, therefore, to be disarmed. On this point the Bordeaux Assembly was sincerity itself. If the roaring rant of its Rurals had not been audible enough, the surrender of Paris by Thiers to the tender mercies of the triumvirate of Vinoy the *Décembriseur*, Valentin the Bonapartist gendarme, and D'Aurelles de Paladine the Jesuit general, would have cut off even the last subterfuge of doubt. But while insultingly exhibiting the true purpose of the disarmament of Paris, the conspirators asked her to lay down her arms on a pretext which was the most glaring, the most barefaced of lies. The artillery of the Paris National Guard, said Thiers, belonged to the State, and to the State it must be returned. The fact is this: From the very day of the capitulation, by which Bismarck's prisoners had signed the surrender of France, but reserved to themselves a numerous bodyguard for the express purpose of cowing Paris, Paris stood on the watch. The National Guard reorganized themselves and intrusted their supreme control to a Central Committee elected by their whole body, save some fragments of the old Bonapartist formation. On the eve of the entrance of the Prussians into Paris, the Central Committee took measures for the removal to Montmartre, Belleville, and La Villette of the cannon and mitrailleuses treacherously abandoned by the capitulards in and about the very quarters the Prussians were to occupy. That artillery had been furnished by the subscriptions of the National Guard. As their private property, it was officially recognized in the capitulation of the 28th of January, and on that very title exempted from the general surrender, into the hands of the conqueror, of arms belonging to the Government. And Thiers was so utterly destitute of even the flimsiest pretext for initiating the war against Paris, that he had to resort to the flagrant lie of the artillery of the National Guard being State property!

The seizure of her artillery was evidently but to serve as the preliminary to the general disarmament of Paris, and, therefore, of the Revolution of the 4th of September. But that revolution had become the legal status of France. The Republic, its work, was recognized by the conqueror in the terms of the capitulation. After the capitulation, it was acknowledged by all the foreign Powers, and in its name the National Assembly had been summoned. The Paris workingmen's revolution of the 4th of September was the only legal title of the National Assembly seated at Bordeaux, and of its executive. Without it, the National Assembly would at once have to give way to the *Corps Législatif*, elected in 1869 by universal suffrage under French, not under Prussian, rule, and forcibly dispersed by the arm of the Revolution. Thiers and his ticket-of-leave men would have had to capitulate for safe-conducts signed by Louis Bonaparte, to save them from a voyage to Cayenne. The National Assembly, with its power of attorney to settle the terms of peace with Prussia, was but an incident of that revolution, the true embodiment of which was still armed Paris, who had initiated it, undergone for it a five months' siege, with its horrors of famine, and made her prolonged resistance, despite Trochu's plan, the basis of an obstinate war of defense in the provinces. And Paris was now either to lay down her arms at the insulting behest of the rebellious slaveholders of Bordeaux, and acknowledge that her revolution of the 4th of September meant nothing but a simple transfer of power from Louis Bonaparte to his royal rivals; or she had to stand forward as the self-sacrificing champion of France, whose salvation from ruin, and whose regeneration were impossible, without the revolutionary overthrow of the political and social conditions that had engendered the Second Empire, and, under its fostering care, matured into utter rottenness. Paris, emaciated by a five months' famine, did not hesitate one moment. She heroically resolved to run all the hazards of a resistance against the French conspirators, even with Prussian cannon frowning upon her from her own forts. Still, in its abhorrence of the civil war into which Paris was to be goaded, the Central Committee continued to persist in a merely defensive attitude, despite the provocations of the Assembly, the usurpations of the Executive, and the menacing concentration of troops in and around Paris.

Thiers opened the civil war by sending Vinoy, at the head of a multitude of *sergents-de-ville* and some regiments of the line, upon a nocturnal expedition against Montmartre, there to seize, by surprise, the artillery of the National Guard. It is well known how this attempt broke down before the resistance of the National Guard and the fraternization of the line with the people. D'Aurelles de Paladine had printed beforehand his bulletin of victory, and Thiers held ready the placards announcing his measures of *coup d'état*. Now these had to be replaced by Thiers' appeals, imparting his magnanimous resolve to leave the National Guard in the possession of their arms, with which, he said, he felt sure they would rally round the Government against the rebels. Out of 300,000 National Guards only 300 responded to this summons to rally round little Thiers against themselves. The glorious workingmen's revolution of the 18th of March took undisputed sway of Paris without striking a blow. The Central Committee was its provisional government. Europe seemed, for a moment, to doubt whether the recent sensational performances of state and war had any reality in them, or whether they were the dreams of a long bygone past.

From the 18th of March to the entrance of the Versailles troops into Paris, the proletarian revolution remained so free from the acts of violence in which the revolutions, and still more the counter-revolutions, of the "better classes" abound, that no facts were left to its opponents to cry out about but the execution of Generals Lecomte and Clement Thomas, and the affair of the Place Vendôme.

One of the Bonapartist officers engaged in the nocturnal attempt against Montmartre, General Lecomte, had four times ordered the 81st line regiment to fire at an unarmed gathering in the Place Pigale, and on their refusal fiercely insulted them. Instead of shooting women and children, his own men shot him. The inveterate habits acquired by the soldiery under the training of the enemies of the working class are, of course, not likely to change the very moment these soldiers change sides. The same men executed Clement Thomas.

"General" Clement Thomas, a malcontent ex-quartermaster-sergeant, had, in the latter days of Louis Philippe's reign, enlisted at the office of the Republican newspaper *Le National,* there to serve in the double capacity of responsible man-of-straw (*gérant responsable*) and the dueling bully to that very combative journal. After the revolution of February, the men of *Le National* having got into power, they metamorphosed this old quartermaster-sergeant into a general on the eve of the butchery of June, of which he, like Jules Favre, was one of the sinister plotters, and became one of the most dastardly executioners. Then he and his generalship disappeared for a long time, to again rise to the surface on the 1st of November, 1870. The day before, the Government of Defense, caught at the Hôtel de Ville, had solemnly pledged their parole to Blanqui, Flourens, and other representatives of the working class, to abdicate their usurped power into the hands of a commune to be freely elected by Paris. Instead of keeping their word, they let loose on Paris the Bretons of Trochu, who now replaced the Corsicans of Bonaparte. General Tamisier alone, refusing to sully his name by such a breach of faith, resigned the commandership-in-chief of the National Guard, and in his place Clement Thomas for once became again a general. During the whole of his tenure of command, he made war, not upon the Prussians, but upon the Paris National Guard. He prevented their general armament, pitted the bourgeois battalions against the workingmen's battalions, weeded out the officers hostile to Trochu's "plan," and disbanded, under the stigma of coward-ice, the very same proletarian battalions whose heroism has now astonished their most inveterate enemies. Clement Thomas felt quite proud of having reconquered his June pre-eminence as the personal enemy of the working class of Paris. Only a few days before the 18th of March, he laid before the War Minister, Leflô, a plan of his own for "finishing off *la fine fleur* (the cream) of the Paris *canaille*." After Vinoy's rout, he must needs appear upon the scene of action in the quality of an amateur spy. The Central Committee and the Paris workingmen were as much responsible for the killing of Clement Thomas and Lecomte as the Princess of Wales was for the fate of the people crushed to death on the day of her entrance into London.

The massacre of unarmed citizens in the Place Vendôme is a myth which M. Thiers and the Rurals persistently ignored in the Assembly, entrusting its propagation exclusively to the servants' hall of European journalism. "The men of order," the reactionists of Paris, trembled at the victory of the 18th of March. To them it was the signal of popular retri-bution at last arriving. The ghosts of the victims assassinated at their hands from the days of June, 1848, down to the 22nd of January, 1871, arose before their faces. Their panic was their only punishment. Even the *sergents-de-ville*, instead of being disarmed and locked up, as ought to have been done, had the gates of Paris flung wide open for their safe retreat to Versailles. The men of order were left not only unharmed, but allowed to rally and quietly to seize more than one strong-hold in the very center of Paris. This indulgence of the Central Committee—this magnanimity of the armed working-men—so strangely at variance with the habits of the "party of order," the latter misinterpreted as mere symptoms of conscious weakness. Hence their silly plan to try, under the cloak of an unarmed demonstration, what Vinoy had failed to perform with his cannon and mitrailleuses. On the 22nd of March a riotous mob of swells started from the quarters of luxury, all the *petits crevés* in their ranks, and at their head the notorious familiars of the Empire—the Heeckeren, Coët-logon, Henri de Pène, etc. Under the cowardly pretense of a pacific demonstration, this rabble, secretly armed with the weapons of the bravo, fell into marching order, ill-treated and disarmed the detached patrols and sentries of the National Guard they met with on their progress, and, on debouching from the Rue de la Paix, with the cry of "Down with the Central Committee! Down with the assassins! The National Assembly forever!" attempted to break through the line drawn up there, and thus to carry by a surprise the headquarters of the National Guard in the Place Vendôme. In reply to their pistol shots, the regular *sommations* (the French equivalent of the English Riot Act) were made, and, proving ineffective, fire was commanded by the general of the National Guard. One volley dispersed into wild flight the silly coxcombs, who expected that the mere exhibition of their "respectability" would have the same effect upon the revolution of Paris as Joshua's trumpets upon the walls of Jericho. The runaways left behind them two National Guards killed, nine severely wounded (among them a number of the Central Committee), and the whole scene of their exploit strewn with revolvers, daggers, and sword-canes, in evidence of the "unarmed" character of their "pacific" demonstration.

When, on the 13th of June, 1849, the National Guard made a really pacific demonstration in protest against the felonious assault of French troops upon Rome, Changarnier, then general of the party of order, was acclaimed by the National Assembly, and especially by M. Thiers, as the saviour of society, for having launched his troops from all sides upon these unarmed men, to shoot and sabre them down, and to trample them under their horses' feet. Paris, then, was placed under a state of siege. Dufaure hurried through the Assembly new laws of repression. New arrests, new proscriptions—a new reign of terror set in. But the lower orders manage these things otherwise. The Central Committee of 1871 simply ignored the heroes of the "pacific demonstration"; so much so, that only two days later they were enabled to muster, under Admiral Saisset, for that *armed* demonstration, crowned by the famous stampede to Versailles. In their reluctance to continue the civil war opened by Thiers' burglarious attempt on Montmartre, the Central Committee made themselves, this time, guilty of a decisive mistake in not at once marching upon Versailles, then completely helpless, and thus putting an end to the conspiracies of Thiers and his Rurals. Instead of this, the party of order was again allowed to try its strength at the ballot-box, on the 26th of March, the day of the election of the Commune. On that day, at the polls, they, these men of order, were blandly exchanging words of conciliation with their too generous conquerors, while muttering in their hearts solemn vows to exterminate them in due time.

Now, look at the reverse of the medal. Thiers opened his second campaign against Paris in the beginning of April. The first batch of Parisian prisoners brought into Versailles was subjected to revolting atrocities, while Ernest Picard, with his hands in his trousers' pockets, strolled about jeering them, and while Mesdames Thiers and Favre, in the midst of their ladies of honor (?) applauded, from the balcony, the outrages of the Versailles mob. The captured soldiers of the line were massacred in cold blood; our brave friend, General Duval, the ironfounder, was shot without any form of trial. Galliffet, the kept man of his wife, so notorious for her shameless exhibitions at the orgies of the Second Empire, boasted in a proclamation of having commanded the murder of a small troop of National Guards, with their captain and lieutenant, surprised and disarmed by his chasseurs. Vinoy, the runaway, was appointed Grand Cross of the Legion of Honor by Thiers, for his general order to shoot down every soldier of the line taken in the ranks of the Federals. Desmarets, the gendarme, was decorated for the treacherous butcherlike chopping in pieces of the high-souled and chivalrous

Flourens, who had saved their heads of the Government of Defense on the 31st of October, 1870. "The encouraging particulars" of his assassination were triumphantly expatiated upon by Thiers in the National Assembly. With the elevated vanity of a parliamentary Tom Thumb, permitted to play the part of a Tamerlane, he denied the rebels against his littleness every right of civilized warfare, up to the right of neutrality for ambulances. Nothing more horrid than that monkey allowed for a time to give full fling to his tigerish instincts, was foreseen by Voltaire.

After the decree of the Commune of the 7th of April, ordering reprisals and declaring it to be its duty "to protect Paris against the cannibal exploits of the Versailles banditti, and to demand an eye for an eye, a tooth for a tooth," Thiers did not stop the barbarous treatment of prisoners, moreover insulting them in his bulletins as follows: "Never have more degraded countenances of a degraded democracy met the afflicted gaze of honest men"—honest, like Thiers himself and his ministerial ticket-of-leave men. Still the shooting of prisoners was suspended for a time. Hardly, however, had Thiers and his Decembrist generals become aware that the Commune decree of reprisals was but an empty threat, that even their gendarme spies caught in Paris under the disguise of National Guards, that even *sergents-de-ville* taken with incendiary shells upon them, were spared—when the wholesale shooting of prisoners was resumed and carried on uninterruptedly to the end. Houses to which National Guards had fled were surrounded by gendarmes, inundated with petroleum (which here occurs for the first time in this war), and then set fire to, the charred corpses being afterwards brought out by the ambulance of the Press at the Ternes. Four National Guards having surrendered to a troop of mounted chasseurs at Belle Épine, on the 25th of April, were afterwards shot down, one after another, by the captain, a worthy man of Galliffet's. One of his four victims, left for dead, Sheffer, crawled back to the Parisian outposts, and deposed to this fact before a commission of the Commune.

When Tolain interpellated the War Minister upon the report of this commission, the Rurals drowned his voice and forbade Leflô to answer. It would be an insult to their "glorious" army to speak of its deeds. The flippant tone in which Thiers' bulletins announced the bayoneting of the Federals surprised asleep at Moulin Saquet, and the wholesale fusillades at Clamart shocked the nerves even of the not over-sensitive London *Times*. But it would be ludicrous to-day to attempt recounting the merely preliminary atrocities committed by the bombarders of Paris and the fomenters of a slaveholders' rebellion protected by foreign invasion. Amidst all these horrors, Thiers, forgetful of his parliamentary laments on the terrible responsibility weighing down his dwarfish shoulders, boasts in his bulletins that *l'Assemblé siège paisiblement* (the Assembly continues meeting in peace), and proves by his constant carousals, now with Decembrist generals, now with German princes, that his digestion is not troubled in the least, not even by the ghosts of Lecomte and Clement Thomas.

CHAPTER III

THE HISTORIC SIGNIFICANCE OF THE COMMUNE

ON the dawn of the 18th of March, Paris arose to the thunderburst of "Vive la Commune!" What is the Commune, that sphinx so tantalizing to the bourgeois mind?

"The proletarians of Paris," said the Central Committee in its manifesto of the 18th of March, "amidst the failures and treasons of the ruling classes, have understood that the hour has struck for them to save the situation by taking into their own hands the direction of public affairs. ... They have understood that it is their imperious duty and their absolute right to render themselves masters of their own destinies, by seizing upon the governmental power." *But the working class cannot simply lay hold of the ready-made State machinery, and wield it for its own purposes.*

The centralized State power, with its ubiquitous organs of standing army, police, bureaucracy, clergy, and judicature

—organs wrought after the plan of a systematic and hierarchic division of labor—originates from the days of absolute monarchy, serving nascent middle class society as a mighty weapon in its struggles against feudalism. Still, its development remained clogged by all manner of medieval rubbish, seignorial rights, local privileges, municipal and guild monopolies, and provincial constitutions. The gigantic broom of the French Revolution of the eighteenth century swept away all these relics of bygone times, thus clearing simultaneously the social soil of its last hindrances to the superstructure of the modern State edifice raised under the First Empire, itself the offspring of the coalition wars of old semifeudal Europe against modern France. During the subsequent régimes the Government, placed under parliamentary control—that is, under the direct control of the propertied classes—became not only a hotbed of huge national debts and crushing taxes; with its irresistible allurements of place, pelf, and patronage, it became not only the bone of contention between the rival factions and adventurers of the ruling classes; but its political character changed simultaneously with the economic changes of society. At the same pace at which the progress of modern industry developed, widened, intensified the class-antagonism between capital and labor, *the State power assumed more and more the character of the national power of capital over labor, of a public force organized for social enslavement, of an engine cf class despotism.* After every revolution marking a progressive phase in the class struggle, the purely repressive character of the State power stands out in bolder and bolder relief. The Revolution of 1830, resulting in the transfer of government from the landlords to the capitalists, transferred it from the more remote to the more direct antagonists of the workingmen. The bourgeois Republicans, who, in the name of the Revolution of 1848, took the State power, used it for the June massacres, in order to convince the working class that "social" republic meant the republic ensuring their social subjection, and in order to convince the royalist bulk of the bourgeois and landlord class that they might safely leave the cares and emoluments of government to the bourgeois "Republicans." However, after their one heroic exploit of June, the bourgeois Republicans had, from the front, to fall back to the rear of the "Party of Order"—a combination formed by all the rival fractions and factions of the appropriating class in their now openly declared antagonism to the producing classes. The proper form of their joint stock Government was the *Parliamentary Republic,* with Louis Bonaparte for its President. Theirs was a régime of avowed class terrorism and deliberate insult towards the "vile multitude." If the Parliamentary Republic, as M. Thiers said, "divided them [the different fractions of the ruling class] least," it opened an abyss between that class and the whole body of society outside their spare ranks. The restraints by which their own divisions had under former régimes still checked the State power, were removed by their union; and in view of the threatening upheaval of the proletariat, they now used that State power mercilessly and ostentatiously as the *national war engine of capital against labor. In their uninterrupted crusade against the producing masses they were,* however, bound not only to invest the executive with continually increased powers of repression, but at the same time to divest their own parliamentary stronghold—the National Assembly —one by one, of all its own means of defense against the Executive. The Executive, in the person of Louis Bonaparte, turned them out. The natural offspring of the "Party-of-Order" Republic was the Second Empire.

The Empire, with the *coup d'état* for its certificate of birth, universal suffrage for its sanction, and the sword for its sceptre, professed to rest upon the *peasantry, the large mass of producers not directly involved in the struggle of capital and labor.* It professed to save the working class by breaking down parliamentarism, and, with it, the undisguised subserviency of Government to the propertied classes. It professed to save the propertied classes by upholding their economic supremacy over the working class; and, finally, it professed to unite all classes by reviving for all the chimera of national glory. In reality, it was the only form of government possible at a time when the bourgeoisie had already lost, and the working class had not yet acquired, the faculty of ruling the nation. It was acclaimed throughout the world as the saviour of society. Under its sway, bourgeois society, freed from political cares, attained a development unexpected even by itself. Its industry and commerce expanded to colossal dimensions; financial swindling celebrated cosmopolitan orgies; the misery of the masses was set off by a shameless display of gorgeous, meretricious, and debased luxury. The State power, apparently soaring high above society, was at the same time itself the greatest scandal of that society and the very hotbed of all its corruptions. Its own rottenness, and the rottenness of the society it had saved, were laid bare by the bayonet of Prussia, herself eagerly bent upon transferring the supreme seat of that régime from Paris to Berlin. *Imperialism is, at the same time, the most prostitute and the ultimate form of the State power which nascent middle-class society had commenced to elaborate as a means of its own emancipation from feudalism, and which full-grown bourgeois society had finally transformed into a means for the enslavement of labor by capital.*

The direct antithesis to the Empire was the Commune. The cry of "Social Republic," with which the revolution of February was ushered in by the Paris proletariat, did but express a vague aspiration after a Republic that was not only to supersede the monarchical form of class-rule, but class-rule itself. The Commune was the positive form of that Republic.

Paris, the central seat of the old governmental power, and, at the same time, the social stronghold of the French working class, had risen in arms against the attempt of Thiers and the Rurals to restore and perpetuate that old governmental power bequeathed to them by the Empire. Paris could resist only because, in consequence of the siege, it had got rid of the army and replaced it by a National Guard, the bulk of which consisted of workingmen. This fact was now to be transformed into an institution. The first decree of the Commune, therefore, was the suppression of the standing army, and the substitution for it of the armed people.

The Commune was formed of the municipal councillors, chosen by universal suffrage in various wards of the town, responsible and revocable at short terms. The majority of its members were naturally workingmen, or acknowledged repre-sentatives of the working class. The Commune was to be a working, not a parliamentary, body, executive and legislative at the same time. Instead of continuing to be the agent of the central Government, the police was at once stripped of its political attributes and turned into the responsible and at all times revocable agent of the Commune. So were the officials of all other branches of the administration. *From the members of the Commune downwards, the public service had to be done at "workmen's wages."* The vested interests and the represen-tation allowances of the high dignitaries of State disappeared along with the high dignitaries themselves. Public functions ceased to be the private property of the tools of the central Government. Not only municipal administration, but the whole initiative hitherto exercised by the State was laid into the hands of the Commune.

Having once got rid of the standing army and the police, the physical force elements of the old Government, the Com-mune was anxious to break the spiritual force of repression, the "parson-power," by the disestablishment and disendow-ment of all churches as proprietary bodies. The priests were sent back to the recesses of private life, there to feed upon the alms of the faithful in imitation of their predecessors, the Apostles. The whole of the educational institutions were opened to the people gratuitously, and at the same time cleared of all interference of Church and State. Thus, not only was education made accessible to all, but science itself freed from the fetters which class prejudice and governmental force had imposed upon it.

The judicial functionaries were to be divested of that sham independence which had but served to mask their abject subserviency to all succeeding governments to which, in turn, they had taken, and broken, the oaths of allegiance. *Like the rest of public servants, magistrates and judges were to be elective, responsible, and revocable.*

The Paris Commune was, of course, to serve as a model to all the great industrial centers of France. The communal régime once established in Paris and the secondary centers, the old centralized Government would in the provinces, too, have to give way to the self-government of the producers. In a rough sketch of national organization which the Commune had no time to develop, it is clearly stated that the Commune was to be the political form of even the smallest country hamlet, *and that in the rural districts the standing army was to be replaced by a national militia, with an extremely short term of service.* The rural communes of each district were to administer their common affairs by an assembly of delegates in the central town, and these district assemblies were again to send deputies to the National Delegation in Paris, each delegate to be at any time revocable and bound by the *mandat impératif (formal instructions) of his constituents.* The few but important functions which still would remain for a central government were not to be suppressed, as has been intentionally misstated, but were to be discharged by communal, and therefore strictly responsible, agents. The unity of the nation was not to be broken; but, on the contrary, to be organized by the Communal Constitution, and to become a reality by the destruction of the State power which claimed to be the embodiment of that unity independent of, and superior to, the nation itself, from which it was but a parasitic excrescence. *While the merely repressive organs of the old governmental power were to be amputated, its legitimate functions were to be wrested from an authority usurping preëminence over society itself, and restored to the responsible agents of society.* Instead of deciding once in three or six years which member of the ruling class was to represent the people in Parliament, universal suffrage was to serve the people, constituted in Communes, as individual suffrage serves every other employer in the search for the workmen and managers in his business. *And it is well known that companies, like individuals, in matters of real business generally know how to put the right man in the right place, and, if they for once make a mistake, to redress it promptly. On the other hand, nothing could be more foreign to the spirit of the Commune than to supersede universal suffrage by hierarchic investiture.*

It is generally the fate of completely new historical creations to be mistaken for the counterpart of older and even defunct forms of social life, to which they may bear a certain likeness. Thus, this new Commune, which breaks the modern State power, has been mistaken for a reproduction of the medieval communes, which first preceded, and afterwards became the substratum of, that very State power. The Communal Constitution has been mistaken for an attempt to break up into a federation of small States, as dreamt of by Montesquieu and the Girondins, that unity of great nations which, if originally brought about by political force, has now become a powerful coefficient of social production. The antagonism of the Commune against the State power has been mistaken for an exaggerated form of the ancient struggle against over-centralization. Peculiar historical circumstances may have prevented the classical development, as in France, of the bourgeois form of government, and may have allowed, as in England, to complete the great central State organs by corrupt vestries, jobbing councillors, and ferocious poor-law guardians in the towns, and virtually hereditary magistrates in the counties. The Communal Constitution would have restored to the social body all the forces hitherto absorbed by the State parasite feeding upon, and clogging the free movement of, society. By this one act it would have initiated the regeneration of France. The provincial French middle class saw in the Commune an attempt to restore the sway their order had held over the country under Louis Philippe, and which, under Louis Napoleon, was supplanted by the pretended rule of the country over the towns. *In reality, the Communal Constitution brought the rural producers under the intellectual lead of the central towns of their districts, and there secured to them, in the workingmen, the natural trustees of their interests. The very existence of the Commune involved, as a matter of course, local municipal liberty,* but no longer as a check upon the now superseded State power. It could only enter into the head of a Bismarck—who, when not engaged on his intrigues of blood and iron, always likes to resume his old trade, so befitting his mental calibre, of contributor to *Kladderadatch* (the Berlin *Punch*)—it could only enter into such a head, to ascribe to the Paris Commune aspirations after that caricature of the old French municipal organization of 1791, the Prussian municipal constitution, which degrades the town

governments to mere secondary wheels in the police machinery of the Prussian State. The Commune made that catchword of bourgeois revolutions, cheap government, a reality, by destroying the two greatest sources of expenditure—the standing army and State functionarism. Its very existence presupposed the non-existence of monarchy, which, in Europe at least, is the normal incumbrance and indispensable cloak of class-rule. It supplied the Republic with the basis of really democratic institutions. But neither cheap government nor the "true Republic" was its ultimate aim; they were its mere concomitants.

The multiplicity of interpretations to which the Commune has been subjected, and the multiplicity of interests which construed it in their favor, show that it was a thoroughly expansive political form, while all previous forms of government had been emphatically repressive. Its true secret was this. *It was essentially a working-class government, the product of the struggle of the producing against the appropriating class, the political form at last discovered under which to work out the economic emancipation of labor.*

Except on this last condition, the Communal Constitution would have been an impossibility and a delusion. The political rule of the producer cannot coexist with the perpetuation of his social slavery. The Commune was therefore to serve as a lever for uprooting the economic foundations upon which rests the existence of classes, and therefore of class rule. With labor emancipated, every man becomes a workingman, and productive labor ceases to be a class attribute.

It is a strange fact. In spite of all the tall talk and all the immense literature, for the last sixty years, about emancipation of labor, no sooner do the workingmen anywhere take the subject into their own hands with a will, than uprises at once all the apologetic phraseology of the mouthpieces of present society with its two poles of Capital and Wage-slavery (the landlord now is but the sleeping partner of the capitalist), as if capitalist society was still in its purest state of virgin innocence, with its antagonisms still undeveloped, with its delusions still unexploded, with its prostitute realities not yet laid bare. The Commune, they exclaim, intends to abolish property, *the basis of all civilization!* Yes, gentlemen, the Commune intends to abolish that class-property which makes the labor of the many the wealth of the few. It aimed at the expropriation of the expropriators. It wanted to make individual property a truth by transforming the means of production, *land* and *capital,* now chiefly the means of enslaving and exploiting labor, into mere instruments of free and associated labor. But this is Communism, "impossible" Communism! Why, those members of the ruling classes who are intelligent enough to perceive the impossibility of continuing the present system—and they are many—have become the obtrusive and full-mouthed apostles of coöperative production. If coöperative production is not to remain a sham and a snare; if it is to supersede the capitalist system; if united coöperative societies are to regulate national production upon a common plan, thus taking it under their own control, and putting an end to the constant anarchy and periodical convulsions which are the fatality of capitalist production—what else, gentlemen, would it be but Communism, "possible" Communism?

The working class did not expect miracles from the Commune. They have no ready-made utopias to introduce *par décret du peuple.* They know that in order to work out their own emancipation, and along with it that higher form to which present society is irresistibly tending, by its own economic agencies, they will have to pass through long struggles, through a series of historic processes, transforming circumstances and men. They have no ideals to realize, but to set free the elements of the new society with which old collapsing bourgeois society itself is pregnant. In the full consciousness of their historic mission, and with the heroic resolve to act up to it, the working class can afford to smile at the coarse invective of the gentlemen's gentlemen with the pen and inkhorn, and at the didactic patronage of well-wishing bourgeois-doctrinaires, pouring forth their ignorant platitudes and sectarian crotchets in the oracular tone of scientific infallibility.

When the Paris Commune took the management of the revolution in its own hands; when plain workingmen for the first time dared to infringe upon the governmental privilege of their "natural superiors," and, under circumstances of unexampled difficulty, performed their work modestly, conscientiously, and efficiently—performed it at salaries the highest of which barely amounted to one-fifth of what, according to high scientific authority, is the minimum required for a secretary to a certain metropolitan school board—the old world writhed in convulsions of rage at the sight of the Red Flag, the symbol of the Republic of Labor, floating over the Hôtel de Ville.

And yet, this was the first revolution in which the working class was openly acknowledged as the only class capable of social initiative, even by the great bulk of the Paris middle class—shopkeepers, tradesmen, merchants—the wealthy capitalist alone excepted. The Commune had saved them by a sagacious settlement of that ever recurring cause of dispute among the middle class themselves—the debtor and creditor accounts. The same portion of the middle class, after they had assisted in putting down the workingmen's insurrection of June, 1848, had been at once unceremoniously sacrificed to their creditors by the then Constituent Assembly. But this was not their only motive for now rallying round the working class. They felt there was but one alternative—the Commune, or the Empire—under whatever name it might reappear. The Empire had ruined them economically by the havoc it made of public wealth, by the wholesale financial swindling it fostered, by the props it lent to the artificially accelerated centralization of capital, and the concomitant expropriation of their own ranks. It had suppressed them politically, it had shocked them morally by its orgies, it had insulted their Voltairianism by handing over the education of their children to the *Frères Ignorantins,* it had revolted their national feeling as Frenchmen by precipitating them headlong into a war which left only one equivalent for the ruins it made—the disappearance of the Empire. In fact, after the exodus from Paris of the high Bonapartist and capitalist *Bohême,* the true middle-class Party of Order came out in the shape of the *Union Républicaine,* enrolling themselves under the colors of the Commune and defending it against the wilful misconstruction of Thiers. Whether the gratitude of this great body of the middle class will stand the present severe trial, time must show.

The Commune was perfectly right in telling the peasants that "its victory was their only hope." Of all the lies hatched at Versailles and reëchoed by the glorious European penny-a-liner, one of the most tremendous was that the Rurals represented the French peasantry. Think only of the love of the French peasant for the men to whom, after 1815, he had to pay the milliard of indemnity! In the eyes of the French peasant, the very existence of a great landed proprietary is in itself an encroachment on his conquests of 1789. The bourgeoisie, in 1848, had burthened his plot of land with the additional tax of forty-five centimes in the franc; but then it did so in the name of the revolution; while now it had fomented a civil war against the revolution, to shift on the peasant's shoulders the chief load of the five milliards of indemnity to be paid to the Prussian. The Commune, on the other hand, in one of its first proclamations, declared that the true originators of the war would be made to pay its cost. The Commune would have delivered the peasant of the blood tax, would have given him a cheap government, transformed his present blood-suckers, the notary, advocate, executor, and other judicial vampires, into salaried communal agents, elected by, and responsible to, himself. It would have freed him of the tyranny of the *garde champêtre*, the gendarme, and the prefect; would have put enlightenment by the schoolmaster in the place of stultification by the priest. As the French peasant is, above all, a man of reckoning, he would find it extremely reasonable that the pay of the priest, instead of being extorted by the tax-gatherer, should only depend upon the spontaneous action of the parishioners' religious instincts. Such were the great immediate boons which the rule of the Commune—and that rule alone—held out to the French peasantry. It is, therefore, quite superfluous here to expatiate upon the more complicated but vital problems which the Commune alone was able, and at the same time compelled, to solve in favor of the peasant, viz., the hypothecary debt (mortgage), lying like an incubus upon his parcel of soil, the *proletariat* *foncier* (land-holding proletariat), daily growing upon the land, and his expropriation from it enforced, at a more and more rapid rate, by the very development of modern agricul* ture and the competition of capitalist farming.

The French peasant had elected Louis Bonaparte president of the Republic; but the Party of Order created the Empire. What the French peasant really wants he commenced to show in 1849 and 1850, by opposing his mayor to the Government's prefect, his schoolmaster to the Government's priest, and himself to the Government's gendarme. All the laws made by the Party of Order in January and February, 1850, were avowed measures of repression against the peasant. The peasant was a Bonapartist, because the Great Revolution, with all its bene* fits to him, was, in his eyes, personified in Napoleon. This de* lusion, rapidly breaking down under the Second Empire (and in its very nature hostile to the Rurals), this prejudice of the past, how could it have withstood the appeal of the Commune to the living interests and urgent wants of the peasantry?

The Rurals—this was, in fact, their chief apprehension—knew that three months' free communication of Communal Paris with the provinces would bring about a general rising of the peasants, and hence their anxiety to establish a police blockade around Paris, so as to stop the spread of the rinderpest.

If the Commune was thus the true representative of all the healthy elements of French society, and therefore the truly national Government, it was, at the same time, a workingmen's Government, as the bold champion of the emancipation of labor, emphatically international. Within sight of the Prussian army, that had annexed to Germany two French provinces, the Commune annexed to France the working people all over the world.

The Second Empire had been the jubilee of cosmopolitan blacklegism, the rakes of all countries rushing in at its call for a share in its orgies and in the plunder of the French people. Even at this moment the right hand of Thiers is Ganesco, the foul Wallachian, and his left hand is Markowski, the Russian spy. The Commune admitted all foreigners to the honor of dying for the immortal cause. Between the foreign war lost by their treason, and the civil war fomented by their conspiracy with the foreign invader, the bourgeoisie had found the time to display their patriotism by organizing police-hunts upon the Germans in France; the Commune made a *German workingman its Minister of Labor*. Thiers, the bourgeoisie, the Second Empire, had continually deluded Poland by loud professions of sympathy, while in reality betraying her to, and doing the dirty work of, Russia; the Commune honored the heroic sons of Poland by placing them at the head of the defenders of Paris. And, to broadly mark the new era of history, it was conscious of initiating, under the eyes of the conquering Prussians on the one side and of the Bonapartist army, led by Bonapartist generals, on the other, the Commune pulled down that colossal symbol of martial glory, the Vendôme column.

The great social measure of the Commune was its own working existence. Its special measures could but betoken the tendency of a government of the people by the people. *Such were the abolition of the nightwork of journeyman bakers;* the prohibition, under penalty, of the employers' practice to reduce wages by levying upon their *workpeople fines under manifold pretexts—a process in which the employer combines in his own person the parts of legislator, judge, and executioner, and filches the money to boot*. Another measure of this class was the surrender, to associations of workmen, under reserve of compensation, of all closed workshops and factories, no matter whether the respective capitalists had absconded or preferred to strike work.

The financial measures of the Commune, remarkable for their sagacity and moderation, could only be such as were compatible with the state of a besieged town. Considering the colossal robberies committed upon the City of Paris by the great financial companies and contractors, under the protection of Haussmann, the Commune would have had an incomparably better title to confiscate their property than Louis Napoleon had against the Orleans family. The Hohenzollern and the English oligarchs, who both have derived a good deal of their estates from Church plunder, were, of course, greatly shocked at the Commune clearing but 8,000 francs out of secularization.

While the Versailles Government, as soon as it had recovered some spirit and strength, used the most violent means against the Commune; while it put down the free expression of opinion all over France, even to the forbidding of meetings of delegates from the large towns; while it subjected Versailles and the rest of France to an espionage far surpassing that of the Second Empire; while it burned by its gendarme inquisitors all papers printed at Paris, and sifted all correspondence from and to Paris; while in the National Assembly the most timid attempts to put in a word for Paris were howled down in a manner unknown even to the *Chambre introuvable* of 1816; with the savage warfare of Versailles outside, and its attempts at corruption and conspiracy inside Paris—would the Commune not have shamefully betrayed its trust by affecting to keep up all the decencies and appearances of liberalism as in a time of profound peace? Had the Government of the Commune been akin to that of M. Thiers, there would have been no more occasion to suppress Party-of-Order papers at Paris than there was to suppress Communal papers at Versailles.

It was irritating, indeed, to the Rurals that at the very same time they declared the return to the Church to be the only means of salvation for France, the infidel Commune unearthed the peculiar mysteries of the Picpus nunnery and of the St. Laurent Church. It was a satire upon M. Thiers that, while he showered grand crosses upon the Bonapartist generals, in acknowledgment of their mastery in losing battles, signing capitulations, and turning cigarettes at Wilhelmshöhe, the Commune dismissed and arrested its generals whenever they were suspected of neglecting their duties. The expulsion from, and arrest by, the Commune of one of its members who had slipped in under a false name, and had undergone at Lyons six days' imprisonment for simple bankruptcy, was it not a deliberate insult hurled at the forger,

Jules Favre, then still the Foreign Minister of France, still selling France to Bismarck, and still dictating his orders to that paragon Government of Belgium? But, indeed, the Commune did not pretend to infallibility, the invariable attribute of all governments of the old stamp. It published its doings and sayings, it initiated the public into all its shortcomings.

In every revolution there intrude, at the side of its true agents, men of a different stamp; some of them survivors of and devotees to past revolutions, without insight into the present movement, but preserving popular influence by their known honesty and courage, or by the sheer force of tradition; others mere bawlers, who by dint of repeating year after year the same set of stereotyped declamation against the Government of the day, have sneaked into the reputation of revolutionists of the first water. After the 18th of March some such men did also turn up, and in some cases contrived to play preëminent parts. As far as their power went, they hampered the real action of the working class, exactly as men of that sort have hampered the full development of every previous revolution. They are an unavoidable evil; with time they are shaken off; but time was not allowed to the Commune.

Wonderful, indeed, was the change the Commune had wrought in Paris! No longer any trace of the meretricious Paris of the Second Empire. No longer was Paris the rendezvous of British landlords, Irish absentees, American ex-slaveholders and shoddy men, Russian ex-serf-owners, and Wallachian boyards. No more corpses at the morgue, no nocturnal burglaries, scarcely any robberies; in fact, for the first time since the days of February, 1848, the streets of Paris were safe, and that without any police of any kind. "We," said a member of the Commune, "hear no longer of assassination, theft, and personal assault; it seems, indeed, as if the police had dragged along with it to Versailles all its conservative friends." The *cocottes* had refound the scent of their protectors—the absconding men of family, religion, and, above all, of property. In their stead, the real women of Paris showed again at the surface—heroic, noble, and devoted, like the women of antiquity. Working, thinking, fighting, bleeding Paris—almost forgetful, in its incubation of a new society, of the cannibals at its gates—radiant in the enthusiasm of its historic initiative!

Opposed to this new world at Paris, behold the old world at Versailles—that assembly of the ghouls of all defunct régimes, Legitimists and Orleanists, eager to feed upon the carcass of the nation—with a tail of antediluvian Republicans, sanctioning, by their presence in the Assembly, the slaveholders' rebellion, relying for the maintenance of their Parliamentary Republic upon the vanity of the senile mountebank at its head, and caricaturing 1789 by holding their ghastly meetings in the *Jeu de Paume*. There it was, this Assembly, the representative of everything dead in France, propped up into a semblance of life by nothing but the swords of the generals of Louis Bonaparte. Paris all truth, Versailles all lie; and that lie vented through the mouth of Thiers.

Thiers tells a deputation of the mayors of the Seine-et-Oise—"You may rely upon my word, which I have *never* broken!" He tells the Assembly itself that "it was the most freely elected and most liberal Assembly France ever possessed"; he tells his motley soldiery that it was "the admiration of the world, and the finest army France ever possessed"; he tells the provinces that the bombardment of Paris by him was a myth: "If some cannonshots have been fired, it is not the deed of the army of Versailles, but of some insurgents trying to make believe that they are fighting, while they dare not show their faces." He again tells the provinces that "the artillery of Versailles does not bombard Paris, but only cannonades it." He tells the Archbishop of Paris that the pretended executions and reprisals (!) attributed to the Versailles troops were all moonshine. He tells Paris that he was only anxious "to free it from the hideous tyrants who oppress it," and that, in fact, the Paris of the Commune was "but a handful of criminals."

The Paris of M. Thiers was not the real Paris of the "vile multitude," but a phantom Paris, the Paris of the *francs-*

fileurs, the Paris of the Boulevards, male and female—the rich, the capitalist, the gilded, the idle Paris, now thronging with its lackeys, its blacklegs, its literary *bohême,* and its *cocottes* at Versailles, Saint-Denis, Rueil, and Saint-Germain; considering the civil war but an agreeable diversion, eyeing the battle going on through telescopes, counting the rounds of cannon, and swearing by their own honor and that of their prostitutes that the performance was far better got up than it used to be at the Porte St. Martin. The men who fell were really dead; the cries of the wounded were cries in good earnest; and, besides, the whole thing was so intensely historical.

This is the Paris of M. Thiers, as the Emigration of Coblentz was the France of M. de Calonne.

CHAPTER IV

THE REPRESSION

THE first attempt of the slaveholders' conspiracy to put down Paris by getting the Prussians to occupy it, was frustrated by Bismarck's refusal. The second attempt, that of the 18th of March, ended in the rout of the army and the flight to Versailles of the Government, which ordered the whole administration to break up and follow in its track. By the semblance of peace-negotiations with Paris, Thiers found the time to prepare for war against it. But where to find an army? The remnant of the line regiments were weak in number and unsafe in character. His urgent appeal to the provinces to succor Versailles, by their National Guards and volunteers, met with a flat refusal. Brittany alone furnished a handful of *Chouans* fighting under a white flag, every one of them wearing on his breast the heart of Jesus in white cloth, and shouting *"Vive le Roi!"* (Long live the King!). Thiers was, therefore, compelled to collect, in hot haste, a motley crew, composed of sailors, marines, Pontifical Zouaves, Valentin's gendarmes, and Piétri's *sergents de ville* and *mouchards*. This army, however, would have been ridiculously ineffective without the instalments of imperialist war-prisoners, which Bismarck granted in numbers just sufficient to keep the civil war a-going, and keep the Versailles Government in abject dependence on Prussia. During the war itself, the Versailles police had to look after the Versailles army, while the gendarmes had to drag it on by exposing themselves at all posts of danger. The forts which fell were not taken but bought. The heroism of the Federals convinced Thiers that the resistance of Paris was not to be broken by his own strategic genius and the bayonets at his disposal.

Meanwhile, his relations with the provinces became more and more difficult. Not one single address of approval came in to gladden Thiers and his Rurals. Quite the contrary. Deputations and addresses demanding, in a tone anything but respectful, conciliation with Paris on the basis of the unequivocal recognition of the Republic, the acknowledgment of the Communal liberties, and the dissolution of the National Assembly, whose mandate was extinct, poured in from all sides, and in such numbers that Dufaure, Thiers' Minister of Justice, in his circular of April 23d to the public prosecutors, commanded them to treat "the cry of conciliation" as a crime. In regard, however, to the hopeless prospect held out by his campaign, Thiers resolved to shift his tactics by ordering, all over the country, municipal elections to take place on the 30th of April, on the basis of the new municipal law dictated by himself to the National Assembly. What with the intrigues of his prefects, what with police intimidation, he felt quite sanguine of imparting, by the verdict of the provinces, to the National Assembly that moral power it had never possessed, and of getting at last from the provinces the physical force required for the conquest of Paris.

His banditti-warfare against Paris, exalted in his own bulletins, and the attempts of his Ministers at the establishment, throughout France, of a reign of terror, Thiers was from the beginning anxious to accompany with a little byplay of conciliation, which had to serve more than one purpose. It was to dupe the provinces, to inveigle the middle-class element in

Paris, and, above all, to afford the professed Republicans in the National Assembly the opportunity of hiding their treason against Paris behind their faith in Thiers. On the 21st of March, when still without an army, he had declared to the Assembly: "Come what may, I will not send an army to Paris." On March 27th he rose again: "I have found the Republic an accomplished fact, and I am firmly resolved to maintain it." In reality, he put down the revolution at Lyons and Marseilles in the name of the Republic, while the roars of his Rurals drowned the very mention of its name at Versailles. After this exploit, he toned down the "accomplished fact" into an hypothetical fact. The Orleans princes, whom he had cautiously warned off Bordeaux, were now, in flagrant breach of the law, permitted to intrigue at Dreux. The concessions held out by Thiers in his interminable interviews with the delegates from Paris and the provinces, although constantly varied in tone and color, according to time and circumstances, did in fact never come to more than the prospective restriction of revenge to the "handful of criminals implicated in the murder of Lecomte and Clement Thomas," on the well-understood premise that Paris and France were unreservedly to accept M. Thiers himself as the best of possible Republics, as he, in 1830, had done with Louis Philippe. Even these concessions he not only took care to render doubtful by the official comments put upon them in the Assembly through his Ministers; he had his Dufaure to act. Dufaure, this old Orleanist lawyer, had always been the justiciary of the state of siege, as now in 1871, under Thiers, so in 1839, under Louis Philippe, and in 1849, under Louis Bonaparte's presidency. While out of office he made a fortune by pleading for the Paris capitalists, and made political capital by pleading against the laws he had himself originated. He now hurried through the National Assembly not only a set of repressive laws which were, after the fall of Paris, to extirpate the last remnant of Republican liberty in France; he foreshadowed the fate of Paris by abridging the, for him, too slow procedure of courts-martial, and by a new-fangled, Draconic code of deportation. The Revolution of 1848, abolishing the penalty of death for political crimes, had replaced it by deportation. Louis Bonaparte did not dare, at least not in theory, to re-establish the *régime* of the guillotine. The Rural Assembly, not yet bold enough even to hint that the Parisians were not rebels, but assassins, had therefore to confine its prospective vengeance against Paris to Dufaure's new code of deportation. Under all these circumstances Thiers himself could not have gone on with his comedy of conciliation, had it not, as he in-tended it to do, drawn forth shrieks of rage from the Rurals, whose ruminating mind could understand neither the play, nor its necessities of hypocrisy, tergiversation, and procrasti-nation.

In sight of the impending municipal elections of April 30th, Thiers enacted one of his great conciliation scenes on April 27th. Amidst a flood of sentimental rhetoric, he exclaimed from the tribune of the Assembly: "There exists no conspiracy against the Republic but that of Paris, which compels us to shed French blood. I repeat it again and again. Let those im-pious arms fall from the hands which hold them, and chastise-ment will be arrested at once by an act of peace excluding only the small number of criminals." To the violent interrup-tion of the Rurals he replied: "Gentlemen, tell me, I implore you, am I wrong? Do you really regret that I could have stated the truth that the criminals are only a handful? Is it not fortunate in the midst of our misfortunes that those who have been capable to shed the blood of Clement Thomas and General Lecomte are but rare exceptions?"

France, however, turned a deaf ear to what Thiers flattered himself to be a parliamentary siren's song. Out of 700,000 municipal councillors returned by the 35,000 communes still left to France, the united Legitimists, Orleanists, and Bona-partists did not carry 8,000. The supplementary elections which followed were still more decidedly hostile. Thus, instead of getting from the provinces the badly needed physical force, the National Assembly lost even its last claim of moral force, that of being the expression of the universal suffrage of the country. To complete the discomfiture, the newly-chosen municipal councils of all the cities of France openly threatened the usurping Assembly at Versailles with a counter Assembly at Bordeaux.

Then the long-expected moment of decisive action had at last come for Bismarck. He peremptorily summoned Thiers to send to Frankfort plenipotentiaries for the definitive settlement of peace. In humble obedience to the call of his master, Thiers hastened to despatch his trusty Jules Favre, backed by Pouyer-Quertier. Pouyer-Quertier, an "eminent" Rouen cotton-spinner, a fervent and even servile partisan of the Second Empire, had never found any fault with it save its commercial treaty with England, prejudicial to his own shop-interest. Hardly installed at Bordeaux as Thiers' Minister of Finance, he denounced that "unholy" treaty, hinted at its near abrogation, and had even the effrontery to try, although in vain (having counted without Bismarck), the immediate enforcement of the old protective duties against Alsace, where, he said, no previous international treaties stood in the way. This man, who considered counter-revolution as a means to put down wages at Rouen, and the surrender of French provinces as a means to bring up the price of his wares in France, was he not *the one* predestined to be picked out by Thiers as the helpmate of Jules Favre in his last and crowning treason?

On the arrival at Frankfort of this exquisite pair of plenipotentiaries, bully Bismarck at once met them with the imperious alternative: "Either the restoration of the Empire, or the unconditional acceptance of my own peace terms!" These terms included a shortening of the intervals in which the war indemnity was to be paid, and the continued occupation of the Paris forts by Prussian troops until Bismarck should feel satisfied with the state of things in France; Prussia thus being recognized as the supreme arbiter in internal French politics! In return for this he offered to let loose, for the extermination of Paris, the captive Bonapartist army, and to lend them the direct assistance of Emperor William's troops. He pledged his good faith by making payment of the first instalment of the indemnity dependent on the "pacification" of Paris. Such a bait was, of course, eagerly swallowed by Thiers and his plenipotentiaries. They signed the treaty of peace on the 10th of May, and had it endorsed by the Versailles Assembly on the 18th.

In the interval between the conclusion of peace and the arrival of the Bonapartist prisoners, Thiers felt the more bound to resume his comedy of conciliation, as his Republican tools stood in sore need of a pretext for blinking their eyes at the preparations for the carnage of Paris. As late as the 18th of May he replied to a deputation of middle-class conciliators: "Whenever the insurgents will make up their minds for capitulation, the gates of Paris shall be flung wide open during a week for all except the murderers of Generals Clement Thomas and Lecomte."

A few days afterwards, when violently interpellated on these promises by the Rurals, he refused to enter into any explanations; not, however, without giving them this significant hint: "I tell you there are impatient men amongst you, men who are in too great a hurry. They must have another eight days; at the end of these eight days there will be no more danger, and the task will be proportionate to their courage and to their capacities." As soon as MacMahon was able to assure him that he could shortly enter Paris, Thiers declared to the Assembly that "he would enter Paris, with the *laws* in his hands, and demand a full expiation from the wretches who had sacrificed the lives of soldiers and destroyed public monuments." As the moment of decision drew near he said to the Assembly, "I shall be pitiless!"; to Paris, that it was doomed; and to his Bonapartist banditti, that they had State license to wreak vengeance upon Paris to their heart's content. At last when treachery had opened the gates of Paris to General Douai, on the 21st of May, Thiers, on the 22d, revealed to the Rurals the "goal" of his conciliation comedy, which they had so obstinately persisted in not understanding. "I told you a few days ago that we were approaching *our* goal; to-day I come to tell you the *goal* is reached. The victory of order, justice, and civilization is at last won!"

So it was. The civilization and justice of bourgeois order comes out in its lurid light whenever the slaves and drudges of that order rise against their masters. Then this civilization and justice stand forth as undisguised savagery and lawless revenge. Each new crisis in the class struggle between the appropriator and the producer brings out this fact more glaringly. Even the atrocities of the bourgeois in June, 1848, vanish before the ineffable infamy of 1871. The self-sacrificing heroism with which the population of Paris—men, women, and children—fought for eight days after the entrance of the Versaillese, reflects as much the grandeur of their cause as the infernal deeds of the soldiery reflect the innate spirit of that civilization of which they are the mercenary vindicators. A glorious civilization, indeed, the great problem of which is how to get rid of the heaps of corpses it made after the battle was over!

To find a parallel for the conduct of Thiers and his bloodhounds we must go back to the times of Sulla and the two Triumvirates of Rome. The same wholesale slaughter in cold blood; the same disregard, in massacre, of age and sex; the same system of torturing prisoners; the same proscriptions, but this time of a whole class; the same savage hunt after concealed leaders, lest one might escape; the same denunciations of political and private enemies; the same indifference for the butchery of entire strangers to the feud. There is but this difference, that the Romans had no mitrailleuses for the despatch, in the lump, of the proscribed, and that they had not "the law in their hands," nor on their lips the cry of "civilization."

And after those horrors, look upon the other, still more hideous, face of that bourgeois civilization as described by its own press!

"With stray shots," writes the Paris correspondent of a London Tory paper, "still ringing in the distance, and untended wounded wretches dying amid the tombstones of Père la Chaise—with 6,000 terror-stricken insurgents wandering in an agony of despair in the labyrinth of the catacombs, and wretches hurried through the streets to be shot down in scores by the mitrailleuse—it is revolting to see the *cafés* filled with the votaries of absinthe, billiards, and dominoes; female profligacy perambulating the boulevards, and the sound of revelry disturbing the night from the *cabinets particuliers* of fashionable restaurants." M. Edouard Hervé writes in the *Journal de Paris,* a Versaillist journal suppressed by the Commune: "The way in which the population of Paris (!) manifested its satisfaction yesterday was rather more than frivolous, and we fear it will grow worse as time progresses. Paris has now a *fête-day appearance,* which is sadly out of place; and, unless we are to be called the *Parisiens de la décadence,* this sort of thing must come to an end." And then he quotes the passage from Tacitus: "Yet, on the morrow of that horrible struggle, even before it was completely over, Rome, degraded and corrupt, began once more to wallow in the voluptuous slough which was destroying its body and polluting its soul—*ali prœlia et vulnera, alibi balnea popinœque* —here fights and wounds, there baths and restaurants." M. Hervé only forgets to say that the "population of Paris" he speaks of is but the population of the Paris of M. Thiers— the *francs-fileurs* returning in throngs from Versailles, Saint-Denis, Rueil, and Saint-Germain—the Paris of the "Decline."

In all its bloody triumphs over the self-sacrificing champions of a new and better society, that nefarious civilization, based upon the enslavement of labor, drowns the moans of its victims in a hue-and-cry of calumny, reverberated by a world-wide echo. The serene workingmen's Paris of the Commune is suddenly changed into a pandemonium by the bloodhounds of "order." And what does this tremendous change prove to the bourgeois mind of all countries? Why, that the Commune has conspired against civilization! The Paris people die enthusiastically for the Commune in numbers unequalled in any battle known to history. What does that prove? Why, that the Commune was not the people's own government, but the usurpation of a handful of criminals! The women of Paris joyfully give up their lives at the barricades and on the place of execution. What does this prove? Why, that the demon of the Commune has changed them into Megæras and Hecates! The moderation of the Commune during two months of undisputed sway is equalled only by the heroism of its defense. What does that prove? Why, that for months the Commune carefully hid, under a mask of moderation and humanity, the bloodthirstiness of its fiendish instincts, to be let loose in the hour of its agony!

The workingmen's Paris, in the act of its heroic self-holocaust, involved in its flames buildings and monuments. While tearing to pieces the living body of the proletariat, its rulers must no longer expect to return triumphantly into the intact architecture of their abodes. The Government of Versailles cries, "Incendiarism!" and whispers this cue to all its agents, down to the remotest hamlet, to hunt up its enemies everywhere as suspected of professional incendiarism. The bourgeoisie of the whole world, which looks complacently upon the wholesale massacre after the battle, is convulsed by horror at the desecration of brick and mortar!

When governments give state-licenses to their navies to "kill, *burn,* and destroy," is that a license for incendiarism? When the British troops wantonly set fire to the Capitol at Washington and to the summer palace of the Chinese Emperor, was that incendiarism? When the Prussians, not for military reasons, but out of the mere spite of revenge, burnt down, by the help of petroleum, towns like Châteaudun and innumerable villages, was that incendiarism? When Thiers, during six weeks, bombarded Paris, under the pretext that he wanted to set fire to those houses only in which there were people, was that incendiarism? In war, fire is an arm as legitimate as any. Buildings held by the enemy are shelled to set them on fire. If their defenders have to retire, they themselves light the flames to prevent the attack from making use of the buildings. To be burnt down has always been the inevitable fate of all buildings situated in the front of battle of all the regular armies of the world. But in the war of the enslaved against their enslavers, the only justifiable war in history, this is by no means to hold good! The Commune used fire strictly as a means of defense. They used it to stop up to the Versailles troops those long straight avenues which Haussmann had expressly opened to artillery fire; they used it to cover their retreat, in the same way as the Versaillese, in their advance, used their shells which destroyed at least as many buildings as the fire of the Commune. It is a matter of dispute, even now, which buildings were set fire to by the defense, and which by the attack. And the defense resorted to fire only then, when the Versaillese troops had already commenced their wholesale murdering of prisoners. Besides the Commune had, long before, given full public notice that, if driven to extremities, they would bury themselves under the ruins of Paris, and make Paris a second Moscow, as the Government of Defense, but only as a cloak for its treason, had promised to do. For this purpose Trochu had found them the petroleum. The Commune knew that its opponents cared nothing for the lives of the Paris people, but cared much for their own Paris buildings. And Thiers, on the other hand, had given them notice that he would be implacable in his vengeance. No sooner had he got his army ready on one side, and the Prussians shutting up the trap on the other, than he proclaimed: "I shall be pitiless! The expiation will be complete, and justice will be stern!" If the acts of the Paris workingmen were vandalism, it was the vandalism of defense in despair, not the vandalism of triumph, like that which the Christians perpetrated upon the really priceless art treasures of heathen antiquity; and even that vandalism has been justified by the historian as an unavoidable and comparatively trifling concomitant to the Titanic struggle between a new society arising and an old one breaking down. It was still less the vandalism of Haussmann, razing historic Paris to make place for the Paris of the sightseer!

But the execution by the Commune of the sixty-four hostages, with the Archbishop of Paris at their head! The bourgeoisie and its army in June, 1848, reëstablished a custom which had long disappeared from the practice of war —the shooting of their defenseless prisoners. This brutal custom has since been more or less strictly adhered to by the suppressors of all popular commotions in Europe and India; thus proving that it constitutes a real "progress of civilization"! On the other hand, the Prussians, in France, had reëstablished the practice of taking hostages—innocent men, who, with their lives, were to answer to them for the acts of others. When Thiers, as we have seen, from the very beginning of the conflict, enforced the humane practice of shooting down the Communal prisoners, the Commune, to protect their lives, was obliged to resort to the Prussian practice of securing hostages. The lives of the hostages had been forfeited over and over again by the continued shooting of prisoners on the part of the Versaillese. How could they be spared any longer after the carnage with which MacMahon's pretorians celebrated their entrance into Paris? Was even the last check upon the unscrupulous ferocity of bourgeois governments—the taking of hostages—to be made a mere sham of? The real murderer of Archbishop Darboy is Thiers. The Commune again and again had offered to exchange the archbishop, and ever so many priests in the bargain, against the single Blanqui, then in the hands of Thiers. Thiers obstinately refused. He knew that with Blanqui he would give to the Commune a head; while the archbishop would serve his purpose best in the shape of a corpse. Thiers acted upon the precedent of Cavaignac. How, in June, 1848, did not Cavaignac and his men of order raise shouts of horror by stigmatizing the insurgents as the assassins of Archbishop Affre! They knew perfectly well that the archbishop had been shot by the soldiers of order. M. Jacquemet, the archbishop's vicar-general, present on the spot, had immediately afterwards handed them in his evidence to that effect.

All this chorus of calumny, which the party of order never fail, in their orgies of blood, to raise against their victims, only proves that the bourgeois of our days considers himself the legitimate successor to the baron of old, who thought every weapon in his own hand fair against the plebeian, while in the hands of the plebeian a weapon of any kind constituted in itself a crime.

The conspiracy of the ruling class to break down the Revolution by a civil war carried on under the patronage of the foreign invader—a conspiracy which we have traced from the very 4th of September down to the entrance of MacMahon's pretorians through the gate of St. Cloud—culminated in the carnage of Paris. Bismarck gloats over the ruins of Paris, in which he saw perhaps the first instalment of that general destruction of great cities he had prayed for when still a mere Rural in the Prussian *Chambre introuvable* of 1849. He gloats over the *cadavres* of the Paris proletariat. For him this is not only the extermination of revolution, but the extinction of France, now decapitated in reality, and by the French Government itself. With the shallowness characteristic of all successful statesmen, he sees but the surface of this tremendous historic event. When has history ever exhibited before the spectacle of a conqueror crowning his victory by turning into, not only the gendarme, but the hired bravo of the conquered government? There existed no war between Prussia and the Commune of Paris. On the contrary, the Commune had accepted the peace preliminaries, and Prussia had announced her neutrality. Prussia was, therefore, no belligerent. She had acted the part of a bravo, a cowardly bravo, because incurring no danger; a hired bravo, because stipulating beforehand the payment of her blood-money of five hundred millions on the fall of Paris. And thus, at last, came out the true character of the war, ordained by Providence as a chastisement of godless and debauched France by pious and moral Germany! And this unparalleled breach of the law of nations, even as understood by the old-world lawyers, instead of arousing the "civilized" governments of Europe to declare the felonious Prussian Government, the mere tool of the St. Petersburg Cabinet, an outlaw amongst nations, only incites them to consider whether the few victims who escape the double cordon around Paris are not to be given up to the hangman at Versailles!

That after the most tremendous war of modern times, the conquering and the conquered hosts should fraternize for the common massacre of the proletariat—this unparalleled event does indicate, not as Bismarck thinks, the final repression of a new society upheaving, but the crumbling into dust of bourgeois society. The highest heroic effort of which old society is still capable is national war; and this is now proved to be a mere governmental humbug, intended to defer the struggle of the classes, and to be thrown aside as soon as that class struggle bursts out in civil war. Class rule is no longer able to disguise itself in a national uniform; the national Governments are *one* as against the proletariat!

After Whit-Sunday, 1871, there can be neither peace nor truce possible between the workingmen of France and the appropriators of their product. The iron hand of a mercenary soldiery may keep for a time both classes tied down in common oppression. But the battle must break out again and again in ever-growing dimensions, and there can be no doubt as to who will be the victor in the end—the appropriating few, or the immense working majority. And the French working class is only the vanguard of the modern proletariat.

While the European Governments thus testify, before Paris, to the international character of class rule, they cry down the International Workingmen's Association—the international counter-organization of labor against the cosmopolitan organization of capital—as the head fountain of all these disasters. Thiers denounced it as the despot of labor, pretending to be its liberator. Picard ordered that all communications between the French Internationals and those abroad should be cut off. Count Jaubert, Thiers' mummified accomplice of 1835, declares it the great problem of all civilized governments to weed it out. The Rurals roar against it, and the whole European press joins the chorus. An honorable French writer, completely foreign to our Association, speaks as follows: "The members of the Central Committee of the National Guard, as well as the greater part of the members of the Commune, are the most active, intelligent, and energetic minds of the International Workingmen's Association; ... men who are thoroughly honest, sincere, intelligent, devoted, pure, and fanatical in the *good* sense of the word." The police-tinged bourgeois mind naturally figures to itself the International Workingmen's Association as acting in the manner of a secret conspiracy, its central body ordering, from time to time, explosions in different countries. Our Association is, in fact, nothing but the international bond between the most advanced workingmen in the various countries of the civilized world. Wherever, in whatever shape, and under whatever conditions the class struggle obtains any constituency, it is but natural that members of our Association should stand in the foreground. The soil out of which it grows is modern society itself. It cannot be stamped out by any amount of carnage. To stamp it out, the Government would have to stamp out the despotism of capital over labor—the condition of their own parasitical existence.

Workingmen's Paris, with its Commune, will be forever celebrated as the glorious harbinger of a new society. Its martyrs are enshrined in the great heart of the working class. Its exterminators, history has already nailed to that eternal pillory from which all the prayers of their priest will not avail to redeem them.

The Best of the World's Best Books

COMPLETE LIST OF TITLES IN

THE MODERN LIBRARY

For convenience in ordering use number at right of title

ADAMS, HENRY	The Education of Henry Adams 76
AIKEN, CONRAD (Editor)	A Comprehensive Anthology of American Poetry 101
AIKEN, CONRAD (Editor)	20th-Century American Poetry 127
ALEICHEM, SHOLOM	Selected Stories of 145
ANDERSON, SHERWOOD	Winesburg, Ohio 104
AQUINAS, ST. THOMAS	Introduction to St. Thomas Aquinas 259
ARISTOTLE	Introduction to Aristotle 248
ARISTOTLE	Politics 228
ARISTOTLE	Rhetoric and Poetics 246
AUGUSTINE, ST.	The Confessions of 263
AUSTEN, JANE	Pride and Prejudice and Sense and Sensibility 264
BACON, FRANCIS	Selected Writings of 256
BALZAC	Droll Stories 193
BALZAC	Père Goriot and Eugénie Grandet 245
BEERBOHM, MAX	Zuleika Dobson 116
BELLAMY, EDWARD	Looking Backward 22
BENNETT, ARNOLD	The Old Wives' Tale 184
BERGSON, HENRI	Creative Evolution 231
BIERCE, AMBROSE	In the Midst of Life 133
BLAKE, WILLIAM	Selected Poetry & Prose of 285
BOCCACCIO	The Decameron 71
BOSWELL, JAMES	The Life of Samuel Johnson 282
BRONTË, CHARLOTTE	Jane Eyre 64
BRONTË, EMILY	Wuthering Heights 106
BROWNING, ROBERT	Selected Poetry of 198
BUCK, PEARL	The Good Earth 15
BURCKHARDT, JACOB	The Civilization of the Renaissance in Italy 32
BURK, JOHN N.	The Life and Works of Beethoven 241
BUTLER, SAMUEL	Erewhon and Erewhon Revisited 136
BUTLER, SAMUEL	The Way of All Flesh 13
BYRNE, DONN	Messer Marco Polo 43
BYRON, LORD	The Selected Poetry of 195
BYRON, LORD	Don Juan 24
CAESAR, JULIUS	The Gallic War and Other Writings of 295
CALDWELL, ERSKINE	God's Little Acre 51
CALDWELL, ERSKINE	Tobacco Road 249
CANFIELD, DOROTHY	The Deepening Stream 200
CARROLL, LEWIS	Alice in Wonderland, etc. 79
CASANOVA, JACQUES	Memoirs of Casanova 165
CELLINI, BENVENUTO	Autobiography of Cellini 150
CERVANTES	Don Quixote 174
CHAUCER	The Canterbury Tales 161
CHEKHOV, ANTON	Best Plays by 171
CHEKHOV, ANTON	The Short Stories of 50
CICERO	The Basic Works of 272
COLERIDGE	Selected Poetry and Prose of 279

COMMAGER, HENRY STEELE & NEVINS, ALLAN	A Short History of the United States 235
CONFUCIUS	The Wisdom of Confucius 7
CONRAD, JOSEPH	Lord Jim 186
CONRAD, JOSEPH	Nostromo 275
CONRAD, JOSEPH	Victory 34
COOPER, JAMES FENIMORE	The Pathfinder 105
CORNEILLE & RACINE	Six Plays of Corneille and Racine 194
CORVO, FREDERICK BARON	A History of the Borgias 192
CRANE, STEPHEN	The Red Badge of Courage 130
CUMMINGS, E. E.	The Enormous Room 214
DANA, RICHARD HENRY	Two Years Before the Mast 236
DANTE	The Divine Comedy 208
DEFOE, DANIEL	Moll Flanders 122
DEFOE, DANIEL	Robinson Crusoe and A Journal of the Plague Year 92
DEWEY, JOHN	Human Nature and Conduct 173
DICKENS, CHARLES	David Copperfield 110
DICKENS, CHARLES	Pickwick Papers 204
DICKENS, CHARLES	A Tale of Two Cities 189
DICKINSON, EMILY	Selected Poems of 25
DINESEN, ISAK	Out of Africa 23
DINESEN, ISAK	Seven Gothic Tales 54
DONNE, JOHN	Complete Poetry and Selected Prose of 12
DOS PASSOS, JOHN	Three Soldiers 205
DOSTOYEVSKY, FYODOR	The Best Short Stories of 293
DOSTOYEVSKY, FYODOR	The Brothers Karamazov 151
DOSTOYEVSKY, FYODOR	Crime and Punishment 199
DOSTOYEVSKY, FYODOR	The Possessed 55
DOUGLAS, NORMAN	South Wind 5
DOYLE, SIR ARTHUR CONAN	The Adventures and Memoirs of Sherlock Holmes 206
DREISER, THEODORE	Sister Carrie 8
DUMAS, ALEXANDRE	Camille 69
DUMAS, ALEXANDRE	The Three Musketeers 143
DU MAURIER, DAPHNE	Rebecca 227
ELLIS, HAVELOCK	The Dance of Life 160
EMERSON, RALPH WALDO	Essays and Other Writings 91
FAULKNER, WILLIAM	Absalom, Absalom! 271
FAULKNER, WILLIAM	Go Down, Moses 175
FAULKNER, WILLIAM	Light in August 88
FAULKNER, WILLIAM	Sanctuary 61
FAULKNER, WILLIAM	The Sound and the Fury and As I Lay Dying 187
FIELDING, HENRY	Joseph Andrews 117
FIELDING, HENRY	Tom Jones 185
FLAUBERT, GUSTAVE	Madame Bovary 28
FORESTER, C. S.	The African Queen 102
FRANCE, ANATOLE	Penguin Island 210
FRANKLIN, BENJAMIN	Autobiography, etc. 39
FREUD, SIGMUND	The Interpretation of Dreams 96
FROST, ROBERT	The Poems of 242
GALSWORTHY, JOHN	The Apple Tree (in Great Modern Short Stories 168)
GAUTIER, THEOPHILE	Mlle. De Maupin and One of Cleopatra's Nights 53
GEORGE, HENRY	Progress and Poverty 36

GOETHE	Faust 177
GOGOL, NIKOLAI	Dead Souls 40
GOLDSMITH, OLIVER	The Vicar of Wakefield and other Writings 291
GRAVES, ROBERT	I, Claudius 20
GUNTHER, JOHN	Death Be Not Proud 286
HACKETT, FRANCIS	The Personal History of Henry the Eighth 265
HAGGARD, H. RIDER	She and King Solomon's Mines 163
HARDY, THOMAS	Jude the Obscure 135
HARDY, THOMAS	The Mayor of Casterbridge 17
HARDY, THOMAS	The Return of the Native 121
HARDY, THOMAS	Tess of the D'Urbervilles 72
HART & KAUFMAN	Six Plays by 233
HARTE, BRET	The Best Stories of 250
HAWTHORNE, NATHANIEL	The Scarlet Letter 93
HEGEL	The Philosophy of 239
HELLMAN, LILLIAN	Four Plays by 223
HENRY, O.	Best Short Stories of 4
HERODOTUS	The Persian Wars 255
HOFFENSTEIN, SAMUEL	The Complete Poetry of 225
HOMER	The Iliad 166
HOMER	The Odyssey 167
HORACE	The Complete Works of 141
HOWELLS, WILLIAM DEAN	The Rise of Silas Lapham 277
HUDSON, W. H.	Green Mansions 89
HUGHES, RICHARD	A High Wind in Jamaica 112
HUGO, VICTOR	The Hunchback of Notre Dame 35
HUXLEY, ALDOUS	Antic Hay 209
HUXLEY, ALDOUS	Brave New World 48
HUXLEY, ALDOUS	Point Counter Point 180
IBSEN, HENRIK	Six Plays by 6
IRVING, WASHINGTON	Selected Writings of 240
JAMES, HENRY	The Bostonians 16
JAMES, HENRY	The Portrait of a Lady 107
JAMES, HENRY	The Turn of the Screw 169
JAMES, HENRY	Washington Square 269
JAMES, HENRY	The Wings of the Dove 244
JAMES, WILLIAM	The Philosophy of William James 114
JAMES, WILLIAM	The Varieties of Religious Experience 70
JEFFERS, ROBINSON	Roan Stallion; Tamar and Other Poems 118
JEFFERSON, THOMAS	The Life and Selected Writings of 234
JOYCE, JAMES	Dubliners 124
KAFKA, FRANZ	Selected Stories of 283
KANT	The Philosophy of 266
KAUFMAN & HART	Six Plays by 233
KEATS	The Complete Poetry and Selected Prose of 273
KIPLING, RUDYARD	Kim 99
KOESTLER, ARTHUR	Darkness at Noon 74
LAOTSE	The Wisdom of 262
LAWRENCE, D. H.	The Rainbow 128
LAWRENCE, D. H.	Sons and Lovers 109
LAWRENCE, D. H.	Women in Love 68
LEWIS, SINCLAIR	Dodsworth 252
LONGFELLOW, HENRY W.	Poems 56
LOUYS, PIERRE	Aphrodite 77
LUDWIG, EMIL	Napoleon 95

MACHIAVELLI	The Prince and The Discourses 65
MALRAUX, ANDRÉ	Man's Fate 33
MANN, THOMAS	Death in Venice (in Great German Short Novels and Stories 108)
MARQUAND, JOHN P.	The Late George Apley 182
MARX, KARL	Capital and Other Writings 202
MAUGHAM, W. SOMERSET	The Best Short Stories of 14
MAUGHAM, W. SOMERSET	Cakes and Ale 270
MAUGHAM, W. SOMERSET	The Moon and Sixpence 27
MAUGHAM, W. SOMERSET	Of Human Bondage 176
MAUPASSANT, GUY DE	Best Short Stories 98
MAUROIS, ANDRÉ	Disraeli 46
McCORD, DAVID (Editor)	What Cheer: An Anthology of Humorous and Witty Verse 190
MEAD, MARGARET	Coming of Age in Samoa 126
MELVILLE, HERMAN	Moby Dick 119
MEREDITH, GEORGE	The Egoist 253
MEREDITH, GEORGE	The Ordeal of Richard Feverel 134
MEREJKOWSKI, DMITRI	The Romance of Leonardo da Vinci 138
MICHENER, JAMES A.	Selected Writings of 296
MILTON, JOHN	The Complete Poetry and Selected Prose of John Milton 132
MOLIÈRE	Plays 78
MONTAIGNE	Selected Essays of 218
MORIER, JAMES	The Adventures of Hajji Baba of Ispahan 289
NASH, OGDEN	The Selected Verse of Ogden Nash 191
NEVINS, ALLAN & COMMAGER, HENRY STEELE	A Short History of the United States 235
NEWMAN, CARDINAL JOHN H.	Apologia Pro Vita Sua 113
NIETZSCHE, FRIEDRICH	Thus Spake Zarathustra 9
NOSTRADAMUS	Oracles of 81
ODETS, CLIFFORD	Six Plays of 67
O'HARA, JOHN	Appointment in Samarra 42
O'HARA, JOHN	Selected Short Stories of 211
O'NEILL, EUGENE	The Emperor Jones, Anna Christie and The Hairy Ape 146
O'NEILL, EUGENE	The Long Voyage Home: Seven Plays of the Sea 111
PALGRAVE, FRANCIS (Editor)	The Golden Treasury 232
PARKER, DOROTHY	The Collected Short Stories of 123
PARKER, DOROTHY	The Collected Poetry of 237
PARKMAN, FRANCIS	The Oregon Trail 267
PASCAL, BLAISE	Pensées and The Provincial Letters 164
PATER, WALTER	Marius the Epicurean 90
PATER, WALTER	The Renaissance 86
PEPYS, SAMUEL	Passages from the Diary of 103
PERELMAN, S. J.	The Best of 247
PETRONIUS ARBITER	The Satyricon 156
PLATO	The Republic 153
PLATO	The Works of Plato 181
POE, EDGAR ALLAN	Selected Poetry and Prose 82
POLO, MARCO	The Travels of Marco Polo 196
POPE, ALEXANDER	Selected Works of 257
PORTER, KATHERINE ANNE	Flowering Judas 284
PORTER, KATHERINE ANNE	Pale Horse, Pale Rider 45
PROUST, MARCEL	The Captive 120
PROUST, MARCEL	Cities of the Plain 220
PROUST, MARCEL	The Guermantes Way 213

PROUST, MARCEL	The Past Recaptured 278
PROUST, MARCEL	Swann's Way 59
PROUST, MARCEL	The Sweet Cheat Gone 260
PROUST, MARCEL	Within a Budding Grove 172
RACINE & CORNEILLE	Six Plays by 194
READE, CHARLES	The Cloister and the Hearth 62
REED, JOHN	Ten Days that Shook the World 215
RENAN, ERNEST	The Life of Jesus 140
RICHARDSON, SAMUEL	Clarissa 10
ROSTAND, EDMOND	Cyrano de Bergerac 154
ROUSSEAU, JEAN JACQUES	The Confessions of 243
RUSSELL, BERTRAND	Selected Papers of Bertrand Russell 137
SAKI	The Short Stories of 280
SANTAYANA, GEORGE	The Sense of Beauty 292
SCHOPENHAUER	The Philosophy of Schopenhauer 52
SCHULBERG, BUDD	What Makes Sammy Run? 281
SHAKESPEARE, WILLIAM	Tragedies, 1, 1A—complete, 2 vols.
SHAKESPEARE, WILLIAM	Comedies, 2, 2A—complete, 2 vols.
SHAKESPEARE, WILLIAM	Histories, 3 }complete, 2 vols. Histories, Poems, 3A
SHAW, BERNARD	Four Plays by 19
SHAW, BERNARD	Saint Joan, Major Barbara, and Androcles and the Lion 294
SHELLEY	The Selected Poetry & Prose of 274
SMOLLETT, TOBIAS	Humphry Clinker 159
SPINOZA	The Philosophy of Spinoza 60
STEINBECK, JOHN	In Dubious Battle 115
STEINBECK, JOHN	The Grapes of Wrath 148
STEINBECK, JOHN	Of Mice and Men 29
STEINBECK, JOHN	Tortilla Flat 216
STENDHAL	The Red and the Black 157
STERNE, LAURENCE	Tristram Shandy 147
STEWART, GEORGE R.	Storm 254
STOKER, BRAM	Dracula 31
STONE, IRVING	Lust for Life 11
STOWE, HARRIET BEECHER	Uncle Tom's Cabin 261
STRACHEY, LYTTON	Eminent Victorians 212
SUETONIUS	Lives of the Twelve Caesars 188
SWIFT, JONATHAN	Gulliver's Travels, A Tale of a Tub, The Battle of the Books 100
SYMONDS, JOHN A.	The Life of Michelangelo 49
TACITUS	The Complete Works of 222
TENNYSON	Selected Poetry of 230
THACKERAY, WILLIAM	Henry Esmond 80
THACKERAY, WILLIAM	Vanity Fair 131
THOMPSON, FRANCIS	Complete Poems 38
THOREAU, HENRY DAVID	Walden and Other Writings 155
THUCYDIDES	The Complete Writings of 58
TOLSTOY, LEO	Anna Karenina 37
TROLLOPE, ANTHONY	Barchester Towers and The Warden 41
TROLLOPE, ANTHONY	The Eustace Diamonds 251
TURGENEV, IVAN	Fathers and Sons 21
TWAIN, MARK	A Connecticut Yankee in King Arthur's Court 162
VEBLEN, THORSTEIN	The Theory of the Leisure Class 63
VIRGIL	The Aeneid, Eclogues & Georgics 75
VOLTAIRE	Candide and Other Writings 47
WALPOLE, HUGH	Fortitude 178

WALTON, IZAAK — The Compleat Angler 26
WARREN, ROBERT PENN — All The King's Men 170
WEBB, MARY — Precious Bane 219
WELLS, H. G. — Tono Bungay 197
WELTY, EUDORA — Selected Stories of 290
WHARTON, EDITH — The Age of Innocence 229
WHITMAN, WALT — Leaves of Grass 97
WILDE, OSCAR — Dorian Gray, De Profundis 125
WILDE, OSCAR — The Plays of Oscar Wilde 83
WILDE, OSCAR — Poems and Fairy Tales 84
WORDSWORTH — Selected Poetry of 268
WRIGHT, RICHARD — Native Son 221
YEATS, W. B. (Editor) — Irish Fairy and Folk Tales 44
YOUNG, G. F. — The Medici 179
ZIMMERN, ALFRED — The Greek Commonwealth 207
ZOLA, EMILE — Nana 142

MISCELLANEOUS

An Anthology of Irish Literature 288
The Arabian Nights' Entertainments 201
Best Amer. Humorous Short Stories 87
Best Russian Short Stories 18
Best Spanish Stories 129
A Comprehensive Anthology of American Poetry 101
The Consolation of Philosophy 226
Eight Famous Elizabethan Plays 94
Eighteenth-Century Plays 224
Famous Ghost Stories 73
The Federalist 139
Five Great Modern Irish Plays 30
Fourteen Great Detective Stories 144
Great German Short Novels and Stories 108
Great Modern Short Stories 168
Great Tales of the American West 238
The Greek Poets 203
The Latin Poets 217
The Making of Man: An Outline of Anthropology 149
The Making of Society: An Outline of Sociology 183
New Voices in the American Theatre 258
Outline of Abnormal Psychology 152
Outline of Psychoanalysis 66
Restoration Plays 287
Seven Famous Greek Plays 158
The Short Bible 57
Six Modern American Plays 276
Three Famous French Romances 85
    Sapho, by Alphonse Daudet
    Manon Lescaut, by Antoine Prevost
    Carmen, by Prosper Merimee
Twentieth-Century Amer. Poetry 127

MODERN LIBRARY GIANTS

A series of full-sized library editions of books that formerly were available only in cumbersome and expensive sets.

THE MODERN LIBRARY GIANTS REPRESENT A SELECTION OF THE WORLD'S GREATEST BOOKS

These volumes contain from 600 to 1,400 pages each

G1. TOLSTOY, LEO. War and Peace.

G2. BOSWELL, JAMES. Life of Samuel Johnson.

G3. HUGO, VICTOR. Les Miserables.

G4. THE COMPLETE POEMS OF KEATS AND SHELLEY.

G5. PLUTARCH'S LIVES (The Dryden Translation).

G6.
G7. GIBBON, EDWARD. The Decline and Fall of the Roman
G8. Empire (Complete in three volumes).

G9. GREAT VOICES OF THE REFORMATION.

G10. TWELVE FAMOUS RESTORATION PLAYS (1660-1820) (Congreve, Wycherley, Gay, Goldsmith, Sheridan, etc.)

G11. JAMES, HENRY. The Short Stories of

G12. THE MOST POPULAR NOVELS OF SIR WALTER SCOTT (Quentin Durward, Ivanhoe and Kenilworth).

G13. CARLYLE, THOMAS. The French Revolution.

G14. BULFINCH'S MYTHOLOGY (Illustrated).

G15. CERVANTES. Don Quixote (Illustrated).

G16. WOLFE, THOMAS. Look Homeward, Angel.

G17. THE POEMS AND PLAYS OF ROBERT BROWNING.

G18. ELEVEN PLAYS OF HENRIK IBSEN.

G19. THE COMPLETE WORKS OF HOMER.

G20. THE LIFE AND WRITINGS OF ABRAHAM LINCOLN.

G21. SIXTEEN FAMOUS AMERICAN PLAYS.

G22. THIRTY FAMOUS ONE-ACT PLAYS.

G23. TOLSTOY, LEO. Anna Karenina.

G24. LAMB, CHARLES. The Complete Works and Letters of

G25. THE COMPLETE PLAYS OF GILBERT AND SULLIVAN.

G26. MARX, KARL. Capital.

G27. DARWIN, CHARLES. Origin of Species & The Descent of Man.

G28. THE COMPLETE WORKS OF LEWIS CARROLL.

G29. PRESCOTT, WILLIAM H. The Conquest of Mexico and The Conquest of Peru.

G30. MYERS, GUSTAVUS. History of the Great American Fortunes.

G31. WERFEL, FRANZ. The Forty Days of Musa Dagh.

G32. SMITH, ADAM. The Wealth of Nations.

G33. COLLINS, WILKIE. The Moonstone and The Woman in White.

G34. NIETZSCHE, FRIEDRICH. The Philosophy of Nietzsche.

G35. BURY, J. B. A History of Greece.

G36. DOSTOYEVSKY, FYODOR. The Brothers Karamazov.

G37. THE COMPLETE NOVELS AND SELECTED TALES OF NATHANIEL HAWTHORNE.

G38. ROLLAND, ROMAIN. Jean-Christophe

G39. THE BASIC WRITINGS OF SIGMUND FREUD.

G40. THE COMPLETE TALES AND POEMS OF EDGAR ALLAN POE.
G41. FARRELL, JAMES T. Studs Lonigan.
G42. THE POEMS AND PLAYS OF TENNYSON.
G43. DEWEY, JOHN. Intelligence in the Modern World: John Dewey's Philosophy.
G44. DOS PASSOS, JOHN. U. S. A.
G45. STOIC AND EPICUREAN PHILOSOPHERS
G46. A NEW ANTHOLOGY OF MODERN POETRY.
G47. THE ENGLISH PHILOSOPHERS FROM BACON TO MILL.
G48. THE METROPOLITAN OPERA GUIDE.
G49. TWAIN, MARK. Tom Sawyer and Huckleberry Finn.
G50. WHITMAN, WALT. Leaves of Grass.
G51. THE BEST-KNOWN NOVELS OF GEORGE ELIOT.
G52. JOYCE, JAMES. Ulysses.
G53. SUE, EUGENE. The Wandering Jew.
G54. AN ANTHOLOGY OF FAMOUS BRITISH STORIES.
G55. O'NEILL, EUGENE. Nine Plays by
G56. THE WISDOM OF CATHOLICISM.
G57. MELVILLE. Selected Writings of Herman Melville.
G58. THE COMPLETE NOVELS OF JANE AUSTEN.
G59. THE WISDOM OF CHINA AND INDIA.
G60. DOSTOYEVSKY, FYODOR. The Idiot.
G61. SPAETH, SIGMUND. A Guide to Great Orchestral Music.
G62. THE POEMS, PROSE AND PLAYS OF PUSHKIN.
G63. SIXTEEN FAMOUS BRITISH PLAYS.
G64. MELVILLE, HERMAN. Moby Dick.
G65. THE COMPLETE WORKS OF RABELAIS.
G66. THREE FAMOUS MURDER NOVELS
　　　Before the Fact, Francis Iles.
　　　Trent's Last Case, E. C. Bentley.
　　　The House of the Arrow, A. E. W. Mason.
G67. ANTHOLOGY OF FAMOUS ENGLISH AND AMERICAN POETRY.
G68. THE SELECTED WORK OF TOM PAINE.
G69. ONE HUNDRED AND ONE YEARS' ENTERTAINMENT.
G70. THE COMPLETE POETRY OF JOHN DONNE AND WILLIAM BLAKE.
G71. SIXTEEN FAMOUS EUROPEAN PLAYS.
G72. GREAT TALES OF TERROR AND THE SUPERNATURAL.
G73. A SUB-TREASURY OF AMERICAN HUMOR.
G74. ST. AUGUSTINE. The City of God.
G75. SELECTED WRITINGS OF ROBERT LOUIS STEVENSON.
G76. GRIMM AND ANDERSEN, TALES OF
G77. AN ANTHOLOGY OF FAMOUS AMERICAN STORIES.
G78. HOLMES, OLIVER WENDELL. The Mind and Faith of Justice Holmes.
G79. THE WISDOM OF ISRAEL.
G80. DREISER, THEODORE. An American Tragedy.